T0281720

Beginning Database Programming Using ASP.NET Core 3

With MVC, Razor Pages, Web API, jQuery, Angular, SQL Server, and NoSQL

Bipin Joshi

Apress®

Beginning Database Programming Using ASP.NET Core 3: With MVC, Razor Pages, Web API, jQuery, Angular, SQL Server, and NoSQL

Bipin Joshi
Thane, India

ISBN-13 (pbk): 978-1-4842-5508-7   ISBN-13 (electronic): 978-1-4842-5509-4
https://doi.org/10.1007/978-1-4842-5509-4

Managing Director, Apress Media LLC: Welmoed Spahr
Acquisitions Editor: Joan Murray
Development Editor: Laura Berendson
Coordinating Editor: Jill Balzano

Cover image designed by Freepik (www.freepik.com)

Distributed to the book trade worldwide by Springer Science+Business Media New York, 233 Spring Street, 6th Floor, New York, NY 10013. Phone 1-800-SPRINGER, fax (201) 348-4505, e-mail orders-ny@springer-sbm.com, or visit www.springeronline.com. Apress Media, LLC is a California LLC and the sole member (owner) is Springer Science + Business Media Finance Inc (SSBM Finance Inc). SSBM Finance Inc is a **Delaware** corporation.

For information on translations, please e-mail rights@apress.com, or visit http://www.apress.com/rights-permissions.

Apress titles may be purchased in bulk for academic, corporate, or promotional use. eBook versions and licenses are also available for most titles. For more information, reference our Print and eBook Bulk Sales web page at http://www.apress.com/bulk-sales.

Any source code or other supplementary material referenced by the author in this book is available to readers on GitHub via the book's product page, located at www.apress.com/9781484255087. For more detailed information, please visit http://www.apress.com/source-code.

Printed on acid-free paper

At the holy feet of Lord Shiva, Goddess Parvati,
and Gurudev Dattatreya.

—Bipin Joshi

Table of Contents

About the Author

Bipin Joshi is an independent software consultant, trainer, author, yoga mentor, and meditation teacher who writes about seemingly unrelated topics: software development and yoga! He conducts online training courses to help developers learn the .NET family of technologies better and faster. Currently, his focus is ASP.NET, C#, Azure, data access technologies, design patterns, and architectural patterns. More details about his online training courses are available at `www.binaryintellect.com`.

Bipin has been programming since 1995 and has worked with the .NET framework since its inception. He is a published author and has authored or co-authored more than 12 books and numerous articles on .NET technologies. He regularly writes about ASP.NET and other cutting-edge web technologies on his web site – `www.binaryintellect.net`. Bipin is a Microsoft Most Valuable Professional (MVP) and a former Microsoft Certified Trainer (MCT).

Having embraced the yoga way of life, he enjoys the intoxicating presence of God and writes about yoga on his web site – `www.bipinjoshi.org`. Bipin has also penned a few books on yoga and teaches meditation to selected individuals. He can be reached through his web sites.

About the Technical Reviewer

 **Alex Thissen** has been involved in application development since the late 1990s and worked as a lead developer, trainer, coach, and architect at large enterprises and small companies. He spends his time teaching other developers the details of the Microsoft development platform and frameworks and coaches architects to design and build modern distributed applications at cloud scale. He has received the Microsoft Most Valuable Professional award for Visual Studio and Development Technologies since 2006. In his spare time, Alex likes to participate in all kinds of sport and loves playing and programming new and retro video games.

Introduction

Welcome to *Beginning Database Programming Using ASP.NET Core 3*! Modern web application development is dominated by open source frameworks that evolve at a rapid pace. At times, it becomes challenging and overwhelming even for experienced developers to keep themselves updated with the latest happenings in the technologies and frameworks of their interest. It goes without saying that beginners aiming to grasp the fundamentals of such technologies and frameworks often look for resources that can introduce them to the subject quickly and efficiently.

This book is about Microsoft's latest web development framework – ASP.NET Core 3.0. While developing real-world web applications using ASP.NET Core, you have many options to choose from: MVC, Razor Pages, Web API, Blazor, jQuery, Angular, Entity Framework (EF) Core, SQL Server data provider, Azure SQL Databases, Cosmos DB, MongoDB, and more. The book attempts to address the difficulties faced by beginners when they decide to jump to the ASP.NET Core family of technologies. It discusses topics that are most frequently needed by beginners. To that end, this book teaches you to

- Work with data entry forms and form validations

- Perform CRUD (Create, Read, Update, and Delete) database operations

- Use jQuery Ajax and Angular with ASP.NET Core applications

- Implement user authentication and authorization

- Store data in NoSQL databases such as Cosmos DB and MongoDB

- Deploy ASP.NET Core web applications to Internet Information Services (IIS) and Azure App Service

What makes this book special is the approach it takes while introducing these technical features. Rather than presenting these features and available options in isolation, this book utilizes them in an integrated manner by building a small CRUD-focused sample application – Employee Manager.

Throughout this book, you build multiple versions of Employee Manager, each version using a particular set of technologies, features, and options. For example, in one of the chapters, you build Employee Manager using ASP.NET Core MVC. In another chapter, you build the same application using ASP.NET Core Razor Pages. In yet another chapter, you build Employee Manager using Blazor, and so on. I hope that this approach will help you to get introduced to various aspects of ASP.NET Core quickly and efficiently.

Who Is This Book For?

This book is intended for beginner-level software developers wanting to get introduced to web development using ASP.NET Core and related technologies. This book doesn't aim at taking a deep dive into the subject; rather, it attempts to quickly familiarize you with an array of technologies, features, and options that can be used while building modern web applications using ASP.NET Core. I make the following assumptions about you:

- You are familiar with C# programming language.

- You possess a basic understanding of ASP.NET and how web applications work.

- You are familiar with Visual Studio IDE. Although the book explains some features of Visual Studio as and when they are required, you should know the basics such as creating/opening project files, compiling and debugging source code, and running an application from within the Visual Studio.

- You know how to work with Microsoft SQL Server tables and stored procedures.

Additionally, in some chapters, familiarity with JavaScript would be a plus.

Software Required

In order to work through the examples discussed in this book, you need the following software:

- Visual Studio 2019 for Windows (make sure to apply the latest updates)

- .NET Core 3.0 and ASP.NET Core 3.0

- SQL Server 2012 or later with the Northwind database

- Access to the Azure portal, Azure SQL Databases, and Azure Cosmos DB in the examples that use these technologies

- MongoDB database server in the example that uses it as a data store

- jQuery 3.x and Angular 8 in the chapters where these are used

- Any modern web browser

I have used Visual Studio 2019 Enterprise edition to create all the example projects. However, you can use any edition of Visual Studio 2019 for Windows such as Community or Professional edition. IIS Express has been used as the development web server. Most of the examples presented in this book use the Northwind sample database, and I strongly suggest that you install it in your SQL Server. I have used the Firefox browser in my illustrations and screenshots, but you can use any other modern browser.

Structure of This Book

As mentioned earlier, this book teaches you about the ASP.NET Core family of technologies by building the Employee Manager sample application. In all, there are ten chapters, out of which the first two are introductory chapters. Chapters 3–9 guide you to build various versions of Employee Manager, each version making use of a particular set of technologies, features, and options. Chapter 10 covers deployment. These ten chapters are briefly outlined as follows:

- **Chapter 1:** This chapter gives you a quick introduction to ASP.NET Core in terms of its prominent features and primary development options. You also build a "Hello World" example using ASP.NET Core MVC, Razor Pages, and Web API.

- **Chapter 2:** This chapter explains the Employee Manager application. It takes a quick look at the Employees table of the Northwind database and also discusses its columns that are used for the sake of CRUD operations. Various pages of the application such as employee listing page, Insert New Employee page, user registration page, and sign-in page are discussed in terms of their functionality. It then proceeds to summarize various technology features and options available to you for building this application. The chapter also guides you to host your source code into GitHub repositories.

- **Chapter 3:** This chapter teaches you to develop Employee Manager using ASP.NET Core MVC. It illustrates various features such as using Tag Helpers to build user interfaces (UIs), creating an Entity Framework Core model, and model validation using data annotations. You also learn to use ASP.NET Core Identity for user authentication and authorization.

- **Chapter 4:** In this chapter, you develop Employee Manager using ASP.NET Core Razor Pages. This chapter also teaches how an EF Core model can be created using reverse engineering techniques. This example also illustrates asynchronous operations (async/await) in Razor Pages and ASP.NET Core Identity.

- **Chapter 5:** In this chapter, you develop Employee Manager using ASP.NET Core Web API. The application consists of two parts – Web API and client. Web API performs the CRUD operations using repositories, raw SQL queries, and stored procedures. The client application is developed using ASP.NET Core MVC and uses HTML Helpers to build the user interface. The client application uses HttpClient to invoke Web API. The client also demonstrates how to write asynchronous actions (async/await) in the MVC controller.

- **Chapter 6:** This chapter teaches you to develop Employee Manager using jQuery and Web API. Data entry forms are designed using HTML5 markup. Data validations are performed using jQuery validation plugin. Communication between the client and the server is facilitated using jQuery Ajax. The CRUD operations are wrapped inside an asynchronous Web API and use asynchronous methods of Entity Framework Core. User authentication is implemented using JSON Web Tokens (JWTs).

- **Chapter 7:** In this chapter, you develop Employee Manager using Angular and Web API. Data entry forms are designed using Angular reactive forms. Form validations are performed using Angular's built-in validation techniques. Angular invokes Web API to perform CRUD operations. Communication between the client and the server is facilitated using Angular's HttpClient. User authentication is implemented using the JWT authentication scheme.

- **Chapter 8:** This chapter teaches you to develop Employee Manager using Blazor. The application uses Blazor's server-side hosting model. You learn to develop Razor Components. Data entry forms complete with validations are developed using Blazor's input components. The CRUD operations are encapsulated in a repository injected into Razor Components. User authentication and authorization are implemented using ASP.NET Core Identity and policy-based authorization.

- **Chapter 9:** In this chapter, you develop Employee Manager using three different data stores: Azure SQL Database, Azure Cosmos DB, and MongoDB. First, you learn to perform CRUD operations on Azure SQL Databases using the Microsoft.Data.SqlClient data provider. Then you learn two ways to access data residing in Azure Cosmos DB, namely, Cosmos DB client library and EF Core provider for Cosmos DB. Finally, you also learn to access data from MongoDB using MongoDB driver for .NET Core.

- **Chapter 10:** This chapter is about deploying Employee Manager you developed in earlier chapters. As an example it illustrates how the ASP.NET Core MVC version of Employee Manager can be deployed to Internet Information Services (IIS) followed by deploying to Azure App Service.

Downloading the Source Code

The complete source code for the book is available for download at the book's companion web site. Visit `www.apress.com`, and go to this book's information page. Then click the Download source code option to go to the book's source code available on GitHub.

Contacting the Author

You can reach me via my web site – `www.binaryintellect.net`. You can also follow me on Facebook, Twitter, and LinkedIn (visit my web site for the links).

CHAPTER 1

Introduction to ASP.NET Core

This chapter introduces you to the basics of ASP.NET Core. It discusses the main development options available in ASP.NET Core, namely, MVC, Razor Pages, and Web API. Since you are going to work extensively with ASP.NET Core projects in the later chapters, it is worthwhile to learn how to create an ASP.NET Core web application using the Visual Studio IDE. To that end, this chapter helps you to

- Understand main development options available in ASP.NET Core.

- Create an ASP.NET Core MVC application.

- Create an ASP.NET Core Razor Pages application.

- Create an ASP.NET Core Web API application.

- Install the Northwind sample database.

Overview of ASP.NET Core

ASP.NET Core is a framework for building modern web applications and services. It's part of .NET Core and is a cross-platform and open source framework. This means you can develop and deploy your web applications targeting all the popular operating systems such as Windows, Linux, and macOS.

ASP.NET Core is a redesigned and rewritten framework for building modern web applications. Although we won't discuss each and every feature of the framework here, some of its important technical features are listed as follows:

- Cross-platform framework. You can develop and run web applications on Windows, Linux, and macOS.

1

© Bipin Joshi 2019
B. Joshi, *Beginning Database Programming Using ASP.NET Core 3*,
https://doi.org/10.1007/978-1-4842-5509-4_1

- Open source with a lot of community involvement.

- Built-in dependency injection (DI) framework.

- ASP.NET Core includes a built-in web server called Kestrel. You can use Kestrel by itself or host your web applications under IIS, Nginx, or Apache.

- Multiple development options for UI including MVC, Razor Pages, and Blazor. (Of course, you can also use client-side JavaScript frameworks to develop the front-end.)

- Unified programming model for MVC web applications and Web APIs.

- High-performance modular request pipeline suitable for modern, cloud-optimized applications.

Figure 1-1 shows the layers of ASP.NET Core.

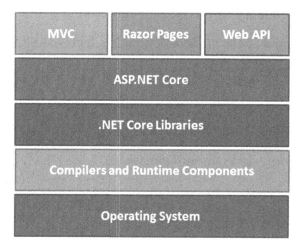

Figure 1-1. *Layers of .NET Core and ASP.NET Core*

As you can see from Figure 1-1, the bottommost layer is the operating system. Because .NET Core is a cross-platform framework, this could be Windows, Linux, or macOS. Your web application code is going to be the same regardless of the underlying operating system.

To develop and run .NET Core applications, you must have language compilers and other necessary runtime components. They are installed when you install .NET Core on the machine.

The next layer primarily consists of the .NET Core libraries and framework-level services. These libraries provide you several features including data types and file IO. ASP.NET Core makes use of the .NET Core libraries and hence is shown sitting on top of this layer.

ASP.NET Core offers three main development options, namely, ASP.NET Core MVC, ASP.NET Core Razor Pages, and ASP.NET Core Web APIs. These options make the top layer of the diagram.

ASP.NET Core is built considering modularity. Most of the ASP.NET Core applications (MVC/Razor Pages/Web APIs) make use of functionality that resides in NuGet packages.

From the preceding discussion, you know that there are three primary development options – MVC, Razor Pages, and Web APIs. Let's discuss each of them briefly before we go into the code-level details.

Note   You can also use Blazor to build interactive rich client-side UI using C#, HTML, and CSS. However, Blazor is a relatively new addition to the ASP.NET Core family and hence is not discussed in this chapter. You learn more about Blazor in Chapter 8.

ASP.NET Core MVC

ASP.NET Core MVC allows you to build web applications using the Model-View-Controller (MVC) pattern. Although detailed discussion of the MVC pattern is beyond the scope of this book, a brief discussion of MVC as applicable to ASP.NET Core follows.

The responsibility of a web application built using ASP.NET Core MVC is divided into three components: model, view, and controller. Model represents the application's data and could be anything from a primitive type to a complex object. View houses the application's user interface (UI) and usually displays data held by the model. View also accepts user input and commands. Controller mediates between a model and a view. Its job is to prepare the model required for a view and also to act upon the user input and commands as captured by the view. It also decides the program flow by deciding which model and view to send next to the user. Thus, a controller might need to deal with many models and many views. An end user never deals with a model and a view directly; rather, it invokes the controller.

Figure 1-2 shows the model, view, and controller relationship.

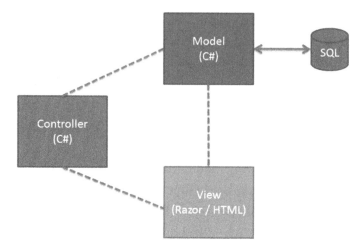

Figure 1-2. *MVC pattern as applied to ASP.NET Core MVC*

As far as ASP.NET Core MVC is concerned, a model typically takes the form of a C# object(s) and often holds data from some data store such as SQL Server. A view physically exists as a .cshtml file and primarily contains markup and Razor code. A controller is a C# class and typically contains one or more methods called actions. The job of a controller as discussed earlier is accomplished by its actions. The end user invokes the controller to get some job done.

ASP.NET Core MVC is a good development choice when your program flow is complex and involves multiple models and views. It's also a preferred development option for Ajax-based scenarios and Single Page Applications (SPAs).

ASP.NET Core Razor Pages

ASP.NET Core Razor Pages allows you to build web applications that use a Model-View-ViewModel (MVVM)-like pattern. The Model-View-ViewModel pattern splits the application functionality into three components: model, view, and ViewModel. The striking difference between MVC and MVVM is the absence of a separate controller class.

In MVVM, the model and the view have the same responsibilities as in the MVC pattern. The ViewModel is closely related to a view and is responsible for view-specific things such as data binding, UI event handling, and UI notifications. It encapsulates view-specific data and behavior. It also updates the underlying data model whenever necessary.

Figure 1-3 shows MVVM as applicable to Razor Pages.

4

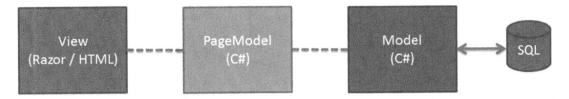

Figure 1-3. *MVVM pattern as applied to ASP.NET Core Razor Pages*

As far as ASP.NET Core Razor Pages is concerned, the view resides in a .cshtml file just like that of an MVC application. For each view, there is a PageModel (ViewModel from MVVM) C# class that houses bindable properties and form processing actions called handlers. The PageModel class also deals with the data model to update or fetch application data.

Razor Pages is the preferred development option for page-focused scenarios with a simple program flow. The lack of a controller class also makes their code organization simpler.

ASP.NET Core Web API

ASP.NET Core Web APIs make use of the same controller-based programming model as used by MVC applications. However, they don't have any views. Web APIs expose certain functionality using REST (REpresentational State Transfer) guidelines. Typically, a Web API consists of a controller that houses five actions. These actions deal with HTTP verbs, namely, GET, POST, PUT, and DELETE. The Web API actions contain processing that you want to execute when the Web API is invoked using a particular HTTP verb.

Once a Web API is ready, it's hosted on a server so that client applications can consume it. The clients could be any type of application such as a JavaScript application, a server-side web application, or even a desktop application.

Figure 1-4 shows the arrangement of a Web API.

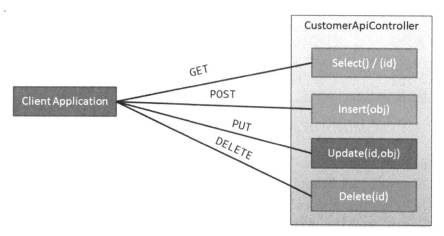

```
http://localhost/api/customer
```

Figure 1-4. *Web API implementing REST guidelines*

As you can see from Figure 1-4, a Web API is a controller named CustomerApiController that contains five actions – Select(), SelectByID(), Insert(), Update(), and Delete(). The action names could be anything, but they are mapped to an HTTP verb. For example, the Select() action is mapped to deal with GET verb, the Insert() action is mapped to deal with POST verb, and so on.

Also notice the parameters of these actions. Two variations of Select() are possible – one that accepts no parameters and the other that accepts an ID of a resource as its parameter. The former variation is intended to retrieve information about multiple resources, whereas the latter is intended to retrieve information about a particular resource matching the specified ID. The Insert() action accepts an object that indicates a new resource to be created on the server. The Update() action accepts an ID of a resource to be updated and an object containing modified values of that resource. The Delete() action accepts an ID of a resource to be deleted.

The Web API is made available at a well-known URL (`http://localhost/api/ customer` in this example). The client application then makes HTTP requests to the Web API in an attempt to invoke the desired functionality.

Web APIs are quite common wherever functionality is to be exposed through a service. This includes Ajax-based scenarios, Single Page Applications (SPA), and also the service layer.

Now that you know the main development options in ASP.NET Core, let's build a simple "Hello World" application using each of them.

> **Note** If you are already comfortable working with Visual Studio IDE and ASP.
> NET Core projects, you may skip to Chapter 2. If you are new to ASP.NET Core
> development or have recently started playing with it, you might want to go
> through the following sections to get an idea of overall project structure and code
> organization.

Creating an ASP.NET Core MVC Project

In this section, you will create a "Hello World" project using ASP.NET Core MVC. The
application you develop will output a message – Hello World! – in the browser and
will also allow you to specify a custom message. Figure 1-5 shows the main page of the
application.

Figure 1-5. *Main page of the "Hello World" application*

As you can see, the page displays a Hello World! message in the heading, but also
allows you to enter a different message in a textbox. Upon clicking the "Submit" button,
the Hello World! will be replaced by the new message you specify. This is shown in
Figure 1-6 where the message is changed to Hello Universe!.

Figure 1-6. *Message changed to "Hello Universe!"*

To begin developing this application, open Visual Studio and click the Create a new project option from the start window (Figure 1-7).

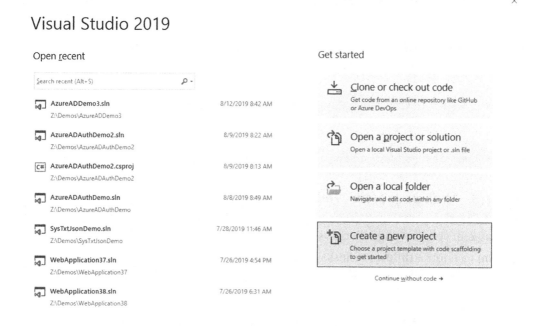

Figure 1-7. *Creating a new project*

Doing so will open another dialog wherein you can select a project template for your new project. This dialog is shown in Figure 1-8.

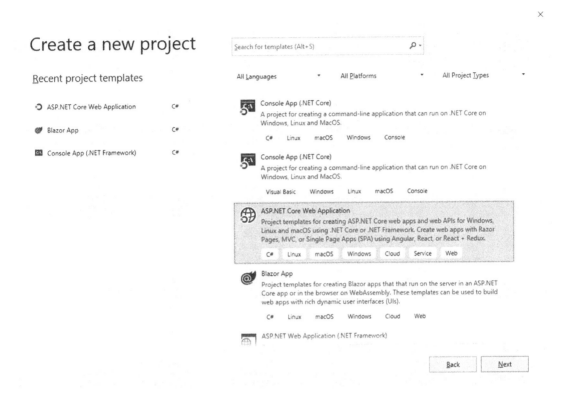

Figure 1-8. *Selecting a project template*

Select ASP.NET Core Web Application in this dialog and click the Next button. You will be asked to enter a project name and its location (Figure 1-9).

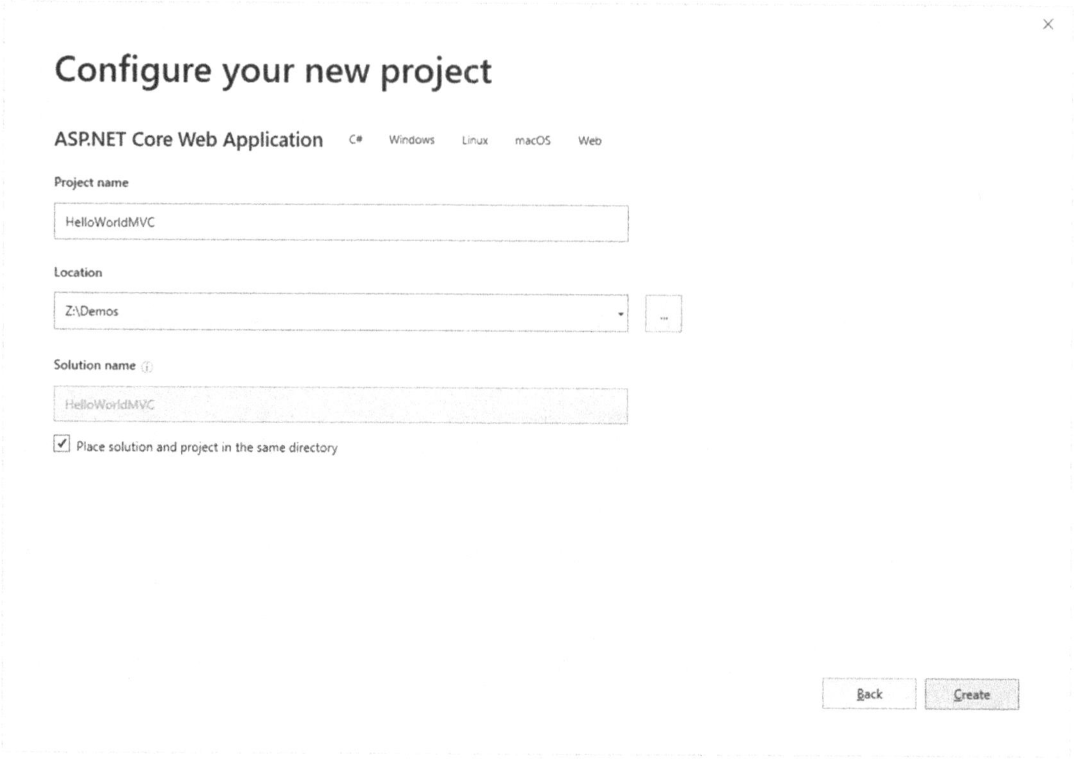

Figure 1-9. *Specifying a project name and location*

Specify those details and click the Create button. As the final step, you need to pick an ASP.NET Core project template (Figure 1-10).

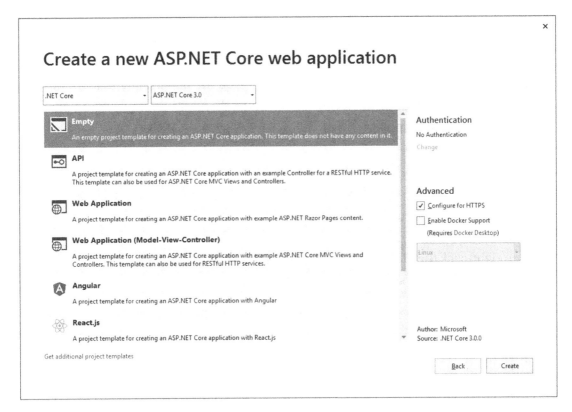

Figure 1-10. *Picking an ASP.NET Core project template*

Here, you will have many project templates such as Empty, API, Web Application, and Web Application (Model-View-Controller). You can also select the .NET framework type – .NET Core or .NET Framework – and the ASP.NET Core version from the dropdown lists at the top. By default, .NET Core and ASP.NET Core 3.0 will be selected in these dropdowns. Keep that selection unchanged. Select the Empty project template from the list.

The Configure for HTTPS checkbox under the Advanced section is checked by default. If this checkbox is checked, the project is configured to use an HTTPS self-signed certificate. Since the certificate is self-signed, your browser might show you a security warning when you run such application. And you will need to configure your browser to trust this certificate (simply follow the browser's instructions). If you uncheck this checkbox, the project uses HTTP. Projects that you create in this book can work with any scheme (HTTP or HTTPS), but in most of the real-world cases, you would prefer HTTPS for security reasons. Now click "Create" to create the project.

Note   While we could have selected the "Web Application (Model-View-Controller)" template for our project, we chose not to, instead selecting the "Empty" project template. This selection will give you the opportunity to learn how to add all the pieces that go in an application yourself, rather than relying on pieces added by the project template.

Once the empty project gets created, add three folders under the project root – Models, Views, and Controllers – by right-clicking the project and then selecting the Add ➤ New Folder shortcut menu option. Also, add a subfolder named Home under the Views folder.

Then right-click the Models folder and select Add ➤ Class from the shortcut menu. This will open a dialog as shown in Figure 1-11.

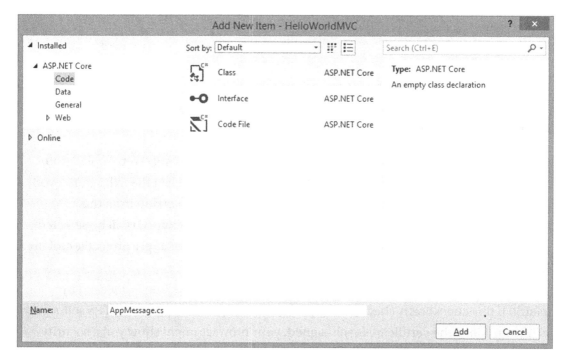

Figure 1-11. *Adding a new class to the Models folder*

Name the class as AppMessage and click the "Add" button. Once the class gets added, write the code shown in Listing 1-1 into it.

Listing 1-1. AppMessage class

```
public class AppMessage
{
    public string Message { get; set; }
}
```

The `AppMessage` class has just one public property called `Message` that represents a message to be displayed in the browser.

Next, right-click the Controllers folder and select Add ➤ "New Item" from the shortcut menu. This will open the Add New Item dialog as shown in Figure 1-12.

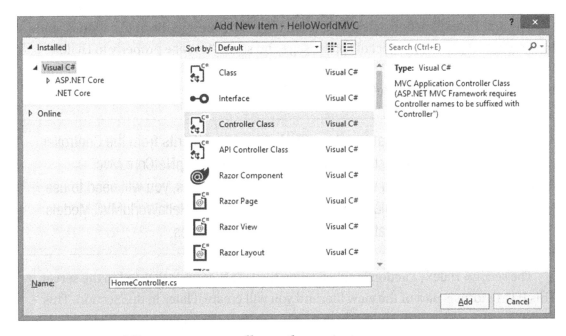

Figure 1-12. *Adding a new controller to the project*

Select "Controller Class" from the list, name the controller `HomeController`, and click the Add button. Once the `HomeController` gets added, remove the default Index() action from it, and add two new actions as shown in Listing 1-2.

Listing 1-2. HomeController contains two actions

```
public IActionResult Index()
{
    AppMessage obj = new AppMessage() {
```

13

```
        Message = "Hello World!"
    };
    return View(obj);
}

[HttpPost]
public IActionResult Index(AppMessage obj)
{
    ViewBag.Message = "Message changed.";
    return View(obj);
}
```

The first Index() action gets called when the first request to the application is made. Inside, you create a new object of AppMessage and set its Message property to Hello World!. This object is passed to the view using the View() method. The View() method exists in the base class of HomeController – Controller.

Note You will observe that the HomeController class inherits from the Controller class. The Controller base class resides in the Microsoft.AspNetCore.Mvc namespace. While working with ASP.NET Core MVC projects, you will need to use this namespace in many places. You also need to use the HelloWorldMVC.Models namespace in order to be able to use the AppMessage class.

The second Index() action is called when the HTML form is POSTed to the server. This HTML form is part of the view file, and you will create it later in this section. This Index() action receives the message entered by the user wrapped in the object of AppMessage. This mapping of textbox value to the Message property of AppMessage is accomplished by the framework through a process called model binding. Inside, you pass the object to the View() method as before. Additionally, you also set the Message property on the ViewBag object. ViewBag is a built-in object provided by ASP.NET Core and is used to pass data from the controller to the view. This Message value will be outputted on the view.

Note that the second Index() action is decorated with the [HttpPost] attribute. The [HttpPost] attribute indicates that the underlying action will be invoked only for POST requests.

Note   In the preceding code, you created two overloads of the Index() action. However, keep in mind that this overloading works as expected because they are dealing with different types of requests. For example, the first Index() handles the initial request to the action, whereas the second Index() handles form submission POST request. If you comment out the [HttpPost] attribute added to the second Index(), you will get AmbiguousMatchException indicating that the framework can't decide which action to use. You can use the [ActionName] attribute to overcome this problem. You will use [ActionName] in later chapters of this book.

So far, you have completed the model and the controller required by the application. Let's add the final piece – view – that houses the user interface of the application.

To add a view, right-click the Views ➤ Home folder and select the Add New Item menu option. This time, select Razor View and specify the name to be Index.cshtml (Figure 1-13).

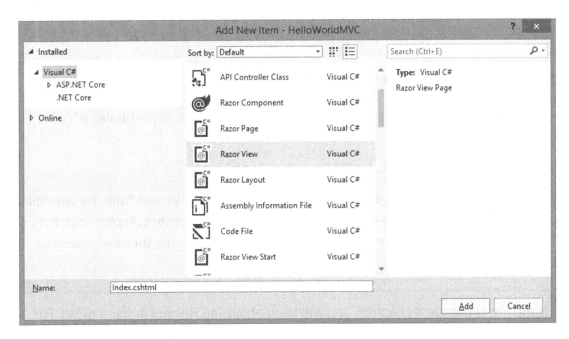

Figure 1-13. *Adding Index view to the project*

Note that the name of the action matches with the name of the view. This way, the View() method assumes that the model is to be supplied to the Index view.

The Index view will use what are known as Tag Helpers to render the user interface. By default, Tag Helpers are not available to a view. To add support for Tag Helpers, open the Add New Item dialog again and select Razor View Imports (Figure 1-14).

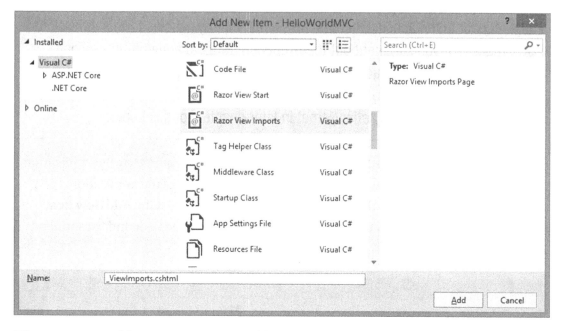

Figure 1-14. *Adding a view imports file*

Once the view imports file (_ViewImports.cshtml) is added, write this line of code into it:

```
@addTagHelper *,Microsoft.AspNetCore.Mvc.TagHelpers
```

Using the @addTagHelper directive adds Tag Helpers to the project from the assembly that follows. In this case, built-in Tag Helpers reside in the Microsoft.AspNetCore.Mvc. TagHelpers assembly. The * indicates that all Tag Helpers from the specified assembly are to be added.

Note   In subsequent chapters, you will learn about Tag Helpers in more detail. For now, keep in mind that they allow you to render the user interface elements of an ASP.NET Core web application.

Next, open the Index.cshtml file and write the markup and code shown in Listing 1-3 into it.

Listing 1-3. Markup and code from Index view

```
@model HelloWorldMVC.Models.AppMessage

<html>
    <head>
        <title>Hello World App</title>
    </head>
    <body>
        <h1>@Model.Message</h1>
        <hr />
        <h2>@ViewBag.Message</h2>
        <form asp-controller="Home" asp-action="Index" method="post">
            <label asp-for="Message">Enter Message :</label>
            <br /><br />
            <input type="text" asp-for="Message" />
            <br /><br />
            <button type="submit">Submit</button>
        </form>
    </body>
</html>
```

The view markup begins with the @model directive that specifies the type of model class being supplied to this view. Recollect that you are supplying an object of AppMessage class to the View() method. Therefore, @model specifies AppMessage as the view's model type.

The actual model object passed through the View() method can be accessed inside a view file using the Model property. In this example, you output the model's Message property on the response using @ razor expression syntax. Similarly, the code also renders ViewBag's Message property on the response.

The Form Tag Helper (<form> tag) renders an HTML form with three fields – a label, a textbox, and a button. Notice that the Form Tag Helper looks quite similar to the standard HTML <form> tag. However, it has some special attributes such as asp-controller and asp-action. The asp-controller and asp-action attributes decide which controller and action will be used to process the form upon submission. In this case, the form will be submitted to the Index() action of HomeController. The method attribute configures the form to use the POST method to submit its content.

The Label and Input Tag Helpers use the asp-for attribute to bind the underlying form field to the model's Message property. This way, the textbox displays the value of the Message property. A user can edit the textbox value and hit the Submit button.

This completes the Index view. Before you run the application, you need to configure the application's startup. To do so, open the Startup.cs file and go to its ConfigureServices() method. Modify ConfigureServices() as shown in Listing 1-4.

Listing 1-4. ConfigureServices() method

```
public void ConfigureServices(IServiceCollection services)
{
    services.AddControllersWithViews();
}
```

The code shown in Listing 1-4 calls the services.AddControllersWithViews() extension method of IServiceCollection. Doing so registers several built-in types related to MVC applications with ASP.NET Core's dependency injection framework.

Now modify the Configure() method inside Startup.cs as shown in Listing 1-5.

Listing 1-5. Configure() method

```
public void Configure(IApplicationBuilder app, IWebHostEnvironment env)
{
    if (env.IsDevelopment())
    {
        app.UseDeveloperExceptionPage();
    }

    app.UseRouting();

    app.UseEndpoints(endpoints =>
    {
      endpoints.MapControllerRoute(
        name: "default",
        pattern: "{controller=Home}/{action=Index}/{id?}");
    });
}
```

The Configure() method is used to configure your application's HTTP pipeline. It adds the required middleware to the HTTP pipeline. In this example, the code checks whether the application is running in development environment or production environment. This is done using the IsDevelopment() method of IWebHostEnvironment. Accordingly, UseDeveloperExceptionPage() is called to add developer exception page middleware to the pipeline. This middleware is responsible for displaying the actual exception details in the browser whenever an error occurs.

Finally, the code adds routing capabilities to the application. The UseRouting() call adds what is known as the endpoint routing middleware to the HTTP pipeline. The UseEndpoints() call wires the endpoint middleware in the application. The pattern mentioned inside the UseEndpoints() handles the request URLs of the form https://localhost:1234/<controller_name>/<action_name>. For example, the Index() can be invoked using this URL: https://localhost:1234/Home/Index. The UseEndpoints() method also configures the HomeController to be the default controller and Index() action to be the default action for the routes.

This completes the application. At this time, your Solution Explorer should resemble Figure 1-15.

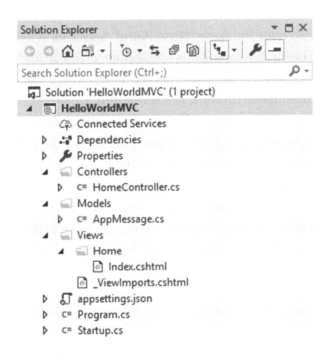

Figure 1-15. *View of Solution Explorer with various files*

Confirm whether you have added various files to the correct folders as shown in Solution Explorer and run the application by pressing F5.

Note   While working with ASP.NET Core MVC projects, you can store models and controllers in any folder though many developers store them in Models and Controllers folders, respectively (like you did in the preceding example). For example, you can store models inside a folder named AppModels. The recommended location for view files is the Views folder (or its subfolders) because by default the framework searches for views in that folder.

If all goes well, Visual Studio will start IIS Express and you will see the application's Index view loaded in the browser. By default, the application will show the Hello World! message. Enter some different message in the textbox and click the Submit button. The heading should now reflect the newly entered message.

Creating an ASP.NET Core Razor Pages Project

In this section, you will create the same "Hello World" application using ASP.NET Core Razor Pages. To begin developing this application, create a new ASP.NET Core project using the Empty project template. This task is exactly the same as before with an exception that the project name this time is HelloWorldRazorPages.

Once the new project gets created, add two folders to it, namely, Models and Pages. The purpose of the Models folder is to store model classes, whereas the Pages folder is used to store Razor Pages and associated page models.

Then add the AppMessage class to the Models folder as in the preceding example. Also place the view imports file (_ViewImports.cshtml) to the Pages folder. Now right-click the Pages folder and select Add New Item from the shortcut menu. This time, add a new Razor Page named Index.cshtml to the Pages folder (Figure 1-16).

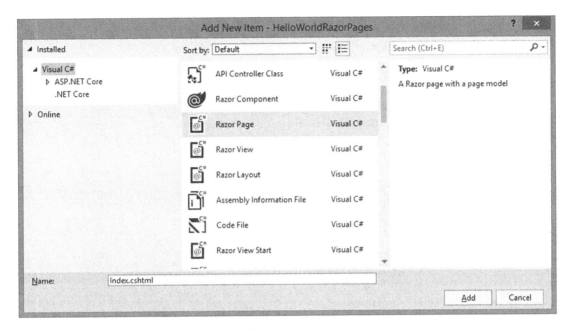

Figure 1-16. *Adding a new Razor Page*

When you add an Index Razor Page, actually two files get added – Index.cshtml and Index.cshtm.cs. The Index.cshtml file houses the Razor code and markup that makes the user interface, whereas the Index.cshtml.cs file represents the page model class.

To get started, your Solution Explorer should resemble Figure 1-17.

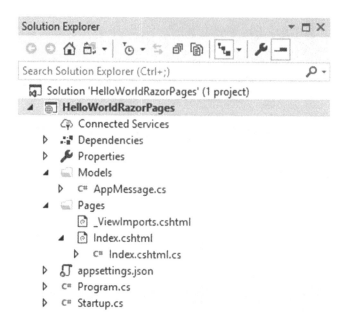

Figure 1-17. *HelloWorldRazorPages project in Solution Explorer*

Now open the Index.cshtml.cs file. This file contains a page model class named IndexModel. Modify the IndexModel class as shown in Listing 1-6.

Listing 1-6. Index page model class

```
public class IndexModel : PageModel
{
    [BindProperty]
    public AppMessage Heading { get; set; }

    public string SubHeading { get; set; }

    public void OnGet()
    {
        this.Heading = new AppMessage();
        this.Heading.Message = "Hello World!";
    }

    public void OnPost()
    {
```

```
        this.SubHeading = "Message changed.";
    }
}
```

The IndexModel class inherits from the PageModel class residing in the Microsoft. AspNetCore.Mvc.RazorPages namespace. The IndexModel class consists of two public properties and two public methods.

The Heading public property is of type AppMessage and is decorated with the [BindProperty] attribute. The [BindProperty] attribute indicates that this property will participate in the model binding.

The SubHeading string property is used to display a message to a user whenever textbox value is changed.

The OnGet() method is called a page handler and handles GET requests to the page. Similar to OnGet(), you can have OnPost(), OnPut(), and OnDelete() page handlers to deal with POST, PUT, and DELETE verbs.

The OnGet() page handler initializes the Heading property to a new AppMessage instance and also sets its Message property to Hello World!. The OnPost() page handler is invoked when a user hits the Submit button and POSTs the form to the server. Inside, the code sets the SubHeading property to a message. The Heading and SubHeading values are displayed on the Index.cshtml file. The markup and code of Index.cshtml is shown in Listing 1-7.

Listing 1-7. Displaying Heading and SubHeading

```
@page

@model HelloWorldRazorPages.Pages.IndexModel

<html>
    <head>
        <title>Hello World App</title>
    </head>
    <body>
        <h1>@Model.Heading.Message</h1>
        <hr />
        <h2>@Model.SubHeading</h2>
        <form method="post">
            <label asp-for="Heading.Message">Enter Message :</label>
```

```
            <br /><br />
            <input type="text" asp-for="Heading.Message" />
            <br /><br />
            <button type="submit">Submit</button>
        </form>
    </body>
</html>
```

Notice that Index.cshtml begins with the @page directive. The @page directive marks the .cshtml file as a Razor Page. The @model directive points to the type of page model class (IndexModel in this case).

The heading of the page displays AppMessage's Message property. Notice how the Heading object from the page model class is accessed using the Model property. This way, all the public properties of the page model class can be accessed using the Model object. The SubHeading is also rendered in a similar way.

The form tag has a method attribute set to post indicating that the form will use the POST method during submission. Inside, the form houses a label, a textbox, and a button as in the preceding example.

This completes the Index Razor Page. Before you run the application, you need to configure the startup using the Startup.cs file. So open the Startup.cs file and modify the ConfigureServices() and Configure() methods as shown in Listing 1-8.

Listing 1-8. Configuring application startup

```
public void ConfigureServices(IServiceCollection services)
{
    services.AddRazorPages();
}

public void Configure(IApplicationBuilder app, IWebHostEnvironment env)
{
    if (env.IsDevelopment())
    {
        app.UseDeveloperExceptionPage();
    }

    app.UseRouting();
```

```
    app.UseEndpoints(endpoints =>
    {
      endpoints.MapRazorPages();
    });
}
```

The code from Listing 1-9 should look familiar to you. This time, we used `AddRazorPages()` to register Razor Pages–related services with the dependency injection framework. Razor Pages uses a slightly different routing mechanism than MVC applications. The routing and URL handling is defined in the individual page using the @page directive. By default, Razor Pages URLs follow this pattern: `https://localhost:1234/<razor_page_name>`. For example, to access the Index page, the URL will be `https://localhost:1234/Index`. This configuration is done using the `MapRazorPages()` method inside the `UseEndpoints()` call.

Now run the application by pressing F5 and test the functionality by specifying a new message.

Note   When you run the MVC and Razor Pages applications, the browser's address bar may show only this URL – `https://localhost:1234` (port number will be different for you). That's because /Home/Index is the default for MVC applications and /Index is the default for Razor Pages applications. You can manually enter the full URL to confirm that they are indeed handled by the appropriate action and page handler, respectively.

Creating an ASP.NET Core Web API Project

Now that you have some idea about ASP.NET Core MVC and Razor Pages applications, let's create a Web API that returns messages when called.

To begin creating a Web API, create a new project named HelloWorldWebApi based on the Empty project template. Web API uses a controller-centric approach to build RESTful services.

Once a project is created, add the Models and Controllers folders to it. Also, add the `AppMessage` class to the Models folder. Since Web API is about services, there won't be any user interface elements in the project.

Then open the "Add New Item" dialog and add a new API controller class to the Controllers folder (Figure 1-18).

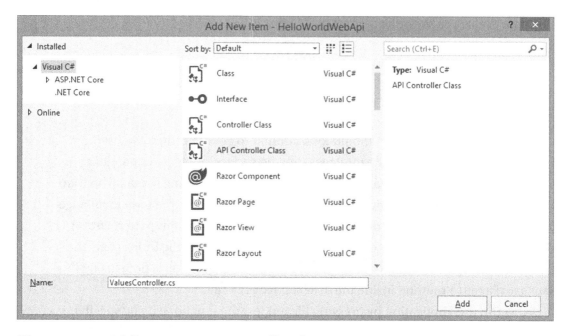

Figure 1-18. *Adding a new API controller class*

The default API controller name is ValuesController; keep that unchanged. You will observe that ValuesController is decorated with the [Route] attribute. This is how routing is configured in Web API applications. The [Route("api/[controller]")] attribute indicates that the API will be available at https://localhost:1234/api/ Values (the port number will vary as per your setup).

Now remove all the actions from within the ValuesController except the first Get() action. In this example, you will handle only GET requests, and hence other actions are not necessary. Modify the Get() action as shown in Listing 1-9.

Listing 1-9. Returning messages from the Get() action

```
[HttpGet]
public List<AppMessage> Get()
{
    List<AppMessage> messages = new List<AppMessage>();
    messages.Add(new AppMessage() { Message = "Hello World!" });
    messages.Add(new AppMessage() { Message = "Hello Galaxy!" });
    messages.Add(new AppMessage() { Message = "Hello Universe!" });
    return messages;
}
```

The Get() action is decorated with the [HttpGet] attribute indicating that it will handle GET requests to the API. Note that the Get() action returns List of AppMessage objects. Inside, the code creates a new List of AppMessage and adds three AppMessage objects to it. These objects have their Message property set to Hello World!, Hello Galaxy!, and Hello Universe!, respectively. Finally, the List of AppMessage objects is returned from the Get() action.

Although the API is ready, you need to configure the startup similar to how you did for MVC and Razor Pages projects. So modify the ConfigureServices() and Configure() methods of the Startup class as shown in Listing 1-10.

Listing 1-10. Configuring Web API startup

```
public void ConfigureServices(IServiceCollection services)
{
    services.AddControllers();
}

public void Configure(IApplicationBuilder app, IWebHostEnvironment env)
{
    if (env.IsDevelopment())
    {
        app.UseDeveloperExceptionPage();
    }

    app.UseRouting();

    app.UseEndpoints(endpoints =>
    {
        endpoints.MapControllers();
    });
}
```

Notice that the code inside ConfigureServices() calls the AddControllers() method to register API-specific services with the dependency injection framework. The Configure() method now uses the MapControllers() method inside the UseEndpoints() to set up the routing for the API.

This completes the Web API. Run the application by pressing F5. When a browser window is opened, go to the browser's address bar and manually enter the API URL – `https://localhost:1234/api/Values` (change the port number as per your setup). This will cause a GET request to be sent to the API, and the `Get()` action will be invoked returning messages as shown in Figure 1-19.

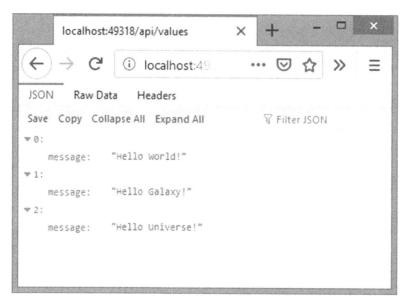

Figure 1-19. *Messages are returned in JavaScript Object Notation (JSON) format*

If you observe the raw data of the response, it will be in JSON format. While working with Web APIs, it's very common to serialize and de-serialize data in JSON format. ASP.NET Core has its own classes to accomplish this task. Additionally, ASP. NET Core supports a popular JSON processing library – Json.NET. Since Json.NET is a quite popular library, you might need to use it instead of ASP.NET Core's default JSON processing mechanism. Luckily, there is an easy way to switch to Json.NET in your ASP. NET Core applications (although you don't need that in this example). You need to add a NuGet package `Microsoft.AspNetCore.Mvc.NewtonsoftJson.` You can do that by right-clicking the Dependencies folder and selecting the Manage NuGet Packages shortcut menu option (Figure 1-20).

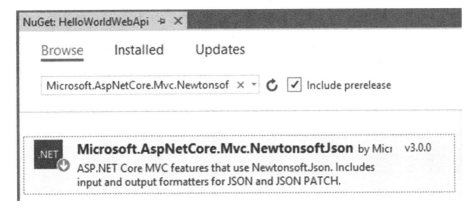

Figure 1-20. Adding `Microsoft.AspNetCore.Mvc.NewtonsoftJson` *NuGet package*

Once you add this NuGet package, you need to change the code from
ConfigureServices() like this:

```
public void ConfigureServices(IServiceCollection services)
{
    services.AddControllers()
            .AddNewtonsoftJson();
}
```

The AddNewtonsoftJson() method adds support for JSON-related features and uses
Json.NET for its functioning.

Installing the Northwind Database

In many examples discussed throughout this book, you use the Northwind sample
database. So you need to install it in your SQL Server instance. You can download
the Northwind database scripts from its GitHub repository at https://github.com/
Microsoft/sql-server-samples/tree/master/samples/databases/northwind-pubs.
Specifically, the instnwnd.sql file contains scripts necessary for creating the Northwind
database. Figure 1-21 shows this file in the GitHub repository.

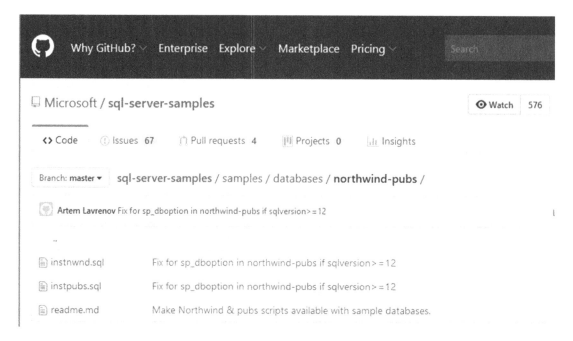

Figure 1-21. *Downloading script for the Northwind sample database*

Once you have the database script, you can run it using SQL Server Management Studio. Figure 1-22 shows the Northwind database created after successful run of the script.

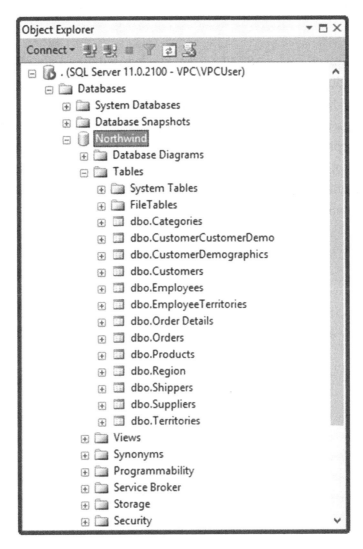

Figure 1-22. *Installing the Northwind sample database*

We mainly need access to the Employees table of the Northwind database. You will observe the Employees table of the Northwind database in the next chapter.

Summary

This chapter introduced you to ASP.NET Core. You learned the basics of MVC and MVVM patterns. You also learned about the main development options offered by ASP. NET Core, namely, MVC, Razor Pages, and Web API. You got acquainted with these three flavors by creating a simple "Hello World" application using Visual Studio. You used the Empty project template and various code files to build the example applications. You also got a glimpse of the application's Startup class, `ConfigureServices()` method, and `Configure()` method. Finally, you installed the Northwind sample database for use in the subsequent chapters.

CHAPTER 2

Sample Application

In this chapter, you will be introduced to the Employee Manager application, specifically its functionality and user interface. Nowadays, many projects use GitHub repositories for collaboration and version control. So it is worthwhile to learn how to host your source code in a private GitHub repository. Learning objectives for this chapter include the following:

- Get familiar with the user interface of the Employee Manager application.

- Understand how the Employee Manager application works.

- Learn about the database structure (column names, data types, sample data, and such details) of the Employees table.

- Explore various technology options used to build the sample application.

- Create a private GitHub repository and work with it from within the Visual Studio IDE.

Features of Employee Manager

As you build and work with the Employee Manager application, it's essential to have some context and insight as to how it functions. This discussion will help you to envision the application functionality as you use various technology features and options to build it.

Modern web application development using frameworks such as ASP.NET Core involves a lot of technology options. For learning purposes, our focus will encompass the following frequently needed features:

- **HTML form processing:** Modern web applications do far more than show pages of information. They accept input from the end user. They also perform data validations and business processing. HTML form processing is, therefore, a common need in such applications.

© Bipin Joshi 2019
B. Joshi, *Beginning Database Programming Using ASP.NET Core 3*,
https://doi.org/10.1007/978-1-4842-5509-4_2

- **CRUD operations:** Modern web applications use data stores such as SQL Server for persisting application data. Performing CRUD operations on a database is a common task in such applications. You accept user input through HTML forms and then based on the application's requirement perform either of the CRUD operations. You will use SQL Server as well as a few NoSQL databases as data stores for your application.

- **User authentication:** Securing web applications using some sort of user authentication scheme is another frequently needed feature. User authentication and authorization helps you restrict access to your web application and also allows you to control what a user can do with your system. To that end, user name and password–based authentication is a widely used approach.

- **JavaScript libraries and frameworks:** Modern web applications heavily utilize client-side scripting. There are many JavaScript libraries and frameworks available today that you can integrate with ASP.NET Core to accomplish your tasks. We will use jQuery and Angular to understand how CRUD operations can be performed using Ajax techniques.

- **Deployment:** Once an ASP.NET Core web application is built, you will need to deploy it on a server. Two common deployment targets for ASP.NET Core are IIS and Azure App Service.

Developing a simple yet fully functional application like Employee Manager introduces you to many different technologies and technology options.

Employee Manager is a web application built using ASP.NET Core. Its main functional and technical aspects are summarized as follows:

- CRUD (Create, Read, Update, and Delete) operations can be implemented on the Employees table of the Northwind database. These CRUD operations are the central theme of Employee Manager. The other features are built around this CRUD functionality.

- Options to add a new employee, modify an existing employee, and delete an existing employee.

- Data entry pages include data validation and basic error handling logic.

- User authentication is included. Features such as user registration, signing in, and signing out are provided to ensure that only authenticated users can use the application.

- Server-side and client-side techniques can be used to build the same application. This will allow you to learn CRUD operations in light of a particular set of technology features and options.

- While the application uses basic CSS styling, user interface technologies such as CSS frameworks, animations, and graphics are downplayed.

- Covers basic exception handling and error checking. Note it does not cover every possible unexpected behavior. This way, you can keep the code base simple and easy to understand.

Now that you know about the functionality of Employee Manager, let's look at the Employees table containing the application's data.

Understanding the Employees Table

In Chapter 1, you installed the Northwind database in SQL Server and glanced at the list of tables. In this section, we'll dive into the Employees table – the main table used in the application – in greater detail.

You can either use SQL Server Management Studio or Visual Studio to work with the Northwind database. In the following scenario, I am going to use Visual Studio to look at the Employees table data as well as schema. So let's get going.

Open Visual Studio and click the Tools ➤ Connect to database menu option. If you are connecting to any database for the first time, Visual Studio asks you to choose a data source (Figure 2-1).

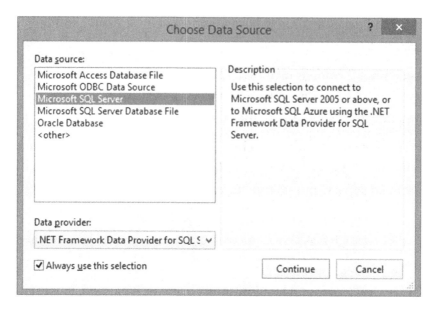

Figure 2-1. *Choosing a data source*

Pick Microsoft SQL Server from the list and keep other settings unchanged, and click the Continue button. You are now required to specify database connection details such as database server name or IP, database name, and security mode. This is shown in Figure 2-2.

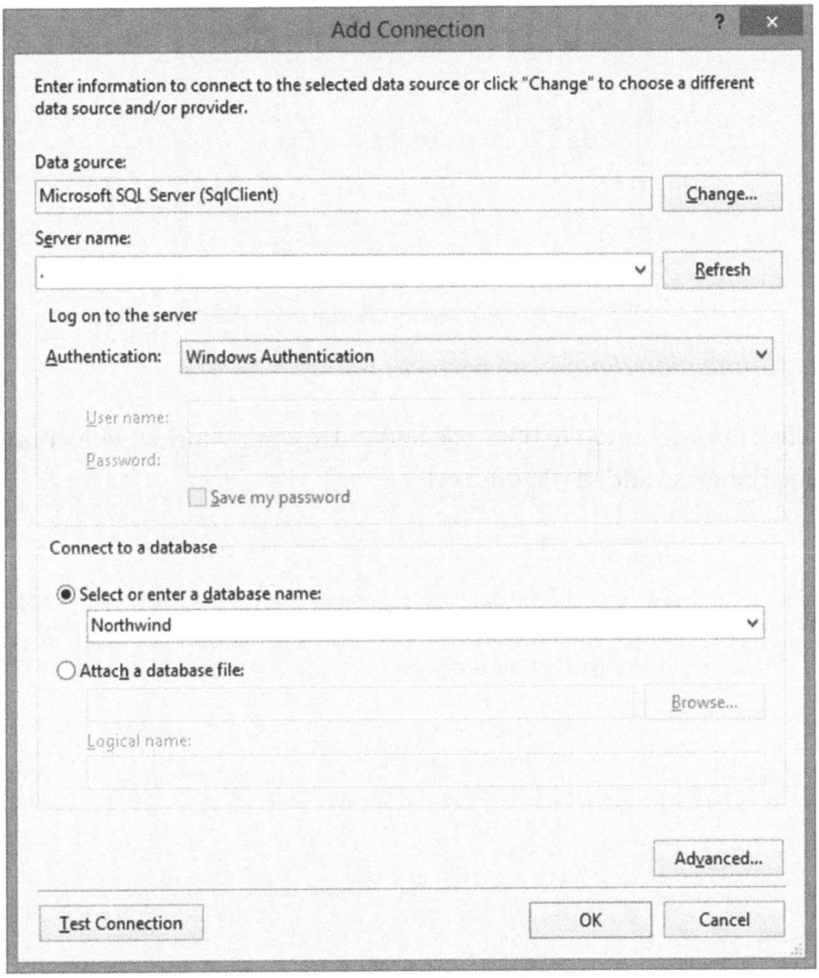

Figure 2-2. *Specifying database connection details*

Specify the server name per your installation. I have specified "." to indicate that SQL Server is installed locally on the same machine and is using the default instance of SQL Server. Security mode is set to "Windows Authentication." You can select the Northwind database from the Select dropdown menu or enter a database name in the combo box. You can quickly confirm whether your connection details are accurate by clicking the "Test Connection" button available at the bottom. If all the details are correct, you will be told that the test connection was successful (Figure 2-3).

Figure 2-3.   *Connection details are correct*

Finally, click the OK button to open the Server Explorer window with connection to the Northwind database added (Figure 2-4).

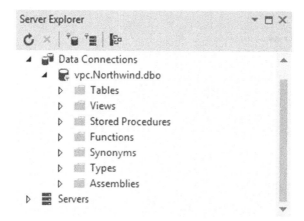

Figure 2-4.   *Data connection added for the Northwind database*

You can now look at the various tables of the Northwind database. Expand the Tables folder to reveal the list of tables and then locate the Employees table from the list. Right-click the Employees table and select Show Table Data from the shortcut menu (Figure 2-5).

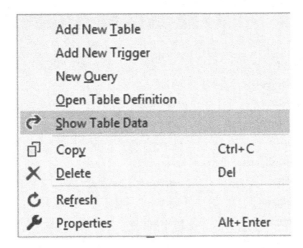

Figure 2-5. *Viewing table data*

This will open the Employees table in editor mode where you can view and modify employee details. Figure 2-6 shows the Employees table opened in the editor.

EmployeeID	LastName	FirstName	Title	TitleOfCourtesy	BirthDate	HireDate	Ac
1	Davolio	Nancy	Sales Represent...	Ms.	12/8/1948 12:00...	5/1/1992 12:00:...	507
2	Fuller	Andrew	Vice President, ...	Dr.	2/19/1952 12:00...	8/14/1992 12:00...	908
3	Leverling	Janet	Sales Represent...	Ms.	8/30/1963 12:00...	4/1/1992 12:00:...	722
4	Peacock	Margaret	Sales Represent...	Mrs.	9/19/1937 12:00...	5/3/1993 12:00:...	411
5	Buchanan	Steven	Sales Manager	Mr.	3/4/1955 12:00:...	10/17/1993 12:0...	14
6	Suyama	Michael	Sales Represent...	Mr.	7/2/1963 12:00:...	10/17/1993 12:0...	Co
7	King	Robert	Sales Represent...	Mr.	5/29/1960 12:00...	1/2/1994 12:00:...	Ed
8	Callahan	Laura	Inside Sales Co...	Ms.	1/9/1958 12:00:...	3/5/1994 12:00:...	47
9	Dodsworth	Anne	Sales Represent...	Ms.	1/27/1966 12:00...	11/15/1994 12:0...	7 H
NULL	NULL	NULL	NULL	NULL	NULL	NULL	NU

Figure 2-6. *Employees table opened in the editor*

Now that you have an understanding of Employees table sample data, let's take a look at the schema to learn more about columns and their data types.

Right-click the Employees table again, but this time select "Open Table Definition" from the shortcut menu. This will open the table definition in editor mode, as shown in Figure 2-7.

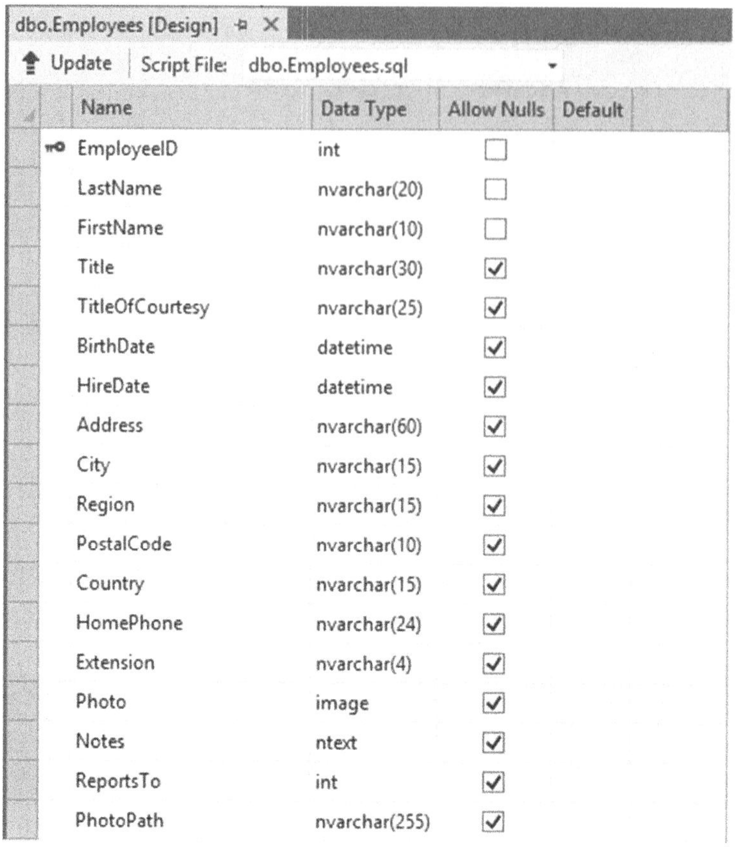

Figure 2-7. *Employees table definition opened in the editor*

The table definition editor allows you to look at the table schema, and you can also modify the table structure if necessary. Although the Employees table contains many columns, you won't use all of them as a part of Employee Manager. You use eight of them, namely, EmployeeID, FirstName, LastName, Title, BirthDate, HireDate, Country, and Notes. These columns, their data types, and their purpose are discussed as follows:

- **EmployeeID:** It's an identity column and acts as the primary key of the table. For example, the first employee record has EmployeeID of 1.

- **FirstName:** Represents an employee's first name. Its data type is nvarchar and length can be up to ten characters. For example, the first employee record has FirstName as Nancy.

- **LastName:** Represents an employee's last name. Its data type is nvarchar and length can be up to 20 characters. For example, the first employee record has LastName value of Davolio.

- **Title:** Represents the designation of an employee. Its data type is nvarchar and length can be up to 30 characters. For example, the first employee record has Title of Sales Representative.

- **BirthDate:** Represents the date of birth of an employee. Its data type is datetime although the time part is not used by the Employee Manager application. For example, the first employee record has BirthDate of 12/8/1948 12:00:00 AM.

- **HireDate:** Represents the date on which an employee was hired by the organization. Its data type is datetime although the time part is not used by the Employee Manager application. For example, the first employee record has HireDate of 5/1/1992 12:00:00 AM.

- **Country:** Represents the country of an employee. Its data type is nvarchar with length of 15 characters. For example, the first employee record has Country set to USA.

- **Notes:** Represents additional information of an employee such as educational background. Its data type is ntext and can contain free-form text such as the following: Education includes a BA in psychology from Colorado State University in 1970. She also completed "The Art of the Cold Call." Nancy is a member of Toastmasters International.

Now that you are aware of the Employees table schema, let's add a supporting table that's required for the working of Employee Manager.

Adding a Countries Table

The Employees table contains a Country column that stores an employee's country. Therefore, on the data entry pages, you need to accept a country from the end user. Instead of accepting the user input in a textbox, it would be nice to display a list of countries to choose from. This requires another table, Countries, that contains a list of countries. The default installation of Northwind doesn't contain such a table, and hence you need to add one.

To add the Countries table, right-click the Tables folder and select Add New Table from the shortcut menu. This will open a table designer that allows you to define the Countries table. Figure 2-8 shows the Countries table definition in Visual Studio.

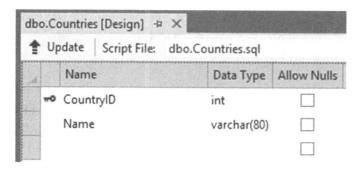

Figure 2-8. *Countries table structure*

The Countries table contains just two columns: CountryID and Name. The CountryID is an integer identity column, whereas Name is a varchar column with length of 80 characters.

Make sure to add a few countries in the Countries table so that you can use it in Employee Manager.

Signing In to Employee Manager

The Employee Manager application requires users to sign in before they can perform the CRUD operations on the Employees table. Therefore, when you start the application, you are presented with a sign-in page as shown in Figure 2-9 (page header and footer have been removed for the sake of clarity).

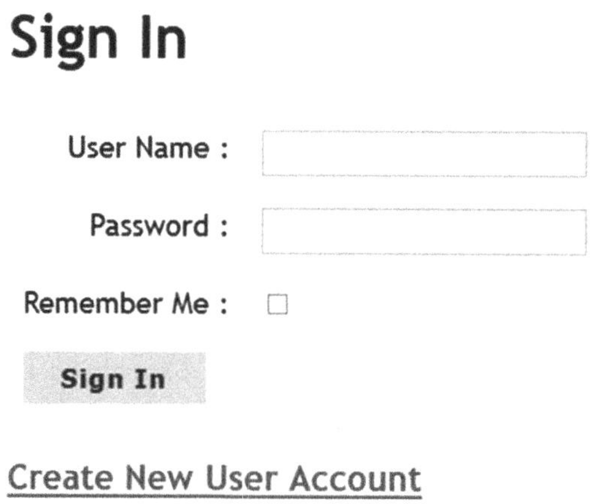

Sign In

User Name :	
Password :	
Remember Me :	☐

Sign In

Create New User Account

Figure 2-9. *The sign-in page*

The sign-in page consists of input controls for entering user name and password. There is also a Remember Me checkbox that decides whether a user's signed-in status is remembered even after the browser is closed. There is a link at the bottom that takes you to the user registration page (discussed in the next section).

The Sign In button triggers the sign-in operation. If there is any error during the signing-in process such as invalid or incomplete credentials, an error message is displayed to the user (Figure 2-10); otherwise, the user is taken to the employee listing page.

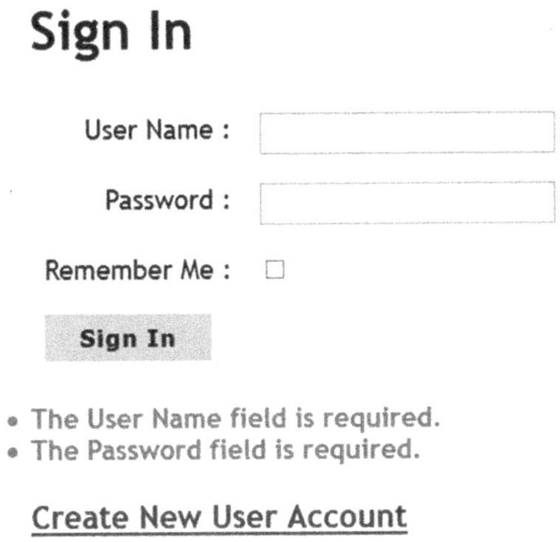

Sign In

User Name :

Password :

Remember Me :   ☐

Sign In

- The User Name field is required.
- The Password field is required.

Create New User Account

Figure 2-10. *Error message being shown for incomplete user input*

Creating a New User Account

You can create a new user account by navigating to the registration page. To go to the user registration page, you need to click the Create New User Account link present at the bottom of the sign-in page. Figure 2-11 shows how the registration page looks like.

Create New User Account

User Name : [   ]

Password : [   ]

Confirm Password : [   ]

Email : [   ]

Full Name : [   ]

Birth Date : [mm / dd / yyyy]

[**Create**]

Go To Sign-In Page

Figure 2-11. *The user registration page*

The user registration page consists of a series of input controls that accept user name, password, confirm password, email, full name, and birth date from a user. You can enter these details and click the Create button to create the user account. After successfully creating an account, you will be automatically taken to the sign-in page. If there are any errors while creating an account, those will be displayed on the registration page, and you can correct them as needed (Figure 2-12).

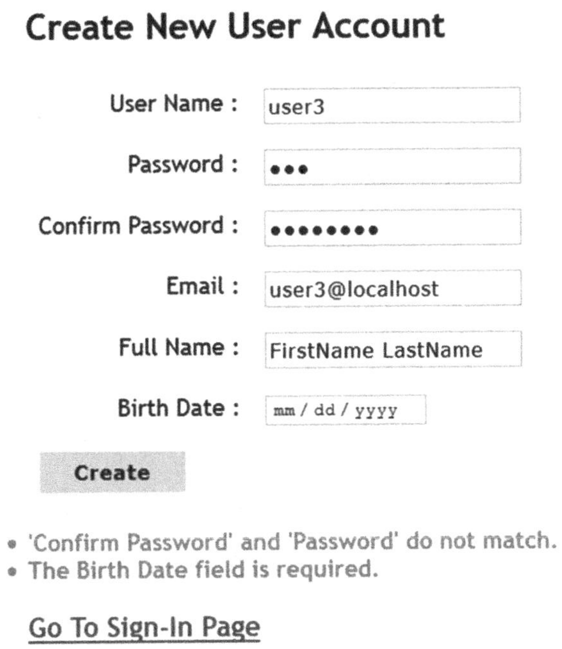

Create New User Account

User Name :	user3
Password :	•••
Confirm Password :	••••••••
Email :	user3@localhost
Full Name :	FirstName LastName
Birth Date :	mm / dd / yyyy

Create

- 'Confirm Password' and 'Password' do not match.
- The Birth Date field is required.

Go To Sign-In Page

Figure 2-12. *Showing errors for invalid or incomplete user details*

The registration page also has a Go To Sign-In Page link at the bottom that takes you to the sign-in page in case you want to skip creating a new account and decide to sign in with an existing account.

Listing All the Employees

After a successful sign-in, the user is presented with a list of all the employees from the Employees table as shown in Figure 2-13.

List of Employees

Insert

Employee ID	First Name	Last Name	Title	Actions	
1	Nancy	Davolio	Sales Representative	Update	Delete
2	Andrew	Fuller	Vice President, Sales	Update	Delete
3	Janet	Leverling	Sales Representative	Update	Delete
4	Margaret	Peacock	Sales Representative	Update	Delete
5	Steven	Buchanan	Sales Manager	Update	Delete
6	Michael	Suyama	Sales Representative	Update	Delete
7	Robert	King	Sales Representative	Update	Delete
8	Laura	Callahan	Inside Sales Coordinator	Update	Delete
9	Anne	Dodsworth	Sales Representative	Update	Delete

Figure 2-13. *Displaying a list of employees*

The employee listing shows EmployeeID, FirstName, LastName, and Title of an employee. Notice that just above the employee listing there is an Insert button. Clicking the Insert button takes the user to another page where a new employee can be added.

Each employee row from the listing also has Update and Delete buttons. Clicking the Update button takes you to another page where details of that employee can be modified. Clicking the Delete button takes you to a confirmation page where details of that employee are shown and a confirmation is sought from the user to delete that employee from the database.

Inserting a New Employee

In order to add a new employee into the Employees table, you need to click the Insert button at the top of the employee listing page. This takes you to the Insert New Employee page as shown in Figure 2-14.

Insert New Employee

First Name :

Last Name :

Title :

Birth Date : `mm / dd / yyyy`

Hire Date : `mm / dd / yyyy`

Country : Please select ⌄

Notes :

Save

Back to Employee Listing

Figure 2-14. *Adding a new employee*

The Insert New Employee page displays a blank data entry page where employee details such as FirstName, LastName, Title, BirthDate, HireDate, Country, and Notes can be entered. The EmployeeID is an automatically generated value (identity column), and therefore it's not accepted from a user.

BirthDate and HireDate values can be picked from the browser's built-in date picker. Most of the modern browsers allow you to pick an input of type date/datetime using a built-in date picker. This simplifies the date entry for the end user.

The Country dropdown list displays a list of countries to choose from. This data comes from the Countries table you added to the Northwind database earlier in this chapter.

The Notes textbox is a multiline textbox (HTML `<textarea>` element) and allows free-form text entry of employee information such as educational background and skills. Specifying notes is optional.

The Insert New Employee page also validates data so that only acceptable values can go into the database. In case one or more form controls contain invalid data, error messages are displayed as shown in Figure 2-15.

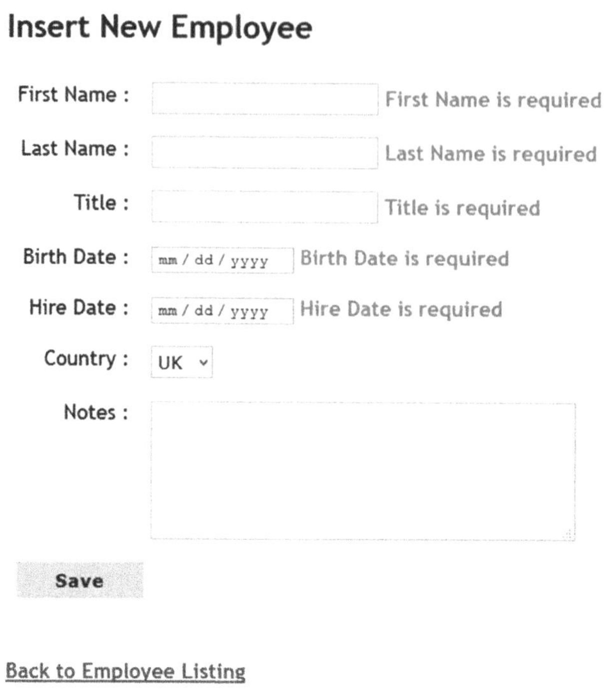

Insert New Employee

First Name : [   ] First Name is required

Last Name : [   ] Last Name is required

Title : [   ] Title is required

Birth Date : [mm / dd / yyyy] Birth Date is required

Hire Date : [mm / dd / yyyy] Hire Date is required

Country : [UK ⌄]

Notes : [   ]

[**Save**]

<u>Back to Employee Listing</u>

Figure 2-15. *Showing validation errors to a user*

Upon clicking the Save button, the new employee gets added to the database, and a success message is displayed as shown in Figure 2-16.

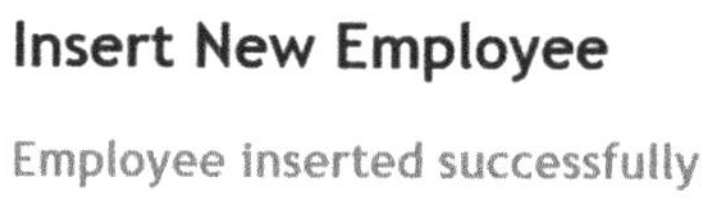

Insert New Employee

Employee inserted successfully

Figure 1-16. *Successful insert operation*

You can insert multiple employee records while you are on the Insert New Employee page. At the bottom of the Insert New Employee page, there is a Back to Employee Listing link. Clicking this link takes you to the employee listing page.

Updating Existing Employee

In order to update details of an existing employee, you need to click the Update button for that employee row in the employee listing page. This takes you to the Update Existing Employee page as shown in Figure 2-17.

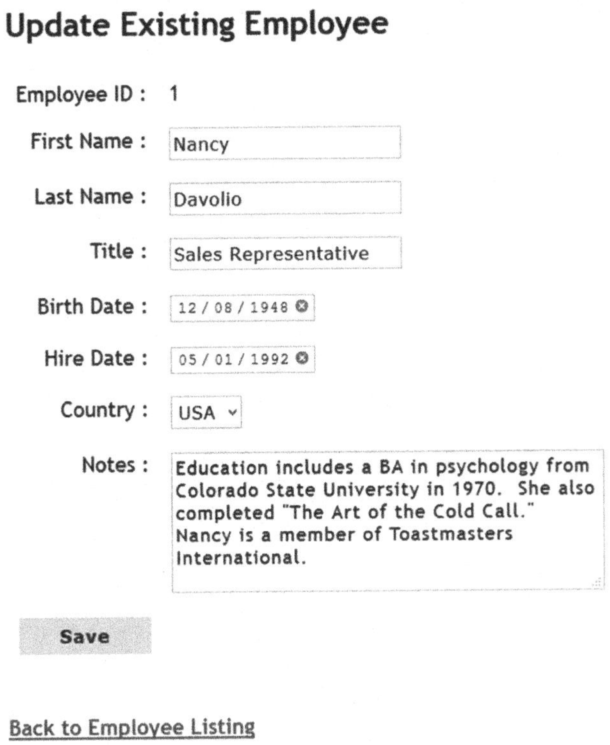

Update Existing Employee

Employee ID : 1

First Name : Nancy

Last Name : Davolio

Title : Sales Representative

Birth Date : 12 / 08 / 1948 ⊗

Hire Date : 05 / 01 / 1992 ⊗

Country : USA ⌄

Notes : Education includes a BA in psychology from Colorado State University in 1970. She also completed "The Art of the Cold Call." Nancy is a member of Toastmasters International.

Save

Back to Employee Listing

Figure 2-17. *Edit existing employee details*

The Update Existing Employee page displays existing details of an employee from the database. This way, you can edit only those pieces that need to be changed. EmployeeID being the primary key of the table can't be modified. Once done, you click the Save button to persist the changes back to the database.

If there are any validation errors, they are displayed beside the control containing erroneous value (Figure 2-18).

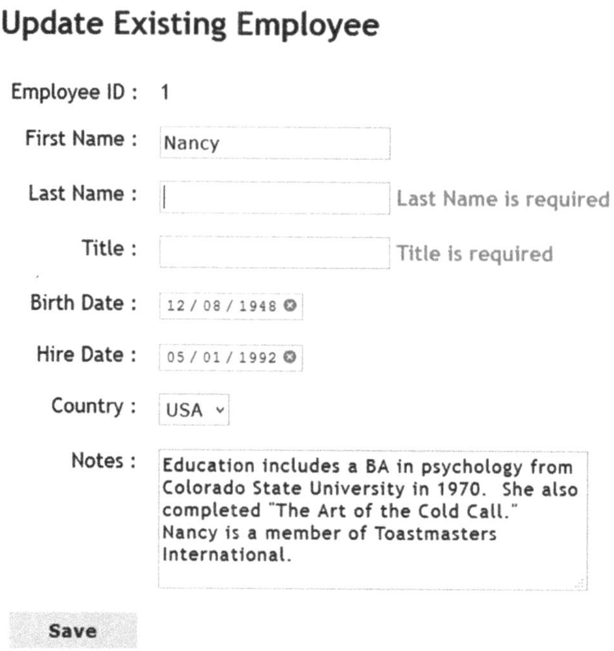

Update Existing Employee

Employee ID :   1

First Name :   Nancy

Last Name :   [   ]   Last Name is required

Title :   [   ]   Title is required

Birth Date :   12 / 08 / 1948 ⊗

Hire Date :   05 / 01 / 1992 ⊗

Country :   USA ⌄

Notes :   Education includes a BA in psychology from
Colorado State University in 1970. She also
completed "The Art of the Cold Call."
Nancy is a member of Toastmasters
International.

Save

Figure 2-18. *Validation errors while modifying employee details*

If there are no validation errors and the update operation is successful, a message is displayed to the user accordingly (Figure 2-19).

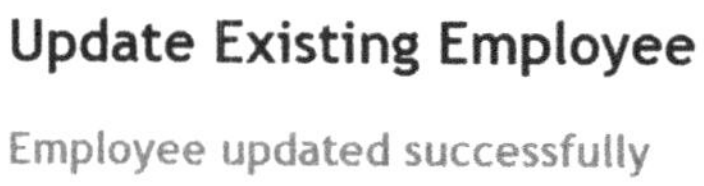

Update Existing Employee

Employee updated successfully

Figure 2-19. *Update operation was successful*

The Update Existing Employee page has a link at the bottom: Back to Employee Listing. Clicking this link takes you to the employee listing page.

Deleting Existing Employee

In order to delete an existing employee, you need to click the Delete button for that record on the employee listing page. Doing so takes you to a confirmation page where the user is warned about the deletion of employee data (Figure 2-20).

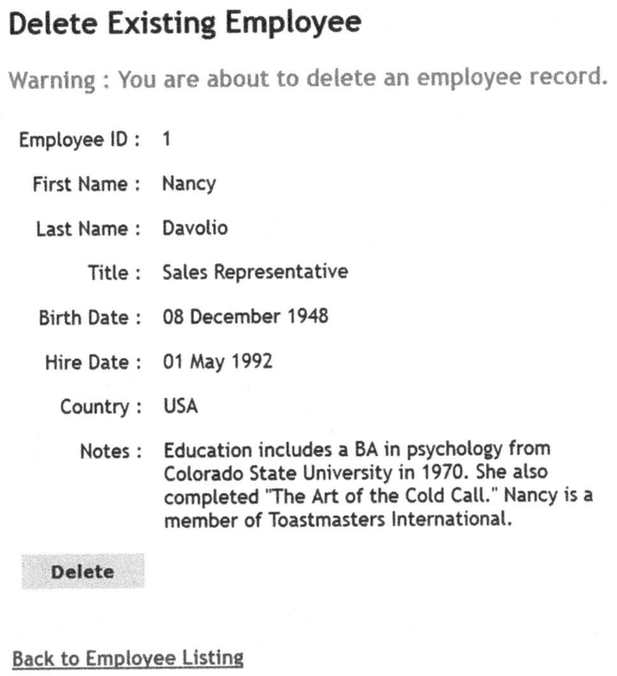

Delete Existing Employee

Warning : You are about to delete an employee record.

Employee ID : 1

First Name : Nancy

Last Name : Davolio

Title : Sales Representative

Birth Date : 08 December 1948

Hire Date : 01 May 1992

Country : USA

Notes : Education includes a BA in psychology from
Colorado State University in 1970. She also
completed "The Art of the Cold Call." Nancy is a
member of Toastmasters International.

Delete

Back to Employee Listing

Figure 2-20. *Seeking confirmation before deleting an employee record*

The Delete Existing Employee page displays existing employee details from the database along with a warning message. You can review the employee details and confirm the deletion by clicking the Delete button. Once the employee record is deleted from the database, the control is automatically taken to the employee listing page, and you are shown a success message (Figure 2-21).

List of Employees

Employee deleted successfully

Figure 2-21. *Employee deletion was successful*

While on the confirmation page, if you decide not to delete an employee record, you can click the Back to Employee Listing link at the bottom of the page. This will cancel the delete operation and will take you to the employee listing page.

Signing Out of Employee Manager

Once you sign in to Employee Manager, all the pages display the signed-in user's user name and the Sign Out button in the footer of the pages. Figure 2-22 shows how this footer looks like.

You are signed in as user1

Sign Out

Figure 2-22. *Page footer showing user name and the Sign Out button*

Upon clicking the Sign Out button, the user is signed out of the system, and control is taken to the sign-in page.

Technology Options Used to Develop Employee Manager

Now that you know how Employee Manager works, it's time to discuss the technical aspects of the application. Earlier in this chapter, it was mentioned that our focus is going to be on these areas: HTML form processing, CRUD operations, user authentication, incorporating JavaScript libraries/frameworks, and deployment. ASP.NET Core offers more than one options to deal with them. In this section, you will learn about these options and also how you are going to utilize them.

Rendering HTML Forms

ASP.NET Core offers three main development options: MVC, Razor Pages, and Web API. Out of these three, MVC and Razor Pages allow you to build web-based user interfaces. HTML forms can be rendered using any of the following approaches no matter whether you use MVC or Razor Pages:

- You can use the standard HTML <form> element and other associated elements such as <input> and <select>.

- You can use HTML Helpers to render HTML elements including form and form fields. This approach allows you to generate a form in a programmatic way rather than using standard HTML tags directly. For example, TextBoxFor() HTML Helper allows you to render an input textbox for a form.

- You can use Tag Helpers to render HTML elements including form and form fields. Tag Helpers are enhancements to standard HTML tags that add functionality to existing elements. For example, Input Tag Helper can be bound to a model's property using the asp-for attribute.

The approaches discussed in the preceding text allow you to render an HTML form. You would also want to process the form input made by the user. Depending on the type of application (MVC or Razor Pages), the form submission is handled either by an action or page handler, respectively.

Performing CRUD Operations

In order to perform database CRUD operations, .NET Core has two main options:

- Entity Framework Core (EF Core)

- Data provider for SQL Server

EF Core is an object relational mapper (O/RM) that also provides many additional services such as change tracking. While working with EF Core, you create entity classes (POCOs) and what is known as a DbContext. The entity classes are mapped to the database tables. The data is exposed through one or more DbSet objects. To perform CRUD operations, you can use LINQ to Entities and methods of DbSet and DbContext. EF Core relies on EF Core providers to communicate with the underlying database.

Although EF Core is a preferred way to working with databases in .NET Core, you can also use the data provider for SQL Server directly. If you ever programmed in .NET Framework before, this approach should be familiar to you. The data provider for SQL Server includes connection, command, and data reader classes that you can use to perform the CRUD operations. There is also a new data provider for SQL Server – Microsoft.Data.SqlClient. The classes from the Microsoft.Data.SqlClient namespace resemble the classes from the System.Data.SqlClient namespace, so their usage is quite similar.

The abovementioned options work great for relational databases. Nowadays NoSQL databases such as MongoDB and Cosmos DB are also becoming popular. These databases typically come with their own drivers or providers that you can use to perform CRUD operations on the respective data stores.

It should be noted that there could be some variations in the way EF Core is used to accomplish the task. For example, EF Core can be used in a synchronous as well as asynchronous manner. You can also use stored procedures or raw SQL queries to perform the CRUD operations instead of using LINQ queries.

Using JavaScript Libraries and Frameworks

Modern web applications heavily rely on client-side JavaScript code for their functionality. Ajax communication between client and server plays a vital role in such applications. For example, you might want to invoke a Web API developed in ASP.NET Core using a client-side library (such as jQuery) or a client-side framework (such as Angular).

There are plenty of JavaScript libraries and frameworks available today. In this book, you use two of them: jQuery and Angular. They are discussed briefly as follows:

- **jQuery** is a popular JavaScript library that has ruled the client-side development for many years. jQuery is being used by thousands of web sites for a variety of tasks ranging from simple hover effects to Document Object Model (DOM) manipulation to validation to Ajax. No wonder that ASP.NET Core client-side validations use jQuery for its functioning. jQuery is a DOM-centric library and also provides Ajax features. jQuery has plenty of third-party plugins that speed up and simplify the client-side development with jQuery.

- **Angular** is a popular JavaScript framework that allows you to build rich client-side applications and SPAs (Single Page Applications). It provides a lot of built-in features such as modular component-based architecture, Ajaxification using HttpClient, testing, animations, and routing. Considering the popularity of Angular, Visual Studio provides a project template for creating Angular projects. In this book, you won't use that template; you rather build an Angular app using Angular CLI (Command Line Interface) and then integrate it with the ASP.NET Core project. This way you can work with the latest version of Angular and can also learn to use Angular CLI (Command Line Interface).

Note   You use jQuery and Angular primarily for the sake of performing CRUD operations. This book doesn't teach you the basics of using these technologies. To learn more, visit `https://jquery.com` and `https://angular.io`, respectively.

User Authentication

Many web applications prohibit anonymous users to access and use the application resources. In such cases, securing the application by means of user authentication becomes essential. ASP.NET Core provides three main options for user authentication:

- **ASP.NET Core Identity** is a framework for providing authentication and authorization services for your web application. It supports many features such as local accounts, external logins, and two-factor authentication. For local user accounts, ASP.NET Core Identity uses a set of tables that store user details such as user name, password, and roles.

- In case you are looking to develop a custom authentication system for you web applications, you might want to skip using ASP.NET Core Identity (which is a complete and full-featured framework). In such cases, you can use the **custom cookie authentication** scheme. Here, you get the chance to define a custom data store and data store schema for persisting user details.

- Cookie-based authentication works well for traditional web-based applications such as the ones developed using ASP.NET Core MVC and Razor Pages. However, using cookies for modern web applications (such as Single Page Applications) is not recommended. In such cases, the preferred way is to use what is known as **JWT (JSON Web Token)-based authentication**. JWT is a standard that defines a way to securely transmit data between two parties as a JSON object. This data is trustworthy because it is digitally signed.

Deployment

Once you build an application, you would like to host it under some production web server. ASP.NET Core is a cross-platform framework; and you can host ASP.NET Core web applications under various popular options such as IIS, Nginx, and Apache. Additionally, you might want to host your apps in a cloud environment such as Azure. You learn to deploy Employee Manager under these two options:

- Internet Information Services (IIS)

- Azure App Service

As you can see from the preceding discussion, ASP.NET Core provides many options to accomplish a task. You learn these options by building more than one version of the Employee Manager application as discussed in the following.

ASP.NET Core MVC

In this version of Employee Manager, you use ASP.NET Core MVC. The user interface is built using Tag Helpers. The model validations are performed using data annotations (validation attributes). The database CRUD operations are performed using Entity Framework Core. The EF Core model is built manually by creating POCOs and mapping them to the table schema. The mapping is done using data annotations (schema attributes). User authentication and authorization is provided using ASP.NET Core Identity.

ASP.NET Core Razor Pages

In this version of Employee Manager, you use ASP.NET Core Razor Pages. The user interface is built using Tag Helpers. The model validations are also performed using data annotations (validation attributes). The database CRUD operations are performed using Entity Framework Core. The EF Core model is built using reverse engineering techniques. Mapping with the table schema is done using data annotations. User authentication and authorization is provided using ASP.NET Core Identity. This example also illustrates asynchronous operations (async/await) with ASP.NET Core Identity.

ASP.NET Core Web API

In this version of Employee Manager, you use ASP.NET Core Web API. The application consists of two parts – Web API and client. The Web API performs the CRUD operations using repositories. The repositories use raw SQL queries and stored procedures to get their job done.

The client application is developed using ASP.NET Core MVC and uses HTML Helpers to build the user interface. The form validations are performed using data annotations (validation attributes). User authentication and authorization is implemented in the client application using ASP.NET Core Identity. The client application uses HttpClient to invoke the Web API. The client also demonstrates how to write asynchronous actions (async/await) in an MVC controller.

jQuery

jQuery is a feature-rich JavaScript library that offers API for DOM manipulation, event handling, Ajax, and more. This version of Employee Manager uses jQuery and HTML5 to build the front-end. The data entry forms are designed using HTML5 markup. The data validations are performed using jQuery validation plugin. The communication between the client and the server is facilitated using jQuery Ajax. The CRUD operations are wrapped inside an asynchronous Web API. The data access is performed using asynchronous methods of EF Core. The user authentication and authorization is implemented using JWT authentication.

Angular

Angular is a JavaScript framework that allows you to build rich client applications including SPAs (Single Page Application). This version of Employee Manager uses Angular to build the front-end. The data entry forms are designed using Angular reactive forms. The form validations are performed using Angular's built-in validation techniques. The communication between the client and the server is facilitated using Angular's HttpClient. The CRUD operations are encapsulated in an asynchronous Web API. The data access is performed using EF Core asynchronous methods. The user authentication and authorization is implemented using JWT authentication.

Blazor

This version of Employee Manager is built using ASP.NET Core Blazor. It uses Blazor's server-side hosting model. The application's user interface is built using Razor Components. CRUD operations are encapsulated in a repository. This repository is injected into Razor Components and invoked from various event handlers. The user authentication and authorization is implemented using ASP.NET Core Identity and Blazor components. This version also illustrates how policy-based authorization can be used in ASP.NET Core applications.

Azure SQL Database

Azure SQL Database offers cloud-based data storage for your applications. This version of Employee Manager uses ASP.NET Core MVC to build the user interface. The application data is persisted in an Azure SQL Database. The CRUD operations are performed using classes from the Microsoft.Data.SqlClient data provider. The data validations are wired using data annotations (validation attributes). The application uses ASP.NET Core Identity to implement user authentication and authorization.

Azure Cosmos DB

Azure Cosmos DB is a cloud-based managed NoSQL database. This version of Employee Manager uses ASP.NET Core MVC to build the user interface. Azure Cosmos DB is used as a data store. The CRUD operations are performed using Microsoft. Azure.DocumentDB.Core classes and the EF Core provider for Cosmos DB. The data validations are wired using data annotations (validation attributes). The application uses custom cookie authentication without ASP.NET Core Identity for user authentication.

MongoDB

MongoDB is a document-based NoSQL database intended for modern applications and cloud environment. This version of Employee Manager uses ASP.NET Core MVC to build the user interface. A local MongoDB installation is used as a data store. The CRUD operations are performed using MongoDB driver for .NET Core. The data validations are wired using data annotations (validation attributes). It uses custom cookie authentication sans ASP.NET Core Identity for user authentication.

Hosting Code in a Private GitHub Repository

Throughout this book, you develop many Visual Studio projects consisting of several code files. I would encourage you to create a private GitHub repository for each version of Employee Manager and house your code in the repository. Although you might not be working with team environment while building Employee Manager, it will give you the chance to familiarize with the GitHub source control model.

Note   Hosting your code in GitHub is optional. Various versions of Employee Manager that you are going to build throughout this book aren't dependent on Git or GitHub. If you do not want to store your code in GitHub, you might skip this section and continue to the next chapter.

GitHub is a popular source code hosting platform. It allows teams to work in collaboration and to implement version control for their code. If you ever used open source software, chances are it is hosted on GitHub. Although I am not going into too much detail of GitHub and working with GitHub here, it's worthwhile to understand how a private GitHub repository can be created from within Visual Studio IDE and how your project's source code can be put into it.

To host your Visual Studio project in a GitHub repository, you need to follow these steps:

- Create a new ASP.NET Core project in Visual Studio.

- Build the application based on your requirements.

- Create a new private GitHub repository.

- Host your project files into the repository just created.

- Continue your work with the project and keep pushing the changes to the repository.

Let's implement these steps by creating a private GitHub repository named HelloWorldMVC that houses the HelloWorldMVC project you created in Chapter 1.

First of all, visit GitHub's web site (`https://GitHub.com`) and create a new account if you don't have one. Keep the account credentials ready because you will need them in a minute.

Next, open Visual Studio and open the Extensions menu. Select Extensions and Updates from the Extensions menu to open a dialog shown in Figure 2-23.

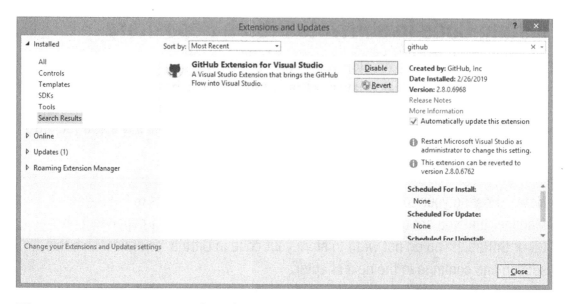

Figure 2-23. *Extensions and Updates dialog*

Search for GitHub to reveal GitHub Extension for Visual Studio. This extension allows you to work with GitHub repositories from within Visual Studio IDE. Install this extension by following the on-screen instructions.

Then create a new folder named GitHubExample and copy the entire HelloWorldMVC project folder into it. Now open the HelloWorldMVC project from the GitHubExample folder using Visual Studio. At this point, your Solution Explorer should resemble Figure 2-24.

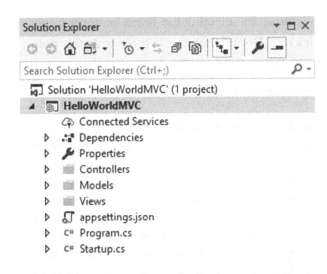

Figure 2-24. *HelloWorldMVC opened in Visual Studio*

Currently, the HelloWorldMVC project is not under any source control. You first need to add it to source control. To do so, select the File ➤ Add to Source Control menu option (Figure 2-25).

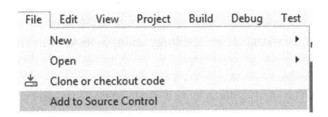

Figure 2-25. *Adding a project to source control*

This will create a local Git repository for the project. You can now publish it to GitHub.

Note   I don't go into much detail about Git and GitHub, but for learning purposes, think of Git as a version control system and GitHub as a hosting platform for repositories managed using Git.

Next, open Team Explorer by selecting the Team Explorer menu option from the Views menu. Then click the "Home" icon in the toolbar. At this point, your Team Explorer should look like Figure 2-26.

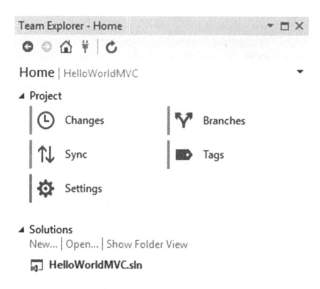

Figure 2-26. *Team Explorer window*

Click the Sync option so that Team Explorer changes its view as shown in Figure 2-27.

Figure 2-27. *Publish to GitHub option in Team Explorer*

As you can see, there is a Publish to GitHub section that allows you to publish the code to a GitHub repository. Click the Publish to GitHub button (if you are not already signed in to GitHub, you will be required to do so). Figure 2-28 shows how Team Explorer looks like after clicking the Publish to GitHub button.

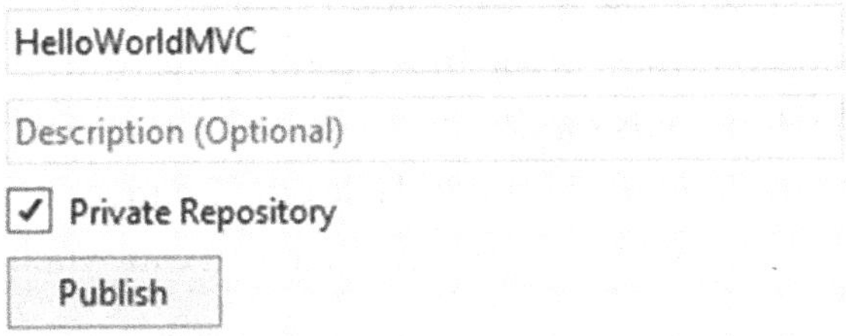

Figure 2-28. *Creating a new GitHub repository*

Here, you can specify the details for a new GitHub repository such as repository name, description, and whether the repository is a private repository. Keep the repository name the same as the project name – HelloWorldMVC. Specifying the description is optional. Check the Private Repository checkbox to indicate that you want to create a new private repository. Private repositories cannot be accessed by others.

Finally, click the Publish button. This will create the specified GitHub repository and publish your project files there. Once the synchronization is done, sign in to the GitHub web site just to confirm that the HelloWorldMVC private repository has been created for you. Figure 2-29 shows how the HelloWorldMVC repository looks like on the GitHub web site.

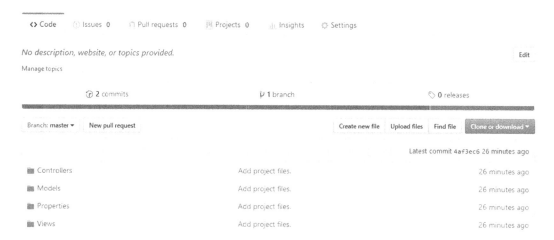

Figure 2-29. *HelloWorldMVC private repository on the GitHub web site*

Try navigating to various folders and files just to confirm that all your source code is now in the GitHub repository.

Now add a new text file named Readme.txt to the project using the Add New Item dialog. Enter some text into it and save the file. Also, open the Index.cshtml file and change the page title to My Hello World App.

Now our code has an additional file that didn't exist at the time of publishing to GitHub and also has a modification in the Index.cshtml file. Now you want to propagate these changes to the GitHub repository.

Click the Home icon of Team Explorer and click the Changes option. You need to first commit the changes to the local repository, and then you can synchronize them to the GitHub repository.

On the Changes screen, specify a commit message – a message that is supposed to indicate why the changes were made – and click the Commit All button (Figure 2-30).

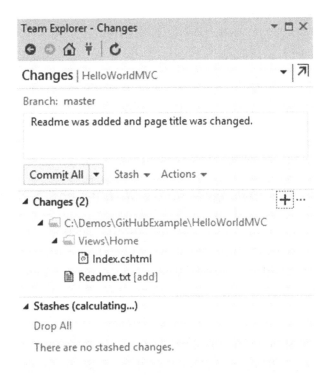

Figure 2-30. *Specifying a commit message and committing changes*

Notice that the changed files are also listed under the Changes section. Once you commit the changes to the local repository, go to the Home screen again and click the Sync option.

Your Team Explorer will now look like Figure 2-31.

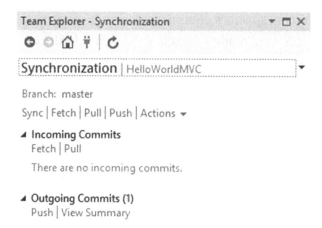

Figure 2-31. *Synchronizing changes with the GitHub repository*

Notice the Push button under the Outgoing Commits section. Click the Push button to publish the changes to the GitHub repository. After successfully pushing the changes, you can confirm with the GitHub repository whether the new changes have been propagated or not.

Note   The complete source code of all the examples developed in this book is available in the book's GitHub repository. Visit this book's page on the Apress web site to know more.

Summary

In this chapter, you were introduced to the Employee Manager application, a project that you are going to work on throughout the book. You learned about various technical options available under ASP.NET Core. You were also introduced to various versions of the application that are developed in the subsequent chapters. Finally, you learned to put a Visual Studio project into a private GitHub repository.

In the next chapter, you will learn how to build Employee Manager using ASP.NET Core MVC.

CHAPTER 3

ASP.NET Core MVC

In this chapter, you develop Employee Manager using ASP.NET Core MVC. The application's user interface is built using Tag Helpers. The database CRUD operations are performed using Entity Framework Core. The EF Core model is built manually by creating POCOs and mapping them to the table schema. To perform the mapping and model validations, data annotation attributes are used. The user authentication and authorization is provided using ASP.NET Core Identity. Specifically, this chapter teaches you to

- Use the Model-View-Controller pattern to build an ASP.NET Core web application

- Utilize Tag Helpers to render HTML form and form fields

- Perform CRUD operations using Entity Framework Core

- Perform data validations using data annotation attributes

- Implement user registration and sign-in using ASP.NET Core Identity

Let's get going.

Create an ASP.NET Core Web Application

Begin by creating a new ASP.NET Core web application based on the Empty project template. Name the application as EmployeeManager.Mvc to indicate that it's the MVC version of the application. This also sets the default namespace for classes you add to the project.

Note   You learned how to create a new ASP.NET Core project in Chapter 1. To avoid repetition, those steps are not explained again. Read Chapter 1 in case you need any help on creating a new ASP.NET Core web application based on the Empty project template.

© Bipin Joshi 2019
B. Joshi, *Beginning Database Programming Using ASP.NET Core 3*,
https://doi.org/10.1007/978-1-4842-5509-4_3

Figure 3-1 shows the EmployeeManager.Mvc project loaded in Solution Explorer once it is complete.

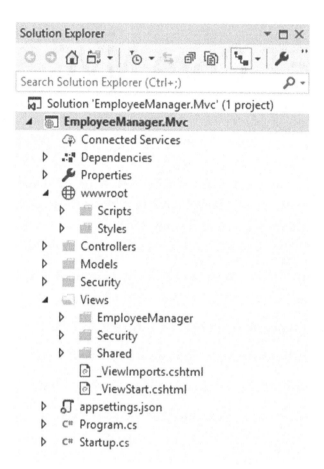

Figure 3-1. *EmployeeManager.Mvc loaded in Solution Explorer*

At this point, you may not understand all the pieces shown in Solution Explorer, and that's alright. Just take a look at the overall project structure and organization. In the sections that follow, you build this application step-by-step.

Create an Entity Framework Core Model

Employee Manager performs database CRUD operations using Entity Framework Core. To work with EF Core, you need to build an EF Core model. In this section, you are going to do just that.

An EF Core model is a set of entity classes and a custom DbContext class. The entity classes represent the application's business objects. For example, an order processing system might have Order entity that represents an order as applicable to the application domain. On the same lines, a contact management software might have Contact entity that represents a contact for that application.

The DbContext class represents a session with the underlying database. It provides various features such as connection management, change tracking, mapping, support for database operations, and more. DbContext houses one or more DbSet objects. A DbSet is a collection of entities. For example, NorthwindDbContext might house a DbSet for exposing Employee entities. Figure 3-2 shows a sample EF Core model.

EF Core Model

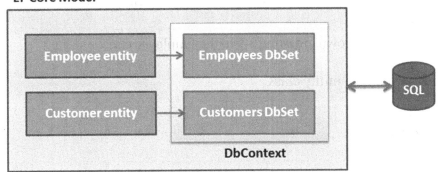

Figure 3-2. *Entity classes, DbSet, and DbContext*

The figure shows an EF Core model consisting of two entity classes (Employee and Customer), two DbSet objects (Employees and Customers), and a DbContext class housing them.

Now that you have some idea about an EF Core model, let's create the model required for the Employee Manager application. Open the Manage NuGet Packages page from the shortcut menu of the Dependencies folder and add these packages to your project:

- Microsoft.EntityFrameworkCore.SqlServer

- Microsoft.EntityFrameworkCore

- Microsoft.EntityFrameworkCore.Relational

The Microsoft.EntityFrameworkCore.SqlServer NuGet package is the SQL Server database provider for Entity Framework Core. Actually, when you install the

Microsoft.EntityFrameworkCore.SqlServer NuGet package, the other two dependent packages are automatically installed for you. These NuGet packages contain classes needed to perform database operations.

Now add a folder named Models in the project. Then using the Add New Item dialog, add three classes to the Models folder, namely, Employee, Country, and AppDbContext.

Then open the Employee entity class and use these namespaces at the top:

```
using System.ComponentModel.DataAnnotations;
using System.ComponentModel.DataAnnotations.Schema;
```

The System.ComponentModel.DataAnnotations namespace includes a set of attributes that allow you to validate data. The System.ComponentModel.DataAnnotations.Schema contains certain attributes that allow you to map entity classes to database tables.

Now add the code shown in Listing 3-1 to the Employee class.

Listing 3-1. Employee entity class

```
[Table("Employees")]
public class Employee
{
    [Column("EmployeeID")]
    [Key]
    [DatabaseGenerated(DatabaseGeneratedOption.Identity)]
    [Required(ErrorMessage = "Employee ID is required")]
    [Display(Name = "Employee ID")]
    public int EmployeeID { get; set; }

    [Column("FirstName")]
    [Display(Name = "First Name")]
    [Required(ErrorMessage = "First Name is required")]
    [StringLength(10,ErrorMessage ="First Name must be less than 10
    characters")]
    public string FirstName { get; set; }

    [Column("LastName")]
    [Display(Name = "Last Name")]
    [Required(ErrorMessage ="Last Name is required")]
```

```
[StringLength(20,ErrorMessage ="Last Name must be less than 20
characters")]
public string LastName { get; set; }

[Column("Title")]
[Display(Name = "Title")]
[Required(ErrorMessage ="Title is required")]
[StringLength(30,ErrorMessage ="Title must be less than 30 characters")]
public string Title { get; set; }

[Column("BirthDate")]
[Display(Name = "Birth Date")]
[Required(ErrorMessage ="Birth Date is required")]
public DateTime BirthDate { get; set; }

[Column("HireDate")]
[Display(Name = "Hire Date")]
[Required(ErrorMessage ="Hire Date is required")]
public DateTime HireDate { get; set; }

[Column("Country")]
[Display(Name = "Country")]
[Required(ErrorMessage ="Country is required")]
[StringLength(15,ErrorMessage ="Country must be less than 15 characters")]
public string Country { get; set; }

[Column("Notes")]
[Display(Name = "Notes")]
[StringLength(500,ErrorMessage ="Notes must be less than 500 characters")]
public string Notes { get; set; }
}
```

Let's analyze the code before moving ahead. The Employee class contains eight public properties, namely, EmployeeID, FirstName, LastName, Title, BirthDate, HireDate, Country, and Notes. You need to map the Employee entity class to the underlying Employees table of the Northwind database. There are three ways to perform this mapping:

- You can follow certain conventions, and the framework will automatically do the mapping for you.

- You can use certain data annotations to explicitly specify the mapping.

- You can use Fluent API to explicitly specify the mapping.

If you observe the `Employee` class, you will find that its name matches with the table name (Employees) and its property names map to the column names of the Employees table. If you follow these conventions, the framework will automatically do the mapping for you. So strictly speaking, the Employee class doesn't need explicit mapping. However, for the sake of learning data annotations, Employee uses the second approach – explicitly specify mapping using data annotations. You get a glimpse of Fluent API in the subsequent chapters. For this example, you use data annotations for mapping and data validation.

Note   The Employee Manager application uses an existing database and table for its working. If you wish, EF Core can also create a database and table(s) for you based on the entity classes you create. In such cases, metadata specified by the data annotations is also used for creating the tables. In this book, we don't need this approach since we have already installed the Northwind database.

The Employee class is decorated with the `[Table]` attribute. The `[Table]` attribute is used to map a class to a table. In this case, the Employee class is mapped to the Employees table.

The `EmployeeID` property represents an employee's numeric ID. It is decorated with `[Column]`, `[Key]`, `[DatabaseGenerated]`, `[Required]`, and `[Display]` attributes. The `[Column]` attribute is used to map the underlying property to a table's column. In this case, the `EmployeeID` property is mapped to the EmployeeID column of the Employees table. If you observe the schema of the Employees table, you will find that EmployeeID is an identity column and is a primary key of the table. The `[DatabaseGenerated]` attribute indicates that the property value is being generated by the database engine. The enumerated value of `DatabaseGeneratedOption.Identity` indicates that the value will be generated by the database when an entity is added to the database. The `[Key]` attribute is used to mark a primary key. The `[Required]` attribute indicates that the EmployeeID property must be assigned some value. The `ErrorMessage` property of the `[Required]` attribute specifies the error message to be displayed on the user interface in case EmployeeID is not assigned any value. The `[Display]` attribute specifies the name of the underlying property used by the user interface. It's useful to display some friendly name instead of the actual property name. For example, you might have a property called CustomerID but would like to show it on a web page as Customer Code.

The FirstName property is decorated with [Column], [Required], [StringLength], and [Display] attributes. The [StringLength] attribute validates the underlying property for certain string length. In this case, you set the maximum length parameter of [StringLength] to 10 indicating that the FirstName can be a string with maximum of ten characters.

The LastName property is decorated with [Column], [Required], [StringLength], and [Display] attributes. This time, [StringLength] sets the maximum length to 20.

The Title property is decorated with [Column], [Required], [StringLength], and [Display] attributes. This time, [StringLength] sets the maximum length to 30.

The BirthDate and HireDate properties hold a DateTime value and are decorated with [Column], [Required], and [Display] attributes.

The Country property is decorated with [Column], [Required], [StringLength], and [Display] attributes. This time, [StringLength] sets the maximum length to 15.

The Notes property is decorated with [Column], [StringLength], and [Display] attributes. This time, [StringLength] sets the maximum length to 500. The Notes column in the Employees table allows NULL values, and hence there is no mention of the [Required] attribute. Although Notes is of type ntext, [StringLength] sets the maximum length to 500 to prohibit users from entering a huge amount of text data.

This completes the Employee entity class. Now, open the Country class and write the code shown in Listing 3-2 in it.

Listing 3-2. Country entity class

```
public class Country
{
    public int CountryID { get; set; }
    public string Name { get; set; }
}
```

For creating the Country entity class, the code relies on the built-in conventions rather than using data annotations for mapping. This way, the Country class is automatically mapped to the Countries table in the database. Moreover, the CountryID and Name properties will be mapped to the respective columns of the Countries table.

The Country class is primarily used to let users pick a country on employee data entry pages. The application doesn't allow the users to add or edit countries. Therefore, the code doesn't use validation attributes such as [Required] and [StringLength].

Now that you completed the Employee and Country entity classes, let's complete the AppDbContext class. Listing 3-3 shows the code of AppDbContext.

Listing 3-3. AppDbContext houses DbSet objects

```
public class AppDbContext:DbContext
{

    public AppDbContext(DbContextOptions<AppDbContext> options) :
    base(options)
    {
    }

    public DbSet<Employee> Employees { get; set; }

    public DbSet<Country> Countries { get; set; }
}
```

The AppDbContext class inherits from the DbContext class that resides in the Microsoft.EntityFrameworkCore namespace. So use that namespace at the top of the class file:

```
using Microsoft.EntityFrameworkCore;
```

Then add two public properties of type DbSet<TEntity> – Employees and Countries. These properties hold entities of type Employee and Country, respectively.

The AppDbContext class also has a public constructor with the specified signature. Although we haven't added any code in it, this constructor is required so that the dependency injection (DI) framework can inject AppDbContext instances when required (more on this in later sections).

This completes the EF Core model required for this example.

Create an EmployeeManager Controller

The Employee Manager application's CRUD functionality occurs inside a controller class – EmployeeManagerController. To add this class, create the Controllers folder under the project root and add a controller class named EmployeeManagerController using the Add New Item dialog (Figure 3-3).

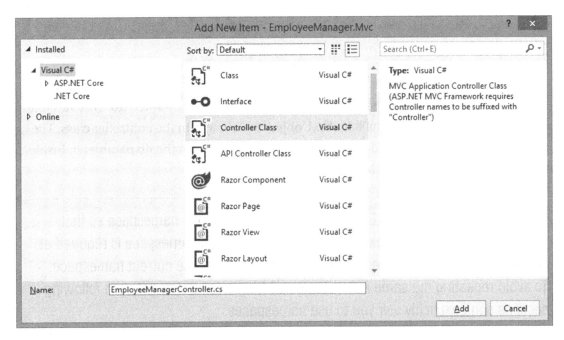

Figure 3-3. *Adding the EmployeeManagerController class to the Controllers folder*

The EmployeeManagerController class inherits from the Controller class. The Controller base class is available in the Microsoft.AspNetCore.Mvc namespace.

Since the EmployeeManagerController needs to perform CRUD operations on the Employees table, it needs an instance of AppDbContext created earlier. Although you can instantiate AppDbContext just like any other C# object, there is a better way to accomplish the task. You can inject an object of AppDbContext into the constructor of EmployeeManagerController with the help of dependency injection (DI) features of ASP. NET Core. To inject such an instance, you need to write a public constructor as shown in Listing 3-4.

Listing 3-4. Injecting AppDbContext into EmployeeManagerController

```
public class EmployeeManagerController : Controller
{
    private AppDbContext db = null;

    public EmployeeManagerController(AppDbContext db)
    {
        this.db = db;
    }
}
```

The code declares a member variable of type AppDbContext named db. This variable is used to store the injected AppDbContext object for use within the controller class. The public constructor receives the injected AppDbContext through the db parameter. Inside, the injected instance is stored in the local reference.

Note   You need to use the EmployeeManager.Mvc.Models namespace so that you access the AppDbContext. The same step of using a namespace is required at all the places where you use a type outside the scope of the current namespace. To avoid repeating the same instructions and for the sake of brevity, the following sections don't explicitly ask you to use namespaces.

Next, you need a private helper method that supplies a list of countries to the Country dropdown list of the insert and update pages. This method – FillCountries()– is shown in Listing 3-5.

Listing 3-5. FillCountries() helper method

```
private void FillCountries()
{
    List<SelectListItem> countries =
    (from c in db.Countries
     orderby c.Name ascending
```

```
    select new SelectListItem()
    { Text = c.Name,
      Value = c.Name }).ToList();
      ViewBag.Countries = countries;
}
```

The `FillCountries()` helper method declares a List of `SelectListItem` objects. The `SelectListItem` from the `Microsoft.AspNetCore.Mvc.Rendering` namespace represents an item of a dropdown list (<select> element of HTML). Since you want to display a list of countries to pick from, a List has been created.

A LINQ to Entities query selects all the entities from the Countries DbSet and projects them into the new `SelectListItem` object. Notice how the `Text` and `Value` properties of `SelectListItem` are assigned to the `Name` property of the `Country` entity. A LINQ to Entities query returns `IQueryable<T>`. The `ToList()` method converts this `IQueryable` into a List of `SelectListItem` objects.

The list of countries is to be passed to the view so that it can be populated in the <select> element. To facilitate this data transfer, the code uses a `ViewBag` object. The `ViewBag` is a dynamic type and allows you to dynamically set or get values using object. property syntax. Here, the code stores countries in the `Countries` property of `ViewBag`.

Add a _ViewImports File

In the following sections, you use ASP.NET Core Tag Helpers to render the user interface elements such as form, form fields, and hyperlinks. In order to use Tag Helpers, you need to enable them in your project.

Add the Views folder under the project root folder. Then add a _ViewImports.cshtml to the Views folder. You can do that by opening the Add New Item dialog and selecting Razor View Imports from the list (Figure 3-4).

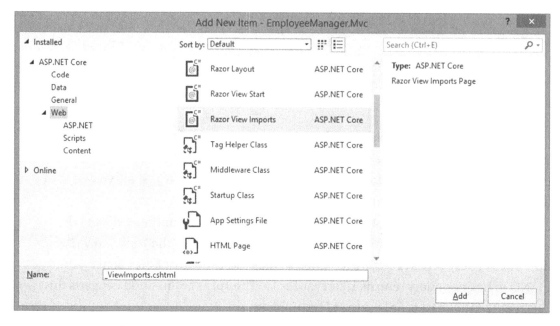

Figure 3-4. *Adding a _ViewImports.cshtml file*

The _ViewImports file is a special file in that it contains namespace imports and directives to enable Tag Helpers. These settings are then applied to all the view files. Then write this to the _ViewImports.cshtml file:

```
@using EmployeeManager.Mvc
@using EmployeeManager.Mvc.Models
@addTagHelper *, Microsoft.AspNetCore.Mvc.TagHelpers
```

The code uses the @using directive to use a few namespaces such as EmployeeManager.Mvc and EmployeeManager.Mvc.Models. Here, the @using directive serves the same purpose as the using directive in C#. Once you import namespaces here, you can use classes from these namespaces in any of the view files.

Notice the @addTagHelper directive that enables Tag Helpers for the views. The first parameter to @addTagHelper is * indicating that all the Tag Helpers available from the assembly that follows are to be added to the project. The second parameter is the name of the assembly that contains the Tag Helpers: Microsoft.AspNetCore.Mvc.TagHelpers in this case.

Note   You can also place the @using and @addTagHelper directives in individual view files. But in that case, they are applied to the view under consideration. If you want to use the namespaces and Tag Helpers in multiple views, _ViewImports. cshtml is a better place.

Displaying a List of Employees

Once a user successfully signs in, you need to display a list of employees. The user can modify existing employees, add new employees, or delete existing employees. Although you learned about the employee listing page in Chapter 2, Figure 3-5 shows it here again for the sake of clarity.

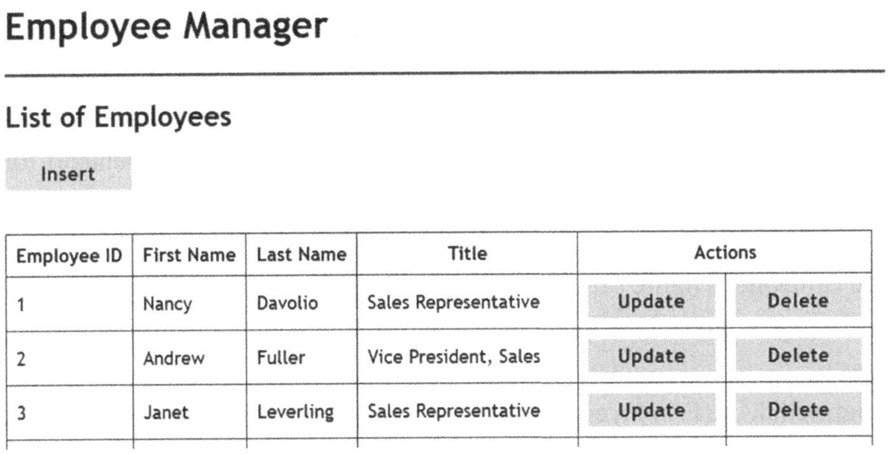

Employee Manager

List of Employees

Insert

Employee ID	First Name	Last Name	Title	Actions	
1	Nancy	Davolio	Sales Representative	Update	Delete
2	Andrew	Fuller	Vice President, Sales	Update	Delete
3	Janet	Leverling	Sales Representative	Update	Delete

Figure 3-5. *Displaying a list of employees*

In order to display a list of employees, you need an action named List() and a view named List.cshtml. To add the List() action, open the EmployeeManagerController class and write the code shown in Listing 3-6.

Listing 3-6. List() action

```
public IActionResult List()
{
    List<Employee> model = (from e in db.Employees
                            orderby e.EmployeeID
                            select e).ToList();
    return View(model);
}
```

The List() action returns IActionResult. The code retrieves a List of Employee objects using a LINQ to Entities query. The List is then passed to the List view using the View() method. The View() method is provided by the Controller base class and accepts a model object to be sent to a view. If no view name is specified, a view with a name the same as the action is assumed. The View() method returns a ViewResult object (ViewResult implements IActionResult) that represents a view to be rendered in the browser.

Now, let's add the List view that uses this employee data and renders it in a table. Add the Views folder under the project root and also add the EmployeeManager folder under the Views folder. The Views folder is intended to store MVC view files. All the views related to a particular controller are grouped inside a folder having a name the same as the controller's name sans the Controller suffix. For example, for storing views of EmployeeManagerController, you create an EmployeeManager subfolder under the Views folder.

Then right-click the EmployeeManager folder and open the Add New Item dialog. Add a Razor View file named List.cshtml (Figure 3-6).

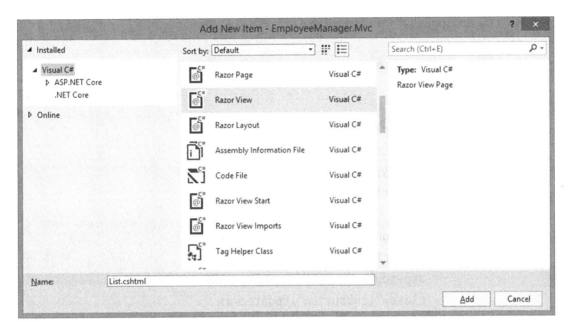

Figure 3-6. *Adding the List view*

Once the List view is added, write the code and markup shown in Listing 3-7 into it.

Listing 3-7. List view renders a list of employees

```
@model List<Employee>

<h2>List of Employees</h2>

<h2 class="message">@TempData["Message"]</h2>

<a asp-controller="EmployeeManager"
   asp-action="Insert"
   class="linkbutton">Insert</a>

<br /><br />

<table border="1">
    <tr>
        <th>Employee ID</th>
        <th>First Name</th>
        <th>Last Name</th>
        <th>Title</th>
```

```
        <th colspan="2">Actions</th>
    </tr>
    @foreach(var item in Model)
    {
        <tr>
            <td>@item.EmployeeID</td>
            <td>@item.FirstName</td>
            <td>@item.LastName</td>
            <td>@item.Title</td>
            <td>
                <a asp-controller="EmployeeManager"
                    asp-action="Update"
                    asp-route-id="@item.EmployeeID"
                    class="linkbutton">Update</a>
            </td>
            <td>
                <a asp-controller="EmployeeManager"
                    asp-action="Delete"
                    asp-route-id="@item.EmployeeID"
                    class="linkbutton">Delete</a>
            </td>
        </tr>
    }
</table>
```

Let's analyze the List view in more detail. The List.cshtml begins with the @model directive. The @model directive specifies the model type used by the view. The List view needs a List of Employee objects to render an employee table. Therefore, the @model directive specifies List<Employee> as the model type. Also recollect that the List() action passes a List of Employee objects to the View() method. A view with the @model directive specifying the model type is called a strongly typed view.

Below the view heading, the code outputs TempData["Message"] on the response stream. This is done using @ syntax of Razor. TempData is a dictionary object and stores data until it's read. You need to use TempData here to display employee deletion messages. The delete employee page sets the Message key of TempData to a success message and redirects the user to the listing page. The List view then displays the Message to the user. The use of `TempData` will be clear when we discuss the delete employee page in later sections.

The markup then displays the Insert link. This is done using the Anchor Tag Helper. Tag Helpers allow server-side code to render HTML elements in Razor files. There are many built-in Tag Helpers such as Form, Select, and Input Tag Helpers. As you develop this application, you will be introduced to more Tag Helpers. For now, you use the Anchor Tag Helper to display a hyperlink that points to the Insert New Employee page. Notice that the `asp-controller` attribute of the anchor Tag Helper is set to the EmployeeManager controller and the `asp-action` attribute is set to the Insert action. You will create the Insert action in later sections.

Then a <table> displays a list of all employees on the page. Although the Employee object has many properties, the table displays only four of them – `EmployeeID`, `FirstName`, `LastName`, and `Title`. In order to render a list of employees, the `foreach` loop is used. Notice the use of `Model` property of the view that represents the model object passed to the view (`List<Employee>` in this case). Each iteration adds a table row consisting of the four property values mentioned in the preceding text.

Note that each row also has Update and Delete links. They take the user to the corresponding pages. These links are rendered using the Anchor Tag Helper. The `asp-controller`, `asp-action`, and `asp-route-id` attributes on the Update link are set to EmployeeManager, Update, and EmployeeID, respectively. For EmployeeID of 1, the resultant link will point to /EmployeeManager/Update/1. This means clicking this link will take a user to the `Update()` action of the `EmployeeManager` controller and `EmployeeID` is also passed to the `Update()` action. The `id` route parameter is needed so that the `Update()` action can know which employee is to be edited.

Note   The id parameter used in the Update and Delete links is a part of the routing configuration of ASP.NET Core MVC. You will learn about the routing configuration when you configure the application's startup later in this chapter.

On the same lines, the Delete link points to the `Delete()` action of `EmployeeManager` and passes `EmployeeID` as a route parameter.

The List view makes use of certain CSS classes such as linkbutton and message. These CSS classes come from the application's style sheet – site.css. The content of site. css is not discussed here. You can grab the style sheet from the book's source code.

Insert a New Employee

Clicking the Insert link on the employee listing page takes you to another page where you can insert a new employee. This page is shown in Figure 3-7.

Insert New Employee

First Name :

Last Name :

Title :

Birth Date : mm / dd / yyyy

Hire Date : mm / dd / yyyy

Country : Please select

Notes :

Save

Back to Employee Listing

Figure 3-7. *Inserting a new employee*

The page has form fields to accept `FirstName`, `LastName`, `Title`, `BirthDate`, `HireDate`, `Country`, and `Notes`. `EmployeeID` being an identity value is not accepted from the end user. Clicking the Save button inserts the employee details into the database. The Back to Employee Listing link takes you to the employee listing page.

To build the insert page, you need two actions and a view. So open the `EmployeeManagerController` class and add the two actions as shown in Listing 3-8.

Listing 3-8. Insert() actions insert a new employee

```
public IActionResult Insert()
{
    FillCountries();
    return View();
}
```

```
[HttpPost]
public IActionResult Insert(Employee model)
{
    FillCountries();
    if (ModelState.IsValid)
    {
        db.Employees.Add(model);
        db.SaveChanges();
        ViewBag.Message = "Employee inserted successfully";
    }
    return View(model);
}
```

The first Insert() action gets called when you click the Insert link on the employee listing page. Inside, the code calls the FillCountries() helper method to store a list of countries into ViewBag. It then displays the Insert view in the browser. The Insert view is discussed shortly.

The second Insert() is called when you submit the form by clicking the Save button. The form is submitted using the POST method, and hence Insert() is decorated with the [HttpPost] attribute. Adding [HttpPost] ensures that the underlying action is invoked only for POST requests. Note that this version of Insert() accepts a parameter of type Employee. Upon submitting the form, ASP.NET Core automatically fills the form field values into an Employee object for you. This is called model binding. While filling the values, ASP.NET Core matches the form field names with the property names. For example, the Employee object's FirstName property will be assigned the value entered in the textbox with name FirstName.

Inside, the Insert() action calls the FillCountries() helper method. Before inserting a new employee into the database, the code checks whether the Employee object holds valid values. Recollect that while creating the Employee entity class, you used data annotations such as [Required] and [StringLength] to specify validation criteria. To check whether Employee contains valid values or not, the code uses ModelState's IsValid property. The IsValid property returns true if all the validations are successful; otherwise, it returns false.

In the former case, the code adds the Employee object to Employees DbSet. This is done using the Add() method of Employees DbSet. The Add() method adds a new employee into the DbSet and marks it as newly added entity. To persist the values into the database, the SaveChanges() method of the AppDbContext is called. A success message is stored into the ViewBag for displaying to the user. The Insert view is rendered again in the browser so that you can insert another employee if you so wish.

This completes the two Insert() actions. Now let's proceed to the Insert view. Open the Add New Item dialog by right-clicking the Views ➤ EmployeeManager folder and add another Razor View named Insert.cshtml. Then write the markup shown in Listing 3-9 in it.

Listing 3-9. Skeleton markup of Insert.cshtml

```
@model Employee

<h2>Insert New Employee</h2>
<h3 class="message">@ViewBag.Message</h3>

<form asp-controller="EmployeeManager" asp-action="Insert" method="post">
    <table border="0">
    </table>
</form>
```

Here, the @model directive sets the view's model type to be Employee. Below the heading, the success message stored in the ViewBag is outputted. Initially when the first Insert() is called, Message property will be empty, and hence no message will be displayed. The subsequent insert operations will display the success message to the user.

Then the markup uses a Form Tag Helper to render an HTML <form> element. The asp-controller attribute of the Form Tag Helper specifies the name of the controller (EmployeeManager), and the asp-action attribute specifies the name of the action (Insert) that processes the form upon submission. The method attribute specifies the method of form submission, POST in this case.

Inside, a table is placed to house various form fields (discussed in the following). Now, add the markup shown in Listing 3-10 inside the <table> element.

Listing 3-10. Input Tag Helpers for FirstName, LastName, and Title

```
<tr>
    <td class="right">
        <label asp-for="FirstName"></label> :
    </td>
```

```
        <td>
            <input type="text" asp-for="FirstName" />
            <span asp-validation-for="FirstName" class="message"></span>
        </td>
    </tr>
    <tr>
        <td class="right">
            <label asp-for="LastName"></label> :
        </td>
        <td>
            <input type="text" asp-for="LastName" />
            <span asp-validation-for="LastName" class="message"></span>
        </td>
    </tr>
    <tr>
        <td class="right">
            <label asp-for="Title"></label> :
        </td>
        <td>
            <input type="text" asp-for="Title" />
            <span asp-validation-for="Title" class="message"></span>
        </td>
    </tr>
```

Notice the code marked in bold letters. The Label Tag Helper displays a label for the FirstName textbox. The `asp-for` attribute is set to `FirstName` indicating that <label> is being rendered for the FirstName textbox. Recollect that the FirstName property is decorated with the `[Display]` attribute, and the Label Tag Helper will automatically use that as the label. If the model property doesn't have [Display], the actual property name is used for the label.

The Input Tag Helper binds the <input> element to a model property. This is done using the `asp-for` attribute. So when you add an <input> element with the `asp-for` attribute set to `FirstName,` it will generate an input element whose name is FirstName and value is the same as the property's value.

The <span> element followed by the input element represents a Validation Message Tag Helper and is used to display the validation error message for that property. The `asp-validation-for` attribute specifies the property name whose validation error message is to be displayed (FirstName in this case). The validation error messages are picked from the data annotations used while creating the model class.

The markup that follows sets up the Tag Helpers for `LastName` and `Title` properties.

Next, add the markup shown in Listing 3-11 that displays `BirthDate` and `HireDate` fields.

Listing 3-11. Displaying BirthDate and HireDate form fields

```
<tr>
    <td class="right">
        <label asp-for="BirthDate"></label> :
    </td>
    <td>
        <input type="date" asp-for="BirthDate" />
        <span asp-validation-for="BirthDate" class="message"></span>
    </td>
</tr>
<tr>
    <td class="right">
        <label asp-for="HireDate"></label> :
    </td>
    <td>
        <input type="date" asp-for="HireDate" />
        <span asp-validation-for="HireDate" class="message"></span>
    </td>
</tr>
```

This markup is quite similar to the one discussed earlier. However, notice that the input fields have their type attribute set to date. Modern browsers such as Firefox and Chrome can display a date picker for entering the date.

Now, add the markup shown in Listing 3-12 in the Insert view.

Listing 3-12. Displaying the Country dropdown list and Notes text area

```
<tr>
    <td class="right">
        <label asp-for="Country"></label> :
    </td>
    <td>
        <select asp-for="Country" asp-items="@ViewBag.Countries">
        <option value="">Please select</option>
        </select>
        <span asp-validation-for="Country" class="message"></span>
    </td>
</tr>
<tr>
    <td class="right">
        <label asp-for="Notes"></label> :
    </td>
    <td>
        <textarea asp-for="Notes" rows="5" cols="40"></textarea>
        <span asp-validation-for="Notes" class="message"></span>
    </td>
</tr>
```

This markup should look familiar to you since it's quite similar to the previous one. However, there are a few differences. Firstly, for displaying a list of countries to pick from, the markup uses the Select Tag Helper. The asp-for attribute of the <select> element is set to the Country property indicating that the control value is bound to the Country property of the Employee model object. The asp-items attribute is set to ViewBag's Countries property. Recollect that the FillCountries() method stores a List of SelectListItem objects into the Countries ViewBag property. Setting it to asp-items will generate <option> elements for each country in the ViewBag. Notice that the <select> also has an empty <option> element that displays a "Please select" item in the dropdown list. The countries from the ViewBag are appended to this <option> element.

Secondly, Notes are entered using the Textarea Tag Helper. Since Notes can be free-form text, the markup renders a <textarea> element with 5 rows and 40 columns.

Finally, add the markup shown in Listing 3-13 in the Insert view.

Listing 3-13. Displaying the Save button and Back to Employee Listing link

```
    <tr>
        <td colspan="2">
            <button type="submit">Save</button>
        </td>
    </tr>
  </table>
</form>

<br /><br />

<a asp-controller="EmployeeManager" asp-action="List">Back to Employee
Listing</a>
```

This markup displays the Save button using a <button> element. Clicking the Save button submits the form. At the bottom of the page, the Anchor Tag Helper is used to render a hyperlink that takes the user back to the employee listing page. The asp-controller and asp-action attributes of the Anchor Tag Helper are set to EmployeeManager and List, respectively. Clicking the link will take the control to the List() action.

Update an Existing Employee

On the employee listing page, each employee row has Update and Delete links. Clicking the Update link takes you to the update employee page where the existing details of that employee are presented for editing (Figure 3-8).

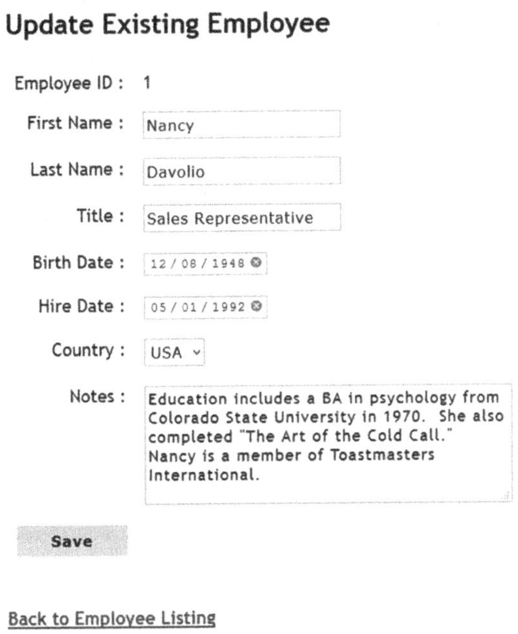

Update Existing Employee

Employee ID :   1

First Name :   Nancy

Last Name :   Davolio

Title :   Sales Representative

Birth Date :   12 / 08 / 1948 ⊗

Hire Date :   05 / 01 / 1992 ⊗

Country :   USA ⌄

Notes :   Education includes a BA in psychology from Colorado State University in 1970. She also completed "The Art of the Cold Call." Nancy is a member of Toastmasters International.

Save

Back to Employee Listing

Figure 3-8. *Updating an existing employee*

The Update Existing Employee page looks similar to the Insert New Employee page except that various control values are now filled with the details of the employee being modified. The EmployeeID being the primary key can't be modified.

In order to complete this page, you need two actions and a view. So open the EmployeeManagerController and add the first action as shown in Listing 3-14.

Listing 3-14. First Update() action

```
public IActionResult Update(int id)
{
    FillCountries();
    Employee model = db.Employees.Find(id);
    return View(model);
}
```

The first Update() action is invoked when the user clicks the Update link on the employee listing page. It has one parameter – id – that indicates the EmployeeID of the employee being modified. Recollect that the EmployeeID is supplied via the id route parameter of the Update link.

Inside, the FillCountries() helper method is called so that a list of countries is available in the ViewBag. The code then finds the Employee entity whose EmployeeID is passed to the Update() action. This is done using the Find() method of Employees DbSet. The Find() method accepts a primary key value(s) and returns an entity matching that primary key. Find() returns null if no match is found. The returned Employee object is passed to the Update view via the View() method.

Then add the second Update() action as shown in Listing 3-15.

Listing 3-15. Second Update() action

```
[HttpPost]
public IActionResult Update(Employee model)
{
    FillCountries();
    if(ModelState.IsValid)
    {
        db.Employees.Update(model);
        db.SaveChanges();
        ViewBag.Message = "Employee updated successfully";
    }
    return View(model);
}
```

The second Update() is called when the user clicks the Save button. Since this version of Update() handles the form submission via the POST method, it's decorated with the [HttpPost] attribute. The Update() method receives the modified values through an Employee object parameter.

Inside, the code calls FillCountries() as before. It then proceeds to check ModelState's IsValid property. To update an employee, the Update() method of Employees DbSet is used and modified Employee object is passed to it. This way, the Employee object gets marked as modified. Then SaveChanges() is called on the AppDbContext to propagate the changes to the database. A success message is stored in the ViewBag, and the Update view is shown in the browser.

Now, add Update.cshtml to the Views ➤ EmployeeManager folder. Add the markup shown in Listing 3-16 into the Update view.

Listing 3-16. Form Tag Helper in the Update view

```
@model Employee

<h2>Update Existing Employee</h2>
<h3 class="message">@ViewBag.Message</h3>
<form asp-controller="EmployeeManager"
      asp-action="Update"
      method="post">
   <table border="0">
      <tr>
         <td class="right">
             <label asp-for="EmployeeID"></label> :
         </td>
         <td>
             <input type="hidden" asp-for="EmployeeID" />
             <span>@Model.EmployeeID</span>
         </td>
      </tr>
```

The @model directive sets the model for the Update view to Employee. Notice the code marked in bold letters. The Form Tag Helper submits the form to the Update() action of EmployeeManagerController using the POST method. Also notice that the EmployeeID is stored in a hidden form field and is also displayed in a <span> element. Storing EmployeeID in the hidden form field ensures that it is filled in the Employee object during model binding.

The rest of the page markup is the same as the Insert view, and hence it's not discussed again. You can either copy-paste it from the Insert view or grab from the book's source code.

Delete an Existing Employee

Deleting an existing employee from the database is a two-step process. First, when you click the Delete link for an employee record in the employee listing page, a confirmation page is shown that warns the user about the employee deletion. Once the user confirms the deletion, the employee gets deleted from the database. Figure 3-9 shows the confirmation page displayed for an employee.

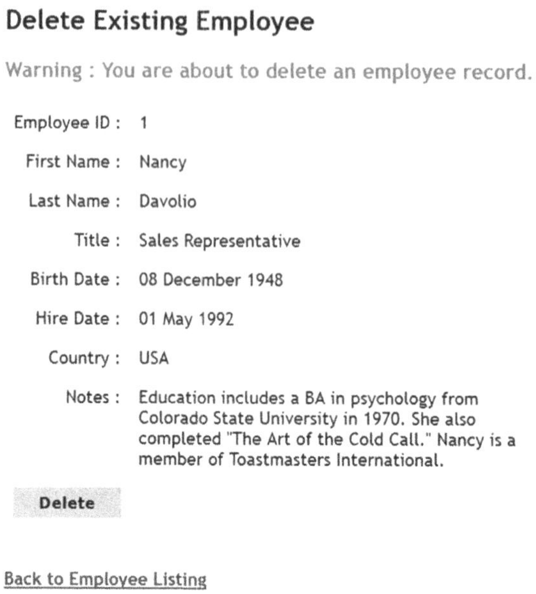

Delete Existing Employee

Warning : You are about to delete an employee record.

Employee ID :   1

First Name :   Nancy

Last Name :   Davolio

Title :   Sales Representative

Birth Date :   08 December 1948

Hire Date :   01 May 1992

Country :   USA

Notes :   Education includes a BA in psychology from
Colorado State University in 1970. She also
completed "The Art of the Cold Call." Nancy is a
member of Toastmasters International.

Delete

Back to Employee Listing

Figure 3-9. *Confirming employee deletion*

In order to implement this piece of functionality, you need two actions and a view. Listing 3-17 shows one of the actions.

Listing 3-17. Action for confirming the delete operation

```
[ActionName("Delete")]
public IActionResult ConfirmDelete(int id)
{
    Employee model = db.Employees.Find(id);
    return View(model);
}
```

The ConfirmDelete() action accepts an EmployeeID of an Employee object that is to be deleted. Recollect that the Delete link from the employee listing page supplies this id as a route parameter. The ConfirmDelete() is decorated with the [ActionName] attribute. Usually, an action name exposed to the external world is the same as the action method name. However, at times you might want to expose an action method with a different name. In this case, the code exposes the ConfirmDelete() method as Delete. This allows us to map the URL /EmployeeManager/Delete to the ConfirmDelete() action.

Inside, the code finds an Employee matching the supplied EmployeeID and passes it to the Delete view.

The second action is shown in Listing 3-18.

Listing 3-18. Delete() action deletes an employee

```
[HttpPost]
public IActionResult Delete(int employeeID)
{
    Employee model = db.Employees.Find(employeeID);
    db.Employees.Remove(model);
    db.SaveChanges();
    TempData["Message"] = "Employee deleted successfully";
    return RedirectToAction("List");
}
```

The Delete() action accepts a single parameter – employeeID. Note that the ConfirmDelete() parameter was named id because it was supplied as a route parameter. On the other hand, Delete() receives the EmployeeID from the confirmation page through model binding. Therefore, it is named employeeID – the same as the property name being model bound. The Delete() action is decorated with the [HttpPost] because we want to invoke it only through POST requests.

Inside, the code finds the employee to be deleted based on the EmployeeID passed in the action. It then calls the Remove() method of DbSet to delete the employee. The Remove() method marks the entity for removal. To delete the employee from the database, the SaveChanges() method is called on the DbContext.

Once an employee is deleted, we want to redirect to the employee listing page. The ViewBag object has a scope of current request. That means whatever you store in ViewBag is available only during the current request. In this case, taking the user to the employee listing page is another request, and hence ViewBag values of earlier requests won't be available. As an alternative, the code uses the TempData object. TempData is a dictionary, and you can store key-value pairs in it. Data stored in TempData remains available until it's read by another request. Here, the code stores a success message in TempData. This success message is outputted on the List view (read the discussion of the employee listing page).

To redirect the user to the employee listing page, the RedirectToAction() method is used. The RedirectToAction() method accepts the name of an action and redirects the control to that action.

> **Note**   EF Core has a ChangeTracker that keeps track of the state of entities
> managed by a DbContext. Calling Add(), Update(), and Remove() methods sets the
> state of an entity to Added, Modified, and Deleted, respectively.

Now, add Delete.cshtml in the Views ➤ EmployeeManager folder. Write the markup shown in Listing 3-19 in it.

Listing 3-19. Delete view displays a warning message along with employee details

```
@model Employee

<h2>Delete Existing Employee</h2>
<h3 class="message">
    Warning : You are about to delete an employee record.
</h3>
<form asp-controller="EmployeeManager" asp-action="Delete" method="post">
    <input type="hidden" asp-for="EmployeeID" />
    <table border="0">
        <tr>
            <td class="right">
                <label asp-for="EmployeeID"></label> :
            </td>
            <td>
                @Model.EmployeeID
            </td>
        </tr>
        <tr>
            <td class="right">
                <label asp-for="FirstName"></label> :
            </td>
            <td>
                @Model.FirstName
            </td>
        </tr>
        ...
```

```
        <tr>
            <td colspan="2">
                <button type="submit">Delete</button>
            </td>
        </tr>
    </table>
</form>
<br /><br />
<a asp-controller="EmployeeManager" asp-action="List">Back to Employee
Listing</a>
```

The Delete view displays a warning message at the top. Below the warning message is a <form> that POSTs to the Delete() action of EmployeeManagerController. Note that EmployeeID is stored in a hidden form field. This is required because when you submit the form by clicking the Delete button, the Delete() action (discussed earlier) should know the EmployeeID for deleting that record.

The table housed inside the form displays existing employee details (for the sake of reducing clutter, only EmployeeID and FirstName properties are shown). You can review these details and click the Delete button at the bottom of the table.

Add Razor Layout and View Start

At this stage, you have completed the functionality related to the CRUD operations. Let's add a few more things before you can run the application. Firstly, you add a Razor Layout for your views. A layout is used to give consistent page layout for various pages of your application. Most of the web sites provide a consistent site layout in terms of logo, header, footer, and navigation structures such as menus. Since these pieces appear on more than one page, they are better kept at a single place. Layout is such a place. If you are familiar with ASP.NET master pages, you will find layouts analogous to them.

Secondly, you will attach this layout to various views of your application. You do this using a View Start file.

Add a subfolder named Shared under Views. The Shared folder is used to store items that are to be shared between multiple controllers or views. For example, a view file might be required by multiple controllers. Rather than keeping two copies of the same view in two controller-specific folders, you can put it in the Shared folder. Since a layout is usually attached with more than one view, it's stored in the Shared folder.

Then right-click the Shared folder and open the Add New Item dialog. Add a layout named _Layout.cshtml to the Views folder (Figure 3-10).

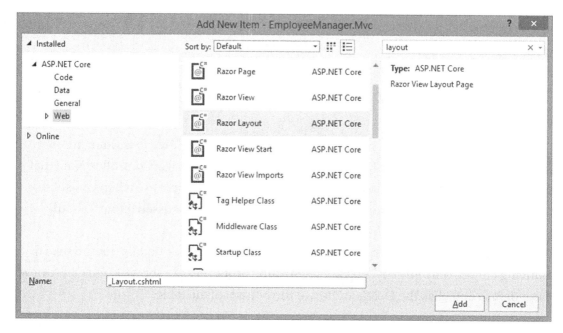

Figure 3-10. *Adding a Razor Layout to the Shared folder*

Next, write the markup shown in Listing 3-20 inside the _Layout file.

Listing 3-20. Markup from _Layout.cshtml

```
<!DOCTYPE html>
<html>
<head>
    <meta name="viewport" content="width=device-width" />
    <title>Employee Manager</title>
    <link href="~/Styles/site.css" rel="stylesheet" />
</head>
<body>
    <h1>Employee Manager</h1>
    <hr />
    <div>
```

```
    @RenderBody()
  </div>
  <hr />
</body>
</html>
```

As you can see, the layout contains HTML elements such as <html>, <head>, <title>, <link>, and <body>. These elements define the skeleton of the page.

Notice the use of the @RenderBody() method. A view's content will be outputted at a place where the @RenderBody() call is placed. This way, the content of the layout and the content of the view are combined to form the final page.

To attach _Layout.cshtml to all the views of the application, add a Razor View Start file in the Views folder (Figure 3-11).

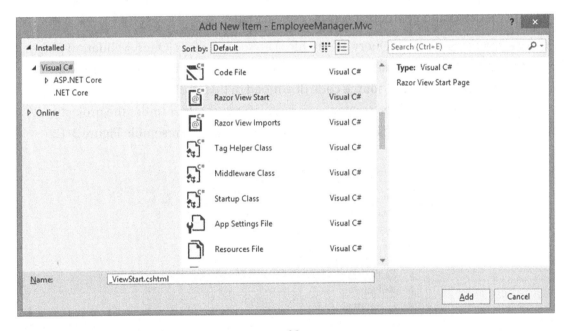

Figure 3-11. *Adding a Razor View Start file*

The View Start file is named _ViewStart.cshtml and contains this code:

```
@{
    Layout = "_Layout";
}
```

This is a Razor code block and sets the Layout property of the views to the name of the layout page (without file extension) to be attached.

Enable Client-Side Validations

The Employee class located in the Models folder is decorated with data annotation attributes such as [Required] and [StringLength] that are capable of performing the validation on the server side as well as on the client side. However, the client-side validations are dependent on jQuery validation. So you need to add certain jQuery files to all the views. These files are as follows:

- jquery.js

- jquery.validate.js

- jquery.validate.unobtrusive.js

The first file is the core jQuery library file. The second file is jQuery validation plugin, and the third file is an add-on to jQuery validation to enable unobtrusive validation. You can grab these files from the source code download of this book.

Once you have these files, create the wwwroot/Scripts folder under the project root folder and place them inside it. Your Solution Explorer should resemble Figure 3-12.

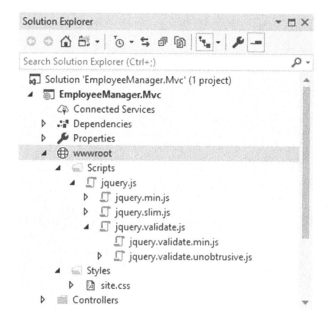

Figure 3-12. *jQuery files added to the wwwroot folder*

Open the _Layout.cshtml file and add <script> elements for these files as shown in Listing 3-21.

Listing 3-21. Enabling client-side validations

```html
<html>
<head>
    <meta name="viewport" content="width=device-width" />
    <title>Employee Manager</title>
    <link href="~/Styles/site.css" rel="stylesheet" />
    <script src="~/Scripts/jquery.js"></script>
    <script src="~/Scripts/jquery.validate.js"></script>
    <script src="~/Scripts/jquery.validate.unobtrusive.js"></script>
</head>
```

Notice the use of ~ to represent the web application's root. In ASP.NET Core, all the static files such as images, scripts, and style sheets are placed inside the wwwroot folder; and wwwroot is considered as the web application's root.

Also notice that the markup also uses a CSS style sheet named site.css. This file contains various CSS classes used by the views. You can download this file from the book's source code.

Note   You can download the latest versions of these jQuery files by visiting `https://jquery.com`, `https://jqueryvalidation.org`, and `https://github.com/aspnet/jquery-validation-unobtrusive`, respectively.

Store the Database Connection String in appsettings.json

The Employee Manager application uses data from the Northwind database you installed earlier. Although you have created an EF Core data model and data entry pages, the database connection information is not mentioned anywhere. It's time to do that now.

The database connection string is a part of the application's configuration, and ASP. NET Core has a special file to store it: appsettings.json. The appsettings.json file stores the application configuration in JSON format. Typically, the configuration is stored as key-value pairs. To add the appsettings.json file, right-click the project in Solution Explorer and open the Add New Item dialog. Then locate the App Settings File entry (Figure 3-13).

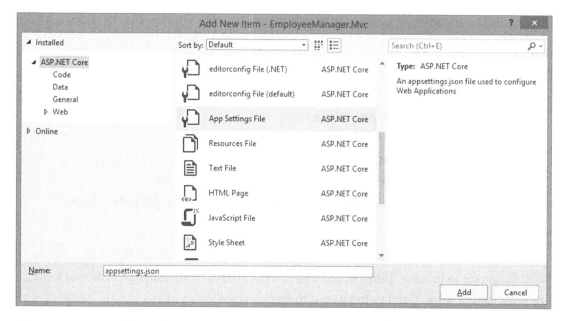

Figure 3-13. *Adding the appsettings.json file*

Once the appsettings.json is added, write the JSON fragment as shown in Listing 3-22 into it.

Listing 3-22. Storing the database connection string in appsettings.json

```
{
  "ConnectionStrings": {
    "AppDb": "data source=.;
             initial catalog=Northwind;
             integrated security=true"
  }
}
```

The ConnectionStrings section is meant for storing database connection strings. An application can have more than one database involved, and all the connection strings can be placed under the ConnectionStrings section. In this case, a key named AppDb stores the Northwind database's connection string.

The data source specifies the name or IP address of the SQL Server installation. Here, dot (.) means local host. The initial catalog specifies the name of the database you want to connect with, Northwind in this case. Integrated security indicates that Windows integrated security is to be used for database-level authentication.

Make sure to change this connection string as per your setup. Storing the connection string inside a configuration file makes it possible to change it at a later stage without needing any change to the source code.

Configure Application Startup

Before running an ASP.NET Core application, you need to specify the application's startup. The application's startup includes three main tasks:

- Read and load the application's configuration so that it can be accessed from the other parts of the application.

- Register services needed by the application. A service is a reusable component that is registered with the dependency injection (DI) framework and can then be used in the other parts of the application.

- Define the application's request processing pipeline.

The startup information mentioned in the preceding text is stored in the Startup class by default. The Startup class usually resides in the project root. Let's see how the Employee Manager's Startup class looks like. Listing 3-23 shows the skeleton of the Startup.cs file.

Listing 3-23. Skeleton of Startup.cs

```
public class Startup
{
    public Startup(IConfiguration config)
    {
    }

    public void ConfigureServices(IServiceCollection services)
    {
    }
```

```
    public void Configure(IApplicationBuilder app,
                          IWebHostEnvironment env)
    {
    }
}
```

The startup code consists of three parts – startup class constructor, ConfigureServices() method, and Configure() method.

The startup class constructor receives an object implementing IConfiguration that represents the application's configuration from the appsettings.json file.

The ConfigureServices() method is used to register services with the DI framework. It receives an object of IServiceCollection and allows you to add services required by your application.

The Configure() method is used to define the application's request pipeline. The request pipeline consists of a series of middleware that process the request in some way. The Configure() method has two parameters – IApplicationBuilder and IWebHostEnvironment. The former allows you to build the request pipeline, and the latter allows reading host environment details.

These three – constructor, ConfigureServices(), and Configure() – are executed in the same sequence when the application is run for the first time. For subsequent requests, the startup information is already available from the previous run. Of course, if the application gets restarted for some reason, these three methods will be executed again.

Now that you know the basics of application startup, let's fill this skeleton with the core required for Employee Manager.

Open Startup.cs and write the code shown in Listing 3-24.

Listing 3-24. Reading application's configuration

```
private IConfiguration config = null;

public Startup(IConfiguration config)
{
    this.config = config;
}
```

The code declares a private variable of type IConfiguration. The startup class constructor receives the configuration from appsettings.json in the form of a config object. The config object is stored in the variable just declared for later use.

Now complete ConfigureServices() as shown in Listing 3-25.

Listing 3-25. Registering MVC in ConfigureServices()

```
public void ConfigureServices(IServiceCollection services)
{
    services.AddControllersWithViews();

    services.AddDbContext<AppDbContext>(
            options => options.UseSqlServer
            (this.config.GetConnectionString("AppDb")));
}
```

The code calls the AddControllersWithViews() method to register MVC-specific services with the DI container.

You created the AppDbContext class earlier and also used it in the EmployeeManagerController. That time, it was mentioned that AppDbContext would be injected into the controller. Here, you are registering AppDbContext with the ASP.NET Core's DI container. The AddDbContext<T>() method registers the specified custom DbContext type (AppDbContext in this case) with the DI container. While registering AppDbContext, the code specifies the database connection string. This is done using the UseSqlServer() method. Notice how the database connection string is retrieved using the GetConnectionString() method of IConfiguration. The connection string's key in the configuration is AppDb, and GetConnectionString() returns its value. This way, AppDbContext is made aware of the underlying database.

Next, complete the Configure() method as shown in Listing 3-26.

Listing 3-26. Configuring request pipeline

```
public void Configure(IApplicationBuilder app,
                    IWebHostEnvironment env)
{
    if (env.IsDevelopment())
    {
        app.UseDeveloperExceptionPage();
    }

    app.UseStaticFiles();
```

```
    app.UseRouting();

    app.UseEndpoints(endpoints => {
endpoints.MapControllerRoute(
 name: "default",
 pattern: "{controller=EmployeeManager}/{action=List}/{id?}");
 });}
}
```

The `Configure()` method checks the `IsDevelopment()` method of `IWebHostEnvironment`. This method returns true if ASPNETCORE_ENVIRONMENT environment variable is set to Development. During development, it will be Development. You can change its value from the project's property page.

If `IsDevelopment()` returns true, the code wires developer exception page middleware using the `UseDeveloperExceptionPage()` method. This middleware displays detailed error messages when any error occurs.

The code then wires static files middleware using the `UseStaticFiles()` method. Calling this method ensures that static files such as images, JavaScript files, and CSS style sheet files can be accessed by the browser.

Then the code calls the `UseRouting()` method to wire the endpoint routing middleware. This middleware enables endpoint routing for your application.

Finally, the code wires endpoint middleware using the `UseEndpoints()` method. The `UseEndpoints()` method configures routing endpoints for the application. Routing maps an incoming request to some controller and action. The `MapControllerRoute()` method defines the default mapping for our application.

The `MapControllerRoute()` has two parameters – the name parameter indicates a unique name given to a route definition under consideration and the pattern parameter specifies a URL pattern. In this case, the pattern consists of three parameters as enclosed in { and }: controller, action, and id. The controller and action parameters indicate that the name of a controller and action will appear in place of the parameters in the URL. They have default values of `EmployeeManager` and `List,` respectively. This indicates that if no controller or action is specified in the URL, `EmployeeManager` and `List` are assumed. The `id` parameter is optional as indicated by ? and is used during update and delete operations.

Recollect how you specified the URLs of the Insert, Update, and Delete links on the employee listing page. The insert URL followed this pattern: /controller/action since id parameter wasn't necessary. On the other hand, the update and delete URLs followed this pattern: /controller/action/id since id parameter was required to perform the respective operations. As you can see, the configuration behind those URLs is specified in the `MapControllerRoute()`.

At this stage, your application can perform CRUD operations. If you run the application, the employee listing page is displayed; and you can test the insert, update, and delete functionality. It is recommended that you do so before going ahead to the next sections.

Add ASP.NET Core Identity Support

Although the Employee Manager application is able to list, insert, update, and delete employees, the application doesn't have any security. In the following sections, you will wire ASP.NET Core Identity into the application to perform user authentication and authorization.

ASP.NET Core Identity is a membership framework that provides authentication and authorization services to your application. You can perform various tasks such as creating a new user account and signing in and signing out of the application. The user data is typically stored in an SQL Server database. ASP.NET Core Identity also supports external login providers such as Facebook, Twitter, and Microsoft account. As far as the Employee Manager application is concerned, you store user data in an SQL Server database.

The first step in adding support to ASP.NET Core Identity is to add the NuGet package for `Microsoft.AspNetCore.Identity.EntityFrameworkCore`. Now proceed to the following sections to build various pieces required to enable ASP.NET Core Identity for Employee Manager.

Add AppIdentityUser, AppIdentityRole, and AppIdentityDbContext Classes

In order to implement authentication and authorization, the system needs to deal with users and roles. Therefore, the Employee Manager application needs to have classes that represent the application's user and role, respectively. These classes allow you to capture user and role details.

Add a folder named Security under the project root and then add three classes into it: `AppIdentityUser`, `AppIdentityRole`, and `AppIdentityDbContext`. The `AppIdentityUser` class represents the application's user, and the `AppIdentityRole` class represents a user role. The `AppIdentityDbContext` class represents a custom

107

DbContext that is used to communicate with the underlying user and role data store. The `AppIdentityUser` class is shown in Listing 3-27.

Listing 3-27. AppIdentityUser class represents the application user

```
public class AppIdentityUser : IdentityUser
{
    public string FullName { get; set; }
    public DateTime BirthDate { get; set; }
}
```

The `AppIdentityUser` class inherits from the `IdentityUser` class residing in the `Microsoft.AspNetCore.Identity` namespace. It provides properties such as `UserName` and `Email`. In addition to these basic properties, you might want to capture more details about a user such as user's first name, last name, address, and any such details. These details can be captured by adding properties to the custom user class. In this case, `AppIdentityUser` adds two properties: `FullName` and `BirthDate`.

The `AppIdentityRole` class represents an application role and is shown in Listing 3-28.

Listing 3-28. AppIdentityRole represents an application role

```
public class AppIdentityRole : IdentityRole
{
    public string Description { get; set; }
}
```

The `AppIdentityRole` class inherits from the `IdentityRole` class residing in the `Microsoft.AspNetCore.Identity` namespace. Properties such as `Name` are available in the `IdentityRole` base class. If you wish to capture any additional information about the role, you can add properties in the derived class. In this case, the Description property is added to capture the description of a role.

Now open the `AppIdentityDbContext` class and write the code shown in Listing 3-29 in it.

Listing 3-29. AppIdentityDbContext for dealing with the data store

```
public class AppIdentityDbContext : IdentityDbContext<AppIdentityUser,App
IdentityRole,string>
{
    public AppIdentityDbContext
        (DbContextOptions<AppIdentityDbContext> options)
        : base(options)
    {

    }
}
```

The `AppIdentityDbContext` is quite similar to the `AppDbContext` class you created earlier. The user and role details need to be stored in and retrieved from some data store such as an SQL Server database. The `AppIdentityDbContext` class communicates to the underlying user and role data store. In this example, you store user and role details in the Northwind database itself. However, if you want, you can store these details in a separate database.

Notice that the `AppIdentityDbContext` class inherits from the `IdentityDbCon text<TUser,TRole,TKey>` class residing in the `Microsoft.AspNetCore.Identity. EntityFrameworkCore` namespace. The TUser parameter indicates the type of application's user (`AppIdentityUser` in this case). The TRole parameter indicates the type of application's role (`AppIdentityRole` in this case), and the TKey parameter indicates the type of the primary key for users and roles (`string` in this case).

The constructor of the `AppIdentityDbContext` class is designed for DI support.

Add ASP.NET Core Identity Configuration to Startup

Now that you created `AppIdentityUser`, `AppIdentityRole`, and `AppIdentityDbContext` classes, it's time to add a few details in the application's startup.

Open the Startup class and add the lines shown in Listing 3-30 to `ConfigureServices()`.

Listing 3-30. Adding ASP.NET Core Identity in ConfigureServices()

```
public void ConfigureServices(IServiceCollection services)
{
```

```
    services.AddControllersWithViews();
    ...
    ...
services.AddDbContext<AppIdentityDbContext>(options =>
        options.UseSqlServer(this.config.GetConnectionString("AppDb")));

services.AddIdentity<AppIdentityUser, AppIdentityRole>()
            .AddEntityFrameworkStores<AppIdentityDbContext>();

    services.ConfigureApplicationCookie(opt =>
    {
        opt.LoginPath = "/Security/SignIn";
        opt.AccessDeniedPath = "/Security/AccessDenied";
    });
}
```

Notice the code marked in bold letters. The AddDbContext() method registers
AppIdentityDbContext with the DI container. In this example, you use the Northwind
database as the identity data store, and hence its connection string from the
configuration is passed to the UseSqlServer().

The AddIdentity() method is used to register ASP.NET Core Identity–related
services with the DI container. The TUser and TRole parameters accept the user and role
types, respectively. The code also calls the AddEntityFrameworkStores() method which
adds an EF Core implementation of identity data stores.

By default, ASP.NET Core Identity issues a cookie to an authenticated user. This
cookie acts like a ticket and is used to decide whether to allow the user to access
the application or not. You can configure various settings of this cookie using the
ConfigureApplicationCookie() method. In this example, the code sets the LoginPath
property to /Security/SignIn. The LoginPath property informs the framework about the
sign-in page of the application. If an unauthenticated user tries to access the application,
the user will be automatically redirected to this page. You create SecurityController
and the SignIn() action in the following sections.

The AccessDeniedPath property sets an error page that is displayed in case access
can't be granted to a user. For example, a user might sign in with valid credentials but
might not belong to the Manager role.

Now, go to the Configure() method and add the authentication and authorization
middleware as shown in Listing 3-31.

Listing 3-31. Adding authentication middleware

```
public void Configure(IApplicationBuilder app, IWebHostEnvironment env)
{
    if (env.IsDevelopment())
    {
        app.UseDeveloperExceptionPage();
    }

    app.UseStaticFiles();
    app.UseRouting();

    app.UseAuthentication();
    app.UseAuthorization();

    app.UseEndpoints(endpoints=> {
        endpoints.MapControllerRoute(
        name: "default",
        pattern: "{controller=EmployeeManager}/{action=List}/{id?}");
            });
}
```

The UseAuthentication() method adds authentication middleware to the request pipeline. Since Employee Manager uses role-based security (as you will see in later sections), you also need to call the UseAuthorization() method. This way, requests are now authenticated and authorized using ASP.NET Core Identity.

Add Database Tables to Store User and Role Details

The Employee Manager application needs to store user and role details in some persistent data store. You use the Northwind database for this purpose. In order to store these details into a database, you need to create certain tables that ASP.NET Core Identity understands. Luckily, there is a command line tool that helps you accomplish this task. To use this command line tool, you need to first install it. To do so, open Visual Studio Developer Command Prompt and issue the following command:

```
> dotnet tool install --global dotnet-ef
```

This command installs the dotnet-ef tool on your machine.

Then add a NuGet package for `Microsoft.EntityFrameworkCore.Design` using the Manage NuGet Packages dialog. After successfully installing the tool and adding the NuGet package, navigate to the Employee Manager project root folder. Then issue this command:

```
> dotnet ef migrations
        add IdentityMigration
        --context AppIdentityDbContext
```

The preceding command generates an EF Core migration named `IdentityMigration` and uses `AppIdentityDbContext`.

Note   The EF Core migrations provide a way to keep the data model and database schema in sync. The existing data is preserved when a migration is executed.

After executing this command, you will notice the Migrations folder under the project root folder. This folder contains certain files used by EF Core migrations (Figure 3-14).

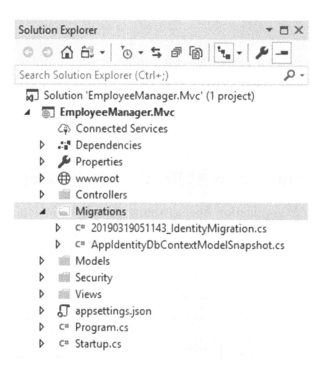

Figure 3-14.   *Migrations folder with EF Core migration–related files*

You don't need to tamper with these files. They are used by EF Core migrations. Next, issue this command on the developer command prompt:

```
> dotnet ef database update --context AppIdentityDbContext
```

This command updates the underlying database by adding ASP.NET Core Identity-specific tables. After invoking this command, if you see the Northwind database, you will find that a few new tables have been added to the database. Figure 3-15 shows these tables.

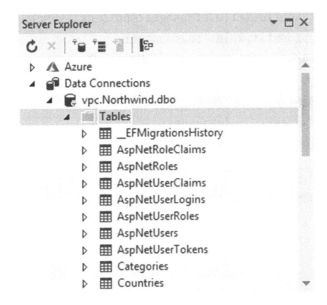

Figure 3-15. *ASP.NET Core Identity–related tables*

Notice the tables that begin with "AspNet" such as AspNetUsers and AspNetRoles. These tables are used by ASP.NET Core Identity to store user and role information.

Add SecurityController to the Controllers Folder

Now that you have wired and configured ASP.NET Core Identity into Employee Manager, you can proceed to create the registration page and sign-in page. However, before you do that, you need to add a controller – SecurityController – that contains necessary actions.

Right-click the Controllers folder and add a new controller class named SecurityController using the Add New Item dialog. Listing 3-32 shows the skeleton of the SecurityController.

Listing 3-32. Skeleton of SecurityController

```
public class SecurityController : Controller
{

    private readonly UserManager<AppIdentityUser> userManager;
    private readonly RoleManager<AppIdentityRole> roleManager;
    private readonly SignInManager<AppIdentityUser> signinManager;

    public SecurityController(UserManager<AppIdentityUser> userManager,
    RoleManager<AppIdentityRole> roleManager,
    SignInManager<AppIdentityUser> signinManager)
    {
        this.userManager = userManager;
        this.roleManager = roleManager;
        this.signinManager = signinManager;
    }

    public IActionResult Register()
    {
    }

    [HttpPost]
    public IActionResult Register(Register obj)
    {
    }

    public IActionResult SignIn()
    {
    }

    [HttpPost]
    public IActionResult SignIn(SignIn obj)
    {
    }
```

```
[HttpPost]
public IActionResult SignOut()
{
}
}
```

The SecurityController contains five actions and a constructor. The class declares three member variables of type UserManager<TUser>, RoleManager<TRole> and SignInManager<TUser>, respectively. The UserManager class allows you to perform user-centric operations such as creating a user account and modifying user details. The RoleManager class allows you to manage application roles and allows you to create or remove roles from the system. The SignInManager class allows you to validate a user and issue the authentication cookie discussed earlier.

The UserManager, RoleManager, and SignInManager objects are injected into the constructor of SecurityController and are stored locally into the variables declared earlier.

The user registration is handled by two Register() actions, whereas user authentication and signing in are handled by two SignIn() actions. The SignOut() action signs the user out of the system.

The Register(), SignIn(), and SignOut() actions are discussed in the following sections.

Create a User Registration Page

The user registration page allows you to create a user account. You can then sign in to the system using the account created (Figure 3-16).

Create New User Account

User Name :

Password :

Confirm Password :

Email :

Full Name :

Birth Date :   mm / dd / yyyy

Create

<u>Go To Sign-In Page</u>

Figure 3-16. *User registration page*

To create a user registration page, you need a view model class named Register, two Register() actions, and the Register view.

Right-click the Models folder and using the Add New Item dialog add a new class named Register to the folder. Listing 3-33 shows the Register class.

Listing 3-33. Register class

```
public class Register
{
    [Required]
    [Display(Name = "User Name")]
    public string UserName { get; set; }

    [Required]
    [Display(Name = "Password")]
    public string Password { get; set; }

    [Required]
    [Compare("Password")]
    [Display(Name = "Confirm Password")]
    public string ConfirmPassword { get; set; }
```

```
[Required]
[Display(Name = "Email")]
[EmailAddress]
public string Email { get; set; }

[Required]
[Display(Name = "Full Name")]
public string FullName { get; set; }

[Required]
[Display(Name = "Birth Date")]
public DateTime BirthDate { get; set; }
}
```

The Register class contains six properties, namely, UserName, Password, ConfirmPassword, Email, FullName, and BirthDate. These properties are also decorated with data annotations. Notice the [Compare] attribute added to the ConfirmPassword property. The [Compare] attribute specifies a property (Password) that is compared with the underlying property (ConfirmPassword). If they don't match, a validation error is generated. Also notice the [EmailAddress] attribute added on top of the Email property to ensure that only a valid email address can be assigned to it.

Now, go to the SecurityController and add two Register() actions as shown in Listing 3-34.

Listing 3-34. Register() action creates a new user account

```
public IActionResult Register()
{
    return View();
}

[HttpPost]
public IActionResult Register(Register obj)
{
    if (ModelState.IsValid)
    {
        if (!roleManager.RoleExistsAsync("Manager").Result)
        {
```

```
            AppIdentityRole role = new AppIdentityRole();
            role.Name = "Manager";
            role.Description = "Can perform CRUD operations.";
            IdentityResult roleResult =
            roleManager.CreateAsync(role).Result;
        }

        AppIdentityUser user = new AppIdentityUser();
        user.UserName = obj.UserName;
        user.Email = obj.Email;
        user.FullName = obj.FullName;
        user.BirthDate = obj.BirthDate;

        IdentityResult result = userManager.CreateAsync
        (user, obj.Password).Result;

        if (result.Succeeded)
        {
            userManager.AddToRoleAsync(user, "Manager").Wait();
            return RedirectToAction("SignIn", "Security");
        }
        else
        {
            ModelState.AddModelError("", "Invalid user details!");
        }
    }
    return View(obj);
}
```

The first `Register()`gets called when you click the Create New User Account link from the sign-in page (discussed later). It simply displays a blank user registration page ready to accept new user details.

The second `Register()` is invoked when you submit the user registration page by entering user details and clicking the Create button. The `Register()` action receives a Register object through model binding.

Inside, the code checks whether the model contains valid data or not using the `IsValid` property of `ModelState`. If the model contains valid values, the code proceeds to create a new user account.

Before proceeding to create a new user account, the code needs to create a system role named Manager. So the RoleManager class checks whether the Manager role exists in the system using the RoleExistsAsync() method. The UserManager, RoleManager, and SignInManager classes are designed for asynchronous operations. So RoleExistsAsync() is an asynchronous call. Accessing the Result property waits for the async call to finish and allows you to check its Boolean return value.

When you run the application for the first time, the Manager role won't be present in the system, and hence RoleExistsAsync() will return false. The code then proceeds to create a new AppIdentityRole object and sets its Name property to Manager. The Description property is also assigned a brief description about that role. Then the CreateAsync() method of RoleManager is called to create the role in the system.

Note   Here, you create the Manager role at the time of user registration. You could have also created it at the time of application initialization. In a more realistic case, you will have separate user management and role management pages that allow you to create roles, remove roles, and assign roles to users.

To create a new user account, the code creates a new object of AppIdentityUser. The AppIdentityUser represents a system user which holds various details such as UserName, Email, FullName, and BirthDate.

To create a new user account, the CreateAsync() method of UserManager is called. The CreateAsync() accepts two parameters. The first parameter is the AppIdentityUser object representing a new system user, and the second parameter is the password. The CreateAsync() method is an asynchronous call. However, since the Register() action isn't asynchronous, the code calls the Result property to wait for the result of the operation.

When complete, the CreateAsync() returns an IdentityResult object, an object that represents the result of an Identity operation. The Succeeded property of IdentityResult returns true if user account creation is successful; otherwise, it returns false.

If the account creation is successful, the code adds the newly created user to the Manager role. This is done using the AddToRoleAsync() method of the UserManager. The AddToRoleAsync() accepts the AppIdentityUser object and a role name (Manager in this case). Users belonging to the Manager role can perform the CRUD operations on the Employees table. The Wait() method waits for the asynchronous operation to complete.

The user is then redirected to the sign-in page wherein he can sign in to the system with the newly created account.

If, for some reasons, the user account creation fails, then an error is added to the ModelState object using the AddModelError() method. This error will be displayed on the registration page.

Now that Register() actions are complete, you can proceed to add the Register view. To do so, add a subfolder named Security under the Views folder and add a new Razor View named Register.cshtml to it. Then write the markup shown in Listing 3-35 to the Register.cshtml file.

Listing 3-35. Markup of Register.cshtml

```
@model Register

<h1>Create New User Account</h1>
<form asp-controller="Security" asp-action="Register" method="post">
    <table>
    </table>
    <div asp-validation-summary="All" class="message"></div>
    <h3>
        <a asp-controller="Security" asp-action="SignIn">
          Go To Sign-In Page
        </a>
    </h3>
</form>
```

The Register class acts as the model for the Register view as specified by the @model directive.

The Form Tag Helper sets the asp-controller and asp-action attributes to Security and Register, respectively. The method attribute is set to post. This indicates that the form will be POSTed to the Register() action of the Security controller.

The <table> housed inside the <form> contains all the form fields (discussed shortly). Notice the Validation Summary Tag Helper in the form of a <div> element below the table. The Validation Summary Tag Helper displays a list of the error messages that have occurred in the form. The asp-validation-summary attribute is set to All indicating that all the validation errors are to be displayed.

Note   The Validation Message Tag Helper displays an error message for a field under consideration. On the other hand, the Validation Summary Tag Helper displays a collective list of error messages occurring in that form.

The Anchor Tag Helper placed at the bottom of the page renders a link to the sign-in page.

Listing 3-36 shows various form fields that go inside the <table> element.

Listing 3-36. Registration form fields

```
<tr>
    <td class="right"><label asp-for="UserName"></label> :</td>
    <td class="left"><input type="text" asp-for="UserName" /></td>
</tr>
<tr>
    <td class="right"><label asp-for="Password"></label> :</td>
    <td class="left"><input type="password" asp-for="Password" /></td>
</tr>
<tr>
    <td class="right"><label asp-for="ConfirmPassword"></label> :</td>
    <td class="left"><input type="password" asp-for="ConfirmPassword" />
</td>
</tr>
<tr>
    <td class="right"><label asp-for="Email"></label> :</td>
    <td class="left"><input type="text" asp-for="Email" /></td>
</tr>
<tr>
    <td class="right"><label asp-for="FullName"></label> :</td>
    <td><input type="text" asp-for="FullName" /></td>
</tr>
<tr>
    <td class="right"><label asp-for="BirthDate"></label> :</td>
    <td class="left"><input type="date" asp-for="BirthDate" /></td>
</tr>
```

```
<tr>
    <td colspan="2">
        <button type="submit">Create</button>
    </td>
</tr>
```

This markup is responsible for rendering various input textboxes for fields such as UserName, Email, Password, ConfirmPassword, FullName, and BirthDate. Notice that Password and ConfirmPassword fields have type set to password. We won't go into the details of this markup since it is quite simple and straightforward.

Create a Sign-In Page

The sign-in page allows the user to sign in to the system and is shown in Figure 3-17.

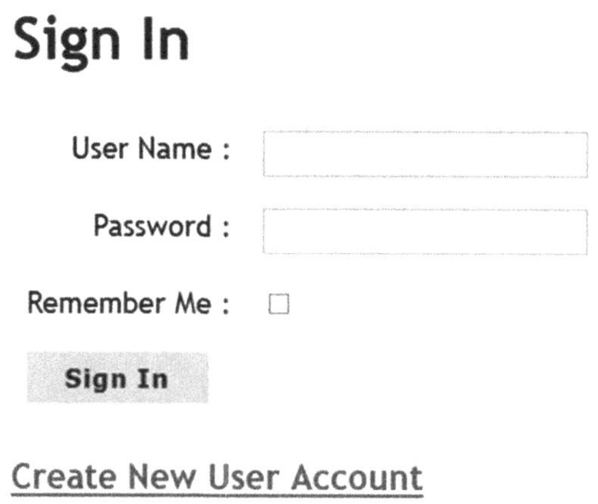

Sign In

User Name : [   ]

Password : [   ]

Remember Me : ☐

Sign In

Create New User Account

Figure 3-17. *Sign-in page*

The sign-in page consists of two input textboxes for entering a UserName and Password. The Remember Me checkbox is used to indicate whether the signed-in status should be preserved even after closing the browser.

To create the sign-in page, you need a SignIn model, two SignIn() actions, and a SignIn view. Begin by adding the SignIn model class into the Models folder (Listing 3-37).

Listing 3-37. SignIn model class

```
public class SignIn
{
    [Required]
    [Display(Name = "User Name")]
    public string UserName { get; set; }

    [Required]
    [Display(Name = "Password")]
    public string Password { get; set; }

    [Required]
    [Display(Name = "Remember Me")]
    public bool RememberMe { get; set; }
}
```

The SignIn model class contains three properties, namely, UserName, Password, and RememberMe. The properties are self-explanatory and hence are not discussed in detail.

Then open the SecurityController and write the code shown in Listing 3-38 into it.

Listing 3-38. SignIn() actions

```
public IActionResult SignIn()
{
    return View();
}

[HttpPost]
public IActionResult SignIn(SignIn obj)
{
    if (ModelState.IsValid)
    {
        var result = signinManager.PasswordSignInAsync
        (obj.UserName, obj.Password,
            obj.RememberMe, false).Result;
```

```
        if (result.Succeeded)
        {
            return RedirectToAction("List", "EmployeeManager");
        }
        else
        {
            ModelState.AddModelError("", " Invalid user details!");
        }
    }
    return View(obj);
}
```

The first `SignIn()` action is called when the user navigates to the sign-in page. Typically, when a user starts the application, he will be navigated to the sign-in page. The `SignIn()` action simply renders the SignIn view into the browser.

The second `SignIn()` is called when the user clicks the Sign In button present on the sign-in page. This action receives the sign-in credentials entered by the user in the form of a `SignIn` object.

Inside, the code checks whether the model object contains valid values. This is done using the `IsValid` property of `ModelState`. If the model contains valid values, the code tries to sign the user into the system by calling the `PasswordSignInAsync()` asynchronous method. The `PasswordSignInAsync()` accepts four parameters. The first three parameters represent the `UserName`, `Password`, and `RememberMe` values. The fourth parameter indicates whether to lock the account if the sign-in attempt fails. We don't want to lock the account, and hence false is passed. Note that the `RememberMe` is a Boolean value. Passing true indicates that the authentication cookie should be preserved even after closing the browser, whereas passing false indicates that the authentication cookie should be destroyed as soon as the browser is closed.

The return value of `PasswordSignInAsync()` is a `SignInResult` object. The `Succeeded` property of `SignInResult` indicates whether the sign-in operation was successful or not. If sign-in is successful, the code redirects the control to the `List()` action of `EmployeeManagerController`; otherwise, an error message is added to the `ModelState` in order to show it to the user.

Now, add the SignIn.cshtml view file in the Views ➤ Security folder and write the markup shown in Listing 3-39.

Listing 3-39. Markup of the SignIn.cshtml view file

```
@model SignIn

<h1>Sign In</h1>
<form asp-controller="Security" asp-action="SignIn" method="post">
    <table>
        <tr>
          <td class="right"><label asp-for="UserName"></label> :</td>
          <td class="left"><input type="text" asp-for="UserName" /></td>
        </tr>
        <tr>
          <td class="right"><label asp-for="Password"></label> :</td>
          <td class="left"><input type="password"
                           asp-for="Password" /></td>
        </tr>
        <tr>
          <td class="right"><label asp-for="RememberMe"></label> :</td>
          <td class="left"><input type="checkbox"
                           asp-for="RememberMe" /></td>
        </tr>
        <tr>
           <td colspan="2">
               <button type="submit">Sign In</button>
           </td>
        </tr>
    </table>
    <div asp-validation-summary="All" class="message"></div>

    <h3><a asp-controller="Security" asp-action="Register">Create New User
    Account</a></h3>
</form>
```

The @model directive sets the view's model type to SignIn. The Form Tag Helper submits the sign-in form to the SignIn() action of the SecurityController.

The input form fields for UserName, Password, and RememberMe are housed inside the <table> element. At the bottom, a Validation Summary Tag Helper is placed to display all the error messages. The Anchor Tag Helper placed at the bottom of the page navigates the user to the user registration page.

Note   The SecurityController also contains the AccessDenied() action that returns the AccessDenied view in case access can't be granted to a user. The AccessDenied action and AccessDenied view are quite straightforward and hence are not discussed here. You can get them from the book's source code.

Add a Sign Out Button

Now that user registration and sign-in functionality is in place, let's complete the sign-out functionality. A user can sign out of the system only if he is signed in to the system. To initiate the sign-out operation, all the pages (list, insert, update, and delete) show a Sign Out button at the bottom (Figure 3-18).

You are signed in as user1

Sign Out

Figure 3-18. *Sign Out button displayed at the bottom of the page*

Since the Sign Out button is common to multiple pages, it's better added to the site's layout. So open the _Layout.cshtml from the Shared folder. Add the code and markup shown in Listing 3-40 at the bottom of the layout.

Listing 3-40. Adding the Sign Out button

```
<body>
    <h1>
        Employee Manager
    </h1>
    <hr />
    <div>
        @RenderBody()
    </div>
```

```
<br />
<hr />
@if (User.Identity.IsAuthenticated)
{
    <h2>You are signed in as @User.Identity.Name</h2>
    <form asp-controller="Security" asp-action="SignOut" method="post">
        <button type="submit">Sign Out</button>
    </form>
}
</body>
```

Notice the code marked in bold letters. The Razor if statement checks whether the current request is coming from an authenticated user. This is done using the IsAuthenticated property. The UserName and the Sign Out button are displayed only if the user is an authenticated user (IsAuthenticated returns true).

The User property of Razor View represents the current application user. The User.Identity.Name property returns the UserName of the user currently signed in to the system. The Sign Out button submits the form to the SignOut() action of SecurityController. The SignOut() action is shown in Listing 3-41.

Listing 3-41. SignOut() action

```
[HttpPost]
public IActionResult SignOut()
{
    signinManager.SignOutAsync().Wait();
    return RedirectToAction("SignIn", "Security");
}
```

The SignOut() action calls the SignOutAsync() method of the SignInManager class. The SignOutAsync() method signs the current user out of the application by removing the authentication cookie. The control is redirected to the SignIn() action of SecurityController so that user is shown the sign-in page again.

Authenticate and Authorize Users

In the preceding sections, you built the infrastructure required to implement user authentication and authorization. However, you haven't applied the infrastructure yet. In this section, you do just that.

In ASP.NET Core MVC, authentication is done at the action level. That's because action is what you invoke from a browser (read the discussion about routing). That means you decide whether an action requires to be protected from anonymous users or not. By default, actions aren't protected, and even unauthenticated users can invoke them. To secure an action, you decorate it with the [Authorize] attribute. The [Authorize] attribute is capable of authenticating as well as authorizing users.

Note   Authentication is a process of deciding whether a user is the one who he claims to be. Authorization is a process of deciding what operations an authenticated user can do with the system. Authorization is often implemented using what is called role-based security. It is obvious from the preceding discussion that authorization is done after authentication.

In the Employee Manager application, you want to secure all the actions that participate in the CRUD operations. These include all the actions of the EmployeeManagerController. So open EmployeeManagerController and decorate all the actions with the [Authorize] attribute. Listing 3-42 shows the List() action as an example.

Listing 3-42. List() action decorated with the [Authorize] attribute

```
[Authorize(Roles = "Manager")]
public IActionResult List()
{
    List<Employee> model = (from e in db.Employees
                            orderby e.EmployeeID
                            select e).ToList();
    return View(model);
}
```

Notice how the code uses the [Authorize] attribute from the Microsoft.AspNetCore. Authorization namespace. It serves a twofold purpose. Firstly, adding [Authorize]

on top of List() secures that action. Secondly, the Roles property of the [Authorize] attribute is set to Manager. This means only the authenticated users belonging to the Manager role can invoke this action. The Roles property takes a comma-delimited string of roles that are granted access to the action. In this example, only the Manager role is involved, but you can easily specify multiple roles by separating them with a comma.

In the preceding discussion, you added [Authorize] on all the actions of the EmployeeManagerController. However, there is a shortcut. You can also add [Authorize] on top of the controller class. Doing so secures all the actions of the controller. Listing 3-43 shows how that can be done.

Listing 3-43. Adding [Authorize] on EmployeeManagerController

```
[Authorize(Roles = "Manager")]
public class EmployeeManagerController : Controller
{
  ...
}
```

There is also an attribute – [AllowAnonymous] – that allows anonymous access to the underlying action. For example, consider a hypothetical action named Help() that displays a help page in the browser and doesn't need security. If the controller has [Authorize] attribute added, Help() will also be secured. In this case, you can add [AllowAnonymous] on top of the Help() action like this:

```
[AllowAnonymous]
public IActionResult Help()
{
  ...
}
```

Protect the Application Against Cross-Site Request Forgery

In the preceding sections, you secured the Employee Manager application from unauthorized access. Although the application is working as expected, in this section, you protect it from cross-site request forgery (CSRF or XSRF) attacks.

> **Note**   Cross-site request forgery attack occurs when a malicious web application triggers interaction between the browser and another web application that trusts that browser. To read more about CSRF attack, visit `https://docs.microsoft.com/en-us/aspnet/core/security/anti-request-forgery`.

Consider the Employee Manager application. Suppose you signed in to the application by supplying a valid user name and password. The authentication cookie issued during the authentication process is passed between the client browser and the server with every request. In other words, Employee Manager now trusts the browser. During CSRF attack, this trust established between the application and the browser is exploited. For example, some malicious web application running in the same browser might send CRUD requests to Employee Manager without your notice and consent (it could be through tricky form submissions or an automated script or any such techniques). Such requests will be executed by Employee Manager because they contain a valid authentication cookie. Luckily, ASP.NET Core provides an easy way to protect your web application against CSRF attack. If you run the application (you might need to comment out the [`Authorize`] attribute from the `EmployeeManagerController` since you are yet to create users) and observe the browser's HTML source for insert, update, or delete pages, you will find a hidden form field automatically generated for you (Figure 3-19).

Figure 3-19. *Antiforgery token generated by the Form Tag Helper*

The Form Tag Helper automatically generates this hidden form field when the form submission method is POST. This hidden form field is called antiforgery token. To be protected from CSRF attack, you should check in your code that all the POST requests to the action include this token issued by the server. To enforce this condition, you use the [ValidateAntiForgeryToken] attribute. Listing 3-44 shows the Register() and SignIn() POST actions decorated with [ValidateAntiForgeryToken].

Listing 3-44. Adding the [ValidateAntiForgeryToken] attribute

```
[HttpPost]
[ValidateAntiForgeryToken]
public IActionResult Register(Register obj)
{
  ...
}

[HttpPost]
[ValidateAntiForgeryToken]
public IActionResult SignIn(SignIn obj)
{
  ...
}
```

Go ahead and add the [ValidateAntiForgeryToken] attribute on top of all POST actions of EmployeeManagerController and SecurityController.

Run the Application

The Employee Manager application is now complete. You can run the application and check whether user account creation, signing in, signing out, and CRUD operations can be performed as expected. For your convenience, a series of steps involved is given as follows:

- Run the application and ensure that you are taken to the sign-in page.

- Click the Create New User Account link on the sign-in page and navigate to the user registration page.

- Create a new user account by entering various form fields such as UserName and Password.

- Upon successful account creation, you are taken to the sign-in page.

- Sign in using the user account you just created.

- If sign-in is successful, you will be taken to the employee listing page.

- Explore insert, update, and delete operations by adding new employees, modifying them, and deleting them.

- Click the Sign Out button present at the bottom of the page and sign out of the system.

- Open the Employees table of the Northwind database in the SQL Server Management Studio and confirm that your data is present in the physical database.

- Open AspNetUsers and AspNetRoles tables and take a look at the users and roles you created during sample runs of the application.

Summary

In this chapter, you created the Employee Manager application using ASP.NET Core MVC. You learned to create an Entity Framework Core model. You were introduced to DbContext and DbSet classes. You then added EmployeeManagerController and several actions for inserting, updating, and deleting employees from the database. You used Razor Views and Tag Helpers to render the user interface of the application.

Once the HTML processing and CRUD functionality was ready, you proceeded to secure the application with ASP.NET Core Identity. ASP.NET Core Identity can be used to implement user authentication and authorization. You learned about UserManager, RoleManager, and SignInManager classes and also about the [Authorize] attribute.

In the next chapter, you build the Employee Manager application using ASP.NET Core Razor Pages.

ASP.NET Core Razor Pages

In this version of Employee Manager, you use ASP.NET Core Razor Pages. The user interface is built using Tag Helpers. The model validations are performed using data annotations. The database CRUD operations are performed using Entity Framework Core. The EF Core model is built using reverse engineering techniques. Mapping with the table schema is illustrated using data annotations as well as Fluent API. The user authentication and security is provided using ASP.NET Core Identity. Specifically, you will learn to

- Use Razor Pages and Tag Helpers to build a web user interface
- Build the EF Core model from the existing database using reverse engineering
- Implement authentication using ASP.NET Core Identity asynchronous operations
- Use exception handling middleware to trap unhandled errors

Create a ASP.NET Core Web Application

Begin by creating a new ASP.NET Core web application based on the Empty project template. Name the application as EmployeeManager.RazorPages to indicate that it's the Razor Pages version of the application. This also sets the default namespace for classes you add to the project.

© Bipin Joshi 2019
B. Joshi, *Beginning Database Programming Using ASP.NET Core 3*,
https://doi.org/10.1007/978-1-4842-5509-4_4

Note   You learned how to create a new ASP.NET Core project in Chapter 1. To avoid repetition, I am not going to explain those steps again. Read Chapter 1 in case you need any help on creating a new ASP.NET Core web application based on the Empty project template.

Since you use EF Core and ASP.NET Core Identity, add NuGet packages for these components as you did in the previous chapter.

Figure 4-1 shows the EmployeeManager.RazorPages project loaded in Solution Explorer once it is complete.

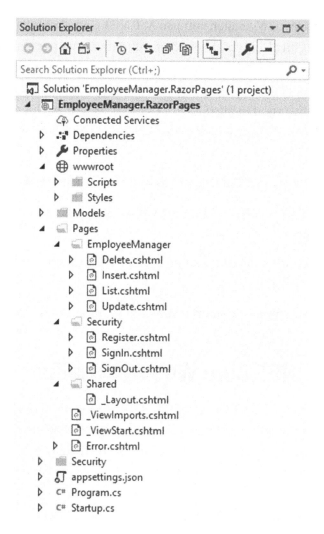

Figure 4-1.   *EmployeeManager.RazorPages loaded in Solution Explorer*

At this point, you may not understand all the pieces shown in Solution Explorer, and that's alright. Just take a look at the overall project structure and organization. In the sections that follow, you build this application step-by-step.

Reverse Engineering the Entity Framework Core Model

In the previous chapter, you created the EF Core model by manually creating POCOs for entity classes (`Employee` and `Country`) and also the `DbContext` class (`AppDbContext`). If you are building an EF Core model for an existing database (similar to our example), you can automate the EF Core model creation using the reverse engineering approach. In this approach, the EF Core command line tool reads the database schema and automatically generates entity classes and `DbContext` for you. Of course, you can modify the generated classes to fine-tune them as per your application requirement.

Note   In order to work with the EF Core command line tool, you need to install the dotnet-ef tool and add the Microsoft.EntityFrameworkCore.Design NuGet package in the project. You may read the previous chapter for related details.

In this section, you will create the EF Core model using the reverse engineering approach. Let's see how that can be done.

Open Visual Studio Developer Command Prompt and navigate to the project root folder. Then issue this command at the command prompt:

```
> dotnet ef dbcontext scaffold
  "Server=.;Database=Northwind;Integrated Security=true;"
  Microsoft.EntityFrameworkCore.SqlServer
  -o Models
  -c AppDbContext
  -t Employees
  -t Countries
```

Here, you use the EF Core scaffold command to generate the DbContext class and entity classes. The command takes a database connection string and data provider name. The connection string points to the Northwind database. Make sure to change the connection string as per your development setup. Since you are using SQL Server, the provider is specified to be `Microsoft.EntityFrameworkCore.SqlServer`.

The `-o` option is used to specify the output folder where all the class files are to be placed. In this example, you store the output in the Models folder under the project root. If the folder doesn't exist, the command creates it for you. The `-c` option specifies the name of the generated `DbContext` class. In this case, the `DbContext` class is named `AppDbContext`. The `-t` option is used to specify a table name whose entity class is to be reverse engineered. In this example, we ask the tool to reverse engineer Employees and Countries tables. If you don't specify the `-t` switch, then entity classes for all the tables from the database are generated. Figure 4-2 shows classes generated after running the command.

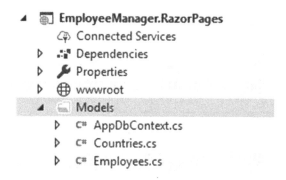

Figure 4-2.   *Generating the EF Core model using reverse engineering*

Let's quickly examine the content of these class files. Open the Countries class, and you should find it similar to Listing 4-1.

Listing 4-1.   Countries entity class

```
public partial class Countries
{
    public int CountryId { get; set; }
    public string Name { get; set; }
}
```

Notice that the class name is `Countries` – the same as the name of the database table. The `Countries` class is marked to be partial. Also, notice that the `CountryId` and Name properties are generated based on the Countries table's column names.

Now open the `Employees` class to reveal its content. Listing 4-2 shows a part of the Employees class.

Listing 4-2. Employees entity class

```
public partial class Employees
{
    public Employees()
    {
        InverseReportsToNavigation = new HashSet<Employees>();
    }
    public int EmployeeId { get; set; }
    public string LastName { get; set; }
    public string FirstName { get; set; }
    public string Title { get; set; }
    public string TitleOfCourtesy { get; set; }
    public DateTime? BirthDate { get; set; }
    public DateTime? HireDate { get; set; }
    ...
    ...
}
```

The Employees class is marked to be partial and contains several properties depending on the Employees table columns. Notice that the BirthDate and HireDate columns allow NULL values, and hence their type is DateTime?.

The Countries and Employees classes don't use data annotations to map them with the underlying tables and columns. This is because the tool by default uses Fluent API to perform the required mapping.

Note   Entity Framework Core Fluent API is a technique used to configure entity classes. Fluent API or Fluent Interface uses method chaining to perform a series of operations to arrive at the result.

To see how Fluent API is used to perform the mapping, open the AppDbContext class and locate the OnModelCreating() overridden method. Here, you will find a series of method calls chained one after the other that configure the Countries and Employees entity classes. Listing 4-3 shows a part of the OnModelCreating() method.

Listing 4-3. OnModelCreating() contains Fluent API calls

```
protected override void OnModelCreating(ModelBuilder modelBuilder)
{
    ...
    modelBuilder.Entity<Countries>(entity =>
    {
        entity.HasKey(e => e.CountryId)
            .HasName("PK__country__3213E83F562F253C");

        entity.Property(e => e.CountryId).HasColumnName("CountryID");

        entity.Property(e => e.Name)
            .IsRequired()
            .HasMaxLength(80)
            .IsUnicode(false);
    });
    ...
    ...
}
```

We won't go into the details of the Fluent API code in this book. It suffices to know that it's a way to configure entity classes.

You just used reverse engineering to generate the EF Core model that uses Fluent API for mapping and configuration. What if you want to use data annotations instead of Fluent API? Luckily, you can specify that data annotations be used during the scaffolding like this:

```
> dotnet ef dbcontext scaffold
  "Server=.;Database=Northwind;Integrated Security=true;"
  Microsoft.EntityFrameworkCore.SqlServer
  -o Models
  -c AppDbContext
  -t Employees
  -t Countries
  --data-annotations
```

This time, you added --data-annotations to the command. This instructs the tool to use data annotations instead of Fluent API for configuring the entity classes.

Run the preceding command and generate the classes in the Models folder again. Let's observe the code generated this time. Listing 4-4 shows the Countries class generated by the tool.

Listing 4-4. Countries class uses data annotations

```
public partial class Countries
{
    [Column("CountryID")]
    public int CountryId { get; set; }

    [Required]
    [StringLength(80)]
    public string Name { get; set; }
}
```

As you can see, the Countries class now uses data annotations such as [Column], [Required], and [StringLength].

Now open the Employees entity class to reveal its content (a part of it is shown in Listing 4-5).

Listing 4-5. Employees class using data annotations

```
public partial class Employees
{
    public Employees()
    {
        InverseReportsToNavigation = new HashSet<Employees>();
    }
    [Key]
    [Column("EmployeeID")]
    public int EmployeeId { get; set; }
    [Required]
    [StringLength(20)]
    public string LastName { get; set; }
    [Required]
    [StringLength(10)]
```

```
    public string FirstName { get; set; }
    ...
    ...
}
```

To keep the Razor Pages version closely matching with the MVC version, you will continue to use data annotations rather than Fluent API.

Note   Data annotations such as [Required] and [StringLength] participate in the UI-level validations. If you use Fluent API, you need to take care of UI-level validations using some alternate technique such as Fluent Validation – a third-party validation library for .NET that uses Fluent Interface for building validation rules. You may read more about Fluent Validation at `https://fluentvalidation.net`.

However, you need to modify the generated `Countries` and `Employees` classes. So go ahead and perform the following changes to the generated classes:

- Change the Countries class (and file name) to Country and ensure that it has all the data annotations and validation error messages.

- Change the Employees class (and file name) to Employee and keep only these properties inside it: EmployeeID, FirstName, LastName, Title, BirthDate, HireDate, Country, and Notes. Also, ensure that it has all the data annotations and validation error messages.

- Open the AppDbContext class and change the DbSet definitions to use Country and Employee classes.

- Remove OnConfiguring() and OnModelCreating() methods from the AppDbContext class.

Once you complete these changes, your EF Core model will look identical to the previous version (see the previous chapter for the ASP.NET Core MVC version of Employee Manager). As you can see, the reverse engineering technique helps you to quickly generate the EF Core model. Although you often need to fine-tune the resultant model, it can save you significant amount of time if the model contains many entity classes.

This completes the EF Core model required for this example.

Create Pages and EmployeeManager Folders

ASP.NET Core Razor Pages offers a page-focused programming model. A page (.cshtml) and its page model (.cs) are stored under the Pages folder. You can further organize your Razor Pages in different subfolders. By default, the folder structure also controls the URL for accessing the page. For example, a Razor Page named Page1.cshtml residing under the Pages folder can be accessed at /Page1, whereas a page named Page2 residing under the Pages ➤ MyFolder folder can be accessed at /MyFolder/Page2.

Create a folder named Pages under the project root folder. Also add the EmployeeManager subfolder under the Pages folder. All the files involved in the CRUD operations are stored under the EmployeeManager subfolder. At this stage, your Solution Explorer should resemble Figure 4-3.

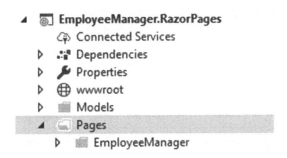

Figure 4-3. *Adding Pages and EmployeeManager folders*

Add a _ViewImports File

In the following sections, you use ASP.NET Core Tag Helpers to render the user interface elements such as form, form fields, and hyperlinks. In order to use Tag Helpers, you need to enable them in your project. This is done using the _ViewImports. cshtml file. So add a _ViewImports.cshtml file to the Pages folder. Then write this to the _ViewImports.cshtml file:

```
@using EmployeeManager.RazorPages
@using EmployeeManager.RazorPages.Pages
@using EmployeeManager.RazorPages.Models

@addTagHelper *, Microsoft.AspNetCore.Mvc.TagHelpers
```

The preceding code should look familiar to you because you used it in the MVC version of Employee Manager. Here, the namespaces are different, and you will add a few more as you proceed.

Displaying a List of Employees

To display a list of employees (Figure 4-4), you need a Razor Page named List.cshtml under the EmployeeManager folder.

Employee Manager

List of Employees

Insert

Employee ID	First Name	Last Name	Title	Actions	
1	Nancy	Davolio	Sales Representative	Update	Delete
2	Andrew	Fuller	Vice President, Sales	Update	Delete
3	Janet	Leverling	Sales Representative	Update	Delete

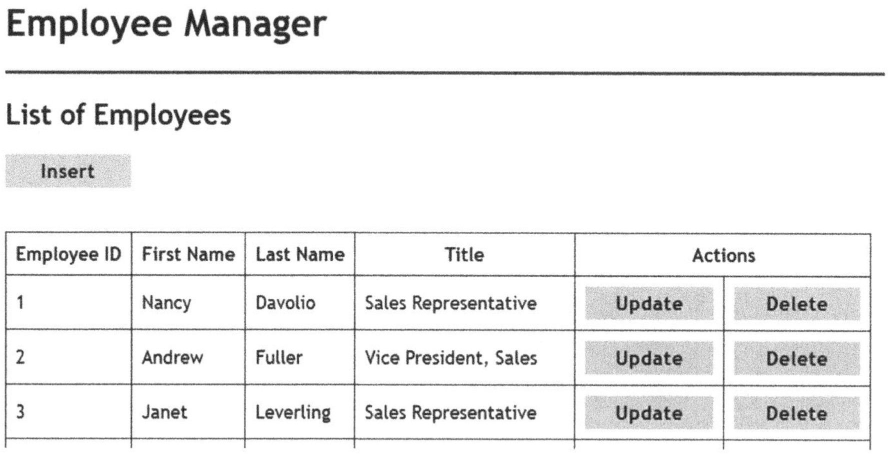

Figure 4-4. *List.cshtml displays a list of employees*

To add this page, right-click the EmployeeManager folder and open the Add New Item dialog. Then pick Razor Page from the list and name the page as List.cshtml (Figure 4-5).

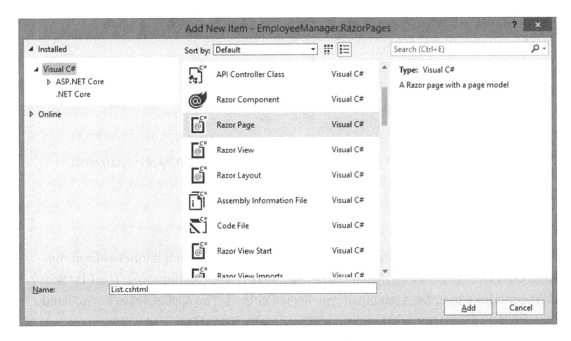

Figure 4-5. *Adding a Razor Page*

Once added, you will find two files associated with the Razor Page: List.cshtml and List.cshtml.cs (Figure 4-6).

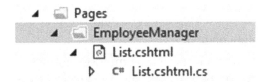

Figure 4-6. *Razor Page and page model files*

The List.cshtml is a Razor file and contains the UI markup and code. The List.cshtml.cs is the page model class file and typically contains properties and page handler methods.

Open the List.cshtml.cs in the IDE and write the code shown in Listing 4-6.

Listing 4-6. Page model class contains the OnGet() page handler

```
public class ListModel : PageModel
{
    private readonly AppDbContext db = null;

    public List<Employee> Employees { get; set; }
```

143

```
    public ListModel(AppDbContext db)
    {
        this.db = db;
    }

    public void OnGet()
    {
        this.Employees = (from e in db.Employees orderby e.EmployeeID
        select e).ToList();
    }
}
```

The List.cshtml.cs file contains a class named ListModel, and it inherits from the PageModel class (Microsoft.AspNetCore.Mvc.RazorPages namespace). The ListModel class contains a member variable of type AppDbContext. The AppDbContext is injected through the constructor and is stored in this member variable.

The Employees property is intended to hold a list of all the Employee entities from the database. The Employees page model property can be accessed from the List.cshtml page while rendering the list of employees.

The Employees property is assigned from within the OnGet() method. The OnGet() is called a page handler and handles GET requests to the page. If you want to handle POST requests, you would have created the OnPost() page handler method (you will do that in the insert, update, and delete pages).

Inside the OnGet(), the code selects all the Employee entities and stores them into a List. Now, open the List.cshtml file and write the code from Listing 4-7 into it.

Listing 4-7. List.cshtml renders a list of employees

```
@page

@model ListModel

<h2>List of Employees</h2>

<h3>@TempData["Message"]</h3>

<a asp-page="Insert" class="linkbutton">Insert</a>

<br /><br />
```

```
<table border="1">
    <tr>
        <th>Employee ID</th>
        <th>First Name</th>
        <th>Last Name</th>
        <th>Title</th>
        <th colspan="2">Actions</th>
    </tr>
    @foreach (var item in Model.Employees)
    {
        <tr>
            <td>@item.EmployeeID</td>
            <td>@item.FirstName</td>
            <td>@item.LastName</td>
            <td>@item.Title</td>
            <td>
                <a asp-page="Update"
                    asp-route-id="@item.EmployeeID"
                    class="linkbutton">Update</a>
            </td>
            <td>
                <a asp-page="Delete"
                    asp-route-id="@item.EmployeeID"
                    class="linkbutton">Delete</a>
            </td>
        </tr>
    }
</table>
```

The List.cshtml begins with the @page directive. The @page directive marks the file as a Razor Page and should be the first line of the file. Following the @page directive is the @model directive that specifies the page model class (ListModel) of this Razor Page.

Below the heading of the page, the TempData["Message"] is outputted. The TempData["Message"] is set during the delete operation and will be clear when you create the Delete Razor Page.

An Anchor Tag Helper renders a hyperlink to the Insert New Employee Razor Page. The `asp-page` attribute of the Anchor Tag Helper points to the Razor Page to navigate to.

The employee data is rendered in a <table>. A for loop iterates through the list of employees. Notice how the `Employees` page model property is accessed using the `Model` property of the Razor Page. The code then outputs `EmployeeID`, `FirstName`, `LastName`, and `Title` properties to generate various table rows.

At the end of each row, there are two hyperlinks: Update and Delete. They are rendered using the Anchor Tag Helper. The `asp-page` and `asp-route-id` attributes point to the target Razor Pages (Update Existing Employee and Delete Existing Employee pages) and `EmployeeID,` respectively.

This completes the List Razor Page.

Inserting a New Employee

Clicking the Insert link on the employee listing page takes you to another page where you can insert a new employee (Figure 4-7). 

Figure 3-7. *Inserting a new employee*

To create this page, add the Insert.cshtml Razor Page to the Pages ➤ EmployeeManager folder. Then open its page model class file – Insert.cshtml.cs – and write the code from Listing 4-8.

Listing 4-8. Member variables and properties of InsertModel

```
public class InsertModel : PageModel
{
    private readonly AppDbContext db = null;
        public string Message { get; set; }

    [BindProperty]
    public Employee Employee { get; set; }
    public List<SelectListItem> Countries { get; set; }

    public InsertModel(AppDbContext db)
    {
        this.db = db;
    }

    public void FillCountries()
    {
        List<SelectListItem> countries = (from c in db.Countries
                                          select new
                                          SelectListItem()
                                          { Text = c.Name,
                                            Value = c.Name
                                          }).ToList();

        this.Countries = countries;
    }
    ...
    ...
}
```

The code declares a variable – db – of type AppDbContext. The AppDbContext is injected through the constructor and stored into this variable. The Message string property indicates a success or error message to be displayed to the user upon inserting a new employee.

Notice the Employee property. It is decorated with the [BindProperty] attribute. The [BindProperty] attribute indicates that the property under consideration will get its value from model binding. While inserting a new employee, you fill various form fields and click the Save button to POST the values. At that time, the form field values are mapped to the properties of Employee due the presence of the [BindProperty] attribute.

The Countries property holds a List<SelectListItem> for the purpose of displaying in the Country dropdown list. The Country property is assigned from within a helper method – FillCountries().

The FillCountries() method queries the Countries table and retrieves all the countries. The countries are filled in a List of SelectListItem objects so that they can be displayed in the Select Tag Helper.

Now, add the OnGet() and OnPost() page handlers to the page model class as shown in Listing 4-9.

Listing 4-9. OnGet() and OnPost() page handlers

```
public void OnGet()
{
    FillCountries();
}

public void OnPost()
{
    FillCountries();

    if (ModelState.IsValid)
    {
        try
        {
            db.Employees.Add(Employee);
            db.SaveChanges();
            Message = "Employee inserted successfully!";
        }
        catch(DbUpdateException ex1)
        {
            Message = ex1.Message;
```

```
        if(ex1.InnerException!=null)
        {
            Message += " : " + ex1.InnerException.Message;
        }
    }
    catch(Exception ex2)
    {
        Message = ex2.Message;
    }
    }
}
```

The OnGet() page handler gets called when the page is requested initially by clicking the Insert link. It simply calls the FillCountries() helper method to prepare a list of countries.

The OnPost() page handler is invoked for POST requests. In this example, the <form> is POSTed when you hit the Save button. Inside, you call FillCountries() again. The code checks the IsValid property of the ModelState object to check whether all the model validations succeeded or not. If model validations are successful, the code attempts to insert a new employee.

This is done by calling the Add() method of AppDbContext and supplying the Employee object. Recollect that the Employee property that returns this object is populated through model binding. The Add() adds the new Employee into the Employees DbSet. The SaveChanges() method persists the change to the database. A success message is set into the Message property and is rendered on the page.

The whole data access code is wrapped inside a try-catch block. If database operation fails for some reason, then EF Core raises DbUpdateException exception. The InnerException property gives a more specific error information. An error message is then stored in the Message property and displayed to the user. Here, the code displays the actual error message to the end user. In a more realistic case, you might want to display a friendly message to the user and log the actual error into a log file.

Now that you know what makes the page model, let's see how the UI markup and code looks like. Listing 4-10 shows the skeleton of Insert.cshtml file.

Listing 4-10. Skeleton of Insert.cshtml

```
@page
@model InsertModel

<h2>Insert New Employee</h2>

<h3 class="message">@Model.Message</h3>

<form method="post">
    <table border="0">
       ...
       ...
    </table>
</form>

<a asp-page="List">Back to Employee Listing</a>
```

The Insert.cshtml begins with the @page directive. The @page directive is followed by the @model directive that sets the page model to be InsertModel. The success or error message from the page model's Message variable is outputted using the Model object.

Notice the Form Tag Helper. It just has the method attribute set to POST. This is because by default the form is submitted to the same Razor Page. In this case, upon clicking the Save button, the form will be submitted to the Insert Razor Page; and since the form's method is POST, the OnPost() page handler will be used to process it.

The <table> element wraps all the form fields. This markup is quite similar to the MVC version of the application. Listing 4-11 shows a part of the form for your understanding.

Listing 4-11. Form fields rendered using Tag Helpers

```
<tr>
    <td class="right">
        <label asp-for="Employee.FirstName"></label> :
    </td>
    <td>
        <input type="text" asp-for="Employee.FirstName" />
        <span asp-validation-for="Employee.FirstName" class="message"></span>
    </td>
```

```
</tr>
...
...
<tr>
    <td class="right">
        <label asp-for="Employee.Country"></label> :
    </td>
    <td>
        <select asp-for="Employee.Country" asp-items="@Model.Countries">
            <option value="">Please select</option>
        </select>
        <span asp-validation-for="Employee.Country" class="message"></span>
    </td>
</tr>
```

The usage of various Tag Helpers such as Input Tag Helper and Validation Message Tag Helper should look familiar to you. However, notice that the asp-for attribute is set to the corresponding property of the Employee page model property. For example, the asp-for attribute of the FirstName textbox is set to Employee.Firstname. On the same lines, the asp-items attribute of the Country dropdown list is set to the Countries property of the Model object.

For the sake of brevity, the complete markup of Insert.cshtml is not given here. You may grab the Insert.cshtml file from the code download and complete the rest of the form fields.

At the bottom of the page, there is a Back to Employee Listing link. This link is generated using the Anchor Tag Helper.

Updating an Existing Employee

On the employee listing page, each employee row has Update and Delete links. Clicking the Update link takes you to the update employee page where the existing details of that employee are presented for editing (Figure 4-8).

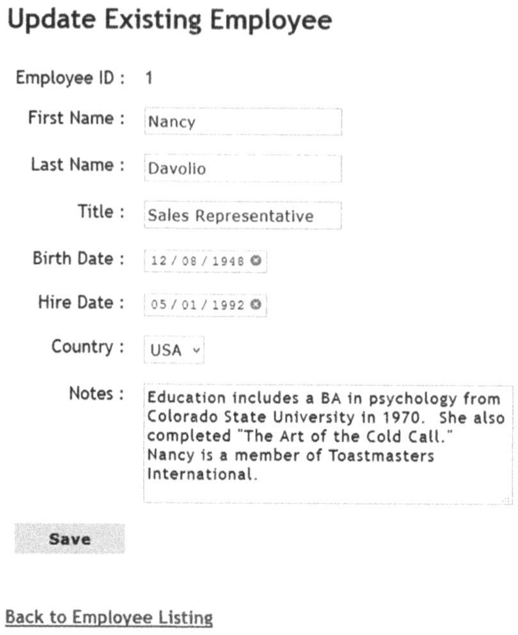

Update Existing Employee

Employee ID :   1

First Name :   Nancy

Last Name :   Davolio

Title :   Sales Representative

Birth Date :   12 / 08 / 1948 ☉

Hire Date :   05 / 01 / 1992 ☉

Country :   USA ˅

Notes :   Education includes a BA in psychology from Colorado State University in 1970. She also completed "The Art of the Cold Call." Nancy is a member of Toastmasters International.

Save

Back to Employee Listing

Figure 4-8. *Updating an existing employee*

The Update Existing Employee page looks similar to the Insert New Employee page except that various control values are now filled with the details of the employee being modified. The EmployeeID being the primary key can't be modified.

In order to complete this page, you need a Razor Page named Update.cshtml. So add Update.cshtml to the Pages ➤ EmployeeManager folder. Then open the UpdateModel class (Update.cshtml.cs) and write the code shown in Listing 4-12.

Listing 4-12. UpdateModel members

```
public class UpdateModel : PageModel
{
    private readonly AppDbContext db = null;

    [BindProperty]
    public Employee Employee { get; set; }

    public List<SelectListItem> Countries { get; set; }

    public string Message { get; set; }

    public bool DataFound { get; set; } = true;
```

```
    public UpdateModel(AppDbContext db)
    {
        this.db = db;
    }
    ...
    ...
}
```

This code is quite similar to the InsertModel class except that a Boolean property DataFound is declared. This property is assigned a false value if the requested EmployeeID is not found in the database. Accordingly, an error message is displayed to the user.

Although not shown in the listing, the FillCountries() method fills the Countries property with a list of countries. You may copy the FillCountries() helper method from the InsertModel class.

When the update page is accessed by clicking the Update link for an employee, the OnGet() handler gets invoked. Listing 4-13 shows this page handler.

Listing 4-13. OnGet() page handler inside UpdateModel

```
public void OnGet(int id)
{
    FillCountries();

    Employee = db.Employees.Find(id);

    if (Employee == null)
    {
        this.DataFound = false;
        this.Message = "EmployeeID Not Found.";
    }
    else
    {
        this.DataFound = true;
        this.Message = "";
    }
}
```

The OnGet() handler has an id parameter. It's the EmployeeID passed from the route. Inside, the code calls the FillCountries() to populate the Countries property with a list of countries. Then the Find() method of Employees DbSet is used to find the specified employee. If the employee couldn't be found, then the Find() method returns null, and the DataFound property is set to false. An error message is also set in the Message page model variable.

If an employee is found, the DataFound property is set to true, and the Message is cleared.

When a user clicks the Save button, the OnPost() page handler gets invoked. This page handler is shown in Listing 4-14.

Listing 4-14. OnPost() page handler of UpdateModel

```
public void OnPost()
{
    FillCountries();

    if (ModelState.IsValid)
    {
        try
        {
            db.Employees.Update(Employee);
            db.SaveChanges();
            Message = "Employee updated successfully!";
        }
        catch (DbUpdateException ex1)
        {
            Message = ex1.Message;
            if (ex1.InnerException != null)
            {
                Message += " : " + ex1.InnerException.Message;
            }
        }
    }
```

```
        catch (Exception ex2)
        {
            Message = ex2.Message;
        }
    }
}
```

The OnPost() handler updates an employee in the Employees DbSet and also persists the changes to the database. This is done using the Update() and SaveChanges() methods. The update operation is wrapped inside a try-catch block for the sake of error handling.

This completes the UpdateModel class. Now open the Update.cshtml file and write the skeleton code shown in Listing 4-15.

Listing 4-15. Skeleton of Update.cshtml

```
@page "{id:int}"
@model UpdateModel

<h2>Update Existing Employee</h2>

<h3 class="message">@Model.Message</h3>

@if (Model.DataFound)
{
<form method="post">
    <table border="0">
      ...
      ...
    </table>
</form>
}
```

Notice the code marked in bold letters. This time, the @page directive includes a route parameter named id. The parameter appears in double quotes and is enclosed in { and }. The id route parameter also has a route constraint that specifies that the id must be an integer value.

The if block checks the DataFound property. The form and form fields are rendered only if DataFound is true.

The content of the form is quite similar to the Insert.cshtml and hence not discussed here in detail. You can grab the complete Update.cshtml from the book's code download.

Deleting an Existing Employee

When the user clicks the Delete link for an employee record in the employee listing page, a confirmation page is shown that warns the user about the employee deletion. Once the user confirms the deletion, the employee gets deleted from the database. Figure 4-9 shows the delete confirmation page displayed for an employee.

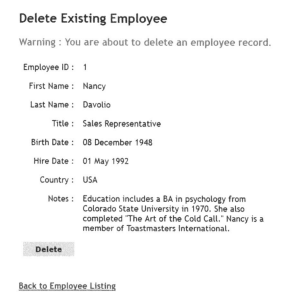

Figure 4-9. *Confirming employee deletion*

In order to implement the delete functionality, you need a Razor Page named Delete. cshtml. So add it in the Pages ➤ EmployeeManager folder. The DeleteModel class is similar to the update page in many respects. The OnGet() handler is identical to that of the UpdateModel class. You can copy the members and the OnGet() handler from the earlier code.

The OnPost() handler deletes an employee from the database and is shown in Listing 4-16.

Listing 4-16. OnPost() page handler of DeleteModel

```
public IActionResult OnPost()
{
    Employee emp = db.Employees.Find(Employee.EmployeeID);
    try
    {
        db.Employees.Remove(emp);
        db.SaveChanges();
        TempData["Message"] = "Employee deleted successfully!";
        return RedirectToPage("/EmployeeManager/List");
    }
    catch (DbUpdateException ex1)
    {
        Message = ex1.Message;
        if (ex1.InnerException != null)
        {
            Message += " : " + ex1.InnerException.Message;
        }
    }
    catch (Exception ex2)
    {
        Message = ex2.Message;
    }
    return Page();
}
```

Inside the OnPost(), the code attempts to find an employee from the DbSet and removes it using the Remove() method. A call to SaveChanges() deletes the employee from the database. Once an employee is deleted, the code stores a success message in the TempData and redirects to the List page using the RedirectToPage() method. Notice that the return type of OnPost() is IActionResult because RedirectToPage() returns the RedirectToPageResult object. Also, after the last catch block, the code calls Page() that returns a PageResult object. This renders the current page in the browser.

Now that the DeleteModel class is complete, open the Delete.cshtml page in the IDE and write the skeleton code shown in Listing 4-17.

Listing 4-17. Skeleton of Delete.cshtml

```
@page "{id}"
@model DeleteModel

<h2>Delete Existing Employee</h2>

<h3 class="message">
    Warning : You are about to delete an employee record!
</h3>

@if (Model.DataFound)
{
<form method="post">
  <input type="hidden" asp-for="Employee.EmployeeID" />
  <table border="0">
    <tr>
        <td class="right">
            <label asp-for="Employee.EmployeeID"></label> :
        </td>
        <td>
            @Model.Employee.EmployeeID
        </td>
    </tr>
  ...
  ...
</form>
}
```

The delete page too defines the id route parameter in the @page directive. The
<form> is rendered only if the DataFound property is true. Since the delete page doesn't
have any data entry controls, the EmployeeID is outputted in a hidden form field. This
way, the model binding will populate the EmployeeID property of the Employee page
property when you click the Delete button. The <table> that displays the existing
employee details is generated based on the Model.Employee properties and is not
discussed here for the sake of brevity. You can grab the complete code of Delete.cshtml
from the book's code download.

Add Razor Layout and View Start

The Razor Pages version of Employee Manager also requires a layout and _ViewStart. cshtml just like the MVC version of the application. The markup and code of both is quite similar to the MVC version, and hence only the differences are discussed here.

Go ahead and add the Shared folder under the Pages folder. Then add _Layout. cshtml in the Shared folder. Also place the _ViewStart.cshtml file under the Pages folder. Figure 4-10 shows these files in Solution Explorer.

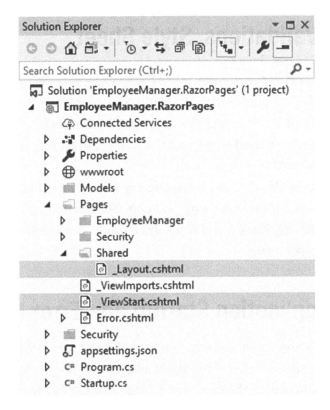

Figure 4-10. *_Layout.cshtml and _ViewStart.cshtml*

Listing 4-18 shows how the Sign Out button is rendered.

Listing 4-18. Rendering the Sign Out button

```
@if (User.Identity.IsAuthenticated)
{
    <h2>You are signed in as @User.Identity.Name</h2>
```

```
<form asp-page="/Security/SignOut" method="post">
    <button type="submit">Sign Out</button>
</form>
}
```

As you can see, the Form Tag Helper is configured to post the form to SignOut page using the asp-page attribute. The SignOut page simply handles the POST operation and redirects to the SignIn page. The SignOut page is discussed later in this chapter.

Client-Side Validations, Style Sheet, and appsettings.json

The process of enabling the client-side validations for Razor Pages is exactly the same as the MVC version of Employee Manager. So just place the Scripts folder under wwwroot with the required jQuery files and also ensure that they are referenced using the <script> tags in the _Layout.cshtml.

The Site.css contains CSS classes and styling used by various pages. The appsettings.json stores the database connection string. Just copy Site.css and appsettings.json from the MVC version of the application and place them under wwwroot/Styles and the project root folder, respectively.

Configure Application Startup and Error Handling

The way you configure the application startup for ASP.NET Core Razor Pages application is quite similar to the MVC version of the application. So all the configuration steps are not discussed here. You can get the complete Startup.cs from the book's code download.

Note   In this section, you learn a few exception handling techniques. Although these techniques are discussed with respect to Razor Pages, they are applicable to MVC applications also. I encourage you to implement them in the MVC version of the application once you finish the Razor Pages version discussed in this chapter.

If you look at the ConfigureServices() method of the Startup class, you will notice the code shown in Listing 4-19.

Listing 4-19. Setting the default page of the application

```
public void ConfigureServices(IServiceCollection services)
{
    services.AddRazorPages()
                    .AddRazorPagesOptions(options =>
                    {
                        options.Conventions
                            .AddPageRoute("/EmployeeManager/List", "");
                    });
    ...
    ...
}
```

The AddRazorPages() method registers services related to Razor Pages with the DI framework.

Recollect that we have stored CRUD-related pages under the Pages/EmployeeManager folder. Razor Pages consider the Index.cshtml under the Pages folder to be the default page of the application. You want to change this and set /EmployeeManager/List page to be the default page. This is done using the AddRazorPagesOptions() method. The AddPageRoute() method of the Conventions object accepts a page name and its route. Empty string means the default page of the application.

Now, go to the Configure() method. There you will find two calls:

```
app.UseStatusCodePagesWithReExecute("/Error","?code={0}");
app.UseExceptionHandler("/Error");
```

These calls add exception handling middleware components to the request pipeline. The UseStatusCodePagesWithReExecute() method adds the status code pages middleware. This middleware is used to handle HTTP-related errors such as Page Not Found (status code 404). The first parameter of the UseStatusCodePagesWithReExecute() method is the error page to be displayed (/Error in this case), and the second parameter is used to pass the status code to the page via the query string. In this example, the status code will be passed to the error page via a query string variable named code. The {0} will be substituted by the actual status code (such as 404).

Next, the code also adds the exception handler middleware using the UseExceptionHandler() method. The exception handler middleware traps any unhandled exception and takes the control to the specified page (/Error) in this case.

To create the error page used by these exception handling middleware components, add a new Razor Page named Error.cshtml in the Pages folder. Listing 4-20 shows the ErrorModel class of this page.

Listing 4-20. ErrorModel page model class

```
public class ErrorModel : PageModel
{
    public string Code { get; set; }

    public void OnGet([FromQuery]int code)
    {
        if (code > 0)
        {
            this.Code = "Status Code : " + code;
        }
    }
}
```

The ErrorModel class defines the Code property to store the HTTP status code. The OnGet() handler receives an integer HTTP status code in the code parameter. Notice the [FromQuery] attribute that instructs the model binding to get the value from the query string.

The if block simply checks whether any status code has been received in the query string, and accordingly it is stored in the Code page model property. The Error.cshtml is shown in Listing 4-21.

Listing 4-21. Error.cshtml displays the error

```
@page
@model ErrorModel

<h2  class="message">
    Unexpected error while processing this request.
</h2>

<h3>@Model.Code</h3>
```

The Error.cshtml simply displays an error message to the user and also outputs the HTTP status code (if any) using the Model.Code property.

The routing-related configuration is done using UseRouting() and UseEndPoints() methods as in the case of the MVC application. However, endpoints are defined like this:

```
app.UseEndpoints(endpoints=> {
    endpoints.MapRazorPages();
});
```

The MapRazorPages() method adds endpoints for Razor Pages.

At this stage, your application is capable of performing the CRUD operations. You can run the application and test the CRUD functionality before you add user authentication to the application.

Add ASP.NET Core Identity Support

In the previous chapter, you added ASP.NET Core Identity support for the MVC version of the Employee Manager application. In this chapter, you will do so for the Razor Pages version. Although the process of adding ASP.NET Core Identity support is quite similar, there are a few differences listed as follows:

- The user registration, signing in, and signing out are now handled by Razor Pages.

- ASP.NET Core Identity is used in an asynchronous fashion, and Razor Pages invoke various methods asynchronously.

Note   Many modern web applications prefer the asynchronous programming model over the synchronous one. Detailed discussion of the benefits offered by the asynchronous programming model is beyond the scope of this book. It suffices to say that asynchronous programming can offer performance and scalability benefits in many situations where database access, web service calls, and other I/O operations are involved.

For the sake of brevity, the following sections discuss only the differences in the implementation. The source code download of this chapter contains the complete code. You may also refer to the MVC version of Employee Manager to brush up the common implementation details.

Add AppIdentityUser, AppIdentityRole, and AppIdentityDbContext Classes

The Razor Pages version of Employee Manager also requires the `AppIdentityUser`, `AppIdentityRole`, and `AppIdentityDbContext` classes for its working. These classes are identical to the MVC version. You may grab them from this chapter's source code or from the MVC version.

These classes reside inside the Security folder under the project root (Figure 4-11). If you copy them from the MVC version of the application, make sure to change their namespace as per the Razor Pages project namespace.

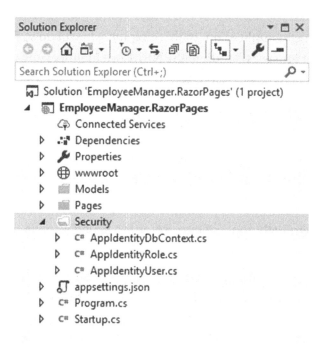

Figure 4-11. *AppIdentityDbContext, AppIdentityUser, and AppIdentityRole classes*

Add ASP.NET Core Identity Configuration and Database Tables

In the MVC version of Employee Manager, you added certain ASP.NET Core Identity-specific configuration in the Startup class. In the `ConfigureServices()`, you used methods such as `AddIdentity()`, `AddEntityFrameworkStores()`, and `ConfigureApplicationCookie()`. And in the `Configure()`, you added the authentication and authorization middleware using the `UseAuthentication()` and `UseAuthorization()` methods. Those method calls remain exactly the same in the Razor Pages version also and are not discussed here.

In addition to the preceding startup configuration, you also need to configure the Northwind database to store users and roles. You have already done so while developing the MVC version of Employee Manager. In case you have cleaned the database, make sure to execute the same commands as before to create the necessary database tables.

Add the Security Subfolder to the Pages folder

For the Razor Pages version of Employee Manager, user registration, signing in, and signing out are taken care of by the respective Razor Pages. These Razor Pages are stored under a subfolder of the Pages folder. So create a subfolder named Security under the Pages folder. Figure 4-12 shows the Security folder containing the required Razor Pages after completing the following sections.

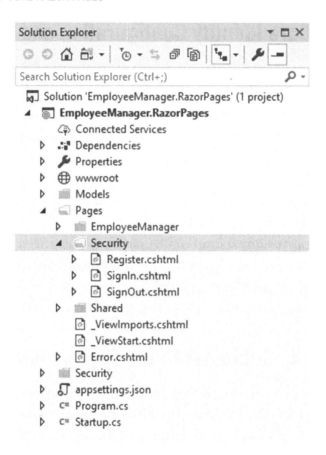

Figure 4-12. *Security subfolder contains security-related Razor Pages*

As you can see, the Security folder contains three Razor Pages, namely, Register.cshtml, SignIn.cshtml, and SignOut.cshtml. You develop these pages in the sections that follow.

Create a User Registration Page

The user registration page allows you to create a user account. You can then sign in to the system using the account created (Figure 4-13).

Create New User Account

User Name :	[ ]
Password :	[ ]
Confirm Password :	[ ]
Email :	[ ]
Full Name :	[ ]
Birth Date :	mm / dd / yyyy

Create

Go To Sign-In Page

Figure 4-13. *User registration page*

To create a user registration page, you need the Register class in the Models folder and a Razor Page named Register under the Pages ➤ Security folder.

You can grab the Register class from the book's source code or the MVC version of the application and place it under the Models folder. Then add a new Razor Page named Register.cshtml in the Pages ➤ Security folder.

Then open the Register.cshtml.cs page model class in the IDE and write the code shown in Listing 4-22.

Listing 4-22. Injecting UserManager and RoleManager

```
public class RegisterModel : PageModel
{
    [BindProperty]
    public Register RegisterData { get; set; }

    private readonly UserManager<AppIdentityUser> userManager;
    private readonly RoleManager<AppIdentityRole> roleManager;
```

167

```
    public RegisterModel(UserManager<AppIdentityUser> userManager,
            RoleManager<AppIdentityRole> roleManager)
    {
        this.userManager = userManager;
        this.roleManager = roleManager;
    }
}
```

The code begins by declaring the `RegisterData` property. The `RegisterData` property is of type `Register` and is marked with the `[BindProperty]` attribute. Due to the `[BindProperty]` attribute, `RegisterData` participates in the model binding, and the form data will be mapped to its properties.

The code then declares two variables of types `UserManager<TUser>` and `RoleManager<TRole>`. The `UserManager<TUser>` and `RoleManager<TRole>` objects are injected into the page model's constructor and are stored into these variables. The `userManager` and `roleManager` are used in the POST page handler.

The POST page handler is invoked when a user clicks the Create button on the form and is shown in Listing 4-23.

Listing 4-23. OnPostAsync() page handler of the register page

```
public async Task<IActionResult> OnPostAsync()
{
    if (ModelState.IsValid)
    {
        if (!await roleManager.RoleExistsAsync("Manager"))
        {
            AppIdentityRole role = new AppIdentityRole();
            role.Name = "Manager";
            role.Description = "Can perform CRUD operations.";
            IdentityResult roleResult = await roleManager.
            CreateAsync(role);
        }

        AppIdentityUser user = new AppIdentityUser();
        user.UserName = RegisterData.UserName;
        user.Email = RegisterData.Email;
```

```
user.FullName = RegisterData.FullName;
user.BirthDate = RegisterData.BirthDate;

IdentityResult result = await userManager.CreateAsync
(user, RegisterData.Password);

if (result.Succeeded)
{
    await userManager.AddToRoleAsync(user, "Manager");
    return RedirectToPage("/Security/SignIn");
}
else
{
    ModelState.AddModelError("", "Invalid user details!");
}
}
return Page();
}
```

Observe the code carefully. Although it looks similar to what you used in the MVC version of the application, there are some differences.

Firstly, the POST handler name is OnPostAsync() and is marked with the async keyword of C#. This indicates that it's an asynchronous method and is using the async-await pattern of C#.

Note   Discussion of asynchronous programming and async/await keywords of C# is beyond the scope of this book. If you are unfamiliar with these concepts, consider reading https://docs.microsoft.com/en-us/dotnet/csharp/programming-guide/concepts/async/.

The OnPostAsync() method returns a Task<TResult> object. The Task class represents an asynchronous operation where TResult is the type obtained as a result of the asynchronous operation. Here, the Task wraps an IActionResult object.

If you observe the code marked in bold letters, you will realize that all those statements use the await operator. The await keyword is followed by an asynchronous operation to be executed, such as RoleExistsAsync(), CreateAsync(), and AddToRoleAsync() in this example.

The code that creates the role and user should look familiar to you since it is similar to the MVC version. To summarize, the code does these things:

- The RoleExistsAsync() checks whether the Manager role already exists in the database. If it doesn't exist, then the role is created using the CreateAsync() method.

- The UserManager's CreateAsync() method creates a new user.

- The UserManager's AddToRoleAsync() method adds the newly created user to the Manager role.

The Register.cshtml renders the user registration page in the browser using various Tag Helpers. Since that markup is quite straightforward and similar to what you used while developing earlier Razor Pages, it has not been discussed here. You can get the complete code of Register.cshtml from this book's code download.

Create a Sign-In Page

The sign-in Razor Page allows the user to sign in to the system and is shown in Figure 4-14.

Sign In

User Name :	
Password :	
Remember Me :	☐

Sign In

Create New User Account

Figure 4-14. *Sign-in Razor Page*

To create the sign-in page, you need the SignIn class and the SignIn Razor Page. The SignIn class is identical to the MVC version. You can grab it from the book's source code or the MVC version and place it under the Models folder.

Then add a new Razor Page named SignIn.cshtml in the Pages ➤ Security folder. Now, open the SignInModel class in the IDE and write the code shown in Listing 4-24 into it.

Listing 4-24. Injecting UserManager, RoleManager, and SignInManager

```
public class SignInModel : PageModel
{
    [BindProperty]
    public SignIn SignInData { get; set; }

    private readonly SignInManager<AppIdentityUser> signinManager;

    public SignInModel(SignInManager<AppIdentityUser> signinManager)
    {
        this.signinManager = signinManager;
    }
}
```

The code begins by creating the SignInData public property. This property is of type SignIn and is decorated with the [BindProperty] attribute.

Then a SignInManager<TUser> variable is declared. This variable gets its value when a SignInManager object is injected into the constructor.

The OnPostAsync() page handler uses asynchronous code to sign the user in to the system and is shown in Listing 4-25.

Listing 4-25. Signing the user in to the system

```
public async Task<IActionResult> OnPostAsync()
{
    if (ModelState.IsValid)
    {
        var result = await signinManager.PasswordSignInAsync
        (SignInData.UserName, SignInData.Password,
            SignInData.RememberMe, false);

        if (result.Succeeded)
        {
            return RedirectToPage("/EmployeeManager/List");
        }
        else
        {
            ModelState.AddModelError("", "Invalid login!");
```

171

```
        }
    }
    return Page();
}
```

Notice the code marked in bold letters. The OnPostAsync() method is marked with the async keyword. To sign the user in to the application, the PasswordSignInAsync() method of SignInManager is used. If the signing-in operation is successful, the control is redirected to the employee listing page. Otherwise, an error messages is added to the ModelState object and is displayed to the user.

The SignIn.cshtml page markup uses Tag Helpers to render the user interface and is not discussed here for the sake of brevity. You can grab the SignIn.cshtml from the book's source code.

Signing the User Out of the Application

Recollect that you added markup to render the Sign Out button (Figure 4-15) in the _Layout. cshtml developed earlier. That time, it was mentioned that the signing-out functionality was wrapped in the SignOut Razor Page. Now it's the time to create the SignOut Razor Page.

You are signed in as user1

Sign Out

Figure 4-15. Sign Out button displayed at the bottom of the page

Add a new Razor Page to the Pages ➤ Security folder and name it SignOut.cshtml. Then open the page model class from the SignOut.cshtml.cs file in the IDE and write the code shown in Listing 4-26 in it.

Listing 4-26. Signing the user out of the application

```
public class SignOutModel : PageModel
{
    private readonly SignInManager<AppIdentityUser> signinManager;

    public SignOutModel(SignInManager<AppIdentityUser> signinManager)
    {
```

```
        this.signinManager = signinManager;
    }

    public async Task<IActionResult> OnPostAsync()
    {
        await signinManager.SignOutAsync();
        return RedirectToPage("/Security/SignIn");
    }
}
```

The code is similar to the SignInModel class in that an object of
SignInManager<TUser> is injected into the constructor. However, this time the
OnPostAsync() method calls the SignOutAsync() method of the SignInManager. Once
the user is signed out of the application, the browser is redirected to the SignIn page by
calling the RedirectToPage() method. The SignOut.cshtml doesn't contain any markup
since it is being used only for signing the user out of the system.

Authenticating and Authorizing Users

At the time of developing the MVC version of Employee Manager, you decorated the
actions or controller with the [Authorize] attribute. In the case of Razor Pages, you can
use the [Authorize] attribute on a page model class. Listing 4-27 shows the ListModel
class using this attribute.

Listing 4-27. [Authorize] added to the ListModel class

```
[Authorize(Roles = "Manager")]
public class ListModel : PageModel
{
  ...
  ...
}
```

Here the ListModel class is decorated with the [Authorize] attribute, and its
Roles property is set to Manager. This way only the authenticated users belonging to
the Manager role can access the List.cshtml Razor Page. You also need to decorate
InsertModel, UpdateModel, and DeleteModel page model classes with the [Authorize]
attribute.

The [Authorize] attribute is added to the SignOutModel class also since only signed-in users can sign out of the system (Listing 4-28).

Listing 4-28. SignOutModel decorated with [Authorize]

```
[Authorize]
public class SignOutModel : PageModel
{
    ...
    ...
}
```

In the ASP.NET Core MVC version of Employee Manager, you used [ValidateAntiForgeryToken] in combination with the Form Tag Helper to prevent the cross-site request forgery (CSRF/XSRF) attacks. Razor Pages are automatically protected from these attacks, and you don't need to explicitly write any code to accomplish the task.

Run the Application

The Razor Pages version of the Employee Manager application is now complete. You can run the application and check whether user account creation, signing in, signing out, and CRUD operations can be performed as expected.

Summary

In this chapter, you created the Employee Manager application using ASP.NET Core Razor Pages. You auto-generated the EF Core model using the reverse engineering techniques. Razor Pages allows a page-focused approach to build web applications. Each Razor Page consists of the page UI housed in a .cshtml file and page processing logic wrapped in a page model .cshtml.cs file. You also learned how to use ASP.NET Core Identity asynchronous methods in Razor Pages using the async and await keywords.

In the next chapter, you develop a Web API for performing the CRUD operations. The Web API is then invoked by a client application.

CHAPTER 5

ASP.NET Core Web API

So far in this book, you developed the Employee Manager application using ASP.NET Core MVC and ASP.NET Core Razor Pages. By now, you are acquainted with the overall development process under ASP.NET Core and EF Core. Continuing this journey further, this chapter shows how Employee Manager can use ASP.NET Core Web API to perform the CRUD operations. It also shows how to use .NET Core's HttpClient class to invoke the API. Specifically, you will learn to

- Understand what are RESTful services

- Create ASP.NET Core Web API

- Execute raw T-SQL queries and stored procedures using EF Core

- Encapsulate CRUD operations in a repository

- Use .NET Core's HttpClient to invoke Web API

Application Architecture

The applications developed so far involved only a single project that contained everything needed by the application. The Web API version of Employee Manager involves two projects – the API project and the client application. Figure 5-1 shows the simplified architectural view of what you are going to develop in this chapter.

© Bipin Joshi 2019
B. Joshi, *Beginning Database Programming Using ASP.NET Core 3*,
https://doi.org/10.1007/978-1-4842-5509-4_5

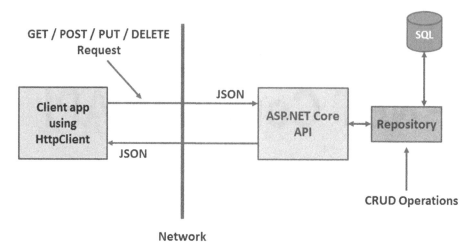

Figure 5-1. *Architecture of Employee Manager*

Let's discuss this architecture in more detail and understand various pieces mentioned therein.

ASP.NET Core and REST Services

Modern web applications often rely on RESTful services for exposing their functionality. Therefore, it's worthwhile to discuss in brief what REST is.

REST stands for REpresentational State Transfer. REST is not a standard; it's a way of architecting your services. Unlike ASMX web services that use complex mechanisms such as Simple Object Access Protocol (SOAP) and Web Services Description Language (WSDL), RESTful services harness the simplicity and power of HTTP. Here are some fundamental characteristics of RESTful services:

- REST services use the HTTP protocol.

- REST services make HTTP requests (using meaningful HTTP verbs such as GET, POST, PUT, and DELETE) to fetch and submit data.

- REST services are stateless in nature.

- REST exposes services as resources accessible and discoverable through URLs.

- REST services typically transfer data in JSON or XML format.

ASP.NET Core Web API is a .NET Core way of developing RESTful services and follows the controller-based programming model of ASP.NET Core MVC. To invoke such an API from the client application, developers commonly use the HttpClient component or Ajax techniques (if it's a JavaScript client).

The HTTP verbs such as GET, POST, PUT, and DELETE indicate the desired action to be performed on a resource. If an API performs create, read, update, and delete (CRUD) operations on a database, you could use POST to indicate an INSERT operation, GET to indicate a SELECT operation, PUT to indicate an UPDATE operation, and DELETE to indicate a DELETE operation. However, merely using a specific verb won't enforce allowing only a particular type of operation. It's up to you to implement these verbs in an API depending on the application's requirements.

Note   When it comes to building RESTful services using ASP.NET Core, you might come across different terms – ASP.NET Core Web API, ASP.NET Core REST API, ASP. NET Core API, or ASP.NET Core REST services. They all mean the same thing.

Understanding the JSON Format

The client and the API often need to exchange data. Two common formats for such a data transfer are JSON and XML, although most of the modern web applications prefer JSON over XML.

JSON, which stands for JavaScript Object Notation, is a lightweight text-based format for data interchange. By using the JSON format, you can represent the data that needs to be transferred between the client and the API. JSON supports strings, numbers, Booleans, objects, and arrays. (If you want to represent any other data type, you must represent it in a supported format.)

An object in JSON format typically consists of one or more name-value pairs. The object begins with { and ends with }. The name-value pairs are placed in between. A property name and its value (if string type) are enclosed in double quotes ("...").
A property and its value are separated by a colon (:). Multiple name-value pairs are delimited by commas (,). The following code shows an object represented in JSON format:

```
var employee={
            "EmployeeID":1,
            "FirstName":"Nancy",
```

```
            "LastName":"Davolio",
            "IsContract":false;
        };
```

If you want to create an array of employee objects, you can write the following:

```
var employeeArray =[
                    {
                      "EmployeeID":1,
                      "FirstName":"Nancy",
                      "LastName":"Davolio",
                      "IsContract":false;
                    },
                    {
                      "EmployeeID":2,
                      "FirstName":"Andrew",
                      "LastName":"Fuller",
                      "IsContract":true;
                    }
                    ];
```

This code creates an array with two employee objects as its elements. Just like a JavaScript array, a JSON array also begins with [and ends with]. Multiple JSON objects that make the array elements are separated by commas (,).

While working with ASP.NET Core Web APIs, you might have to deal with JSON format inside your client- and server-side code. For example, you might be receiving data from some Web API in JSON format and want to process that JSON data in your client code. Or you might want to send data in JSON format to the API so that it can be processed on the server.

Role of the Repository

So far in this book, you have been performing the CRUD operations from the controller classes or Razor Page handlers. In a more realistic situation, you might want to isolate the code performing the CRUD operations into a separate class. You may want that the controllers or page handlers use this class to get the job done.

In such cases, the repository pattern comes handy. **The repository pattern mediates between the data access layer and the rest of the system. Moreover, it does so by providing a collection-like access to the underlying data**.

Once the repository is implemented, the Web API code won't invoke the EF Core code directly. Instead, it will invoke the repository to get the job done. The repository offers a collection interface by providing methods to add, modify, remove, and fetch domain objects.

It would be interesting to know that Entity Framework Core already implements the repository pattern. For example, you can add, modify, remove, and access entities from a DbSet quite similar to a collection. In this example, you use EF Core's capabilities to execute raw T-SQL queries and stored procedures to perform the CRUD operations. And you wrap them into a repository. The Web API then calls the repository to perform the necessary operation. This arrangement is shown in Figure 5-2.

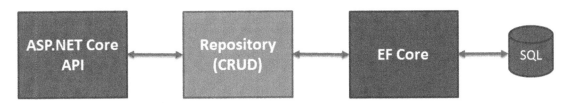

Figure 5-2. *ASP.NET Core API uses the repository to perform CRUD operations*

Note   In the following sections, you develop two ASP.NET Core projects – the API and its client. For the sake of brevity, I won't explain the basics of creating and configuring an ASP.NET Core project again. You may read the previous chapters to know these basics. You may also grab the complete source code of this chapter from the book's code download.

Creating an EmployeeManager.Api Project

Now that you know the overall architecture of the application, let's begin the development process by creating the API project. In order to do so, create a new ASP.NET Core project based on the Empty project template. Name the project as EmployeeManager.Api. Figure 5-3 shows how this project looks like in Solution Explorer upon completion.

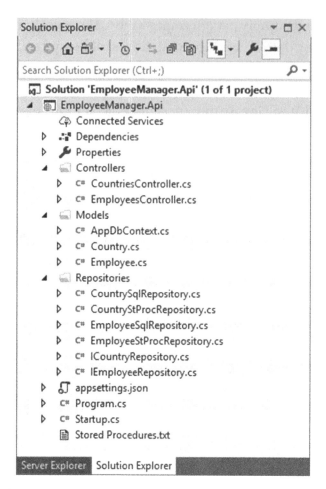

Figure 5-3. *EmployeeManager.Api project after completion*

As you can see, the project has three folders – Models, Controllers, and Repositories. These folders store the respective classes that you are going to add in the following sections. This project depends on EF Core for the sake of performing CRUD operations. Therefore, you need to set it up to use EF Core. These details are identical to the MVC and Razor Pages applications you developed earlier and hence are not discussed again. You may read the previous chapters for information on setting up EF Core in ASP.NET Core projects. You can also get the complete code of this example from the book's code download.

Creating the EF Core Model and Repositories

Although the EmployeeManager.Api project is going to use repositories for the sake of performing the CRUD operations, you still need to create the EF Core model. The process of creating the EF Core model is identical to the previous versions of Employee Manager. You may create AppDbContext, Employee, and Country classes yourself or get them from this book's code download. Make sure to place them in the Models folder.

Once you have these classes, you may proceed to creating the repositories. In this example, you learn to execute raw SQL queries as well as stored procedures using EF Core. So you create two sets of repositories – one using SQL statements and the other using stored procedures.

Creating EmployeeSqlRepository and CountrySqlRepository

In this section, you create the first set of repositories consisting of two classes and two interfaces defining the structure of the repositories. So begin by adding the Repositories folder if you haven't done so already. Then add a new interface named IEmployeeRepository in the Repositories folder. Listing 5-1 shows the IEmployeeRepository interface with its members.

Listing 5-1. IEmployeeRepository interface

```
public interface IEmployeeRepository
{
    List<Employee> SelectAll();
    Employee SelectByID(int id);
    void Insert(Employee emp);
    void Update(Employee emp);
    void Delete(int id);
}
```

The IEmployeeRepository interface consists of five methods, namely, SelectAll(), SelectByID(), Insert(), Update(), and Delete(). These methods dictate the structure of the EmployeeSqlRepository repository as you will see later in this section.

Now add another interface named ICountryRepository into the Repositories folder and write the code shown in Listing 5-2 in it.

Listing 5-2. ICountryRepository interface

```
public interface ICountryRepository
{
    List<Country> SelectAll();
}
```

The ICountryRepository interface contains just a single method – SelectAll(). Since you aren't interested to perform insert, update, and delete operations on the Countries table, those methods aren't necessary here.

Now that you have IEmployeeRepository and ICountryRepository interfaces ready, let's implement them in EmployeeSqlRepository and CountrySqlRepository classes, respectively.

Add a new class to the Repositories folder named EmployeeSqlRepository and implement the IEmployeeRepository interface in it (Listing 5-3).

Listing 5-3. EmployeeSqlRepository implements IEmployeeRepository

```
public class EmployeeSqlRepository : IEmployeeRepository
{
    private readonly AppDbContext db = null;

    public EmployeeSqlRepository(AppDbContext db)
    {
        this.db = db;
    }

    public List<Employee> SelectAll()
    {
        ...
    }

    public Employee SelectByID(int id)
    {
        ...
    }
```

```
  public void Insert(Employee emp)
  {
    ...
  }

  public void Update(Employee emp)
  {
    ...
  }

  public void Delete(int id)
  {
    ...
  }
}
```

As you can see, the EmployeeSqlRepository declares a variable of type AppDbContext. The AppDbContext is injected into the constructor and is stored into this variable. The db variable is then used by other methods to execute the respective queries.

Now that you have the skeleton of EmployeeSqlRepository ready, let's add implementation of various methods one by one. Listing 5-4 shows the implementation of the SelectAll() method.

Listing 5-4. Implementing SelectAll()

```
public List<Employee> SelectAll()
{
    List<Employee> data = db.Employees. FromSqlRaw("SELECT EmployeeID,
FirstName, LastName, Title, BirthDate, HireDate, Country, Notes FROM
Employees ORDER BY EmployeeID ASC").ToList();
    return data;
}
```

The SelectAll() method is intended to return all the employees from the database. Hence, its return type is List<Employee>. Inside, the code executes a SELECT statement that fetches EmployeeID, FirstName, LastName, Title, BirthDate, HireDate, Country, and Notes columns from the Employees table. To execute this SQL statement, the FromSqlRaw() method of the DbSet class is used. The FromSqlRaw() method accepts an SQL query and converts it into a LINQ query. The `FromSqlRaw()` method returns `IQueryable<T>`. To get the data as a `List<Employee>`, the code uses the `ToList()` method. The `List<Employee>` is then returned to the caller. Note that the SELECT statement must return columns that match with the underlying entity properties (`Employee` class in this case).

Listing 5-5 shows how the `SelectByID()` method looks like.

Listing 5-5. Implementing the SelectByID() method

```
public Employee SelectByID(int id)
{
    Employee emp = db.Employees. FromSqlRaw("SELECT EmployeeID, FirstName,
LastName, Title, BirthDate, HireDate, Country, Notes FROM Employees WHERE
EmployeeID={0}", id).SingleOrDefault();
    return emp;
}
```

The `SelectByID()` method is intended to return a specific `Employee` and hence accepts an `EmployeeID` as a parameter. Inside, the code executes an SQL statement that fetches that particular `EmployeeID`. Notice the use of `{0}` that indicates a query parameter. The second parameter of `FromSqlRaw()` specifies a value of this query parameter. This value is converted into a DbParameter object. You could have also supplied a `DbParameter` or `SqlParameter` yourself (you do that while using stored procedures later in this chapter).

Note   While building SQL statements, it is always recommended to use parameters instead of using string concatenation. SQL statements built by concatenating strings can be prone to SQL injection attacks and hence should be avoided.

Since the query is going to return a single employee (or null if no match is found), the code uses the `SingleOrDefault()` method to retrieve that `Employee`. The retrieved employee is returned to the caller.

The `Insert()`, `Update()`, and `Delete()` methods are similar in that all of them execute action queries – INSERT, UPDATE, and DELETE. For the sake of brevity, only the `Update()` method is shown in Listing 5-6. You may get the other methods from the book's source code.

Listing 5-6. Implementing the Update() method

```
public void Update(Employee emp)
{
    int count = db.Database.ExecuteSqlRaw("UPDATE Employees SET
FirstName={0}, LastName={1}, Title={2}, BirthDate={3}, HireDate={4},
Country={5}, Notes={6} WHERE EmployeeID={7}", emp.FirstName, emp.LastName,
emp.Title, emp.BirthDate, emp.HireDate, emp.Country, emp.Notes, emp.
EmployeeID);
}
```

The Update() method updates a specific employee and hence accepts an Employee object as a parameter. Inside, an UPDATE action query is formed and executed using the ExecuteSqlRaw() method. Note that ExecuteSqlRaw() is called on the Database property of the DbContext. The Database property provides access to database-related information and operations for the underlying DbContext.

The ExecuteSqlRaw() specifies a parameterized query. Notice how the parameters are specified: {0}...{7}. The values of these query parameters are picked from the Employee object and are specified in the ExecuteSqlRaw() call in the same sequence. The ExecuteSqlRaw() executes the action query and returns the number of records affected by it. This value is stored in the count variable. Although our implementation doesn't use the count, you may use it for further processing if you so wish.

For the sake of reducing the clutter, the code doesn't add any exception handling code. But in a more realistic case, you should add exception handling to these methods (see earlier chapters for more details on exception handling).

To complete the EmployeeSqlRepository, add Insert() and Delete() methods in the same manner (or grab them from the book's source code).

Next, add a new class named CountrySqlRepository in the Repositories folder and implement the ICountryRepository interface in it. Listing 5-7 shows CountrySqlRepository after implementing the SelectAll() method.

Listing 5-7. CountrySqlRepository implements ICountryRepository

```
public class CountrySqlRepository : ICountryRepository
{
    private readonly AppDbContext db = null;

    public CountrySqlRepository(AppDbContext db)
```

```
    {
        this.db = db;
    }

    public List<Country> SelectAll()
    {
        List<Country> data = db.Countries. FromSqlRaw("SELECT
                            CountryID, Name FROM Countries
                            ORDER BY Name ASC").ToList();
        return data;
    }
}
```

The CountrySqlRepository implementation should look familiar to you because it uses the same FromSqlRaw() method on the Countries DbSet to retrieve a list of all countries from the Countries table.

Creating EmployeeStProcRepository and CountryStProcRepository

In the preceding section, you created two repositories that use raw SQL statements to perform the CRUD operations. In many real-world applications, you might want to use stored procedures over SQL queries. So it would be worthwhile to see how stored procedures can be executed using EF Core. To that end, this section shows you how to create another set of repositories using stored procedures.

In order to work with this set of repositories, you first need to create certain stored procedures in the Northwind database. The complete script for creating these stored procedures can be found in the book's source code download. Here, we discuss a few stored procedures so that you get some idea about them. Take a look at Listing 5-8 that shows the Employees_SelectAll stored procedure.

Listing 5-8. Stored procedure for selecting all employees

```
CREATE PROCEDURE [dbo].[Employees_SelectAll]
AS
SELECT EmployeeID, FirstName, LastName, Title, BirthDate, HireDate,
Country, Notes FROM Employees ORDER BY EmployeeID ASC
RETURN 0
```

The Employees_SelectAll stored procedure returns all the employee records from the Employees table. Listing 5-9 shows the Employees_Update stored procedure.

Listing 5-9. Employees_Update stored procedure

```
CREATE PROCEDURE [dbo].[Employees_Update]
    @EmployeeID INT,
    @FirstName NVARCHAR(10),
    @LastName NVARCHAR(20),
    @Title NVARCHAR(30),
    @BirthDate DATETIME,
    @HireDate DATETIME,
    @Country NVARCHAR(15),
    @Notes NTEXT
AS
    UPDATE Employees SET
    FirstName=@FirstName,
    LastName=@LastName,
    Title=@Title,
    BirthDate=@BirthDate,
    HireDate=@HireDate,
    Country=@Country,
    Notes=@Notes
    WHERE EmployeeID = @EmployeeID;
RETURN 0
```

The Employees_Update stored procedure is intended to update an employee record from the Employees table. It has several parameters for passing values for the modified FirstName, LastName, Title, BirthDate, HireDate, Country, and Notes for a particular

EmployeeID. Inside, it invokes an UPDATE action query and performs the necessary update operation.

Before going ahead, complete all the stored procedures: Employees_SelectAll, Employees_SelectByID, Employees_Insert, Employees_Update, Employees_Delete, and Countries_SelectAll.

Next, add the EmployeeStProcRepository class to the Repositories folder and implement the IEmployeeRepository interface in it. The EmployeeStProcRepository class uses the stored procedures you just created to perform the CRUD operations. It uses the same FromSqlRaw() and ExecuteSqlRaw() methods as before but with a few differences. Listing 5-10 shows the implementation of SelectAll() and SelectByID() methods.

Listing 5-10. Implementing SelectAll() and SelectByID() methods

```
public List<Employee> SelectAll()
{
    List<Employee> data = db.Employees. FromSqlRaw("EXEC Employees_
    SelectAll").ToList();
    return data;
}

public Employee SelectByID(int id)
{
    SqlParameter p = new SqlParameter("@EmployeeID", id);
    Employee emp = db.Employees. FromSqlRaw("EXEC Employees_SelectByID
    @EmployeeID", p).ToList().SingleOrDefault();
    return emp;
}
```

This code should look familiar to you. Notice the code marked in bold letters. The FromSqlRaw() call from the SelectAll() method executes the Employees_SelectAll stored procedure using the EXEC command.

The EXEC call from the SelectByID() method is followed by the name of the stored procedure to execute and also a parameter list that the stored procedure takes. In this case, Employees_SelectByID takes only one parameter – @EmployeeID. The @EmployeeID parameter is represented by a SqlParameter object (Microsoft.Data.SqlClient namespace) that wraps the parameter name and value. The SqlParameter is passed to FromSqlRaw() as the second parameter.

Listing 5-11 shows the Update() method of EmployeeStProcRepository.

Listing 5-11. Implementing the Update() method

```
public void Update(Employee emp)
{
    SqlParameter[] p = new SqlParameter[8];
    p[0] = new SqlParameter("@EmployeeID", emp.EmployeeID);
    p[1] = new SqlParameter("@FirstName", emp.FirstName);
    p[2] = new SqlParameter("@LastName", emp.LastName);
    p[3] = new SqlParameter("@Title", emp.Title);
    p[4] = new SqlParameter("@BirthDate", emp.BirthDate);
    p[5] = new SqlParameter("@HireDate", emp.HireDate);
    p[6] = new SqlParameter("@Country", emp.Country);
    p[7] = new SqlParameter("@Notes", emp.Notes ?? SqlString.Null);

    int count = db.Database.ExecuteSqlRaw("EXEC Employees_Update
    @EmployeeID,@FirstName,@LastName,@Title,@BirthDate,@HireDate,@Country,
    @Notes", p);
}
```

This time, the EXEC command specifies Employees_Update as the stored procedure name followed by eight parameters. These parameters are wrapped in an array of SqlParameter objects. The SqlParameter array is passed in the second parameter of the ExecuteSqlRaw() method.

Note   You will find that developers implement the repository pattern in different ways. For example, you might have repositories that support batch operations and have a separate method, such as Save(), that takes care of persisting data into the database. You will also observe that Unit of Work pattern often goes hand in hand with the repository pattern. Here, you use a simplistic approach to create the repositories.

For the sake of brevity, we won't discuss all the methods of EmployeeStProc Repository and CountryStProcRepository. You may complete these methods yourself or grab them from the book's source code.

Registering Repositories with the DI Container

In the previous chapters, you injected AppDbContext into the controller or page model classes. The controller actions and page handler methods then used the AppDbContext to perform the CRUD operations. In this example, the CRUD operations are being performed by the repositories you just created. So you need to inject the repositories into the controller/page model. In order to inject the repositories in the controllers/page models, you need to register them with the ASP.NET Core's dependency injection (DI) container.

So open the Startup class and go to the ConfigureServices() method. There, add the code shown in Listing 5-12.

Listing 5-12. Registering the repositories with the DI container

```
public void ConfigureServices(IServiceCollection services)
{
  ...
  ...
    services.AddScoped<IEmployeeRepository, EmployeeSqlRepository>();
    services.AddScoped<ICountryRepository, CountrySqlRepository>();
}
```

Note   You also need to set up your ConfigureServices() and Configure() methods for API, EF Core, and routing. These details are discussed in Chapter 1 and Chapter 3. You may read those chapters or look into this chapter's code download.

Notice the code marked in bold letters. It calls the AddScoped<TService, TImplementation>() method to register the EmployeeSqlRepository and CountrySqlRepository. The AddScoped() method creates an instance of a specified type and sets its lifetime to be the current request. That means anytime EmployeeSqlRepository is requested during a request, the same object instance will be supplied by the DI container. Note that IEmployeeRepository is passed as the TService, whereas EmployeeSqlRepository is passed as TImplementation. The CountrySqlRepository is registered in a similar manner.

Note   In DI terms, a type being registered with the DI container is called a service. Just like the AddScoped() method, there are AddTransient() and AddSingleton() methods that can be used to control the lifetime of the service being registered with the DI container. You may read more about them in the ASP.NET Core official documentation at `https://docs.microsoft.com/en-us/aspnet/core/fundamentals/dependency-injection`.

To register `EmployeeStProcRepository` and `CountryStProcRepository` with the DI container, you would have written this code:

```
services.AddScoped<IEmployeeRepository, EmployeeStProcRepository>();
services.AddScoped<ICountryRepository, CountryStProcRepository>();
```

Creating Employees Web API and Countries Web API

Now that you have completed the repositories, let's proceed to create Web APIs required by the application. We need two Web APIs – one to perform CRUD operations on employees and one to return countries from the database.

Begin by adding a new API controller class named `EmployeesController` to the Controllers folder (Figure 5-4).

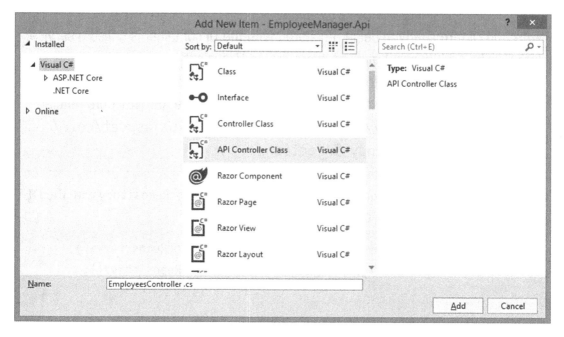

Figure 5-4. *Adding EmployeesController to the project*

The newly added `EmployeesController` class inherits from the `Controller` class. You need to modify the class by adding the skeleton code as shown in Listing 5-13.

Listing 5-13. Skeleton of EmployeesController

```
[Route("api/[controller]")]
public class EmployeesController : Controller
{
    private readonly IEmployeeRepository employeeRepository = null;

    public EmployeesController(IEmployeeRepository employeeRepository)
    {
        this.employeeRepository = employeeRepository;
    }

    [HttpGet]
    public List<Employee> Get()
    {
    }
```

```csharp
    [HttpGet("{id}")]
    public Employee Get(int id)
    {
    }
    [HttpPost]
    public void Post(Employee emp)
    {
    }

    [HttpPut("{id}")]
    public void Put(int id, Employee emp)
    {
    }

    [HttpDelete("{id}")]
    public void Delete(int id)
    {
    }
}
```

The EmployeesController is decorated with the [Route] attribute. In the case of ASP.NET Core Web APIs, routing is defined using the [Route] attribute (also called attribute routing). The [Route] attribute specifies the URL template used for accessing the underlying Web API. In this case, the template is api/[controller]. The api URL segment is added to indicate that you are accessing an API. It's an optional segment, but adding it in the URL makes your API URL more readable.

The attribute routing supports what is known as token replacement. The [controller] specified in the URL template is replaced with the actual controller name (Employees in this case) while building the route. Just like [controller], you can also use [action] in case you want to substitute the action name in the URL template. The URL template used here exposes the API at https://localhost:12345/api/Employees (the port number will vary as per your setup).

The EmployeesController declares a variable of type IEmployeeRepository (employeeRepository). This variable is assigned in the constructor of the class where an implementation of IEmployeeRepository (EmployeeSqlRepository or EmployeeStProcRepository) will be injected by the framework. The repository thus injected is used by five actions, namely, `Get()`, `Get(id)`, `Post()`, `Put()`, and `Delete()`, to perform the CRUD operations.

Now that you know the skeleton of `EmployeesController`, let's add these five actions step-by-step.

First, add the `Get()` and `Get(id)` actions as shown in Listing 5-14.

Listing 5-14. Get() and Get(id) actions of EmployeesController

```
[HttpGet]
public List<Employee> Get()
{
    return employeeRepository.SelectAll();
}

[HttpGet("{id}")]
public Employee Get(int id)
{
    return employeeRepository.SelectByID(id);
}
```

The `Get()` and `Get(id)` actions are intended to return all the employees and a specific employee, respectively. The `Get()` action returns a `List<Employee>` and is decorated with the `[HttpGet]` attribute. Recollect that earlier it was mentioned that the HTTP verbs such as GET, POST, PUT, and DELETE control which API action is invoked by the framework. Adding `[HttpGet]` on top of the `Get()` action means that GET requests will be handled by the `Get()` action. Inside, the code invokes the `SelectAll()` method of the repository to fetch all the employees.

The `Get(id)` action is also decorated with the `[HttpGet]` attribute, but it also takes the id route parameter as indicated by `{id}`. The `Get()` action has an integer id parameter that represents an `EmployeeID`. Inside, the code calls the `SelectByID()` method of the repository to return a particular employee matching the specified `EmployeeID`.

Listing 5-15 shows the `Post()` action of `EmployeesController`.

Listing 5-15. Post() action inserts a new employee

```
[HttpPost]
public void Post([FromBody]Employee emp)
{
    if (ModelState.IsValid)
    {
        employeeRepository.Insert(emp);
    }
}
```

The Post() action is intended to insert a new employee into the database. It's decorated with the [HttpPost] attribute to map it to the POST requests. The Post() action takes an Employee object as a parameter. This object represents the new employee to be added to the database. Note that the emp parameter has the [FromBody] attribute indicating that the value of the parameter is to be picked from the request body.

Inside, the code checks whether the Employee object (the model) contains valid values using the ModelState.IsValid property. If the model contains valid values, the Insert() method of the repository is called to insert a new employee to the database.

Note   There is the [ApiController] attribute that can simplify the API actions by automatically performing the model validation and parameter binding. Read the official documentation to know more about the [ApiController] attribute and its usage.

Listing 5-16 shows the Put() action of the EmployeesController.

Listing 5-16. Put() action updates an employee

```
[HttpPut("{id}")]
public void Put(int id, [FromBody]Employee emp)
{
    if (ModelState.IsValid)
    {
        employeeRepository.Update(emp);
    }
}
```

The Put() action is indented to update an employee record from the database. It is decorated with the [HttpPut] attribute indicating that it's mapped to the PUT verb. Since update operation requires an EmployeeID to be modified, the {id} parameter is added to the route. The Put() action takes two parameters: an EmployeeID to be updated and an Employee object containing the modified value. The id value comes from the route parameter, whereas the Employee object comes from the request body as indicated by the [FromBody] attribute.

Inside, the code calls the Update() method of the repository if the model validation succeeds. Note that in this example, the Employee object itself contains the EmployeeID property and hence the id parameter is not used during the processing. However, as a part of the Put() signature, it's available to you in case you want to use it for some processing.

Listing 5-17 shows the Delete() action of EmployeesController.

Listing 5-17. Delete() action deletes an employee

```
[HttpDelete("{id}")]
public void Delete(int id)
{
    employeeRepository.Delete(id);
}
```

The Delete() action is intended to delete an employee from the database. It's decorated with the [HttpDelete] attribute indicating that it is mapped to the DELETE verb. It receives an id parameter from the route that indicates an EmployeeID to be deleted. Inside, the code calls the Delete() method of the repository to delete the employee.

Note   In the preceding example, you used action names such as Get(), Post(), Put(), and Delete(). This was primarily done for the sake of readability. However, you can name the actions as per your choice. As long as they are mapped to the correct HTTP verbs using the attributes such as [HttpGet], [HttpPost], [HttpPut], and [HttpDelete], the API will behave as expected. For example, you may have an action named SelectAll() that is marked with the [HttpGet] attribute.

You just completed the EmployeesController class. In a similar manner, also complete the CountriesController class. The CountriesController uses CountrySqlRepository or CountryStProcRepository and has only one action: Get() – for returning all the countries to the caller. For the sake of brevity, the CountriesController class is not discussed here. You can also get it from the book's source code. Just for the sake of your quick reference, Listing 5-18 shows the completed CountriesController class.

Listing 5-18. Get() action of CountriesController

```
[Route("api/[controller]")]
public class CountriesController : ControllerBase
{
    private readonly ICountryRepository countryRepository = null;

    public CountriesController(ICountryRepository countryRepository)
    {
        this.countryRepository = countryRepository;
    }

    [HttpGet]
    public List<Country> Get()
    {
        return countryRepository.SelectAll();
    }
}
```

Running the Employees Web API

Now that the Web APIs needed by Employee Manager are ready, let's check whether they are working as expected. Since you haven't created the client application yet, not all the actions can be tested using the browser. However, you can check the Get() and Get(id) actions easily as discussed in the following.

Run the EmployeeManager.Api project from the Visual Studio IDE by pressing F5. When the browser window opens, enter https://localhost:12345/api/Employees in the browser's address bar (change the port number as per your setup). This will initiate a GET request to the EmployeesController. Recollect that GET requests are mapped to the Get() action. Therefore, the Get() action will be invoked, and a List of Employee objects is returned to the browser. Figure 5-5 shows a sample run of the Web API.

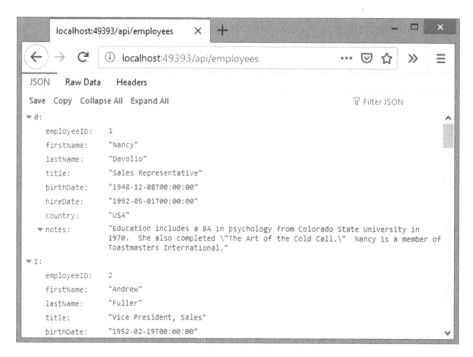

Figure 5-5. *Employees API returns JSON*

Notice how the API returns data in JSON format. You can invoke Get(id) by adding an EmployeeID in the URL. For example, specifying the URL to be https://localhost:12345/api/Employees/1 returns just a single employee whose EmployeeID is 1 (Figure 5-6).

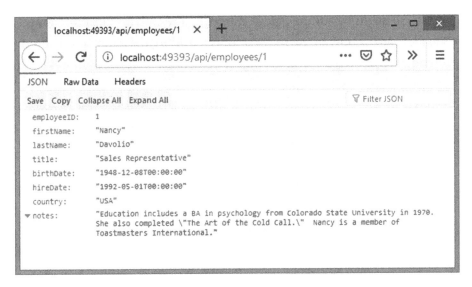

Figure 5-6. *Get(id) returns a single employee*

Note   Although you may not be able to test Post(), Put(), and Delete() actions using the technique discussed in the preceding text, you can use a tool such as Postman to test all the HTTP verbs with your API. Consider visiting www.getpostman.com for more details about the Postman tool.

Creating a Client for Web API

In the preceding sections, you created ASP.NET Core Web API that performs CRUD operations on the Employees table. In the sections that follow, you build a client application that consumes the Web API.

A client to the Web API can be any kind of application such as another web application, a desktop application, another service, or a JavaScript client. As long as the client has network connectivity and access to the Web API, it can invoke the API by making appropriate GET, POST, PUT, and DELETE requests.

Since your focus is ASP.NET Core, you develop an ASP.NET Core MVC application as a client to the Web API. In terms of project organization, the client application looks just like the ASP.NET Core MVC application you developed in the past. However, it resorts to the Web API for performing the CRUD operations rather than using the EF

Core code itself. So begin by adding a new ASP.NET Core web application named EmployeeManager.ApiClient to the same solution. Adding the client application to the same solution makes debugging and testing easy. Figure 5-7 shows Solution Explorer when the client application is complete.

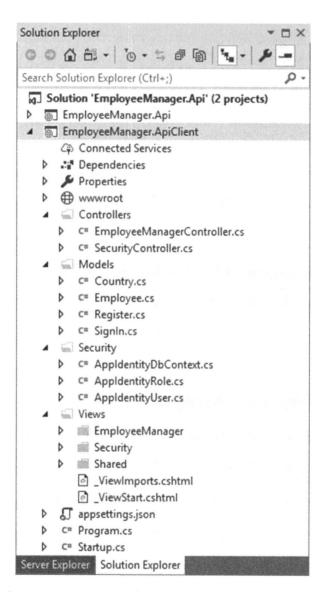

Figure 5-7. *EmployeeManager.ApiClient project in Solution Explorer*

Since the client application is an ASP.NET Core MVC application, the overall development process and the project organization should look familiar to you. For the sake of brevity, I am not going to repeat the basic steps. The steps necessary to consume the API are discussed in the following sections. You can get the complete source code of the client application from this book's source code download.

Creating View Models

While developing the API project, you created the EF Core model required by the application. And the CRUD operations are encapsulated in the repositories. Therefore, the client application won't have any EF Core model or database access code. However, since the Web API project deals with the data in terms of Employee and Country classes, the client needs to have these view model classes. For example, the Get() action of EmployeesController returns a List<Employee>. So to receive that data, the client application too needs a matching data structure. This calls for adding Employee and Country view model classes in the client's Models folder. These classes are quite similar to the Employee and Country entity classes you created earlier. But they won't use database schema–related data annotations such as [Table] and [Column]. Listing 5-19 shows a part of the Employee view model class just to give you an idea.

Listing 5-19. Employee view model class

```
public class Employee
{
    [Required(ErrorMessage ="Employee ID is required")]
    [Display(Name = "Employee ID")]
    public int EmployeeID { get; set; }

    [Display(Name = "First Name")]
    [Required(ErrorMessage = "First Name is required")]
    [StringLength(10,ErrorMessage ="First Name must be less than 10
    characters")]
    public string FirstName { get; set; }

    [Display(Name = "Last Name")]
    [Required(ErrorMessage ="Last Name is required")]
```

```
[StringLength(20,ErrorMessage ="Last Name must be less than 20
characters")]
public string LastName { get; set; }
...
...
}
```

As you can see, the Employee class properties have only those data annotations that are necessary for validations and UI display.

On the same lines, add the Country class as shown in the following:

```
public class Country
{
    public int CountryID { get; set; }
    public string Name { get; set; }
}
```

Adding the EmployeeManagerController

Now that the view models are ready, add a new controller class named EmployeeManagerController in the Controllers folder. Just like the ASP.NET Core MVC version of Employee Manager, the EmployeeManagerController also has seven actions (one for listing, two for insert, two for update, and two for delete) and a helper method (to fill countries in the ViewBag). However, the differences this time are as follows:

- The actions use the HttpClient class to invoke the Web API.

- The actions use the async-await pattern.

- Since the Web API returns data in JSON format, the client code uses classes from the System.Text.Json namespace to deal with the JSON data.

Note   You could have also used a third-party JSON library such as Json.NET (Newtonsoft.Json NuGet package) to process the JSON data returned by the Web API.

You have used the async-await pattern in the previous chapters, so the skeleton of the EmployeeManagerController shown in Listing 5-20 should look familiar to you.

Listing 5-20. Skeleton of EmployeeManagerController

```
public class EmployeeManagerController : Controller
{
    public EmployeeManagerController(HttpClient client, IConfiguration config)
    {
    }

    public async Task<bool> FillCountriesAsync()
    {
    }

    public async Task<IActionResult> ListAsync()
    {
    }

    public async Task<IActionResult> InsertAsync()
    {
    }

    [HttpPost]
    [ValidateAntiForgeryToken]
    public async Task<IActionResult> InsertAsync(Employee model)
    {
    }

    public async Task<IActionResult> UpdateAsync(int id)
    {
    }

    [HttpPost]
    [ValidateAntiForgeryToken]
    public async Task<IActionResult> UpdateAsync(Employee model)
    {
    }
```

```
    [ActionName("Delete")]
    public async Task<IActionResult> ConfirmDeleteAsync(int id)
    {
    }

    [HttpPost]
    [ValidateAntiForgeryToken]
    public async Task<IActionResult> DeleteAsync(int employeeID)
    {
    }
}
```

Now that you have some idea about the EmployeeManagerController, let's complete it in steps.

Setting Up the HttpClient

The EmployeeManagerController uses the HttpClient class to invoke the Web API. The HttpClient class resides in the System.Net.Http namespace and is asynchronous by design. An object of HttpClient is created and configured in the ConfigureServices() of the Startup class. An instance of HttpClient is then registered with the DI container so that it can be injected into the controllers. Listing 5-21 shows how this is done.

Listing 5-21. Creating and configuring HttpClient

```
HttpClient client = new HttpClient();
string baseUrl = config.GetValue<string>("AppSettings:BaseUrl");
client.BaseAddress = new Uri(baseUrl);
var contentType = new MediaTypeWithQualityHeaderValue("application/json");
client.DefaultRequestHeaders.Accept.Add(contentType);
services.AddSingleton<HttpClient>(client);
```

The code begins by creating an object of HttpClient. A string variable (baseAddress) is also declared to hold the API URL. To avoid hard-coding of the API URLs in the code, the client application stores them in the appsettings.json file:

```
"AppSettings": {
  "BaseUrl": "https://localhost:12345",
  "EmployeesApiUrl": "/api/employees",
  "CountriesApiUrl": "/api/countries"
}
```

Notice the use of the GetValue<T>() method for reading the configuration information. The GetValue<T>() method specifies the key whose value you wish to retrieve and the data type of the value (string in this case). Notice how the key is specified. For example, AppSettings:BaseUrl indicates that the BaseUrl key from the AppSettings section is to be retrieved. An example of BaseUrl would be https://localhost:12345. The BaseAddress property of the HttpClient class is a Uri that indicates the base address of the API.

A Web API can return data either in JSON format or XML format (you can also customize the format). To indicate that the client needs data in JSON format, the code sets the Accept HTTP header of HttpClient. This is done using the DefaultRequestHeaders.Accept.Add() method of HttpClient. The Add() method takes a MediaTypeWithQualityHeaderValue object specifying the content type of the returned data. Note that MediaTypeWithQualityHeaderValue resides in the System.Net.Http. Headers namespace.

Once the HttpClient object is configured, it is registered with the DI system using the AddSingleton<T>() method. The AddSingleton() method indicates that only one instance of HttpClient will serve all the requests to the object. Also notice that we supply the previously configured instance of HttpClient to the AddSingleton() method so that this configured instance is made available as a singleton.

Note   You can also use IHttpClientFactory for creating instances of HttpClient. Discussion of using IHttpClientFactory is beyond the scope of this book. You may read https://docs.microsoft.com/en-us/aspnet/core/fundamentals/http-requests for more details.

The HttpClient can now be injected into the EmployeeManagerController class. Listing 5-22 shows how that can be done.

Listing 5-22. Creating and configuring HttpClient

```
private readonly HttpClient client = null;
private string employeesApiUrl = "";
private string countriesApiUrl = "";

public EmployeeManagerController(HttpClient client, IConfiguration config)
{
    this.client = client;
    employeesApiUrl = config.GetValue<string>("AppSettings:EmployeesApiUrl");
    countriesApiUrl = config.GetValue<string>("AppSettings:CountriesApiUrl");
}
```

An object of HttpClient and IConfiguration is injected into the constructor. The IConfiguration object provides access to the configuration information. The HttpClient object injected into the constructor is stored into a local variable for using it in the actions.

The constructor retrieves two keys from the configuration's AppSettings section, namely, EmployeesApiUrl and CountriesApiUrl. An example of EmployeesApiUrl and CountriesApiUrl would be /api/Employees and /api/Countries, respectively.

Strongly Typed Configuration

In the preceding section, you injected the IConfiguration object into EmployeeManagerController and then used the GetValue() method to retrieve EmployeesApiUrl and CountriesApiUrl values. Although this works well in this simple example, there is a better way to access configuration information. You can fill the required configuration information into an object and then access it in a strongly typed manner. Let's quickly see how that can be done.

Suppose you have a class called WebApiConfig that looks like this:

```
public class WebApiConfig
{
    public string BaseUrl { get; set; }
    public string EmployeesApiUrl { get; set; }
    public string CountriesApiUrl { get; set; }
}
```

As you can see, the WebApiConfig class has three properties, namely, BaseUrl, EmployeesApiUrl, and CountriesApiUrl. These properties have the same names as the corresponding configuration keys stored under the AppSettings section of appsettings. json.

You can load values from AppSettings into an object of WebApiConfig in the ConfigureServices() method like this:

```
services.Configure<WebApiConfig>
(config.GetSection("AppSettings"));
```

The Configure<T>() method accepts a configuration section (AppSettings in this case) and registers an object of WebApiConfig filled with the required values. You can access this configuration information in the EmployeeManagerController like this:

```
public EmployeeManagerController(HttpClient client, IOptions<WebApiConfig>
options)
{
    WebApiConfig config = options.Value;
}
```

As you can see, the constructor now accepts the IOptions<T> parameter. The actual WebApiConfig object can be accessed using the Value property. Once retrieved, you can use its EmployeesApiUrl and CountriesApiUrl properties wherever required.

Displaying a List of Employees

In order to display a list of employees (Figure 5-8), you need to create the ListAsync() action and List view.

Employee Manager

List of Employees

Insert

Employee ID	First Name	Last Name	Title	Actions	
1	Nancy	Davolio	Sales Representative	Update	Delete
2	Andrew	Fuller	Vice President, Sales	Update	Delete
3	Janet	Leverling	Sales Representative	Update	Delete

Figure 5-8. *Displaying a list of employees*

Note   Since the actions of the EmployeeManagerController are marked as async methods, the action names are suffixed with Async. For example, instead of having the List() action, the controller has the ListAsync() action.

The ListAsync() action is responsible for fetching all the employees from the API and is shown in Listing 5-23.

Listing 5-23. ListAsync() action makes a GET request to the API

```
public async Task<IActionResult> ListAsync()
{
    HttpResponseMessage response = await client.GetAsync(employeesApiUrl);
    string stringData =await response.Content.
ReadAsStringAsync();
    var options = new JsonSerializerOptions
    {
        PropertyNameCaseInsensitive = true
    };

    List<Employee> data = JsonSerializer.Deserialize
<List<Employee>>(stringData, options);
    return View(data);
}
```

The `ListAsync()`action is marked with the `async` keyword and returns a
`Task<IActionResult>`. Inside, the code invokes the `Get()` action of the API by sending a
GET request. This is done using the `GetAsync()` method of `HttpClient`. The `GetAsync()`
method accepts the part of URL where Employees API can be located (e.g., /api/
Employees) and returns the response wrapped in the `HttpResponseMessage` object.

The `ReadAsStringAsync()` method reads the actual JSON content from the
`HttpResponseMessage` object.

To render this JSON content on the List view, you need to convert it into a
`List<Employee>`. This is done using the `Deserialize()` method of the `JsonSerializer`
class (`System.Text.Json` namespace). The `Deserialize<T>()` method accepts content
as a JSON string and converts it into a type specified by T (`List<Employee>` in this case).
You can also specify settings to be used while parsing the JSON data in the second
parameter of the `Deserialize()` method. In this case, the `JsonSerializerOptions`
object sets the `PropertyNameCaseInsensitive` property to true indicating that the
parsing operation should be case insensitive.

The `List<Employee>` is then passed to the List view for the sake of rendering the
employee listing.

In the projects created so far, you used Tag Helpers to render the user interface. This
time, you use HTML Helpers to do that. The HTML Helpers are similar to Tag Helpers in
purpose, but they use code-oriented syntax rather than tag-oriented syntax used by Tag
Helpers. The ASP.NET Core contains the `HtmlHelper` class that exposes various methods
to render HTML elements. The Razor files have a `Html` property that's an instance of the
`HtmlHelper` class. Using the `Html` property, you can call various methods of `HtmlHelper`
and render the user interface as required.

Listing 5-24 shows the content of List.cshtml that illustrates how HTML Helpers are used.

Listing 5-24. Content of List.cshtml

```
@model List<Employee>

<h2>List of Employees</h2>

<h3 class="message">@TempData["Message"]</h3>

@Html.ActionLink("Insert","Insert","EmployeeManager",null,new { @class=
"linkbutton" })

<br /><br />
```

```
<table border="1">
    <tr>
        <th>Employee ID</th>
        <th>First Name</th>
        <th>Last Name</th>
        <th>Title</th>
        <th colspan="2">Actions</th>
    </tr>
    @foreach(var item in Model)
    {
        <tr>
            <td>@item.EmployeeID</td>
            <td>@item.FirstName</td>
            <td>@item.LastName</td>
            <td>@item.Title</td>
            <td>
                @Html.ActionLink("Update", "Update", "EmployeeManager", new
{ id=item.EmployeeID },new { @class="linkbutton"})
            </td>
            <td>
                @Html.ActionLink("Delete", "Delete", "EmployeeManager", new
{ id = item.EmployeeID }, new { @class = "linkbutton" })
            </td>
        </tr>
    }
</table>
```

This code should look familiar to you because you used similar code while developing the MVC version of Employee Manager. Notice the code marked in bold letters. It uses the ActionLink HTML Helper to generate Insert, Update, and Delete links. The first parameter of ActionLink() is the text of the link, whereas the second and third parameters indicate action name and controller name, respectively.

Note   Although the asynchronous actions are suffixed with Async, while using these action names in the ActionLink() HTML Helper (and in any URLs in general), the Async suffix is omitted. The framework automatically routes them to the correct action.

You can also specify the id route parameter and a CSS class to be applied to the link using the fourth and fifth parameters. These parameters are objects of anonymous types that specify the route id value and CSS class name, respectively.

Inserting a New Employee

To insert a new employee, you need to add InsertAsync() actions and the Insert view (Figure 5-9).

Figure 5-9. *Inserting a new employee*

The InsertAsync() actions dealing with the GET and POST requests are shown in Listing 5-25.

Listing 5-25. InsertAsync() actions add a new employee

```
public async Task<IActionResult> InsertAsync()
{
    await FillCountriesAsync();
    return View();
}

[HttpPost]
[ValidateAntiForgeryToken]
public async Task<IActionResult> InsertAsync(Employee model)
{
    await FillCountriesAsync();
    if (ModelState.IsValid)
    {
        string stringData = JsonSerializer.Serialize(model);
        var contentData = new StringContent(stringData, System.Text.
        Encoding.UTF8, "application/json");
        HttpResponseMessage response = await client.PostAsync
        (employeesApiUrl, contentData);
        if (response.IsSuccessStatusCode)
        {
          ViewBag.Message = "Employee inserted successfully!";
        }
        else
        {
          ViewBag.Message = "Error while calling Web API!";
        }
    }
    return View(model);
}
```

The first InsertAsync() is called when you click the Insert link from the employee listing page. Inside, it calls FillCountriesAsync() to put all the countries in the ViewBag for the purpose of displaying them in the dropdown list. The FillCountriesAsync() helper method is discussed later in this chapter. As a result of InsertAsync(), an empty Insert view is displayed in the browser.

The second InsertAsync() receives the Employee object through model binding. Inside, it calls FillCountries() as before. It then proceeds to checking the validity of the model using the ModelState.IsValid property. If the model contains valid data, the code inserts a new employee by calling the API. To insert an employee, first you need to represent the Employee object in JSON format. This is done using the Serialize() method of the JsonSerializer class. The Serialize() method accepts an object and returns a JSON-formatted string representing that object. The JSON string thus obtained is wrapped into a StringContent object.

To initiate the insert operation, the PostAsync() method of HttpClient is called. The PostAsync() method makes a POST request to the supplied URL (/api/Employees in this case) and also carries a StringContent object containing the JSON data to be sent along with the POST request. The PostAsync() call invokes the Post() action of the Employees API.

The PostAsync() returns the HttpResponseMessage object. The code checks its IsSuccessStatusCode property to determine whether the API call was successful or not. The IsSuccessStatusCode property returns true if the HTTP status code of the response is in the range of 200–299; otherwise, it returns false. Accordingly, a success or error is stored in the ViewBag so that it can be displayed on the Insert view.

The InsertAsync() actions return the Insert view (Insert.cshtml) to the browser. The Insert view is rendered using HTML Helpers. The skeleton of the Insert view is shown in Listing 5-26.

Listing 5-26. Skeleton of the Insert view

```
@model Employee

<h2>Insert New Employee</h2>

<h3 class="message">@ViewBag.Message</h3>

@using (Html.BeginForm("Insert", "EmployeeManager", FormMethod.Post))
{
  . . .

  . . .
}
```

Notice the code marked in bold letters. It uses the `BeginForm()` HTML Helper to render the `<form>` element. The first parameter to the `BeginForm()` is the name of the action that processes the form upon submission (`InsertAsync()` POST action in this case). The second parameter indicates the name of the controller that houses the action specified earlier (`EmployeeManager` in this case). The third parameter indicates the HTTP method of submitting the form (POST in this case). The form content is enclosed inside the `@using` statement. This ensures that the `</form>` tag is also outputted after the block.

The form fields such as labels, textboxes, dropdown list, and button are housed inside the `@using` block. These elements are rendered using various HTML Helpers. Listing 5-27 shows a part of this form for your understanding.

Listing 5-27. Form fields are rendered using HTML Helpers

```
<tr>
    <td class="right">
        @Html.LabelFor(m => m.FirstName) :
    </td>
    <td>
        @Html.TextBoxFor(m => m.FirstName)
        @Html.ValidationMessageFor(m => m.FirstName, null, new { @class =
        "message" })
    </td>
</tr>
...
<tr>
    <td class="right">
        @Html.LabelFor(m => m.BirthDate) :
    </td>
    <td>
        @Html.TextBoxFor(m => m.BirthDate, null, new { type = "date" })
        @Html.ValidationMessageFor(m => m.BirthDate, null, new { @class =
        "message" })
    </td>
</tr>
...
<tr>
```

```
    <td class="right">
        @Html.LabelFor(m => m.Country) :
    </td>
    <td>
        @Html.DropDownListFor(m => m.Country, ViewBag.Countries as
        List<SelectListItem>,"Please select")
        @Html.ValidationMessageFor(m => m.Country, null, new { @class =
        "message" })
    </td>
</tr>
<tr>
    <td class="right">
        @Html.LabelFor(m => m.Notes) :
    </td>
    <td>
        @Html.TextAreaFor(m => m.Notes, 5, 40, null)
        @Html.ValidationMessageFor(m => m.Notes, null, new { @class =
        "message" })
    </td>
</tr>
<tr>
    <td colspan="2">
        <button type="submit">Save</button>
    </td>
</tr>
```

Notice the code marked in bold letters. The code uses strongly typed HTML Helpers such as LabelFor, TextBoxFor, ValidationMessageFor, DropDownListFor, and TextAreaFor to render the form fields.

The LabelFor() HTML Helper accepts a model property in the form of a lambda expression and renders a <label> element. Similarly, the TextBoxFor() HTML Helper renders a textbox (<input type="text" />) for the specified model property (FirstName in this case).

Notice how the BirthDate date picker is displayed. The <input> element's type attribute is set through an anonymous object and indicates that the type is date rather than text.

The `DropDownListFor()` HTML Helper (`<select>` and `<option>` HTML elements) displays a list of countries. The countries are picked from the `ViewBag.Countries` property. Recollect that the `FillCountries()` helper method stores a `List<SelectListItem>` into the `ViewBag`. The `List` is being bound to the dropdown list here. The third parameter indicates the default empty `<option>` element (Please select in this case) to be added to the dropdown list.

The `TextAreaFor()` HTML Helper renders a `<textarea>` element with 5 rows and 40 columns to enter Notes.

To display field-level validation errors, the `ValidationMessageFor()` HTML Helper is placed after each data entry control. It accepts the model property for which the error message is to be displayed (if any).

Finally, the Save button submits the form to the specified action (`InsertAsync()` POST action in this case).

For the sake of brevity, all the form fields of the form are not discussed here. You may get the completed Insert.cshtml from this book's code download.

Note   The client-side validation using jQuery can also be used with HTML Helpers. The process is essentially the same as that of the Tag Helpers and hence is not discussed here again. Read the earlier chapters in case you need to refresh those steps. You can get the complete set of code files from this book's code download.

Updating an Existing Employee

You reach the Update Existing Employee page (Figure 5-10) when you click the Update link of an employee from the employee listing page.

Update Existing Employee

Employee ID : 1

First Name : Nancy

Last Name : Davolio

Title : Sales Representative

Birth Date : 12 / 08 / 1948 ⊗

Hire Date : 05 / 01 / 1992 ⊗

Country : USA ⌄

Notes : Education includes a BA in psychology from Colorado State University in 1970. She also completed "The Art of the Cold Call." Nancy is a member of Toastmasters International.

Save

Back to Employee Listing

Figure 5-10. *Update view displays employee details for editing*

In order to update an existing employee, you need two `UpdateAsync()` actions and the Update view. The `UpdateAsync()` action that handles the GET request is shown in Listing 5-28.

Listing 5-28. Fetching an existing employee to be updated

```
public async Task<IActionResult> UpdateAsync(int id)
{
    await FillCountriesAsync();

    HttpResponseMessage response = await client.
GetAsync($"{employeesApiUrl}/{id}");
    string stringData = await response.Content.ReadAsStringAsync();
    var options = new JsonSerializerOptions
    {
      PropertyNameCaseInsensitive = true
    };
    Employee model = JsonSerializer.Deserialize<Employee>(stringData, options);
    return View(model);
}
```

The `UpdateAsync()` action has the `id` parameter that represents the `EmployeeID` of the employee to be modified. This `EmployeeID` is received as a route parameter from the employee listing page.

Inside, the code calls the `FillCountriesAsync()` helper method to store a list of countries into the `ViewBag`. The code then makes a GET request to the Employees API using the `GetAsync()` method of `HttpClient`. This time, the `EmployeeID` is also passed as a part of the URL. This maps the request with the `Get(id)` action of the Employees API.

The `Employee` returned by the API is unpacked from the `HttpResponseMessage` object using the `ReadAsStringAsync()`. This data being in JSON format needs to be converted into an `Employee` object. This is done using the `Deserialize<T>()` method of `JsonSerializer`. The `Employee` object thus obtained is supplied to the Update view as its model.

Upon clicking the Save button, the form is submitted to the `UpdateAsync()` action (POST request). This `UpdateAsync()` action is shown in Listing 5-29.

Listing 5-29. UpdateAsync() action calls PutAsync() of HttpClient

```
[HttpPost]
[ValidateAntiForgeryToken]
public async Task<IActionResult> UpdateAsync(Employee model)
{
    await FillCountriesAsync();

    if (ModelState.IsValid)
    {
        string stringData = JsonSerializer.Serialize(model);
        var contentData = new StringContent(stringData,
    System.Text.Encoding.UTF8, "application/json");
        HttpResponseMessage response = await client.PutAsync
    ($"{employeesApiUrl}/{model.EmployeeID}", contentData);
        if (response.IsSuccessStatusCode)
        {
            ViewBag.Message = "Employee updated successfully!";
        }
        else
```

```
    {
        ViewBag.Message = "Error while calling Web API!";
    }
    }
    return View(model);
}
```

The `UpdateAsync()` action is quite similar to the `InsertAsync()` POST action discussed earlier. However, this time it makes a PUT request to the API using the `PutAsync()` method of `HttpClient`. The `PutAsync()` method accepts the API URL and `StringContent` object that wraps the modified `Employee` object. Notice that the URL also contains the `EmployeeID` of the `Employee` being modified. Depending on the `IsSuccessStatusCode` property of `HttpResponseMessage`, a success or error message is displayed on the Update view via the `ViewBag.Message` property.

The Update view (Update.cshtml) renders its user interface using HTML Helpers and is quite similar to the Insert view discussed in the previous section. Listing 5-30 shows the skeleton of the Update view.

Listing 5-30. Skeleton of the Update view

```
@model Employee

<h2>Update Existing Employee</h2>

<h3 class="message">@ViewBag.Message</h3>

@using (Html.BeginForm("Update", "EmployeeManager", FormMethod.Post))
{
    ...
}
```

The `BeginForm()` HTML Helper renders a `<form>` element. This time the form is configured to POST its content to the `UpdateAsync()` action of `EmployeeManager`. The `<form>` contains almost the same set of form fields as in the case of the Insert view. The only difference is that the `EmployeeID` is not displayed for editing. It is made available to the model binding via a hidden field, and its value is displayed in a `<span>` element. Listing 5-31 shows how this is done.

Listing 5-31. EmployeeID is stored in a hidden form field

```
<tr>
    <td class="right">
        @Html.LabelFor(m => m.EmployeeID) :
    </td>
    <td>
        @Html.HiddenFor(m=>m.EmployeeID)
        <span>@Model.EmployeeID</span>
    </td>
</tr>
```

As you can see, the HiddenFor() HTML Helper stores the EmployeeID in a hidden form field.

Deleting an Existing Employee

When you click the Delete link for an employee, a confirmation page is displayed (Figure 5-11), and the user can delete the employee.

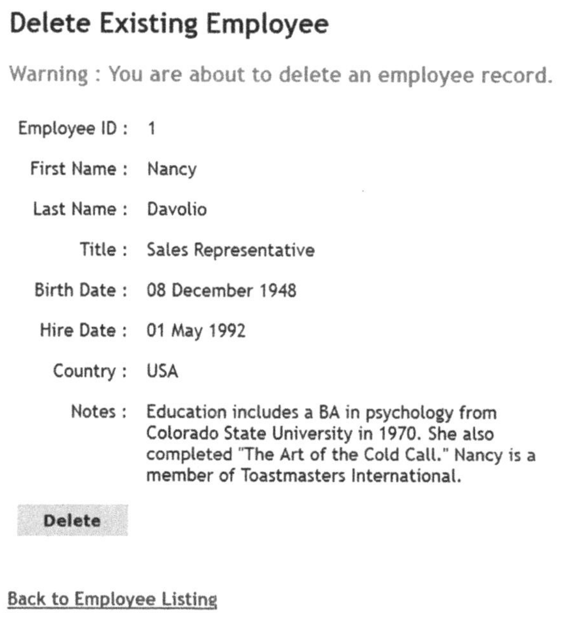

Delete Existing Employee

Warning : You are about to delete an employee record.

Employee ID :	1
First Name :	Nancy
Last Name :	Davolio
Title :	Sales Representative
Birth Date :	08 December 1948
Hire Date :	01 May 1992
Country :	USA
Notes :	Education includes a BA in psychology from Colorado State University in 1970. She also completed "The Art of the Cold Call." Nancy is a member of Toastmasters International.

Delete

Back to Employee Listing

Figure 5-11. *Seeking confirmation before deleting an employee*

To add this functionality, you need two actions and the Delete view (Delete. cshtml). The Delete action that displays the confirmation page is identical to the UpdateAsync(id) action discussed earlier and is not discussed here. For your quick reference, its code is shown in Listing 5-32.

Listing 5-32. Delete action that displays the confirmation page

```
[ActionName("Delete")]
public async Task<IActionResult> ConfirmDeleteAsync(int id)
{
    HttpResponseMessage response = await client.
GetAsync($"{employeesApiUrl}/{id}");
    string stringData = await response.Content.ReadAsStringAsync();
    var options = new JsonSerializerOptions
    {
        PropertyNameCaseInsensitive = true
    };
    Employee model = JsonSerializer.Deserialize<Employee>(stringData,
    options);
    return View(model);
}
```

Notice the use of the [ActionName] attribute that exposes the ConfirmDeleteAsync() method as the Delete action.

Upon clicking the Delete button, the form is submitted to the DeleteAsync() action. The DeleteAsync() action is shown in Listing 5-33.

Listing 5-33. DeleteAsync() action deletes an employee

```
[HttpPost]
[ValidateAntiForgeryToken]
public async Task<IActionResult> DeleteAsync(int employeeID)
{
    HttpResponseMessage response = await client.
    DeleteAsync($"{employeesApiUrl}/{employeeID}");
    if (response.IsSuccessStatusCode)
    {
```

```
      TempData["Message"] = "Employee deleted successfully!";
    }
    else
    {
      TempData["Message"] = "Error while calling Web API!";
    }
    return RedirectToAction("List");
}
```

The DeleteAsync() action receives an EmployeeID as its parameter. Inside, the code invokes the DeleteAsync() method of HttpClient. This initiates a DELETE request to the API and executes its Delete() action. Notice that the DeleteAsync() method appends the EmployeeID of an Employee to be deleted as a part of the URL.

Depending on the value of IsSuccessStatusCode, a success or error message is stored in the TempData dictionary, and the control is redirected to the ListAsync() action of EmployeeManagerController.

The skeleton of the Delete.cshtml view that seeks confirmation from the user is shown in Listing 5-34.

Listing 5-34. Skeleton of Delete.cshtml

```
@model Employee

<h2>Delete Existing Employee</h2>

<h3 class="message">
    Warning : You are about to delete an employee record.
</h3>

@using (Html.BeginForm("Delete", "EmployeeManager", FormMethod.Post))
{
    @Html.HiddenFor(m=>m.EmployeeID)
        ...
        ...
}
```

Notice the code marked in bold letters. The BeginForm() HTML Helper renders the <form> element that houses the employee details. The form is POSTed to the DeleteAsync() action of EmployeeManager.

222

In addition to displaying employee details of the employee being deleted, the
EmployeeID is also stored in a hidden form field using the HiddenFor() HTML Helper.
This way, model binding binds the EmployeeID to the employeeID parameter of the
DeleteAsync() action.

FillCountriesAsync() Helper Method

In the InsertAsync() and UpdateAsync() actions you used FillCountriesAsync()
method that puts a list of countries into the ViewBag. The FillCountriesAsync()
method invokes the Countries API. The Listing 5-35 shows this method.

Listing 5-35. FillCountries invokes Countries API

```
public async Task<bool> FillCountriesAsync()
{
    HttpResponseMessage response = await client.GetAsync(countriesApiUrl);
    string stringData = await response.Content.ReadAsStringAsync();
    var options = new JsonSerializerOptions
    {
        PropertyNameCaseInsensitive = true
    };
    List<Country> listCountries = JsonSerializer.Deserialize<List<Country>>
    (stringData,options);
    List<SelectListItem> countries = (from c in listCountries select new
    SelectListItem() { Text = c.Name, Value = c.Name }).ToList();
    ViewBag.Countries = countries;
    return true;
}
```

The FillCountriesAsync() method is an asynchronous method and makes a GET
request to the Countries API. This is done using the GetAsync() method of HttpClient.
The code should look familiar to you because you used similar code while invoking the
Employees API. The difference is that the data is received using the Country view model.
Upon converting the countries into a List<SelectListItem>, the data is stored into
the Countries property of the ViewBag. Recollect that Insert and Update views bind the
Country dropdown lists with the ViewBag.Countries property.

Integrating ASP.NET Core Identity

In the preceding sections, you completed the `EmployeeManagerController`. You have built everything to perform the CRUD operations on the Employees table. You can also integrate ASP.NET Core Identity into the Employee Manager client application so that users are required to supply user name and password to sign in to the system.

The process of integrating ASP.NET Core Identity is the same as discussed for the ASP.NET Core MVC and ASP.NET Core Razor Pages versions of the application. For the sake of brevity, I leave it up to you to do this integration yourself. You can also get the client project from this book's source code download to study how the integration can be done.

Note   In this example, authentication and authorization are enforced in the client application (EmployeeManagerController). In the upcoming chapters, you will also learn to apply the security to the API itself.

Running the Application

Now that the Employee Manager API and the client application are ready, you can run the projects to check whether everything works as expected. Since the client application uses the API, you need to run the API project first and then run the client project. Luckily, Visual Studio allows you to configure this using the Solution Property Pages dialog. Figure 5-12 shows this dialog.

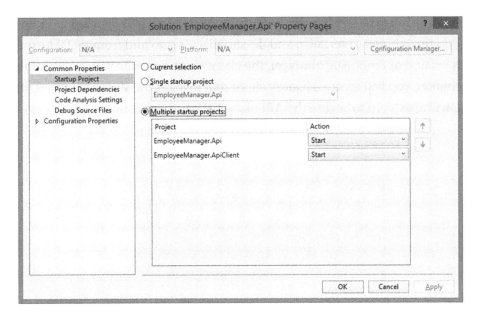

Figure 5-12. *Configuring multiple startup projects*

The Startup Project section of the dialog allows you to configure the startup of the solution. Here, you need to pick the Multiple startup projects option and then arrange the projects in the required order using the arrows on the right.

With this configuration in place, if you press F5, first the API project will be launched followed by the client project. You can then test the CRUD operations using the client project.

Summary

In this chapter, you learned to build ASP.NET Core Web APIs. You built two APIs, namely, Employees and Countries. To perform CRUD operations on the Employees table from within the Employees API, you created repositories. In the process, you learned how to execute raw SQL queries and stored procedures using EF Core. The repositories are registered with the DI framework using the AddScoped() method. You then proceeded to build the client application in ASP.NET Core MVC. The client application uses the HttpClient class to invoke the APIs. The HttpClient class is asynchronous by design, and therefore you also created asynchronous actions in the EmployeeManagerController. The HttpClient is registered with the DI framework using the AddSingleton() method. The API and the client transfer data in JSON format.

You used classes from the `System.Text.Json` namespace such as `JsonSerializer` and `JsonSerializerOptions` to serialize and de-serialize data to and from JSON format.

In this version of Employee Manager, the client was a separate web application. In the next chapter, you will create a jQuery client that invokes the Web APIs to get the job done. You will also learn to secure the API using JWT authentication.

CHAPTER 6

jQuery

In the preceding chapter, you created Web APIs and consumed them using HttpClient. Another popular way to invoke Web APIs is to invoke them using jQuery Ajax. jQuery is a feature-rich JavaScript library for performing HTML-centric operations such as DOM manipulation, event handling, animations, and Ajax. jQuery is being used by thousands of web sites, and it would be worthwhile to learn how to perform CRUD operations using this popular client-side library. To that end, this chapter teaches you to

- Build asynchronous Web APIs

- Invoke Web APIs using Ajax capabilities of the jQuery library

- Use asynchronous methods of Entity Framework Core

- Perform user authentication using the JSON Web Token (JWT)-based authentication scheme

Let's get started.

Note This chapter assumes that you have basic familiarity with the jQuery library. Although jQuery Ajax features used by the sample application are discussed as and when they are encountered, this chapter doesn't teach you the basics of jQuery. You may consider reading the jQuery official documentation at `https://jquery.com` to familiarize yourself with the library.

Overview of Ajax

Before we actually look into any code of the example discussed in this chapter, it's worthwhile to understand what Ajax is and how your web application benefits by integrating it with ASP.NET Core.

© Bipin Joshi 2019
B. Joshi, *Beginning Database Programming Using ASP.NET Core 3,*
https://doi.org/10.1007/978-1-4842-5509-4_6

Originally, Ajax was an acronym for Asynchronous JavaScript and XML. However, modern web applications prefer JSON over XML as a format of data transfer. Simply put, Ajax is a way of communication between a browser client and a server that utilizes existing technologies such as HTML, XML, JSON, and JavaScript.

Let's briefly understand what an asynchronous communication is in the context of JavaScript. Consider a data entry page that allows you to enter certain data and then submit that data to the server. The data is processed by the server, and the result of the processing is sent back to the browser.

Without Ajax in place, this communication takes this form:

- The user makes an initial request to the data entry page.

- The server sends the requested page to the browser.

- The user fills the data entry form and then sends the data to the server by submitting the form.

- Once the form is submitted, the user can't work with the form anymore because the browser is waiting for the server to send the response.

- The server processes the data and sends some response back to the browser.

- Once the response is rendered in the browser, the user can again interact with the page.

The operation outlined in the preceding text is a synchronous operation because data entry (client-side activity) and data processing (server-side activity) happen one after the other.

Now suppose that the same page is built using Ajax. The sequence of operations in this case would be as follows:

- The user makes an initial request to the data entry page.

- The server sends the requested page to the browser.

- The user fills the data entry form and then sends the data to the server by submitting the form.

- This time the form is submitted using Ajax. Ajax being an asynchronous operation can be performed in the background through JavaScript code.

- User interaction with the page isn't interrupted even if the browser is awaiting response from the server.

- The server processes the data and sends some response back to the browser.

- The browser can notify the user about the response so that further action (if any) can be taken.

Thus, in Ajax communication, user interaction with the page and server processing can occur in parallel. It should be noted that during Ajax communication, you need to choose the data format such as XML or JSON. The Ajax communication outlined in the preceding text is triggered using JavaScript and the XMLHttpRequest object provided by the browser.

The jQuery library wraps its Ajax functionality into a set of methods, the most important being $.ajax(). Other methods depend on the $.ajax() method to get their job done. So you use $.ajax() in the example application built in this chapter.

Note   The example developed in this chapter uses the $.ajax() method of jQuery to accomplish its tasks. To know more about other Ajax methods, consider reading `https://api.jquery.com/category/ajax`.

Create an ASP.NET Core Web Application

The example that you develop in this chapter exists as a EmployeeManager.Jquery project. This project includes the required Web APIs and also the jQuery client that consumes those APIs. The EmployeeManager.Jquery application uses asynchrony at three places:

- The Web API actions now asynchronous in nature.

- The Entity Framework Core code that performs the CRUD operations makes use of asynchronous methods (wherever applicable).

- jQuery client code uses $.ajax() which is asynchronous communication.

In the previous examples, you have been using ASP.NET Core Identity to implement user authentication. In this example, you learn to use the JSON Web Token (JWT)-based authentication system. More details about JWT authentication are available in later sections of this chapter.

You can create and configure the EmployeeManager.Jquery project just like the MVC and Web API projects you created in earlier chapters. Figure 6-1 shows the EmployeeManager.Jquery project loaded in Solution Explorer once it is complete.

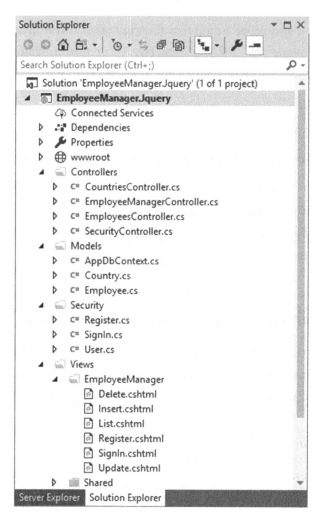

Figure 6-1. *EmployeeManager.Jquery loaded in Solution Explorer*

The overall project organization is quite similar to the previous examples, but there are some differences. For example, the Controllers folder contains API controllers as well as MVC controllers. In the sections that follow, you develop several pieces that make this application with primary focus on Ajax communication. You can get the complete code of this application from this book's code download. For the sake of brevity, steps that you already know (such as EF Core model creation) are not discussed here again.

Note   In the Web APIs that you develop in the next section, the data access code is added directly to the actions. This is done for the sake of brevity and simplicity. Once you finish this application, you can move the data access code to repositories.

Employees Web API and Countries Web API

The EmployeesController and CountriesController represent the Web API classes that perform the CRUD operations. The GetAsync() and GetAsync(id) actions of EmployeesController are shown in Listing 6-1.

Listing 6-1. GetAsync() and GetAsync(id) actions of EmployeesController

```
[HttpGet]
public async Task<IActionResult> GetAsync()
{
    List<Employee> data = await db.Employees.ToListAsync();
    return Ok(data);
}

[HttpGet("{id}")]
public async Task<IActionResult> GetAsync(int id)
{
    Employee emp = await db.Employees.FindAsync(id);
    return Ok(emp);
}
```

The GetAsync() action is marked as an asynchronous action using the async keyword, and it returns a Task<IActionResult>. Inside, the code retrieves all the employees using the ToListAsync() method of IQueryable. As you might have guessed, ToListAsync() is an asynchronous method. Notice that the ToListAsync() line is marked with the await keyword. The List<Employee> is returned to the caller using the Ok() method. The Ok() method returns the OkObjectResult object to the caller and sets the HTTP status code to 200 (Ok). In this case, List<Employee> is also returned to the caller.

The GetAsync(id) action is similar to the GetAsync() action just discussed. However, it returns a Task<Employee> since only one Employee is to be returned. Inside, it uses the FindAsync() asynchronous method to find an Employee with matching EmployeeID. The Employee object is then returned to the caller after wrapping inside the Ok() method.

Note   An API action can return data to the caller in three ways. It can return a concrete type such as a string or Employee. Or it can wrap the data in an implementation of IActionResult. Or it can return ActionResult<T> to the caller. In the previous chapter, you used the first technique. In this chapter, you use the second technique to return data to the jQuery client.

Listing 6-2 shows the PostAsync() action of the EmployeesController that inserts a new employee to the Employees table.

Listing 6-2. PostAsync() action inserts a new employee

```
[HttpPost]
public async Task<IActionResult> PostAsync([FromBody]Employee emp)
{
    if (ModelState.IsValid)
    {
        await db.Employees.AddAsync(emp);
        await db.SaveChangesAsync();
        return CreatedAtAction("Get", new { id = emp.EmployeeID }, emp);
    }
```

```
    else
    {
        return BadRequest();
    }
}
```

The `PostAsync()` action is an asynchronous method and returns the `IActionResult` object wrapped inside a `Task`. The `PostAsync()` action accepts an `Employee` object as its parameter that indicates a new employee to be added to the database.

Notice the code marked in bold letters. The first line uses the `AddAsync()` method to add an employee to the DbSet. Then the code calls the `SaveChangesAsync()` method to persist the changes to the database. Note that `AddAsync()` and `SaveChangesAsync()` are asynchronous methods and hence the respective calls use the `await` keyword.

The `PostAsync()` action returns either a success status code or error status code to the caller. The successful completion of the action is indicated by returning the `CreatedAtActionResult` object using the `CreatedAtAction()` method. The `CreatedAtAction()` method sets HTTP status code to 201 (Created) and also sets the Location HTTP header indicating the URI of the newly created resource. It accepts three parameters: name of an action to use for generating the Location URL, route data to use while generating the URL, and newly created resource. A sample Location URL would be /api/Employees/1234 where 1234 is EmployeeID of a newly created employee.

The error status is returned to the caller using the `BadRequest()` method. The `BadRequest()` method returns `BadRequestObjectResult` to the caller and sets the HTTP status code to 400 (Bad request) indicating that the server can't process the request due to some client error.

Listing 6-3 shows the `PutAsync()` action of the Web API that updates an existing employee.

Listing 6-3. PutAsync() action updates an employee

```
[HttpPut("{id}")]
public async Task<IActionResult> PutAsync(int id, [FromBody]Employee emp)
{
    if (ModelState.IsValid)
    {
        db.Employees.Update(emp);
        await db.SaveChangesAsync();
```

```
        return NoContent();
    }
    else
    {
        return BadRequest();
    }
}
```

This code should look familiar to you since it's quite similar to the PostAsync() action. This time the code uses the Update() method of Employees DbSet to update an employee. The SaveChangesAsync() method then saves the changes to the database.

A successful completion of the action is indicated by returning a NoContentResult object using the NoContent() method. The NoContent() method sets the HTTP status code to 204 (No Content). An error status is returned by calling the BadRequest() method as before.

The DeleteAsync() action of EmployeesController that deletes an employee is shown in Listing 6-4.

Listing 6-4. DeleteAsync() action deletes an employee

```
[HttpDelete("{id}")]
public async Task<IActionResult> DeleteAsync(int id)
{
    Employee emp = await db.Employees.FindAsync(id);
    db.Employees.Remove(emp);
    await db.SaveChangesAsync();
    return NoContent();
}
```

Notice the code marked in bold letters. The DeleteAsync() action first finds an employee to be deleted using the FindAsync() method of Employees DbSet. It then removes that employee from the DbSet using the Remove() method. The SaveChangesAsync() method then deletes the employee from the database. As before, a success status code 204 is returned to the caller by calling the NoContent() method.

This completes the EmployeesController. On the same lines, you can create CountriesController. The CountriesController contains only the GetAsync() action and is shown in Listing 6-5.

Listing 6-5. Returning countries through CountriesController

```
[HttpGet]
public async Task<IActionResult> GetAsync()
{
    List<Country> countries=await db.Countries.ToListAsync();
    return Ok(countries);
}
```

The GetAsync() action is quite straightforward and uses ToListAsync() to realize all the Country entities. The countries are then returned to the caller by wrapping them in the Ok() method.

EmployeeManager Controller

The EmployeeManagerController is quite simple and straightforward. Since actual CRUD calls are initiated from jQuery code, the EmployeeManagerController doesn't have much code. It contains actions that simply return the views to the client. Listing 6-6 shows these actions for your quick reference.

Listing 6-6. EmployeeManagerController contains actions that render views in the browser

```
public IActionResult List()
{
    return View();
}

public IActionResult Insert()
{
    return View();
}

public IActionResult Update(int id)
{
    ViewBag.EmployeeID = id;
    return View();
}
```

```
public IActionResult Delete(int id)
{
    ViewBag.EmployeeID = id;
    return View();
}
```

As you can see, the `List()`, `Insert()`, `Update()`, and `Delete()` actions render the respective views. The `Update()` and `Delete()` actions have an id parameter that is stored in `ViewBag` so that `EmployeeID` can be accessed on the respective views. This **E**mployeeID is required during the Ajax update and delete operations.

Make sure to add views returned by these actions – List.cshtml, Insert.cshtml, Update.cshtml, and Delete.cshtml – into the Views/EmployeeManager folder.

Add a jQuery Library to the Project

In the previous versions of the Employee Manager application, you included a set of jQuery files in the wwwroot\Scripts folder. These files were required for client-side validation of various data entry forms. You added the <script> reference to these files in the _Layout.cshtml file like this:

```
<script src="~/Scripts/jquery.js"></script>
<script src="~/Scripts/jquery.validate.js"></script>
```

In this example, also you need to include those files in the wwwroot\Scripts folder. Especially the core jQuery library (jquery.js) and jQuery validation plugin (jquery.validate.js) are important for us in this chapter's example. Figure 6-2 shows these files placed inside the Scripts folder.

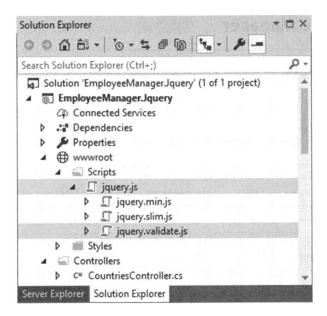

Figure 6-2. *jQuery library and jQuery validation plugin files placed in the wwwroot\Scripts folder*

Since EmployeeManager.Jquery uses jQuery Ajax to invoke the Web API, there will be changes to how the forms are rendered and processed:

- Data entry forms no longer use Tag Helpers or HTML Helpers. They use plain HTML markup.

- The forms are not preloaded with data when they are sent from the server. Instead, the data is loaded from the client-side script.

- Since forms aren't using Tag Helpers/HTML Helpers, data annotation validations aren't used for performing the validations. You need to set the validation rules using the jQuery validation plugin.

- Insert, update, and delete operations are initiated programmatically by capturing the click event of the Save/Delete button.

Display a List of Employees

A list of employees is rendered by the List.cshtml view (Figure 6-3) using jQuery Ajax. jQuery code invokes the GetAsync() action of Employees API and generates the employee listing on the fly.

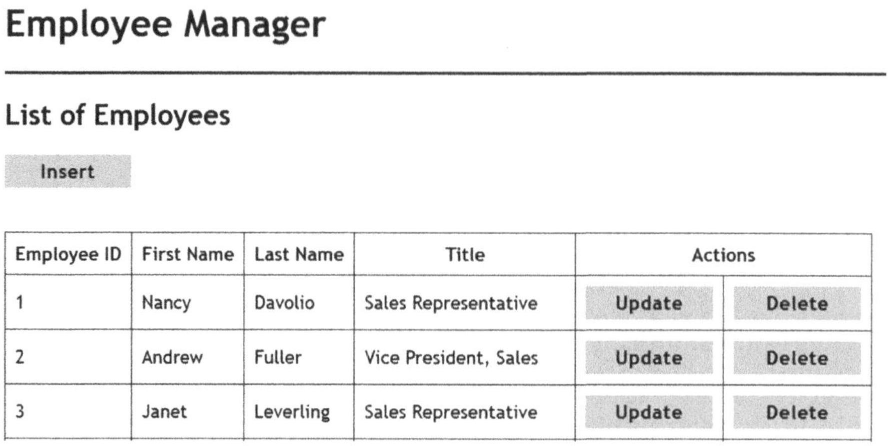

Employee Manager

List of Employees

Insert

Employee ID	First Name	Last Name	Title	Actions	
1	Nancy	Davolio	Sales Representative	Update	Delete
2	Andrew	Fuller	Vice President, Sales	Update	Delete
3	Janet	Leverling	Sales Representative	Update	Delete

Figure 6-3. *Displaying a list of employees*

In order to accomplish this functionality, open the List.cshtml file and add the HTML markup as shown in Listing 6-7.

Listing 6-7. Markup of List.cshtml

```
<h2>List of Employees</h2>

<h3 class="message"></h3>

<a asp-controller="EmployeeManager"
   asp-action="Insert"
   class="linkbutton">Insert</a>

<br /><br />

<table id="employeeList" border="1">
    <tr>
        <th>Employee ID</th>
        <th>First Name</th>
        <th>Last Name</th>
        <th>Title</th>
        <th colspan="2">Actions</th>
    </tr>
</table>
```

This markup is quite straightforward and should look familiar to you. At the top of the page, there is the Insert link rendered using the Anchor Tag Helper. What's more important is the HTML table that follows. The <table> has an id of employeeList. This id is used by the jQuery code while adding various rows to the table. Since rows are added dynamically, even the Update and Delete links are rendered via code.

Now, at the top of List.cshtml (just above the page heading), add a script block as shown in Listing 6-8.

Listing 6-8. jQuery ready() method

```
<script>
    $(document).ready(function () {

    });
</script>
```

In this code, $ refers to the jQuery object. What follows in brackets is called a jQuery selector. Here, it's document selector. There are various types of selectors, and you use some of them in later sections. A jQuery selector returns zero or more DOM elements. Here, the code selects the page's document object and calls the ready() method on it.

The ready() method accepts an anonymous function that will be called once the HTML Document Object Model (DOM) of the page is accessible in the browser. You want to call the Employees API only after the List.cshtml is loaded in the browser so that the employeeList table is accessible. The ready() method helps you ensure this easily.

The jQuery code that actually calls the Employees API goes inside the anonymous function passed to the ready() method and is shown in Listing 6-9.

Listing 6-9. Making Ajax call to the GetAsync() action of Employees API

```
var options = {};
options.url = "/api/employees";
options.type = "GET";
options.dataType = "json";
options.beforeSend = function (request) {
   ...
};
options.success = function (data) {
   ...
};
```

```
options.error = function (xhr) {
  ...
}
$.ajax(options);
```

The code creates a new JavaScript object named `options`. Then a series of properties are set on this `options` object. These properties configure the Ajax call made to the Employees API and are summarized as follows (remember that jQuery, being a JavaScript library, is case sensitive):

- The url property indicates the API endpoint URL. An Ajax request is made to this target URL.

- The type property indicates the HTTP verb to be used to invoke the API. In this case, the GET verb is used since you want to call the GetAsync() action of the API.

- The dataType property indicates the type of data returned from the API. In this case, it's JSON. Other possibilities include XML, HTML, and string.

- The beforeSend property is a callback function that gets invoked just before initiating the Ajax call.

- The success property is a callback function that gets invoked when the API call successfully completes.

- The error property is a callback function that gets called in case the API call fails.

Finally, the code calls the `$.ajax()` method of jQuery to initiate the Ajax call. The options object containing the configuration settings is passed to the `$.ajax()` call as a parameter.

Now, let's discuss the three callback functions mentioned in the code – `beforeSend`, `success`, and `error`. The `beforeSend` callback is quite simple and is shown in Listing 6-10.

Listing 6-10. beforeSend callback function

```
options.beforeSend = function (xhr) {
    $("h3.message").html("Wait...");
};
```

Here, the callback function accepts an object of type jqXHR. The jqXHR is basically a superset of the XMLHttpRequest object. Although the code doesn't make use of the xhr parameter at the moment, you still add it to the signature because you use it while implementing JWT authentication.

Inside, the callback function uses a CSS selector of jQuery and grabs the <h3> element that has message CSS class applied to it. It then sets the HTML content of the <h3> element to a progress message using the html() method. This way a user can be notified that Ajax progress is going on in the background. You could have also used a fancy graphics or animation instead of a text message.

The success function that gets called upon successful completion of the Ajax call is shown in Listing 6-11.

Listing 6-11. Success callback function adds rows to the table

```
options.success = function (data) {
    data.forEach(function (element) {
        var row = "<tr>";
        row += "<td>";
        row += element.employeeID;
        row += "</td>";
        row += "<td>";
        row += element.firstName;
        row += "</td>";
        row += "<td>";
        row += element.lastName;
        row += "</td>";
        row += "<td>";
        row += element.title;
        row += "</td>";
        row += "<td>";
```

```
        row += "<a href='/EmployeeManager/Update/" + element.employeeID +
        "'' class='linkbutton'>Update</a>";
        row += "</td>";
        row += "<td>";
        row += "<a href='/EmployeeManager/Delete/" + element.employeeID +
        "'' class='linkbutton'>Delete</a>";
        row += "</td>";
        row += "</tr>";
        $("#employeeList").append(row);
    });
    $("h3.message").html("");

    if (sessionStorage.hasOwnProperty("message")) {
$("h3.message").html(sessionStorage.getItem("message"));
        sessionStorage.removeItem("message");
    }
};
```

The success function receives the value returned from the API as its parameter. Recollect that the GetAsync() action of the Employees API returns a List of Employee objects. Therefore, the success function receives an array of Employee objects as its parameter.

Inside, the code iterates through the array using its forEach() method. Every iteration forms a table row (<tr> element). Each row contains columns that output employeeID, firstName, lastName, and title of an employee. Notice that server-side property names such as EmployeeID, FirstName, and LastName automatically get converted to their camel-casing equivalent names. This is done because in the JavaScript world camel-casing is quite common and popular.

Note that a table row also contains Update and Delete links. These links point to the Update() and Delete() actions of EmployeeManagerController, respectively. Also note that employeeID is passed to these actions through a route parameter.

Once the HTML markup for a row is created, the row is added to the employeeList table using the append() method. To get hold of the employeeList table, the ID selector of jQuery (# followed by the id of an HTML element) is used. Once the table rows are added, the progress message is cleared by setting its value to an empty string.

Next, during delete operation, the delete page sets a success message into the client-side sessionStorage object. The sessionStorage object is a client-side storage mechanism that allows you to store arbitrary key-value pairs. The sessionStorage object exists as long as the current session lasts. If you close the browser tab or browser window, then all the data from sessionStorage is discarded. The code checks whether the sessionStorage object contains a key named message. This is done using the hasOwnProperty()method. If the message property exists, the hasOwnProperty() method returns true. The message is then retrieved using the getItem() method and is assigned to the <h3> element. The message key is then removed from the sessionStorage using the remove() method.

The error callback function is called in case there is any error while calling the Employees API and is shown in Listing 6-12.

Listing 6-12. Error callback is executed in case the API call fails

```
options.error = function (xhr) {
    $("h3.message").html("Error while calling the API");
}
```

The error callback receives a jqXHR just like the beforeSend callback. Inside, an error message is displayed in the <h3> element so that the user can be notified of the error.

Insert a New Employee

Clicking the Insert link on the employee listing page takes you to another page where you can insert a new employee (Figure 6-4).

Insert New Employee

First Name :

Last Name :

Title :

Birth Date :   mm / dd / yyyy

Hire Date :   mm / dd / yyyy

Country :   Please select ⌄

Notes :

Save

Back to Employee Listing

Figure 6-4. *Inserting a new employee*

The Insert.cshtml uses plain HTML markup to render the data entry form. This markup is shown in Listing 6-13. Note that for the sake of clarity, markup not directly related to the insert operation is omitted from the listing.

Listing 6-13. Markup of Insert.cshtml

```
<h2>Insert New Employee</h2>

<h3 class="message"></h3>

<form id="insertForm">
    <table border="0">
       ...
       <label for="firstName">First Name :</label>
       ...
       <input type="text" id="firstName" name="firstName"/>
       ...
       <label for="lastName">Last Name :</label>
       ...
    <input type="text" id="lastName" name="lastName" />
    ...
```

```
    <label for="title">Title :</label>
    ...
    <input type="text" id="title" name="title"/>
    ...
    <label for="birthDate">Birth Date :</label>
    ...
    <input type="date" id="birthDate" name="birthDate"/>
    ...
    <label for="hireDate">Hire Date :</label>
    ...
    <input type="date" id="hireDate" name="hireDate"/>
    ...
    <label for="country">Country :</label>
    ...
    <select id="country" name="country">
      <option value="">Please select</option>
    </select>
    ...
    <label for="notes">Notes :</label>
    ...
    <textarea id="notes" name="name" rows="5" cols="40">
    </textarea>
      ...
      <button id="save" type="button">Save</button>
      ...
    </table>
</form>
```

The <form> element's id is insertForm. The action and method attributes for the form are not set because the form is not submitted through the traditional HTML way; rather, Ajax call is used to send the data to the server.

Inside, there is a series of form fields for entering various pieces of data. Note that id and name attributes of these elements are set to firstName, lastName, title, birthDate, hireDate, country, and notes, respectively. The id attribute is primarily used by jQuery code, and the name attribute is used while wiring the validation rules using the jQuery validation plugin.

The form validations are configured in the `ready()` callback of jQuery. This code involves setting the validation rules, validation messages, and such tasks. Here, for the sake of simplicity, only the essential configuration is done. You may visit the official web site of the jQuery validation plugin (`https://jqueryvalidation.org`) for more detailed information. The jQuery code that configures the validation is shown in Listing 6-14.

Listing 6-14. Configuring form validation rules

```
$("#insertForm").validate({
    rules: {
        firstName: {
            required: true,
            maxlength: 10
        },
        lastName: {
            required: true,
            maxlength: 20
        },
        title: {
            required: true,
            maxlength: 30
        },
        birthDate: "required",
        hireDate: "required",
        country:"required",
        notes: {
            maxlength: 500
        }
    },
    messages: {
        firstName: "Invalid First Name",
        lastName: "Invalid Last Name",
        title: "Invalid Title",
        birthDate: "Invalid Birth Date",
        hireDate: "Invalid Hire Date",
        country:"Invalid Country",
```

```
        notes: "Invalid Notes"
    },
    errorClass: "message"
});
```

This code initializes the jQuery validation plugin on the insertForm. The insertForm is selected using the ID selector of jQuery (#insertForm), and then the validate() method is called on it passing configuration details. The configuration details are passed through a JavaScript object literal and are summarized as follows:

- There are three main configuration properties used here – rules, messages, and errorClass.

- The rules property holds a set of form fields and validation rules applied to them. For example, validation rules for the firstName input field include required and maxlength. The required property is set to true indicating that the field is required. The maxlength property is set to 10 indicating that a maximum of ten characters can be entered in that field. On the same lines, validation rules for the other form fields are configured.

- The messages property includes a set of validation error messages to be displayed for the form fields. For example, the firstName input field displays Invalid First Name in case any of the validation rules fails.

- The errorClass property indicates a CSS class that is applied to the form fields and error messages in case they contain invalid data.

Instead of specifying validation rules, you could have also specified them in the form of HTML5 attributes. For example, validation rules for firstName could have been specified like this also:

```
<input type="text"
id="firstName"
name="firstName"
maxlength="10" required/>
```

So depending on your requirement and preferred coding style, you can pick one of the ways of specifying the validation rules.

As soon as the Insert.cshtml loads in the browser, you need to initiate an Ajax request to the Countries API to get a list of all the countries. This list is then filled in the Country dropdown list. Listing 6-15 shows how this is done (place this code immediately after initializing the jQuery validation plugin).

Listing 6-15. Filling the Country dropdown list

```
var options = {};
options.url = "/api/countries";
options.type = "GET";
options.dataType = "json";

options.beforeSend = function (request) {
    $("h3.message").html("Wait...");
};

options.success = function (countries) {
  for (var i = 0; i < countries.length; i++) {
      $("#country").append("<option>" + countries[i].name
      + "</option>");
  }
  $("h3.message").html("");
};

options.error = function (xhr) {
    $("h3.message").html("Error while calling the API!");
};

$.ajax(options);
```

This code should look familiar to you since you used similar code in List.cshtml. Here, the code invokes the GetAsync() action of the Countries API by making a GET request. The url and type properties of the options object are set accordingly.

Have a look at the success callback function. It receives a countries array as its parameter because Countries API returns a List of Country objects. Inside, a for loop iterates through the countries array and one by one adds countries to the Country dropdown list. The append() method of jQuery accepts an HTML markup and appends it to the selected element. A <select> element contains <option> child elements, and hence various <option> elements are appended to the Country dropdown list.

The Ajax call is initiated by calling the $.ajax() method of jQuery and passing the options object to it.

When the user fills various form fields and clicks the Save button, you need to invoke the PostAsync() action of the Employees API and save the new employee to the database. This calls for handing click event of the Save button (Listing 6-16).

Listing 6-16. Invoking the PostAsync() action of Employees API

```
$("#save").click(function () {
    if ($("#insertForm").valid()) {
        var options = {};
        options.url = "/api/employees";
        options.type = "POST";

        var obj = {};
        obj.firstName = $("#firstName").val();
        obj.lastName = $("#lastName").val();
        obj.title = $("#title").val();
        obj.birthDate = $("#birthDate").val();
        obj.hireDate = $("#hireDate").val();
        obj.country = $("#country").val();
        obj.notes = $("#notes").val();

        options.data = JSON.stringify(obj);
        options.contentType = "application/json";

        options.beforeSend = function (request) {
            $("h3.message").html("Wait...");
        };
        options.success = function () {
                        $("h3.message").html("Employee inserted successfully!");
                };
        options.error = function (xhr) {
            $("h3.message").html("Error while calling
                            the  API!");
        };
        $.ajax(options);
    }
});
```

The code uses the `click()` method of jQuery to specify a callback function that gets executed when the user clicks the Save button. An Ajax request is to be made only if all the form fields contain valid values. This is checked using the `valid()` method of the jQuery validation plugin. If the form is valid (`valid()` returns true), then the options object is created and its various properties are set.

Since you want to invoke the `PostAsync()` action of the Employees API, the type is set to POST.

While making the POST request, you also need to send the new employee details. These details are filled in a JavaScript object named `obj`. Notice how the values from the form fields are retrieved using the `val()` method. Remember that the property names of obj must match the property names of Employee.

Then the `obj` JavaScript object is converted into its JSON equivalent using the `JSON.stringify()` method. The `JSON.stringify()` method is available in all the modern browsers. It accepts a JavaScript object and converts into its JSON equivalent. The resultant JSON string is assigned to the data property of the options object.

The `contentType` property is used to indicate the content type of the data accompanying the request. Since employee data is being sent in JSON format, the `contentType` is set to application/json.

The `beforeSend` callback function displays a progress message to the user that indicates that an Ajax call is in progress.

The `success` callback function is called if the Web API call is successful, and it displays a success message to the user.

The `error` callback is invoked in case the API call fails and displays an error message to the user.

Finally, the Ajax call is initiated using the `$.ajax()` method of jQuery.

Update an Existing Employee

On the employee listing page, each employee row has Update and Delete links. Clicking the Update link takes you to the update employee page where the existing details of that employee are presented for editing (Figure 6-5).

Update Existing Employee

Employee ID : 1

First Name : Nancy

Last Name : Davollo

Title : Sales Representative

Birth Date : 12 / 08 / 1948 ⊘

Hire Date : 05 / 01 / 1992 ⊘

Country : USA ⌄

Notes : Education includes a BA in psychology from Colorado State University in 1970. She also completed "The Art of the Cold Call." Nancy is a member of Toastmasters International.

Save

Back to Employee Listing

Figure 6-5. *Updating an existing employee*

The Update Existing Employee page looks similar to the Insert New Employee page except that various control values are now filled with the details of the employee being modified. The EmployeeID being the primary key can't be modified.

The Update.cshtml contains a <form> that is quite similar to the preceding section. This time, however, it also embeds the EmployeeID being modified in a hidden form field. This is shown in Listing 6-17.

Listing 6-17. Update.cshtml embeds EmployeeID as a hidden form field

```
<form id="updateForm">
    ...
    <label for="firstName">Employee ID :</label>
    ...
    <span>@ViewBag.EmployeeID</span>
    <input type="hidden" id="employeeID" name="employeeID"
           value="@ViewBag.EmployeeID" />
    ...
</form>
```

As you can see, the updateForm displays the EmployeeID in a <span> element and also stores its value in a hidden form field. Recollect that the Update() action of EmployeeManagerController stores the EmployeeID into ViewBag. The same ViewBag property is being retrieved here and assigned to the hidden form field.

The other form fields of updateForm are quite similar to the earlier form and hence are not discussed here. The process of wiring the form validations and filling the Country dropdown list is exactly the same as before and hence not discussed here again.

Once the Country dropdown list is filled, you need to make an Ajax request to Employees API that invokes the GetAsync(id) action. This is necessary because you need to populate the existing employee details into various form fields so that the user can modify them as required. This Ajax call is shown in Listing 6-18.

Listing 6-18. Filling form fields with existing employee details

```
var options = {};
options.url = "/api/employees/" + $("#employeeID").val();
options.type = "GET";
options.dataType = "json";
options.beforeSend = function (request) {
    $("h3.message").html("Wait...");
};
options.success = function (data) {
 $("#firstName").val(data.firstName);
 $("#lastName").val(data.lastName);
 $("#title").val(data.title);
 $("#birthDate").val(data.birthDate.substring(0, 10));
 $("#hireDate").val(data.hireDate.substring(0, 10));
 $("#country").val(data.country);
 $("#notes").val(data.notes);
 $("h3.message").html("");
};
options.error = function () {
    $("h3.message").html("Error while calling the API!");
};
$.ajax(options);
```

Notice the code shown in bold letters. This time, the `url` property of the options object also includes the `EmployeeID` whose details are to be retrieved. The `EmployeeID` is retrieved from the hidden form field.

The `success` function receives the Employee object whose details are fetched from the server. The code then fills various form fields such as `firstName`, `lastName`, `title`, `birthDate`, `hireDate`, `country`, and `notes` with the details received from the API. Notice the use of the `val()` method to set the form field values. Also notice how the `birthDate` and `hireDate` values are assigned. By default, Web API returns dates in ISO date format: yyyy-MM-ddThh:mm:ss. Since these fields are date fields, the time portion needs to be trimmed before you assign the value to the input field. This is done using the JavaScript `substring()` method (you can also use some other JavaScript technique to get date values in yyyy-MM-dd format). Once the form field values are assigned, the progress message is removed.

The Ajax call is initiated using the `$.ajax()` method as before.

When a user makes changes to the employee details and clicks the Save button, you need to invoke the `PutAsync()` action of the Employees API so that the changes can be saved in the database. This calls for handling the click event of the Save button and is shown in Listing 6-19.

Listing 6-19. Invoking the PutAsync() action of Employees API

```
$("#save").click(function () {
    if ($("#updateForm").valid()) {
        var options = {};
        options.url = "/api/employees/" + $("#employeeID").val();
        options.type = "PUT";

        var obj = {};
        obj.employeeID = parseInt($("#employeeID").val());
        obj.firstName = $("#firstName").val();
        obj.lastName = $("#lastName").val();
        obj.title = $("#title").val();
        obj.birthDate = $("#birthDate").val();
        obj.hireDate = $("#hireDate").val();
        obj.country = $("#country").val();
        obj.notes = $("#notes").val();
```

```
        options.data = JSON.stringify(obj);
        options.contentType = "application/json";

    options.beforeSend = function (request) {
        $("h3.message").html("Wait...");
    };
    options.success = function () {
        $("h3.message").html("Employee updated
                            successfully!");
    };
    options.error = function (xhr) {
        $("h3.message").html("Error while calling
                            the API!");
    };
    $.ajax(options);
    }
});
```

This code is quite similar to the one that inserts a new employee. Notice the code marked in bold letters. This time the url property also includes the EmployeeID. This EmployeeID is supplied to the id parameter of the PutAsync() API action. Also, the HTTP verb specified in the type property is PUT since this is an update operation. Also notice the use of the parseInt() JavaScript method to convert string EmployeeID from the hidden input field to an integer.

Finally, $.ajax() accepts the options object with the configuration settings and initiates the Ajax call.

Delete an Existing Employee

When you click the Delete link for an employee record in the List.cshtml, a confirmation page is shown that warns the user about the employee deletion. Once the user confirms the deletion, the employee gets deleted from the database (Figure 6-6).

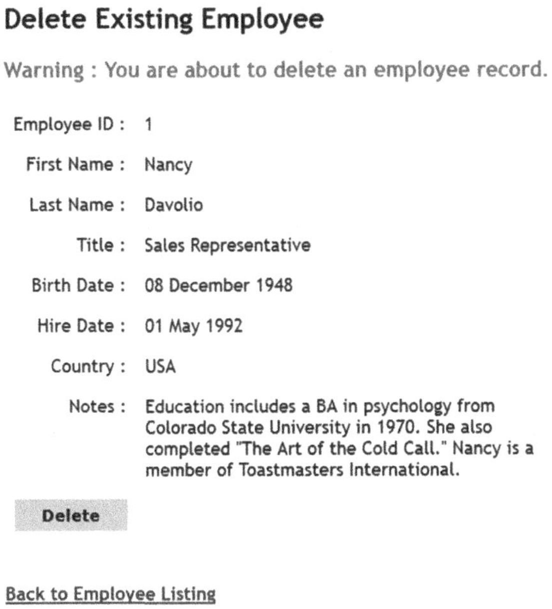

Delete Existing Employee

Warning : You are about to delete an employee record.

Employee ID :   1

First Name :   Nancy

Last Name :   Davolio

Title :   Sales Representative

Birth Date :   08 December 1948

Hire Date :   01 May 1992

Country :   USA

Notes :   Education includes a BA in psychology from Colorado State University in 1970. She also completed "The Art of the Cold Call." Nancy is a member of Toastmasters International.

Delete

Back to Employee Listing

Figure 6-6. *Confirming employee deletion*

When Delete.cshtml is rendered in the browser, you need to make an Ajax call and retrieve employee details for a specific EmployeeID. To display these details, you make use of <span> elements as shown in Listing 6-20. For the sake of clarity, only a part of the whole markup is shown here.

Listing 6-20. Displaying employee details in <span> elements

```
<h2>Delete Existing Employee</h2>
<h3 class="message">
    Warning : You are about to delete an employee record.
</h3>
<form id="deleteForm">
    <table border="0">
        <tr>
            <td class="right">Employee ID :</td>
            <td>
                <span>@ViewBag.EmployeeID</span>
                <input type="hidden"
                       id="employeeID"
```

```
                    name="employeeID"
                    value="@ViewBag.EmployeeID" />
        </td>
    </tr>
    <tr>
        <td class="right">First Name :</td>
        <td><span id="firstName"></span></td>
    </tr>
    <tr>
        <td class="right">Last Name :</td>
        <td><span id="lastName"></span></td>
    </tr>
    ...
    ...
    <tr>
        <td colspan="2">
            <button id="delete" type="button">
              Delete
            </button>
        </td>
    </tr>
    </table>
</form>
```

Recollect that the Delete() action of EmployeeManagerController stores the EmployeeID in ViewBag. That EmployeeID is stored in a hidden input field so that jQuery Ajax code knows which employee is to be deleted. The <span> elements that display employee details have id attributes – firstName, lastName, title, birthDate, hireDate, country, and notes. These <span> elements are assigned the respective values from jQuery code discussed shortly. There is also a Delete button that can be used to initiate the delete operation.

The jQuery code that loads the employee details goes inside the ready() method as before. Listing 6-21 shows how this is done.

Listing 6-21. jQuery code loads employee details from the Employees API

```
var options = {};
options.url = "/api/employees/" + $("#employeeID").val();
options.type = "GET";
options.dataType = "json";
options.beforeSend = function (request) {
    $("h3.message").html("Wait...");
};
options.success = function (data) {
    $("#firstName").html(data.firstName);
    $("#lastName").html(data.lastName);
    $("#title").html(data.title);
    $("#birthDate").html(data.birthDate.substring(0, 10));
    $("#hireDate").html(data.hireDate.substring(0, 10));
    $("#country").html(data.country);
    $("#notes").html(data.notes);
    $("h3.message").html("");
};
options.error = function (xhr) {
    $("h3.message").html("Error while calling the API!");
};
$.ajax(options);
```

The code makes a GET request to the Employees API and passes `EmployeeID` in the URL. This way, the `GetAsync(id)` action of the Employees API is invoked and returns a particular employee. This Employee object is received in the success callback function. Inside the success callback, the code assigns values to various `<span>` elements using the `html()` method.

The `beforeSend` callback and error callback are quite straightforward and are identical to the previous calls.

Finally, the `$.ajax()` method accepts the options object with various configuration settings and initiates the Ajax call.

When the user clicks the Delete button, another Ajax call is made to the server to delete the employee. This requires handling the click event of the Delete button from jQuery code. Listing 6-22 shows how this is done.

Listing 6-22. Deleting an employee by invoking the DeleteAsync() action

```
$("#delete").click(function () {
    var options = {};
    options.url = "/api/employees/" + $("#employeeID").val();
    options.type = "DELETE";
    options.contentType = "application/json";
    options.beforeSend = function (request) {
        $("h3.message").html("Wait...");
    };
    options.success = function () {
        sessionStorage.setItem("message", "Employee deleted
                                        successfully!");
        window.location.href = "/EmployeeManager/List";
    };
    options.error = function (xhr) {
        $("h3.message").html("Error while calling the API!");
    };
    $.ajax(options);
});
```

The click callback function first configures the options object. Note that the type property of the options object is set to DELETE so that the DeleteAsync() action of the Employees API is invoked. Also note that EmployeeID stored in the hidden input field is appended to the URL specified in the url property.

Once the employee is deleted successfully, the success callback is invoked. Inside, a success message is stored in the sessionStorage object's message key. The user is then redirected to the employee listing page. Recollect that List.cshtml shows the success message stored in sessionStorage to the user. Finally, the Ajax call is initiated using the $.ajax() method.

At this stage, your application is ready to perform CRUD operations. You can run the application and check whether all the jQuery Ajax calls are working as expected. In the sections that follow, you integrate the JSON Web Token (JWT)-based authentication scheme into the Employee Manager application.

Overview of the JSON Web Token (JWT)-Based Authentication

In the earlier chapters, you used ASP.NET Core Identity to authenticate and authorize the users. You are aware that ASP.NET Core Identity uses a cookie-based authentication for its functionality. Although cookie-based authentication works great for many applications, there are situations when developers prefer to use alternatives. Consider the following:

- Cookies are transferred between a browser and server automatically as a part of a request-response cycle. This automatic cookie transfer can expose the web application to CSRF/XSRF attacks.

- Automatic sending of cookies by the browser works only for requests belonging to the same origin. That means cross-domain calls can't use the cookie authentication effectively.

- Cookies work primarily for the browser-based clients. Non-browser clients such as mobile apps may not be able to deal with the cookies.

Considering this, an increasing number of modern web applications, especially Single Page Applications (SPAs) and Web APIs, prefer alternatives over the traditional cookie authentication. One such popular alternative is what is known as JSON Web Token or JWT.

What Is JWT?

JWT is an open standard to pass user data between client and server. JWT is more secure and can also be used with non-browser clients. A JWT consists of three parts, namely, header, payload, and signature:

```
header.payload.signature
```

The header part consists of information such as algorithm used to generate the signature and is a JSON object.

The payload part consists of the data or claims to be stored inside the JWT. For example, user ID and roles can go as a part of payload in a JWT.

Based on the header and payload, a cryptographic hash is generated using some algorithm such as HS256 (HMAC with SHA-256). A secret key is used while generating this hash. The resultant hashed data is then appended as the signature part of JWT.

Note   Here, only a simplified version of JWT is presented just to give you a brief understanding of the overall JWT generation process. Discussion of all the encoding and hashing techniques involved is beyond the scope of this book.

Unlike cookies, which are passed automatically by the browser to the server, JWT needs to be explicitly passed to the server. So a simplified flow of operations would be as follows:

- The client sends security credentials such as user name and password to the server for validation.

- The server validates the user name and password.

- If found correct, the server generates and issues a JWT to the client.

- The client receives the token and stores it somewhere.

- While requesting any resource from the server, the client adds the JWT issued earlier in the Authorization header.

- The server reads the Authorization header to retrieve the JWT.

- If the token is valid, the server performs the action requested by the client.

This flow of operations is pictorially shown in Figure 6-7.

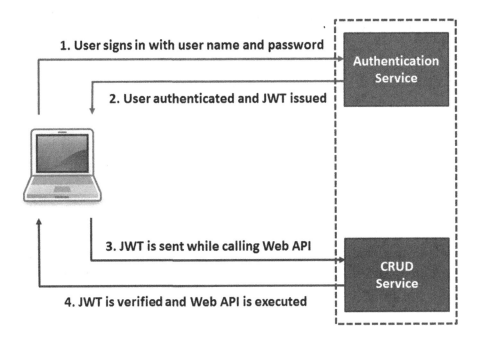

1. User signs in with user name and password

Authentication Service

2. User authenticated and JWT issued

3. JWT is sent while calling Web API

CRUD Service

4. JWT is verified and Web API is executed

Figure 6-7. *JWT authentication flow in a nutshell*

As you can see from the figure, there are three distinct parts – client, authentication service, and CRUD service. A user signs in to the system by sending user name and password to the authentication service. Here, it is assumed that the authentication service and CRUD service are part of the same application. However, the authentication service can also be a third-party service. The authentication service first authenticates the user by validating supplied user name and password. If the details are valid, it creates a JWT and issues it to that user.

The user can now invoke CRUD service (or any other application-specific service). While doing so, the user sends the JWT through the Authorization header. The CRUD service verifies the incoming JWT. If the JWT is valid, it proceeds to invoke the requested operation. The response of the operation is sent back to the user.

As far as Employee Manager is concerned, a JWT is created by SecurityController – a Web API that takes care of user registration and sign-in. The SecurityController is discussed in later sections.

Add Support for JWT Authentication

Now that you are familiar with JWT-based authentication, let's add JWT authentication support to Employee Manager developed earlier in this chapter. In the sections that follow, you add this support in steps, the first step being defining a data store for the user information.

Storing User Details

ASP.NET Core Identity stores user and role details such as UserName, Password, and Email in certain SQL Server tables; and you are familiar with those tables from the examples of previous chapters. Now that you want to use a different authentication scheme (JWT in this case), you also need to decide the data store for these details. In this example, you create a new table in the Northwind database for that purpose. It is a common practice to create three tables, namely, Users, Roles, and UserRoles, to store user details, role details, and user-to-role mapping. However, for the sake of simplicity here, you create just one table named Users with schema as shown in Figure 6-8.

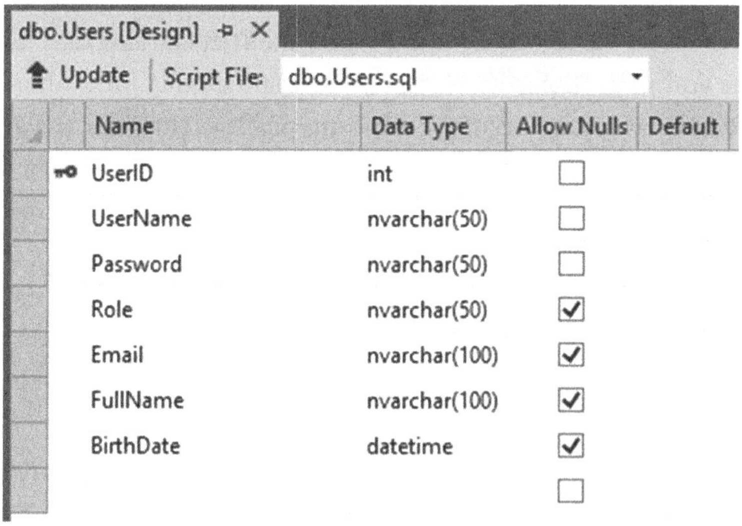

Figure 6-8. *Users table added to the Northwind database*

As you can see, the Users table consists of these columns – UserID, UserName, Password, Email, FullName, BirthDate, and Role. The column names are self-explanatory. The Role column holds a role name assigned to a user. In this example, a user has only one role assigned – Manager. So this simple arrangement works for Employee Manager. Note that all these details are stored as plain text. In a more realistic scenario, you should consider some encryption strategy for storing these details.

Once you add the Users table to the Northwind database, you can create the User entity class that maps to this table. The User class is shown in Listing 6-23.

Listing 6-23. User class maps to the Users table

```
public class User
{
    [DatabaseGenerated(DatabaseGeneratedOption.Identity)]
    [Required]
    [Display(Name ="User ID")]
    public int UserID { get; set; }

    [Required]
    [StringLength(20)]
    [Display(Name = "User Name")]
    public string UserName { get; set; }

    [Required]
    [StringLength(20)]
    [Display(Name = "Password")]
    public string Password { get; set; }

    [Required]
    [Display(Name = "Email")]
    [EmailAddress]
    public string Email { get; set; }

    [Required]
    [Display(Name = "Full Name")]
    public string FullName { get; set; }

    [Required]
    [Display(Name = "Birth Date")]
    public DateTime BirthDate { get; set; }
```

```
[Required]
[StringLength(50)]
[Display(Name = "Role")]
public string Role { get; set; }
}
```

The User class contains several properties such as UserID, UserName, Password, Email, FullName, BirthDate, and Role. These properties map to the columns of the Users table you just created.

Make sure to add Users DbSet to the AppDbContext so that user data can be accessed via EF Core:

```
public class AppDbContext:DbContext
{
    ...
    public DbSet<User> Users { get; set; }
}
```

Enable and Configure JWT Authentication

Now that you created the Users table and User entity class, you are ready to enable JWT authentication for your web application. You do this in the ConfigureServices() method of the Startup class. Before you proceed to ConfigureServices(), however, you need to add this NuGet package – Microsoft.AspNetCore.Authentication.JwtBearer. This package represents an ASP.NET Core middleware that enables JWT authentication features.

Now, add the configuration information shown in Listing 6-24 to appsettings.json.

Listing 6-24. Adding JWT configuration to appsettings.json

```
"Jwt": {
  "Key": "c65decd0-c396-4083-a71e-f8ad42cf7f7d",
  "Issuer": "Employee Manager Security API",
  "Audience": "Employee Manager Client App"
}
```

Here, a configuration section named Jwt is added that contains three keys – Key, Issuer, and Audience. The Key is a secret key that is used to sign a JWT. In this case, a GUID is used just as an example. The Issuer key indicates a string value that represents the issuer of JWT. An issuer is a party that issues JWT. In this example, SecurityController Web API is the issuer. Audience is a party that indicates the intended recipient of a JWT. In this example, the jQuery client is the recipient.

A JWT carries issuer and audience details that can be used while validating it. A JWT issued to one application shouldn't be used with another application. This is ensured using the issuer and audience values. In a more real-world case, you should set these keys to more meaningful values such as URIs indicating the respective parties.

These details (Key, Issuer, and Audience) are used at two distinct places in the code. Firstly, they are used while creating a new JWT. This happens in SecurityController (discussed later). Secondly, these details are used while configuring JWT authentication so that a JWT supplied while calling Employees Web API and Countries Web API can be validated against these details. This happens in the application startup (discussed shortly). These values are stored in appsettings.json to avoid hard-coding them in the source code.

Then open the Startup class and use these namespaces:

```
using Microsoft.AspNetCore.Authentication.JwtBearer;
using Microsoft.IdentityModel.Tokens;
```

Next, go to the ConfigureServices() method and add the configuration shown in Listing 6-25 at the end of the method.

Listing 6-25. Configuring JWT authentication in the ConfigureServices() method

```
public void ConfigureServices(IServiceCollection services)
{
    ...
    ...
    services.AddAuthentication
(JwtBearerDefaults.AuthenticationScheme)
            .AddJwtBearer(options =>
            {
                options.TokenValidationParameters =
                new TokenValidationParameters
```

```
            {
                ClockSkew = TimeSpan.Zero,
                ValidateIssuer = true,
                ValidateAudience = true,
                ValidateLifetime = true,
                ValidateIssuerSigningKey = true,
                ValidIssuer = config["Jwt:Issuer"],
                ValidAudience = config["Jwt:Audience"],
                IssuerSigningKey = new SymmetricSecurityKey(Encoding.
                UTF8.GetBytes(config["Jwt:Key"]))
            };
        });

}
```

The code uses the AddAuthentication() method to specify the authentication scheme to be JwtBearerDefaults.AuthenticationScheme.

Then the AddJwtBearer() method configures various parameters used while validating JWTs. The ValidateIssuer, ValidateAudience, ValidateLifetime, and ValidateIssuerSigningKey properties are set to true indicating that issuer, audience, lifetime, and signing key of a JWT should be validated against the specified values. The values for these pieces of information are supplied via properties – ValidIssuer, ValidAudience, and IssuerSigningKey properties. The lifetime of a JWT is specified at the time of generating it. The values of ValidIssuer, ValidAudience, and IssuerSigningKey are picked from the appsettings.json (read earlier discussion).

Notice that IssuerSigningKey is assigned a SymmetricSecurityKey object. The SymmetricSecurityKey object is constructed by passing the byte array of the secret key stored in the appsettings.json.

Once ConfigureServices() is complete, go to Configure() and call UseAuthentication() and UseAuthorization() methods as you normally do (Listing 6-26).

Listing 6-26. Enabling authentication and authorization

```
public void Configure(IApplicationBuilder app, IWebHostEnvironment env)
{
    ...
    app.UseStaticFiles();
```

```
    app.UseRouting();
        app.UseAuthentication();
        app.UseAuthorization();
    ...
}
```

These methods wire authentication and authorization middleware in the HTTP pipeline.

Create a New User Account

Creating a new user account and signing a user in to the application is done inside SecurityController. The Register() action of SecurityController does this and is shown in Listing 6-27.

Listing 6-27. Register() action of SecurityController creates a new user account

```
[HttpPost]
[Route("[action]")]
public IActionResult Register([FromBody]Register userDetails)
{
    var usr = from u in db.Users
                where u.UserName == userDetails.UserName
                select u;

    if (usr.Count() <= 0)
    {
        var user = new User();
        user.UserName = userDetails.UserName;
        user.Password = userDetails.Password;
        user.Email = userDetails.Email;
        user.FullName = userDetails.FullName;
        user.BirthDate = userDetails.BirthDate;
        user.Role = "Manager";
        db.Users.Add(user);
        db.SaveChanges();
        return Ok("User created successfully.");
    }
```

```
    else
    {
        return BadRequest("UserName already exists.");
    }
}
```

Usually an API action getting invoked is decided by the HTTP verb. The Security API consists of two public actions – Register() and SignIn(). Both of these actions are invoked using a POST request. Therefore, to distinguish between the two requests, they need to be identified through routing. That's what the [Route] attribute added to the Register() action does. Adding the [Route] attribute with [action] token means that the underlying action will be invoked using this URL – /api/Security/Register.

The Register() action receives details about the new user account via the Register model class. The Register model class is identical to the one used in previous chapters and hence not discussed here again.

Inside, the Register() action checks whether a user with the same UserName already exists or not. If the UserName doesn't exist, the code proceeds to creating a new User object and adds it to the Users DbSet. Then SaveChanges() is called to save the user details to the Users database table. Note that the Role property of the User object is set to Manager. Once a user is added to the database, a success message is sent to the caller.

Note   Here, you assigned the Manager role to a user at the time of user registration. In a more realistic case, you will have separate user management and role management pages that allow you to create roles, remove roles, and assign roles to users.

In case the UserName already exists in the database, an error message is sent to the caller.

The Register() action is called from Register.cshtml using jQuery Ajax. For the sake of brevity, the HTML markup of Register.cshtml and jQuery validation plugin configuration are not discussed here. You can grab those pieces from the book's source code. The jQuery Ajax call that invokes the Register() action is shown in Listing 6-28.

Listing 6-28. Invoking the Register() action using jQuery Ajax

```javascript
$("#create").click(function () {

    if ($("#registerForm").valid()) {
        var options = {};
        options.url = "/api/security/register";
        options.type = "POST";

        var obj = {};
        obj.userName = $("#userName").val();
        obj.password = $("#password").val();
        obj.confirmPassword = $("#confirmPassword").val();
        obj.email = $("#email").val();
        obj.fullName = $("#fullName").val();
        obj.birthDate = $("#birthDate").val();

        options.data = JSON.stringify(obj);
        options.contentType = "application/json";
        options.dataType = "text";

        options.success = function (msg) {
            $("h3.message").html(msg);
            $("#userName").val("");
            $("#password").val("");
            $("#confirmPassword").val("");
            $("#email").val("");
            $("#fullName").val("");
            $("#birthDate").val("");
        };
        options.error = function () {
            $("h3.message").html("Error while calling API!");
        };
        $.ajax(options);
    }
});
```

This code should look familiar to you because you used similar code while writing the CRUD operations. The code creates the options object as before. This time the url property of the options object is set to /api/security/register since you want to invoke the Register() action. The type property is set to POST. The user account details such as UserName, Password, Email, FullName, and BirthDate are picked from various form fields and then wrapped in a JavaScript object. The JSON equivalent of that object is set to the data property of the options object. This data is send to the Security API along with the Ajax request.

The success callback receives a success message from the Security API. That message is displayed in the <h3> element, and various form fields are made empty.

Finally, the code initiates an Ajax call using the $.ajax() method.

Signing In to the Application

In order to sign in to the application, a user specifies user name and password on the sign-in page. The sign-in page makes an Ajax request to the SignIn() action of the Security API. The SignIn() action is shown in Listing 6-29.

Listing 6-29. SignIn() action issues a JWT

```
[HttpPost]
[Route("[action]")]
public IActionResult SignIn([FromBody]SignIn loginDetails)
{
    var query = from u in db.Users
                where u.UserName == loginDetails.UserName
                && u.Password == loginDetails.Password
                select u;

    if (query.Count() > 0)
    {
        var tokenString = GenerateJWT(loginDetails.UserName);
        return Ok(new { token = tokenString });
    }
}
```

```
    else
    {
        return Unauthorized();
    }
}
```

The SignIn() action is also decorated with the [Route] attribute just like the Register() action. It accepts a SignIn object that contains a UserName and Password as a parameter. The SignIn class is quite similar to the earlier examples except that it doesn't have the RememberMe property (since cookies aren't used in this example). For the sake of brevity, the SignIn class is not discussed here again.

Inside the SignIn() action, the code checks whether the UserName and Password combination exists in the Users table. If it does exists, then query.Count() is greater than 0; it indicates that the user's sign-in credentials are valid. If user credentials are valid, the code proceeds to generate a new JWT using the GenerateJWT() helper method. The GenerateJWT() method is discussed shortly.

The JWT generated by the GenerateJWT() method is wrapped into a OkObjectResult using the Ok() method. The OkObjectResult returns HTTP status code 200 to the caller along with the specified content (JWT in this case). In this case, content is an anonymous object with token property set to the generated JWT.

If the user validation fails, then the UnauthorizedResult object is returned to the caller using the Unauthorized() method. The UnauthorizedResult object returns HTTP status code 401 to the browser indicating that the user is not authorized to access a resource.

The GenerateJWT() helper method used by the SignIn() action is shown in Listing 6-30.

Listing 6-30. GenerateJWT() method creates a new JWT

```
private string GenerateJWT(string userName)
{
    var usr = (from u in db.Users
               where u.UserName == userName
               select u).SingleOrDefault();

    var claims = new List<Claim>();
    claims.Add(new Claim(ClaimTypes.Name,usr.UserName));
    claims.Add(new Claim(ClaimTypes.Role, usr.Role));
```

```
    var securityKey = new SymmetricSecurityKey(
                    Encoding.UTF8.GetBytes(config["Jwt:Key"]));
    var credentials = new SigningCredentials(
                    securityKey,
                    SecurityAlgorithms.HmacSha256);

    var token = new JwtSecurityToken(
        issuer: config["Jwt:Issuer"],
        audience: config["Jwt:Audience"],
        expires: DateTime.Now.AddHours(12),
        signingCredentials: credentials,
        claims: claims);

    var tokenHandler = new JwtSecurityTokenHandler();
    var stringToken = tokenHandler.WriteToken(token);
    return stringToken;
}
```

The GenerateJWT() method accepts a user name as its parameter. Inside, it fetches a User object containing details of that user. It then creates a List of Claim objects (make sure to use the System.Security.Claims namespace). A claim is a statement about a user. For example, the user's name, email, or role can be treated as a claim made by that user. Here, two Claim objects are added to the list – one that holds UserName and the other that holds Role assigned to the user. Notice that type of the claim being added is specified using the ClaimTypes class.

Then a SymmetricSecurityKey object (Microsoft.IdentityModel.Tokens namespace) is created based on the security Key specified in the configuration file. The SymmetricSecurityKey class represents a key used for cryptographic purposes generated using a symmetric algorithm. Recollect that you used this class earlier in the ConfigureServices() method of the Startup class.

Next, a SigningCredentials object (Microsoft.IdentityModel.Tokens namespace) is created by passing the security key created earlier and security algorithm to be used. In this case, HmacSha256 algorithm is used. Based on these details, the SigningCredentials object can generate a digital signature used to sign a JWT.

Then a new JwtSecurityToken object is created. The JwtSecurityToken class represents a JWT, and several pieces of information are supplied in its constructor.

The issuer parameter indicates an issuer of this JWT, and its value is picked from the configuration file. The audience parameter indicates the intended recipient or audience of this JWT, and its value is picked from the configuration file. The expires parameter indicates a DateTime at which the JWT being created is considered expired. In this case, the expiry is set to 12 hours, but you can change this value as per your requirement. The signingCredentials parameter indicates a SigningCredentials object that is used to digitally sign the JWT being created. The claims parameter indicates a list of claims belonging to this JWT.

Then an object of JwtSecurityTokenHandler class is created. The JwtSecurityTokenHandler class is used for creating and validating JWTs. The WriteToken() method of JwtSecurityTokenHandler accepts the JwtSecurityToken object created earlier and creates a string representing the JWT. Finally, the string token is returned to the caller (SignIn() action in this case).

Now that you know how a JWT is created and issued from the Security API, let's discuss the jQuery Ajax code that invokes the SignIn() action of the Security API. For the sake of brevity, the HTML markup and configuration of the validation rules are not discussed here. The click event handler of the Sign In button that contains the necessary jQuery Ajax code is shown in Listing 6-31.

Listing 6-31. Invoking the SignIn() action and storing JWT on the client side

```
$("#signin").click(function () {
    if ($("#signinForm").valid()) {
        var options = {};
        options.url = "/api/security/signin";
        options.type = "POST";

        var obj = {};
        obj.userName = $("#userName").val();
        obj.password = $("#password").val();

        options.data = JSON.stringify(obj);
        options.contentType = "application/json";
        options.dataType = "json";
```

```
            options.success = function (obj) {
                sessionStorage.setItem("token", obj.token);
                sessionStorage.setItem("userName", $("#userName").
                val());
                window.location.href = "/EmployeeManager/List";
            };
        options.error = function () {
            $("h3.message").html("Unable to Sign-in");
        };
        $.ajax(options);
    }
});
```

This code should look familiar to you because you used similar code many times earlier in this chapter. Note that the `url` property of the options object points to the `SignIn()` action. The user name and password entered by a user are wrapped in the `obj` JavaScript object and are sent along with the `POST` request.

Notice the code marked in bold letters. It shows the `success` callback that gets executed upon successful API call. The `success` callback receives an object containing the JWT issued by the `SignIn()` action. The JWT is saved in the `sessionStorage` object of the browser with a key name of `token`. The user's sign-in name is also stored in the `username` key of the sessionStorage. This way the JWT issued by the server is stored on the client machine. You can use this persisted JWT while making calls to the Employees API (discussed later).

Once the JWT and user name are stored in the `sessionStorage`, the user is redirected to the /EmployeeManager/List so that the employee listing page can be rendered. This is done using the `window.location.href` property.

Note   Here, you use the sessionStorage object to persist the JWT issued by the server. The sessionStorage is emptied when you close the browser window or tab. And you will be required to get another token the next time you access the application. If you want, you can also store the token in the localStorage object which is remembered across browser sessions.

If there is an error during the signing-in operation, `error` callback is invoked that displays an error message to the user.

Signing Out of the Application

Signing out of the application requires you to remove the JWT stored in the sessionStorage object. jQuery code that does that resides in the layout file (Layout. cshtml). Have a look at Listing 6-32 that shows a fragment of the _Layout.cshtml

Listing 6-32. Displaying user name and the Sign Out button

```
<h2 id="userName"></h2>
<form id="signoutForm">
    <button id="signout" type="button">Sign Out</button>
</form>
```

The markup shows an <h2> element with id of userName and a <form> element with id of signoutForm. The signoutForm contains the signout button. The userName element is used to display the user's name who is currently signed in to the application, whereas clicking the signout button removes the JWT stored in the sessionStorage.

Listing 6-33 shows how these elements are used by the jQuery code.

Listing 6-33. jQuery code for showing user name and signing the user out of the application

```
$(document).ready(function () {
    if (sessionStorage.hasOwnProperty("userName")) {
        $("#userName").html("You are signed in as " + sessionStorage.
        getItem("userName"));
    }
    else {
        $("#signoutForm").hide();
    }

    $("#signout").click(function () {
        sessionStorage.removeItem("token");
        sessionStorage.removeItem("userName");
        window.location.href = "/EmployeeManager/SignIn";
    });
});
```

When any page is displayed in the browser, the code from the ready() method is executed. The code checks whether the sessionStorage object contains the userName key. If it contains the userName key, it indicates that some user is currently signed in to the application. So the code shows the user name in the <h2> element. If the userName key doesn't exist, it indicates that no user is currently signed in to the application, and hence the signoutForm is kept hidden.

The click event handler of the signout button removes token and userName keys from the sessionStorage object. The user is redirected to the sign-in page by setting the window.location.href property to /EmployeeManager/SignIn.

Enforce Authentication on All Pages

Now that sign-in and sign-out operations are complete, you can proceed to secure the Employees API and pages doing the CRUD operations.

Open Employees API and decorate the controller class with the [Authorize] attribute:

```
[Route("api/[controller]")]
[Authorize(Roles = "Manager")]
public class EmployeesController : ControllerBase
{
    ...
}
```

As you can see, the usage of the [Authorize] attribute is identical to the previous examples even though this time you are using JWT authentication. The only difference is EmployeesController is an API controller class. When you add the [Authorize] attribute, the Employees API will allow only the authorized users to invoke its actions.

Since the Employees API now requires JWT authentication, you should send the JWT stored in the sessionStorage while making the Ajax calls. Listing 6-34 shows part of List. cshtml illustrating how this can be done.

Listing 6-34. Sending JWT from client to the server

```
$(document).ready(function () {

    if (!sessionStorage.hasOwnProperty("token")) {
         window.location.href = "/EmployeeManager/SignIn";
      }
```

```
...
    options.beforeSend = function (xhr) {
        xhr.setRequestHeader("Authorization",
                "Bearer " + sessionStorage.getItem("token"));
        $("h3.message").html("Wait...");
    };
...
```

Notice the code shown in bold letters. When a page is loaded in the browser, the code checks whether JWT is stored in the sessionStorage or not. This is done by checking the existence of the token key in the sessionStorage. If no JWT exists, then the user is redirected to the sign-in page.

The beforeSend callback sets the Authorization HTTP header before making an Ajax request. This is done using the setRequestHeader() method of the jqXHR object. The Authorization header contains the credentials to authenticate a user with the server. Here, you want to send a JWT bearer token to the server. So the value of the Authorization header is a string – Bearer followed by the actual JWT from the sessionStorage.

If a request doesn't contain the JWT or the token has expired or the token is invalid, then the Employees API returns HTTP status code 401 (Unauthorized). You need to check this code in the error callback as shown in Listing 6-35.

Listing 6-35. Employees API returns 401 – Unauthorized status code if JWT is invalid

```
options.error = function (xhr) {
        if (xhr.status == 401) {
            window.location.href = "/EmployeeManager/SignIn";
        }
    $("h3.message").html("Error while calling the API");
}
```

The status property of the jqXHR object indicates the HTTP status code returned from the server. If it's 401 (Unauthorized), then the user is redirected to the sign-in page.

Make sure to add the code discussed in the preceding text in all the pages participating in the CRUD operations.

This completes the Employee Manager application that uses jQuery Ajax. Verify whether user registration, sign-in, and sign-out operations are working as expected along with the CRUD operations.

Summary

In this chapter, you created the Employee Manager application using ASP.NET Core MVC, Web API, and jQuery Ajax. You learned how a Web API can be invoked using jQuery's $.ajax() method. You programmed the CRUD operations using jQuery Ajax and then implemented JWT-based authentication.

JWT authentication is a popular authentication scheme when it comes to securing APIs and SPAs. You learned to configure and generate JWT using .NET Core classes. You also learned to store and send a JWT issued by the server using client-side script.

Although the example discussed in this chapter makes heavy use of jQuery Ajax, it isn't a Single Page Application (SPA). In the next chapter, you develop Employee Manager as a SPA using ASP.NET Core and Angular.

CHAPTER 7

Angular

In this chapter you develop the Employee Manager application as an Angular SPA (Single Page Application). Angular is a JavaScript framework that allows you to build rich client applications and provides many features such as components, directives, data binding, form processing, services, and dependency injection. Angular applications are written using TypeScript, a superset of JavaScript. TypeScript is a typed language and provides many object-oriented features such as classes, interfaces, and data types. TypeScript code is compiled (often called Transpilation) into plain JavaScript so that it can be used by any browser.

Employee Manager that you develop in this chapter exposes its CRUD functionality using ASP.NET Core Web APIs. User authentication is also done using Web API and JWT. An Angular front-end utilizes those Web APIs using Angular's HttpClient. Specifically, this chapter teaches you to

- Build SPA using Angular

- Utilize ASP.NET Core Web APIs using Angular's HttpClient class

- Use Angular Command Line Interface (CLI) to create Angular applications, components, and services

- Validate and process forms using Angular's reactive forms (also called Model Driven Forms)

- Integrate ASP.NET Core's JWT authentication scheme with the Angular application

Let's get started.

© Bipin Joshi 2019
B. Joshi, *Beginning Database Programming Using ASP.NET Core 3*,
https://doi.org/10.1007/978-1-4842-5509-4_7

> **Note**   This chapter assumes that you have basic familiarity with Angular and TypeScript. Although Angular features used by the sample application are discussed as and when they are encountered, this chapter doesn't attempt to teach you the basics of Angular. You may consider reading the Angular official documentation at `https://angular.io` and TypeScript official documentation at `www.typescriptlang.org` for more details. This chapter also assumes that you have installed Node.js and Angular CLI on your development machine. Read the Angular official web site for more details.

Overview of the Project Structure

The Employee Manager application that you build in this chapter is divided into two applications for the sake of development. The first application is an ASP.NET Core API application that hosts Web APIs used by Employee Manager. That means Employees API, Countries API, and Security API are part of this application. These Web APIs are identical to the ones that you built in the previous chapter, and hence they are not discussed here again.

The second application is an Angular application that represents the front-end to the Web APIs. It contains various pieces of the Angular application such as classes, components, and services.

During development, the ASP.NET Core application and the Angular application exist as two independent projects. Therefore, communication between them is cross-domain communication. Since by default browsers prohibit cross-domain calls, you need to enable CORS (Cross Origin Resource Sharing) in the ASP.NET Core application.

> **Note**   Communication is said to be cross-domain if the origin of the two parties taking part in the communication is not the same. An origin consists of a scheme, a host, and a port. To accept requests from different origins, the web server should be configured to have the Access-Control-Allow-Origin HTTP header. You may read more about CORS at `https://docs.microsoft.com/en-us/aspnet/core/security/cors`.

Once the development is over, the resultant Angular application becomes a part of the ASP.NET Core application and hence doesn't need CORS enabled. Figure 7-1 shows the overall arrangement of the ASP.NET Core project containing the Web APIs.

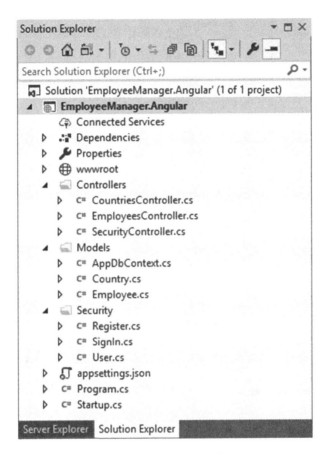

Figure 7-1. *ASP.NET Core project containing Web APIs*

As you can see, most of the pieces of the EmployeeManager.Angular project are identical to the EmployeeManager.Jquery project you developed in the previous chapter. Here, there is no Views folder because the application's user interface is provided by Angular. Also notice that EF Core model and associated classes are identical to the EmployeeManager.Jquery project. You can get the completed EmployeeManager. Angular from this chapter's source code download.

Figure 7-2 shows the Angular SPA that represents the front-end of Employee Manager.

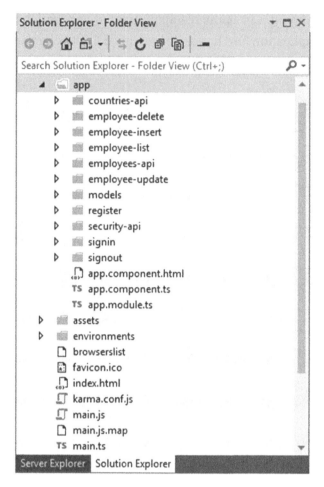

Figure 7-2. *Angular application provides the front-end of Employee Manager*

Note   Simply put, a Single Page Application or SPA generates its user interface on the fly by rewriting the current page instead of fetching different pages from the web server. Such an application can also provide additional features such as client-side routing. So the application appears to be "navigating" between pages, but in reality it is just rendering different parts of the UI on the same page.

You can see from the figure that Angular code files are organized in several subfolders under the app folder (the project root folder is named EmployeeManager AngularApp, but you could name it anything of your choice). You will know about various parts that make the front-end in due course of time. For now just try to acquaint yourself with the overall project structure. You can also grab the complete source of this Angular application from the book's source code.

Once the Angular application is complete, it is compiled to produce plain JavaScript code. The resultant JavaScript code is then placed inside the wwwroot folder of the EmployeeManager.Angular project. This is shown in Figure 7-3.

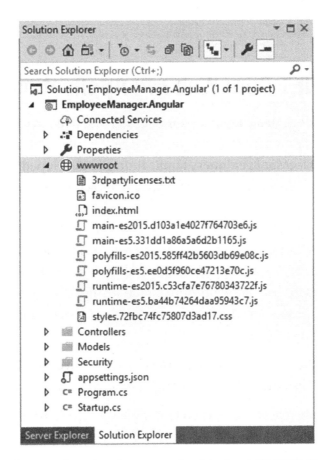

Figure 7-3. *Angular application integrated with the ASP.NET Core application*

So once the development is complete, you can run and deploy Employee Manager as a single ASP.NET Core application. The Index.html seen inside the wwwroot folder is the launching page of the Angular SPA.

> **Note**   Visual Studio also provides a project template for creating Angular applications. However, you won't use it in this book. Dealing with the Angular application independently of the ASP.NET Core application allows you to clearly understand how an Angular application works and how it can be integrated into an ASP.NET Core application. Once you know these details, you can easily use the Visual Studio Angular project template to build Angular applications.

Create ASP.NET Core Web API Application

In order to work through this chapter's example, you first need to create an ASP.NET Core Web API application named EmployeeManager.Angular. This application is quite similar to the EmployeeManager.Jquery application you developed in the previous chapter. So, you can utilize that code base while creating the EmployeeManager. Angular project.

The EmployeeManager.Angular application serves three Web APIs, namely, EmployeesController, CountriesController, and SecurityController. Additionally it also contains EF Core model classes (AppDbContext, Employee, and Country classes) and view models required for user authentication functionality (User, Register, and SignIn classes). Since these classes are identical to the previous example, they are not discussed here again. Note, however, that

- The EmployeeManager.Angular project doesn't have the Views folder because UI is rendered using an Angular application

- For the same reason, there is no EmployeeManagerController class in the Controllers folder

- The wwwroot folder can be made empty because jQuery files and style sheet files are not required in this project

- Since the Web APIs are to be made available to an independent Angular application, CORS must be enabled in the Web API project

If you wish, you can simply grab the EmployeeManager.Angular project from this chapter's code download and run it as discussed in the following.

Enabling CORS in Web API Project

To enable CORS in the EmployeeManager.Angular application, go to the Startup class and add this line to the `ConfigureServices()` method:

```
public void ConfigureServices(IServiceCollection services)
{
    services.AddCors();

    ...
}
```

The `AddCors()` method adds CORS services to the `IServiceCollection`. Further, go to the `Configure()` method and add the code shown in Listing 7-1.

Listing 7-1. Configuring CORS midleware

```
public void Configure(IApplicationBuilder app, IWebHostEnvironment env)
{
    ...
    app.UseCors(builder => builder
            .AllowAnyOrigin()
            .AllowAnyMethod()
            .AllowAnyHeader());
    ...
}
```

The `UseCors()` method wires the CORS middleware to the HTTP pipeline. It also configures a CORS policy by specifying three settings:

- AllowAnyOrigin() means an external request from any origin is allowed to access resources of this application.

- AllowAnyMethod() means any HTTP method (GET, POST, etc.) can be used to make a request.

- AllowAnyHeader() means that any HTTP headers are allowed.

> **Note**   Here you granted Web API access to any external request. However, in a more realistic case, you should ensure that only specific origins and specific HTTP methods are allowed to access the Web API. Detailed discussion of CORS and CORS policies is beyond the scope of this book. You may read more about CORS in ASP.NET Core at `https://docs.microsoft.com/en-us/aspnet/core/security/cors`.

The code discussed in the preceding text should be used only during development. Once you integrate the Angular application with the ASP.NET Core application, you should remove this code.

Running Web API Application

Once the Web APIs are ready in the EmployeeManager.Angular application, they need to be made available to the Angular application being developed in later sections. Normally, you run a web application from within Visual Studio so that you can debug and test it. Here, you would use another approach to run the application since the Web APIs are already ready.

Locate the Visual Studio program group and click the Developer Command Prompt entry. This will open a console window. Change the working folder to the EmployeeManager.Angular project root folder and issue this command:

```
> dotnet run
```

Here, you are using .NET Core Command Line Interface (CLI) to run the application. Once you issue this command, your console window should resemble Figure 7-4.

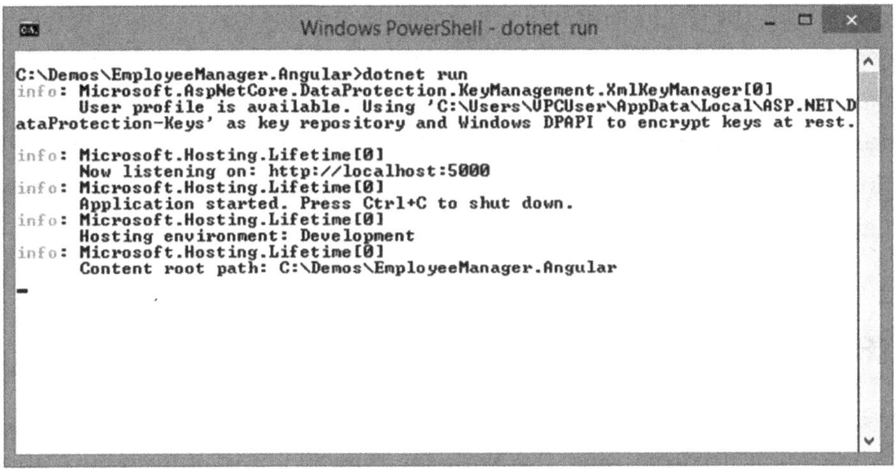

Figure 7-4. Running the Web API project using .NET Core CLI

Notice that the Web API application is now available at http://localhost:5000 (this URL might be different depending on your project setup). If you wish to check whether the Web APIs are available or not, just comment out the [Authorize] attribute added to them, and then run the project as mentioned in the preceding text. You can then try accessing them using a browser. Figure 7-5 shows a browser accessing the Employees API.

Figure 7-5. Accessing Employees Web API using browser

As you can see, the `Get()` action of the Employees API is invoked, and list of employees is returned to the browser. Before going further make sure to uncomment the [`Authorize`] attribute and then run the application again. You can either keep this application running in the background as you begin developing the Angular application, or you can run it as and when needed by the Angular application. You can terminate the Web API application by pressing Ctrl + C.

Create Angular Application

Now that EmployeeManager.Angular project is ready, you can proceed to create an Angular application. To do so, open the Node.js command prompt from the Node.js program group. Go to a folder where you want to place the newly created Angular application. To create an Angular application, issue this Angular CLI command at the command prompt:

```
> ng new EmployeeManagerAngularApp
```

Upon issuing this command, you will be asked whether you like to add Angular routing or not. Enter Y because you want to implement client-side routing to the application and press the enter key. You will then be asked which style sheet format would you like to use. Select CSS (default) from the list and press the enter key. The project creation starts and a new Angular application gets created in the EmployeeManagerAngularApp folder.

Once you are notified about the project creation, go inside the EmployeeManager AngularApp folder and issue this command at the command prompt:

```
> ng serve --open
```

This command builds the Angular application and also starts listening at `http://localhost:4200`. The --open switch opens the default browser and launches the URL just mentioned. To terminate the Angular application, you can press Ctrl + C. Figure 7-6 shows how the newly created Angular application looks in the browser.

Figure 7-6. *Newly created Angular application launched in browser*

Before beginning the Angular application development, it is worthwhile to note that the ASP.NET Core Web API application is available at `http://localhost:5000` and the Angular application is available at `http://localhost:4200`. Thus communication between them is going to be a cross-domain communication and will require CORS enabled in the Web API application (see earlier section on enabling CORS).

Angular Application Architecture

Now that you have created an Angular application, it would be worthwhile to briefly understand the overall architecture of an Angular application. Rather than discussing each and every piece of an Angular application, here you will focus on the parts that you are going to utilize in the EmployeeManagerAngularApp application.

An Angular application consists of one or more modules or NgModules. A module wraps related functionality together. At a minimum, an application has what is known as a root module. You can also have additional modules called feature modules (they are optional). NgModules can import functionality from other NgModules. They can also export their own functionality to other NgModules. The root module is responsible for loading the application (often called bootstrapping). If you look at the code files created during the application creation, the app.module.ts contains the root module named AppModule.

An Angular application contains one or more components. A component deals with a part of the user interface. A component consists of a view and associated data and logic. A view is an HTML file that typically contains HTML markup and data binding code. The data needed by a view can be bundled into model classes. At a minimum, an Angular application needs to have one component. The app.component.ts file contains a default component named AppComponent.

An Angular application can contain many views (provided by different components of the application). You can "navigate" through these views using Angular's routing service. The router can define client-side routes and associated navigational features.

In a typical Angular application, you would also want to isolate reusable pieces of code into one or more services. This way your application's code base can be made modular, reusable, and maintainable. A service is injected into components through Angular's dependency injection system.

At code level, the building blocks mentioned in the preceding text – NgModules, components, and services – exist as TypeScript classes. These classes are decorated with what is known as decorators that provide metadata information about the class under consideration. For example, NgModule classes are decorated with the @NgModule() decorator, component classes are decorated with the @Component() decorator, and service classes are decorated with the @Injectable() decorator.

Editing Angular Project Files in Visual Studio

Angular project files can be edited using any text editor of your choice. However, here you use Visual Studio to do so. Some other popular applications for working with Angular projects include Visual Studio Code, WebStorm, Atom, and Sublime Text.

To open the Angular project that is just created in Visual Studio, click the File ➤ Open ➤ Folder menu option. Then select the EmployeeManagerAngularApp folder in the Select Folder dialog and click Select Folder button. This opens the selected folder in Visual Studio and your Solution Explorer looks as shown in Figure 7-7.

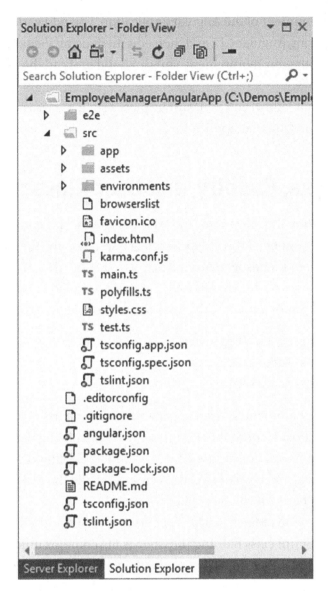

Figure 7-7. *EmployeeManagerAngularApp folder opened in Visual Studio*

Out of all the folders and files shown in Solution Explorer, files under the EmployeeManagerAngularApp ➤ src ➤ app folder are more important to you because they represent your application's code. Many of the other files are used by Angular internally, and you don't need to change them in any way.

During the development of the Angular application, you add various parts needed by the application using Angular CLI and then edit them using Visual Studio IDE. Once you edit the files as per your requirement, you can build and run the application using Angular CLI.

In the sections that follow, you add various pieces such as classes, components, and services that make your Angular application.

Add Employee, Country, and User Classes

The Angular application that consumes the Web APIs deals with employees, countries, and users. Therefore, you need three TypeScript classes, namely, Employee, Country, and User, that represent the respective entities.

You add these classes to the Models folder and use Angular CLI to create them. Go to Node.js Command Prompt and issue these commands one after the other:

```
> ng generate class models/Employee
> ng generate class models/Country
> ng generate class models/User
```

The ng generate command is used to generate various parts of an Angular application such as classes, components, and services. Specifying the class option indicates that you want to create a class. The class option is followed by path and name of the class. In this case, the Employee class is created inside the Models folder. If the Models folder doesn't exist, it will be created for you.

Issuing this command creates two files per class – *.ts file and *.spec.ts file. The .ts file is the main TypeScript class file, and the .spec.ts file contains unit tests for your code. You won't use the .spec.ts files in this book, and they can even be deleted to reduce the clutter from the folder.

Next, open the Employee class (Employee.ts) in Visual Studio and modify it as shown in Listing 7-2.

Listing 7-2. Employee TypeScript class

```
export class Employee {
  employeeID: number;
  firstName: string;
  lastName: string;
```

```
  title: string;
  birthDate: Date;
  hireDate: Date;
  country: string;
  notes: string;
}
```

The export keyword indicates that the class under consideration can be accessed from other parts of your application. The class keyword followed by a class name indicates the class you wish to create (Employee in this case).

The Employee class consists of several members such as employeeID, firstName, lastName, title, birthDate, hireDate, country, and notes. Note that these member names correspond to the server-side Employee class property names. That's because you need to transport data between Angular application and the ASP.NET Core application through these properties. Also note that these members have data types such as number, string, and Date.

Note   In a TypeScript class, members are public by default. You can explicitly use public or private access modifiers if you want.

On the same lines, you can create Country and User classes. These classes are shown in Listing 7-3.

Listing 7-3. Country and User TypeScript classes

```
export class Country {
  countryID: number;
  name: string;
}

export class User {
  userName: string;
  password: string;
  email: string;
  fullName: string;
  birthDate: Date;
}
```

Add Service to Invoke Employees Web API

To invoke the Web APIs, you use Angular's HttpClient class. Rather than writing the HttpClient-related code at several places, it would be better if you isolate it in one place. You can then reuse that code wherever you want in the application.

You can accomplish this by creating an Angular service. Once created, an Angular service can be injected into other parts of your application. A service exposes certain reusable functionality and doesn't contain any user interface elements.

In this section you create EmployeesApi service that helps you invoke various actions of the Employees Web API. To create this service, go to the Node.js command prompt and issue this command:

```
> ng generate service employees-api/EmployeesApi
```

The preceding command creates a service EmployeesApiService (the Service suffix is automatically added to the name you specify) under the employees-api folder. The service physically exists in the employees-api.service.ts file. If you open this file, you will see the code shown in Listing 7-4.

Listing 7-4. Newly created EmployeesApiService class

```
import { Injectable } from '@angular/core';

@Injectable({
  providedIn: 'root'
})
export class EmployeesApiService {
  constructor() { }
}
```

The `import` statement at the top indicates that you wish to use the `Injectable` symbol from the `@angular/core` package. The `EmployeesApiService` class is decorated with `@Injectable()` decorator. Using the `@Injectable()` decorator means that the underlying class can be injected by Angular's dependency injection system.

The `@Injectable()` decorator accepts a metadata object. In this case, the `providedIn` property of the metadata object is set to `root` indicating that you want to provide the service under consideration at the application's root level. This means Angular will create one shared instance of the service under consideration and will inject it into a component that requests the service.

The EmployeesApiService class also has an empty constructor. The constructor can be used to initialize the service and is similar to C# constructor.

Now let's modify the EmployeesApiService so that it invokes the Employees Web API using Angular's HttpClient class.

Go to the top of the .ts file and add these two import statements:

```
import { HttpClient, HttpHeaders } from '@angular/common/http';
import { Employee } from '../models/employee';
```

The first import statement indicates that you want to use HttpClient class and HttpHeaders class from the specified Angular package. The second import statement indicates that you want to use Employee model class residing in the specified .ts file (you created this class earlier in the previous section).

Then go to the EmployeesApiService class and declare a couple of members and also define the constructor as shown in Listing 7-5.

Listing 7-5. HttpClient injected into the constructor

```
baseUrl: string = 'http://localhost:5000/api/employees';
client: HttpClient;

constructor(client: HttpClient) {
  this.client = client;
}
```

The code first declares baseUrl member that holds the URL where Employees Web API is located. Recollect that dotnet run command made the Web API available at the specified URL and port.

Then a member of type HttpClient is declared that holds an instance of HttpClient class. The HttpClient class is injected into the constructor as shown. The HttpClient class allows you to make HTTP requests to a web resource such as a Web API. You will find this constructor injection mechanism quite similar to ASP.NET Core's constructor injection.

Next, add a method called selectAll() that is intended to invoke the Get() action of the Employees Web API (Listing 7-6).

Listing 7-6. selectAll() method invokes the Get() action of Employees Web API

```
selectAll() {
  return this.client.get(this.baseUrl, {
    headers: new HttpHeaders({
      "Authorization": "Bearer " + sessionStorage.getItem('token')
    })
  });
}
```

The `selectAll()` method calls the `get()` method of the `HttpClient` class. The `get()` method makes a GET request to the specified resource. In this case the resource is the Employees Web API. Since the Employees Web API is protected with JWT authentication, the code also passes the JWT issued and stored in the `sessionStorage` object when the user signs in to the system. The JWT is passed to the server as a part of the Authorization header. The Authorization header is wrapped inside the `HttpHeaders` object and passed in the headers parameter of `get()` method.

The `get()` method of `HttpClient` returns what is known as an `Observable`. An observable uses publisher-subscriber pattern for sending one or more values to its subscribers. So the observable publishes the values, and subscribers interested in receiving the values subscribe to it. Here, a list of employees is published to the subscribers. It should be noted that an observable executes only if it has at least one subscriber. In this example, the Angular component displaying a list of employees acts as the subscriber to the observable.

Note   Detailed discussion of observables is beyond the scope of this book. You may read more about observables at `https://angular.io/guide/observables`.

The `selectByID()` method is similar to the `selectAll()` method and is shown in Listing 7-7.

Listing 7-7. selectByID() invokes the Get(id) action of Employees Web API

```
selectByID(id: number) {
  return this.client.get(this.baseUrl + "/" + id, {
    headers: new HttpHeaders({
      "Authorization": "Bearer " + sessionStorage.getItem('token')
    })
  });
}
```

The selectByID() method accepts a numeric id parameter indicating an EmployeeID whose data is to be retrieved. Inside, the code calls the get() method of HttpClient as before. But this time the id is appended in the URL so that Get(id) action of the Employees Web API is invoked.

To make a POST request to the Employees Web API, you need to add the insert() method as shown in Listing 7-8.

Listing 7-8. insert() method makes a POST request to Employees Web API

```
insert(emp: Employee) {
  return this.client.post(this.baseUrl, emp, {
    headers: new HttpHeaders({
      "Authorization": "Bearer " + sessionStorage.getItem('token'),
      "Content-Type": "application/json"
    })
  });
}
```

The insert() method accepts a parameter of type Employee that represents a new employee to be added to the database. Inside, the code calls post() method of HttpClient to make a POST request to the Employees Web API. In addition to the URL and HttpHeaders, the emp object is also passed as a second parameter.

Note that HttpHeaders object contains Content-Type header in addition to the Authorization header. This way you indicate that JSON data is being passed along with the request.

Just like selectAll() and selectByID() methods, post() method also returns an Observable to the caller.

To send a PUT request to the Web API, you need to write the update() method as shown in Listing 7-9.

Listing 7-9. update() method makes a PUT request to the Employees Web API

```
update(emp: Employee) {
  return this.client.put(this.baseUrl + '/' + emp.employeeID, emp, {
    headers: new HttpHeaders({
      "Authorization": "Bearer " + sessionStorage.getItem('token'),
      "Content-Type": "application/json"
    })
  });
}
```

The update() method is quite similar to insert() method in that it accepts an Employee object to be sent along with the PUT request and returns an Observable to the caller. However, it calls the put() method of HttpClient (so that the Put() action of the Web API is invoked) and appends the employeeID to the URL.

As in the previous case, you pass the Authorization and Content-Type headers using the HttpHeaders object.

Finally, the delete() method sends a DELETE request to the Web API in order to invoke its Delete() action (Listing 7-10).

Listing 7-10. delete() method makes a DELETE request to Employees Web API

```
delete(id: number) {
  return this.client.delete(this.baseUrl + "/" + id, {
    headers: new HttpHeaders({
      "Authorization": "Bearer " + sessionStorage.getItem('token')
    })
  });
}
```

The delete() method accepts a numeric EmployeeID and returns an Observable. Inside, the code calls the delete() method of HttpClient by appending the id parameter to the URL. The Authorization HTTP header is assigned a value as before.

This completes the EmployeeApiService service. On the same lines, you can create CountriesApiService inside the countries-api folder. The CountriesApiService class will have only one method – selectAll(). Since this class is quite simple, it's not discussed here. You can get the complete CountriesApiService class from this chapter's code download. For your quick reference, the selectAll() method is shown in Listing 7-11.

Listing 7-11. selectAll() method of the CountriesApiService class

```
selectAll() {
  return this._http.get(this.baseUrl, {
    headers: new HttpHeaders({
      "Authorization": "Bearer " + sessionStorage.getItem('token')
    })
  });
}
```

As you can see, the selectAll() method calls the get() method of HttpClient and returns an Observable.

Add Service to Invoke Security Web API

Now that EmployeesApiService and CountriesApiService are ready, let's move ahead and create an Angular service that invokes the Security Web API. Go to the Angular CLI and issue this command:

```
> ng generate service security-api/SecurityApi
```

This will create a new service class named SecurityApiService under the security-api folder. At the top of this class, add these two import statements:

```
import { HttpClient, HttpHeaders } from '@angular/common/http';
import { User } from '../models/user';
```

Here, you import HttpClient and HttpHeaders classes as before. Additionally you also import the User model class created earlier.

The SecurityApiService contains a constructor that injects HttpClient and two methods – one for registering a user and another for signing the user in to the system. The complete SecurityApiService class is shown in Listing 7-12.

Listing 7-12. SecurityApiService class

```
@Injectable()
export class SecurityApiService {
  baseUrl: string = 'http://localhost:5000/api/security';
  client: HttpClient;

  constructor(client: HttpClient) {
    this.client = client;
  }

  signIn(usr: User) {
    return this.client.post<any>(this.baseUrl + "/signin", usr);
  }

  register(usr: User) {
    return this.client.post(this.baseUrl + "/register", usr,
                          { responseType: 'text'});
  }
}
```

This code should look familiar to you since it is similar to the earlier services. The baseURL and client members store the URL of the Security Web API and HttpClient object, respectively. The HttpClient is injected in the constructor.

The signIn() method accepts a parameter of User type and returns an Observable. Inside, it makes a POST request to SignIn() action of the Security Web API using the post() method of HttpClient. Notice that the post<T>() method specifies the response body of type any (any type indicates that the exact data type is not known at development time). This is because SignIn() action returns either a JSON object with token property (if user credentials are valid) or HTTP status code 401 (Unauthorized). Also note that User object containing user name and password is passed to the post() method's second parameter.

The register() method accepts a User object and returns an Observable. Inside, the code makes a POST request to the Register() action of Security Web API. This time in addition to the URL and User object, you also pass the responseType to be text. This is because the Register() action returns a string success or error message.

This completes all the Angular services needed by the application. These services are consumed by a set of Angular components. In the following sections, you create these components.

Display a List of Employees

To display a list of employees (Figure 7-8), you need to create an Angular component named EmployeeListComponent.

Employee Manager

List of Employees

Insert

Employee ID	First Name	Last Name	Title	Actions	
1	Nancy	Davolio	Sales Representative	Update	Delete
2	Andrew	Fuller	Vice President, Sales	Update	Delete
3	Janet	Leverling	Sales Representative	Update	Delete

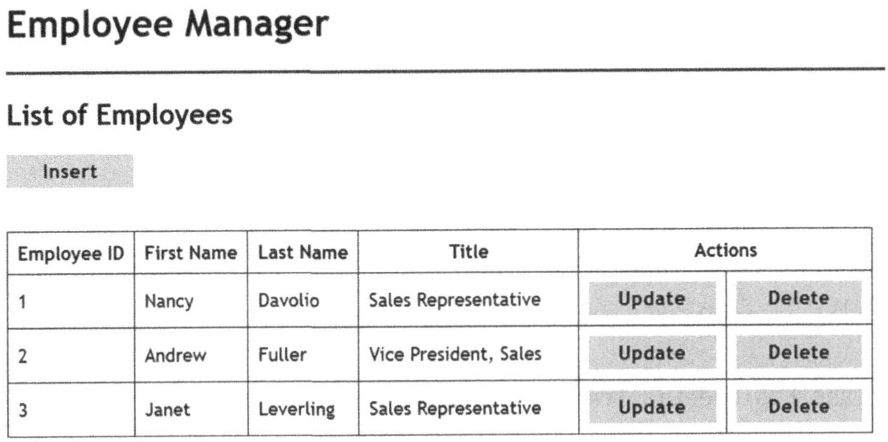

Figure 7-8. *Displaying a list of employees*

To create a skeleton of this component, open the Angular CLI and go inside the project folder. Then issue this command:

```
> ng generate component EmployeeList
```

The preceding command creates a new component class named EmployeeListComponent (Component suffix is added automatically for you) and places the component files inside the employee-list folder (the folder named is derived from the component name and it gets created automatically for you). If you look inside the employee-list folder, you will find four files:

- employee-list.component.ts

- employee-list.component.html

- employee-list.component.css

- employee-list.component.spec.ts

The first file contains a class that houses component's data and logic. The second file represents component's view and contains UI markup. The third file is optional and can include CSS styling used by the view. The fourth file is also optional and contains unit tests for the component. In this example, you don't need the .css and .spec.ts files of components, and you may delete them to reduce clutter.

If you open the employee-list.component.ts file, you will see code as shown in Listing 7-13.

Listing 7-13. Skeleton of EmployeeListComponent

```
import { Component, OnInit } from '@angular/core';

@Component({
  selector: 'app-employee-list',
  templateUrl: './employee-list.component.html',
  styleUrls: ['./employee-list.component.css']
})
export class EmployeeListComponent implements OnInit {
  constructor() { }
  ngOnInit() {
  }
}
```

The code imports the `Component` symbol and `OnInit` interface from the specified package. Then the code declares a class named `EmployeeListComponent`. The class is decorated with `@Component()` decorator. The `@Component()` decorator indicates that the underlying class is a component. The `@Component()` decorator also specifies the following metadata information:

- **selector**: A component exists on a view in the form of a markup tag. The selector property indicates the name of that markup tag. In this case the EmployeeListComponent is represented by

  .

- **templateUrl**: This is the path of the view file of the component.

- **styleUrls**: One or more paths pointing to the CSS files used by the component. Since CSS files are optional, you can remove this property.

Notice that the `EmployeeListComponent` class implements `OnInit` interface. Implementing `OnInit` interface means the class must include `ngOnInit()` method. Angular provides several lifecycle hooks that provide opportunity to developers to execute some code when certain lifecycle event occurs. One of the lifecycle hooks is `ngOnInit()`. The `ngOnInit()` method gets executed automatically once when a component is initialized.

Note   At first glance, the ngOnInit lifecycle hook looks similar to the constructor. However, they are different. A constructor is called when the class is instantiated and is typically used for member initialization and dependency injection. The ngOnInit lifecycle hook, on the other hand, is executed when the framework initializes the component. For more information about Angular lifecycle hooks, read `https://angular.io/guide/lifecycle-hooks`.

Now that you know the basic skeleton of a component, let's modify EmployeeListComponent as per application requirement.

Go to the top of the component class file and add these import statements below the existing ones:

```
import { Router } from '@angular/router';
import { EmployeesApiService } from '../employees-api/employees-api.
service';
import { Employee } from '../models/employee';
```

The first import statement imports Router class. This class provides routing and navigational capabilities to your component. Then the code imports EmployeesApiService service because the component needs to fetch data from the Employees Web API. Finally, Employee class is also imported.

Next, go to the EmployeeListComponent class and add the members and constructor as shown in Listing 7-14.

Listing 7-14. Members and constructor of EmployeeListComponent

```
employees: Array<Employee> = [];
message: string;
employeesApi: EmployeesApiService;
router: Router;

constructor(employeesApi: EmployeesApiService, router: Router) {
  this.employeesApi = employeesApi;
  this.router = router;
}
```

The employees member is intended to hold an array of Employee objects returned from the Web API. So, its type is Array<Employee>. The message string variable holds a message that is displayed to the end user (it could be a success message or an error message). The employeeApi variable is of type EmployeesApiService and holds a reference to the injected EmployeesApiService service instance. The router variable is a Router object injected into the constructor.

The constructor receives EmployeesApiService object and Router object through dependency injection. Inside, references to the injected objects are stored in the respective class members.

To display a list of employees, you need to fetch employee data from the Web API. This is done inside the ngOnInit() method as shown in Listing 7-15.

Listing 7-15. ngOnInit() fetches employee data

```
ngOnInit() {
  if (!sessionStorage.hasOwnProperty("token")) {
    this.router.navigate(['/signin']);
  }

  this.employeesApi.selectAll().subscribe(
    data => this.employees = data as Array<Employee>,
    error => {
      if (error.status === 401) {
        this.router.navigate(['/signin']);
      }
```

```
      this.message = error.message
    }
  );

  if (sessionStorage.hasOwnProperty("message")) {
    this.message = sessionStorage.getItem("message");
    sessionStorage.removeItem("message");
  }
}
```

Before making a call to the Employees Web API, the code checks whether a user has signed in to the system or not. This is done by checking JWT in the sessionStorage object. If JWT doesn't exist, the control is taken to the sign-in page (discussed later) accessible at /signin (e.g., http://localhost:1234/signin). This client-side URL is defined by routing configuration discussed in the later sections. To navigate to this URL, the code uses the navigate() method of the Router object. The navigate() method accepts a link parameters array that specifies a target URL (/signin in this case).

Next, the code calls the selectAll() method of EmployeesApiService. Recollect that selectAll() returns an Observable. So, the code subscribes to it using the subscribe() method. The subscribe() method takes two parameters. The first parameter is a handler function that receives the value returned by the Observable. This function is written using the Arrow Function syntax. The data parameter of the arrow function holds the employees returned by the Web API. These employees are stored in the employees member after typecasting data to Array<Employee>.

The second arrow function receives an error object in case there is any error while executing the call. The error handler checks the HTTP status code, and if it's 401 (Unauthorized), then the user is navigated to the sign-in page. If there is any error other than 401, the error message is stored in message member. This message is displayed on the view.

Note   An observable can send three types of notifications: next, error, and complete. Accordingly you can supply three callback functions to handle these notifications. A next handler is called (zero or more times) when a value is received. An error handler callback gets called in case there is any error while executing the observable. A `complete` handler gets called when the execution of observable is complete. In this example, you use the next handler and error handler to handle the respective notifications. For more details about observables, consider reading `https://angular.io/guide/observables`.

The delete employee page (discussed later) sets a message in the `sessionStorage` object. If a user is coming to the employee listing page after deleting an employee, that message is stored in the `message` member, and the `sessionStorage` entry is removed.

The employee listing page has three buttons – Insert, Update, and Delete that takes a user to the respective pages. Click event handlers of these buttons are also found in the `EmployeeListComponent` and are shown in Listing 7-16.

Listing 7-16. Click event handlers of Insert, Update, and Delete buttons

```
insert_click() {
  this.router.navigate(['/employees/insert']);
}

update_click(id) {
  this.router.navigate(['/employees/update', id]);
}

delete_click(id) {
  this.router.navigate(['/employees/delete', id]);
}
```

The `insert_click()` method represents the click event handler of Insert button. It calls the `navigate()` method of `Router` object to take the user to the Insert New Employee page.

The `update_click()` method represents the click event handler of Update button. This event handler receives `employeeID` as its `id` parameter. Inside, it calls the `navigate()` method of the `Router` object to navigate the user to the Update Existing Employee page. Notice that the array passed to the `navigate()` method now has a second element that holds the `id`. This will append the `id` to the URL specified in the first parameter.

The delete_click() method represents the click event handler of the Delete button. This event handler is quite similar to update_click() but navigates the user to Delete Existing Employee page.

This completes the EmployeeListComponent's class. Now let's complete its view. So open employee-list.component.html in Visual Studio and write the markup shown in Listing 7-17 in it.

Listing 7-17. Markup of EmployeeListComponent's view file

```
<h2>List of Employees</h2>
<button (click)="insert_click()" title="Insert">Insert</button>
<h3 class="message">{{message}}</h3>
<br />
<table border="1" cellpadding="10">
  <thead>
    <tr>
      <th>Employee ID</th>
      <th>First Name</th>
      <th>Last Name</th>
      <th>Title</th>
      <th colspan="2">Action</th>
    </tr>
  </thead>
  <tbody>
    <tr *ngFor="let emp of employees">
      <td>{{emp.employeeID}}</td>
      <td>{{emp.firstName}}</td>
      <td>{{emp.lastName}}</td>
      <td>{{emp.title}}</td>
      <td>
        <button (click)="update_click(emp.employeeID)">Update</button>
      </td>
```

```
      <td>
        <button (click)="delete_click(emp.employeeID)">Delete</button>
      </td>
    </tr>
  </tbody>
</table>
<hr />
<app-signout></app-signout>
```

Below the heading, the Insert button is placed using the `<button>` tag. Note the Angular's event binding syntax – `(click)` – where the `click` event is put in parenthesis and its event handler function (`insert_click()`) is also specified.

Below the Insert button, the `<h3>` element is placed for displaying notifications and messages to the user. The component class contains `message` member that holds a message to be displayed to the user. To output the message on the page, Angular's interpolation syntax is used – `{{expression}}`.

Then a table renders a list of employees. The table consists of a static header and dynamically generated rows. To generate table rows dynamically, the markup uses Angular's `*ngFor` syntax. The `ngFor` structural directive is like foreach loop used in C# in that it iterates through supplied data and renders the inner content for each data item. In this case, the `employees` member of the component class (`Array<Employee>`) is the data to be iterated upon. The value of individual data item is accessed through the `emp` local variable. First four `<td>` elements inside a table row use interpolation syntax and `emp` variable to display `employeeID`, `firstName`, `lastName`, and `title` values.

Note   Detailed discussion of ngFor and other structural directives of Angular is beyond the scope of this book. You may read more about them in Angular official documentation available at `https://angular.io/guide/structural-directives`.

Each table row also renders an Update and a Delete button. An `employeeID` is passed to the click event handler of Update and Delete button (`update_click(id)` and `delete_click(id)` functions).

At the bottom of the view, `SignOutComponent` is placed using its selector – `<app-signout>`. The `SignOutComponent` manages the sign-out functionality and is discussed later in this chapter.

This completes the `EmployeeListComponent`.

Insert a New Employee

Clicking the Insert link on the employee listing page takes you to another page where you can insert a new employee (Figure 7-9).

Insert New Employee

First Name :

Last Name :

Title :

Birth Date : mm / dd / yyyy

Hire Date : mm / dd / yyyy

Country : Please select

Notes :

Save

Back to Employee Listing

Figure 7-9. *Inserting a new employee*

The Insert New Employee page is represented by a component named Employee InsertComponent. So add this component to the project by issuing this command:

```
> ng generate component EmployeeInsert
```

Once the component is added, open the employee-insert.component.ts file in Visual Studio and add import statements shown in Listing 7-18.

Listing 7-18. Importing required classes

```
import { Component, OnInit } from '@angular/core';
import { FormBuilder, FormGroup, Validators } from '@angular/forms';
import { Router } from '@angular/router';
import { Country } from '../models/country';
import { EmployeesApiService } from '../employees-api/employees-api.service';
import { CountriesApiService } from '../countries-api/countries-api.service';
```

The second `import` statement imports three classes, namely, `FormBuilder`, `FormGroup`, and `Validators`. The `FormBuilder` class is used to construct an Angular form based on developer-defined configuration. The `FormGroup` class represents a group of form controls and tracks their value and validations. The `Validators` class provides access to Angular's built-in validators that can be used to validate form controls.

Note   There are two ways to create forms in Angular – Template Driven Forms and reactive forms (also called Model Driven Forms). The former is suitable for simple forms, whereas the latter is suitable for complex and scalable forms. In this book you use reactive forms. To know more, visit `https://angular.io/guide/forms-overview`.

The next import statement imports the `Router` class. This should look familiar too since you imported it in EmployeeListComponent also.

The next three import statements import `Country` model class, `EmployeesApiService`, and `CountriesApiService` services. You are already aware of their purpose.

Next, go to the EmployeeInsertComponent class and declare a set of members as shown in Listing 7-19.

Listing 7-19. Members of the EmployeeInsertComponent class

```
formBuilder: FormBuilder;
insertForm: FormGroup;
router: Router;
employeesApi: EmployeesApiService;
```

```
countriesApi: CountriesApiService;
countries: Array<Country>;
message: string;
```

The class member declarations are quite straightforward. Many of these objects are injected into the constructor (discussed shortly) and stored in the respective member variable. Notice that an array of Country objects is declared so that Country dropdown list can be populated with a list of countries.

The constructor that injects required objects and constructs the required data entry form is shown in Listing 7-20.

Listing 7-20. Constructor defines an insert new employee form

```
constructor(formBuilder: FormBuilder,
    router: Router,
    employeeApi: EmployeesApiService,
    countriesApi:CountriesApiService) {

    this.formBuilder = formBuilder;
    this.router = router;
    this.employeesApi = employeeApi;
    this.countriesApi = countriesApi;

    this.insertForm = this.formBuilder.group({
        firstName: [", [Validators.required, Validators.maxLength(10)]],
        lastName: [", [Validators.required, Validators.maxLength(20)]],
        title: [", [Validators.required, Validators.maxLength(30)]],
        birthDate: [", [Validators.required]],
        hireDate: [", [Validators.required]],
        country: [", [Validators.required, Validators.maxLength(15)]],
        notes: [", [Validators.maxLength(500)]]
    });
}
```

The constructor injects objects required by the component. They include FormBuilder, Route, EmployeesApiService, and CountriesApiService instances.

Inside, the injected objects and services are stored in class members declared earlier. Next, you need to construct a form consisting of form controls based on your requirements. A form control is represented by FormControl class. One or more FormControl objects make a FormGroup. To create a FormGroup required for inserting a new employee, the group() method of the FormBuilder class is used.

The group() method accepts an object containing configuration of form controls and returns a FormGroup instance. The form control configuration is specified in key-value format where key represents the name of a form control and value represents its configuration. Just to understand how a form control configuration is specified, have a look at this fragment:

```
firstName: [", [Validators.required,
             Validators.maxLength(10)]]
```

Here, a form control for first name is being defined. Therefore, key is firstName. The value is an array – the first element of the array is a default value for the control, and the second element is another array containing validators to be attached to the control. In this case two validators are attached to the firstName control. The required validator indicates that some value must be entered into this control. The maxLength validator indicates that a maximum of ten characters can be entered into the control (although not used in the preceding code, if a control has just one validator attached with it, you can specify just that validator in the second element rather than specifying it as an array).

Note   The Validators class also provides many other validators such as minLength, min, max, email, and pattern. As you might have guessed, many of these validators provide validation functionality as provided by HTML5 validation attributes.

Other controls, namely, lastName, title, birthDate, hireDate, country, and notes, are configured on similar lines.

The FormGroup returned by the group() method is assigned to insertForm member.

When this component is displayed, you need to fetch a list of countries from Countries Web API. This is done in the ngOnInit() method and is shown in Listing 7-21.

Listing 7-21. Countries Web API is called from ngOnInit()

```
ngOnInit() {
  if (!sessionStorage.hasOwnProperty("token")) {
    this.router.navigate(["/signin"]);
  }
  this.countriesApi.selectAll()
  .subscribe(data => this.countries = data as Array<Country>
  , error => this.message = error.message);
}
```

Notice the code shown in bold letters. It subscribes to the selectAll() method of CountriesApiService object and retrieves an array of Country objects. The first handler function stores the retrieved countries into countries member. The second handler function stores an error message in the message member.

When a user enters data in various form controls and clicks the Save button, the save_click() event handler method in the component class gets executed. This method is shown in Listing 7-22.

Listing 7-22. save_click() invokes the insert() method EmployeesApiService

```
save_click() {
  if (this.insertForm.invalid) {
    this.message = "One or more values are invalid.";
    return;
  }
  this.employeesApi.insert(this.insertForm.value)
    .subscribe(() => this.message = "Employee inserted
      successfully!", error => {
      if (error.status === 401) {
        this.router.navigate(["/signin"]);
      }
      this.message = error.message
    });
}
```

The code begins by observing the `invalid` property of `insertForm` FormGroup. The `invalid` property returns `true` if one or more controls from the `FormGroup` contain invalid values. It returns `false` if all the form controls contain valid values (just like the `invalid` property, there is also the `valid` property that returns `true` if all controls contain valid values; otherwise, it returns `false`). If the form contains one or more invalid values, an error message is displayed to the user through the message member. If all form controls contain valid values, the code proceeds to inserting a new employee into the database.

To insert a new employee, the code calls the `insert()` method of the `EmployeesApiService` class. Recollect that the `insert()` method expects an employee object containing employee details. This object is obtained through the `value` property of `FormGroup`. The `value` property returns an object containing all the form control values. For example, a sample object returned by value property would look like this:

```
{
  birthDate: "1948-12-08",
  country: "USA",
  employeeID: 1,
  firstName: "Nancy",
  hireDate: "1992-05-01",
  lastName: "Davolio",
  notes: "Education includes...",
  title: "Sales Representative"
}
```

As you can see, the property names are picked from control names, and property values hold the respective control values.

To handle the success or error while calling the Employees Web API, the code subscribes to the `Observable` returned by the `insert()` method. The first handler function is called when the Web API call is successful. Inside, a success message is assigned to the `message` member. In case there is some error, the second handler gets executed. If the HTTP status code indicates that a request is unauthorized (401 – Unauthorized), then the user is navigated to the sign-in page. Otherwise, the error message is assigned to the `message` member.

The Insert New Employee page has a link at the bottom that takes the user back to the employee listing page. The click event handler of this link is shown in Listing 7-23.

Listing 7-23. Taking the user back to the employee listing page

```
cancel_click() {
  this.router.navigate(["/employees/list"]);
}
```

When a user clicks the link, the navigate() method of the Router class navigates the user to the employee listing page.

This completes the component class. Now let's proceed to the component view. Listing 7-24 shows a part of the employee-update.component.html file (for the sake of reducing clutter, unwanted markup has been omitted).

Listing 7-24. EmployeeInsertComponent's view file

```
<h2>Insert New Employee</h2>
<h3 class="message">{{message}}</h3>
<form [formGroup]="insertForm" (ngSubmit)="save_click()" novalidate>
...
<td class="right">First Name :</td>
<td><input type="text" formControlName="firstName"></td>
...
<td class="right">Last Name :</td>
<td><input type="text" formControlName="lastName"></td>
...
<td class="right">Title :</td>
<td><input type="text" formControlName="title"></td>
...
<td class="right">Birth Date :</td>
<td><input type="date" formControlName="birthDate"></td>
...
<td class="right">Hire Date :</td>
<td><input type="date" formControlName="hireDate"></td>
...
<td class="right">Country :</td>
```

315

```
<td>
  <select formControlName="country">
    <option value="">Please select</option>
    <option *ngFor="let c of countries" [value]="c.name">
      {{c.name}}
    </option>
  </select>
</td>
...
<td class="right">Notes :</td>
<td>
<textarea rows="3" cols="50" formControlName="notes">
</textarea>
</td>
</tr>
...
<button type="submit">Save</button>
...
</form>
...
<a href="#" (click)="cancel_click()">Back to Employee Listing</a>
...
<app-signout></app-signout>
```

At the top, just below the page heading, the code displays the message member using interpolation syntax. Below there is the `<form>` element that needs to be bound to the `FormGroup` defined inside the class file (`insertForm`). To do this, Angular's `formGroup` directive is used. A directive is a special attribute added to HTML elements that attaches certain behavior to the element. Notice the binding syntax: the `formGroup` directive is put inside square brackets, and the member to be bound (`insertForm`) is assigned as its value.

The `FormGroup` captures submit event of the `<form>` element and raises `ngSubmit` event. Therefore, `ngSubmit` is put inside parenthesis and the event handler function `save_click()` also specified.

You have configured validation rules while defining the FormGroup. So, `novalidate` HTML attribute is added to the form to suppress browser's native validations.

316

Inside the form element, there is a series of `<input>` elements for accepting inputs from the user. These elements use Angular's `formControlName` directive to associate an input element with a form control from the `FormGroup`. For example, setting `formControlName` to `firstName` associates that input element to the `firstName` form control from the `insertForm` FormGroup.

Notice how the Country dropdown list is filled with a list of all countries. In addition to the first `<option>` element (Please select), it dynamically adds more `<option>` elements by iterating through the `countries` member (Array<Country>). This is done using the `ngFor` structural directive discussed earlier. Every new option element gets its `value` from the `Name` property of `Country` object. The `Name` property is also rendered within the `<option>` and `</option>` using the interpolation syntax.

The form can be submitted using the Save submit button. Below the Save button, there is a link that takes the user back to the employee listing page. The `click` event handler of the link (`cancel_click()`) is attached using the event binding syntax.

At the bottom of the view, `SignOutComponent` (discussed later) is placed that allows the user to sign out of the system.

Note In this form, you didn't display any field-level validations. This was done merely to reduce the clutter. While creating the sign-in form later in this chapter, you learn to use field-level validation messages. Once you learn how that can be done, you can modify EmployeeInsertComponent to display field-level validation error messages.

This completes the EmployeeInsertComponent's view. Save your work so far and proceed to the next component.

Update an Existing Employee

Clicking the Update button on the employee listing page takes you to the Update Existing Employee page where existing details of an employee are presented for editing (Figure 7-10).

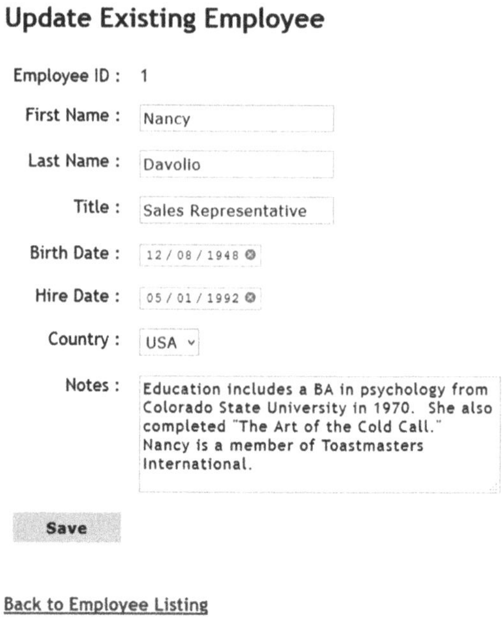

Update Existing Employee

Employee ID : 1

First Name : Nancy

Last Name : Davolio

Title : Sales Representative

Birth Date : 12 / 08 / 1948 ⊗

Hire Date : 05 / 01 / 1992 ⊗

Country : USA ⌄

Notes : Education includes a BA in psychology from
Colorado State University in 1970. She also
completed "The Art of the Cold Call."
Nancy is a member of Toastmasters
International.

Save

Back to Employee Listing

Figure 7-10. *Updating an existing employee*

The Update Existing Employee page looks similar to the Insert New Employee page except that various controls are now filled with the details of the employee being modified. The EmployeeID being the primary key can't be modified. The following text discusses only the differences that you need to be aware of. You can get the complete source of this component from the book's code download.

To develop the update existing page, you need to add EmployeeUpdateComponent using Angular CLI. Recollect that the Update link contains the EmployeeID to be modified. You need to grab this EmployeeID and fetch details for that employee. To get the EmployeeID passed in the current route URL, you use Angular's ActivatedRoute interface. So import it by modifying the import statement as shown in the following:

```
import { Router, ActivatedRoute } from '@angular/router';
```

An object of ActivatedRoute is injected into the constructor and stored in a member variable. This is shown in Listing 7-25.

Listing 7-25. Injecting the ActivatedRoute object

```
formBuilder: FormBuilder;
route: ActivatedRoute;
id: number;
router: Router;
employeesApi: EmployeesApiService;
countriesApi: CountriesApiService;
updateForm: FormGroup;
message: string;
countries: Array<Country>;

constructor(formBuilder: FormBuilder,
  router: Router,
  route: ActivatedRoute,
  employeesApi: EmployeesApiService,
  countriesApi: CountriesApiService) {

  this.formBuilder = formBuilder;
  this.route = route;
  this.router = router;
  this.employeesApi = employeesApi;
  this.countriesApi = countriesApi;

  if (this.route.snapshot.params["id"]) {
     this.id = this.route.snapshot.params["id"];
   }
  ...
}
```

Notice the code marked in bold letters. Two additional members are declared in the class – route and id. They represent the ActivatedRoute object and id passed in the URL, respectively.

To retrieve id passed in the URL, the snapshot property (snapshot property is of type ActivatedRouteSnapshot) of the ActivatedRoute object is used. The id value is then retrieved from the params collection. The retrieved id is stored in a member variable.

319

The remainder of the constructor defines the updateForm FormGroup similar to how you defined insertForm in the previous section. For the sake of brevity, that configuration is not repeated.

The ngOnInit() method retrieves details of the given employee by calling the selectByID() method of the EmployeesApiService object. This is shown in Listing 7-26.

Listing 7-26. Fetching details of an employee using selectByID()

```
...
this.employeesApi.selectByID(this.id)
  .subscribe((data:any) => {
    data.birthDate = data.birthDate.substring(0, 10);
    data.hireDate = data.hireDate.substring(0, 10);
    this.updateForm.setValue(data);
  }, error => {
    if (error.status === 401) {
      this.router.navigate(["/signin"]);
    }
    this.message = error.message
  });
...
```

The code calls the selectByID() method of EmployeesApiService by passing the id member to it. The subscribe() method supplies a value handler and error handler functions. Notice that the data parameter is marked to be of any type because you need to manipulate inside the value handler function. The BirthDate and HireDate values returned by the Web API are in ISO date format and include time zone information. However, while displaying these dates in the browser's date input field, you need to trim the time zone part. This is done inside the value handler function using the substring() method of JavaScript. To display the employee details fetched from the Web API, the code uses setValue() method of FormGroup. The setValue() method accepts an object and fills the form controls with the corresponding values. The error handler function works as before.

The click event handler of the Save button is quite similar to the one you used while inserting an employee except that it invokes the update() method of EmployeesApiService. Hence, it's not discussed here again.

The view for `EmployeeUpdateComponent` is quite similar to the one you developed in the previous section. The only difference is that the update view also displays EmployeeID. This is shown in Listing 7-27.

Listing 7-27. Update view displays EmployeeID

```
<form [formGroup]="updateForm" (ngSubmit)="save_click()" novalidate>
  <table border="0" cellpadding="10">
    <tr>
      <td class="right">Employee ID :</td>
      <td>
        <span>{{id}}</span>
        <input type="hidden" formControlName="employeeID">
      </td>
    </tr>
...
...
```

The `formGroup` directive associates the `updateForm` FormGroup member with the form element. The `EmployeeID` is displayed in read-only fashion using a `<span>` element and interpolation syntax. Although a user can't edit the `EmployeeID`, it must be passed between the component class and view because it's used during update operation. Therefore, the `EmployeeID` is also persisted in a hidden form field. This way `setValue()` will assign the current `EmployeeID` to this hidden form field. And calling `value` property of `updateForm` will return it along with other form control values.

Delete an Existing Employee

Upon clicking the Delete button on the employee listing page, you navigate to the Delete Existing Employee page (Figure 7-11).

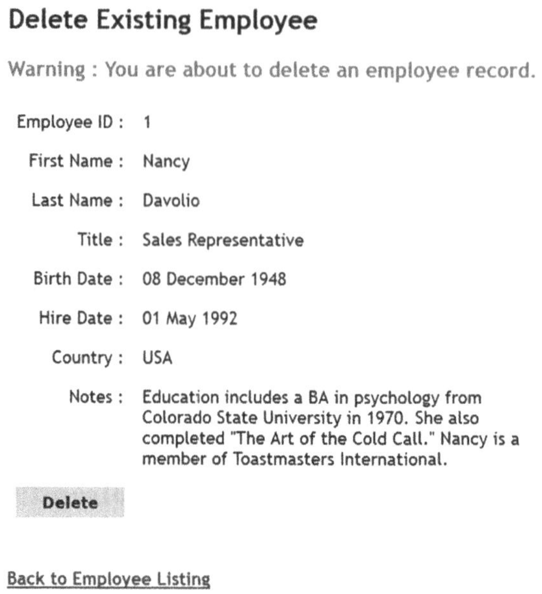

Delete Existing Employee

Warning : You are about to delete an employee record.

Employee ID : 1

First Name : Nancy

Last Name : Davolio

Title : Sales Representative

Birth Date : 08 December 1948

Hire Date : 01 May 1992

Country : USA

Notes : Education includes a BA in psychology from
Colorado State University in 1970. She also
completed "The Art of the Cold Call." Nancy is a
member of Toastmasters International.

Delete

Back to Employee Listing

Figure 7-11. *Seeking delete confirmation from user*

This page is represented by EmployeeDeleteComponent and is similar to update form discussed earlier in that it fetches a particular employee based on an id passed in the route. The employee details are displayed in read-only fashion. Clicking the Delete button invokes the delete() method of EmployeesApiService. For the sake of brevity, only the calls to selectByID() and delete() methods are discussed in the following. You can get the complete code of this component (including the view file) from this chapter's code download.

The selectAll() method of EmployeesApiService fetches an employee object whose id is specified in the route. This is shown in Listing 7-28.

Listing 7-28. selectAll() retrieves an employee object

```
this.employeesApi.selectByID(this.id)
  .subscribe(data => {
    this.employee = data as Employee;
    this.deleteForm.controls['employeeID']
    .setValue(this.employee.employeeID);
  }
    , error => {
```

```
    if (error.status === 401) {
      this.router.navigate(["/signin"]);
    }
    this.message = error.message
  });
```

Notice the value handler function passed to the subscribe() method. The data object is stored in the employees member of the component class. You can use the employees member to display employee details on the view.

Since employee details are displayed in read-only fashion, there are no data entry controls on the form. The only form control you need is a hidden form field that stores EmploeeID. So, the code directly sets the employeeID hidden form field using the controls collection of deleteForm FormGroup. The setValue() method of a form control accepts a value to be assigned to the control.

The click event handler of the Delete button calls the delete() method of EmployeesApiService as shown in Listing 7-29.

Listing 7-29. Calling the delete() method to delete an employee

```
this.employeesApi.delete(
  this.deleteForm.controls["employeeID"].value)
  .subscribe(() => {
              sessionStorage.setItem("message", "Employee
              deleted successfully!");
              this.router.navigate(['/employees/list']);
  }, error => {
    if (error.status === 401) {
      this.router.navigate(["/signin"]);
    }
    this.message = error.message
  });
```

The delete() method accepts an EmployeeID to be deleted. This EmployeeID is retrieved from the hidden form field using the controls collection. The value property of a form control from the collection returns its value.

The value handler function stores a success message into sessionStorage object. Recollect that this sessionStorage message is displayed on the employee listing page. The user is then navigated to the employee listing page.

Sign-In Component

When you run the application initially, you are taken to the sign-in page represented by the SignInComponent (the UI rendered by this component is similar to the sign-in page of the jQuery example discussed in the previous chapter). This component invokes the Security Web API to get a JWT. The token is then stored in sessionStorage object. It is recommended that you get the component class file (signin.component.ts) and view file (signin.component.html) from the book's code download. Although the complete code of SignInComponent is not discussed here, a few things are worth noting:

- How to display field-level validation errors

- How to invoke the Security API and get a JWT

The SignInComponent class configures signinForm in the constructor as shown in Listing 7-30.

Listing 7-30. Configuration of signinForm

```
this.signinForm = this.formBuilder.group({
  userName: [", [Validators.required, Validators.maxLength(20)]],
  password: [", [Validators.required, Validators.maxLength(20)]]
});
```

As you can see, the signinForm consists of two form controls – one for accepting user name and one for accepting password. Both the form controls have required and maxLength validators attached with them. You would like to display field-level validation error messages in the view so that you can know which of the form control is invalid. To display validation errors on the view, you can use Angular's ngIf structural directive as shown in Listing 7-31.

Listing 7-31. Displaying field-level validation error messages

```
<div *ngIf="signinForm.controls.userName.dirty && signinForm.controls.
userName.invalid">
  <div *ngIf="signinForm.controls.userName.errors.required"
  [ngClass]="'message'">
    User Name is required
  </div>
  <div *ngIf="signinForm.controls.userName.errors.maxlength"
  [ngClass]="'message'">
    User Name must be smaller than 20 characters
  </div>
</div>
```

This code shows how validation error messages can be displayed for user name input field. The ngIf structural directive applied to the outer <div> element is similar to the if statement of C# in that it checks for one or more Boolean expressions. Here, the code checks for two Boolean expressions. Firstly, it checks whether the userName form control has been edited or not. This is done by accessing the userName form control from the controls collection of signinForm FormGroup and then checking its dirty property. The dirty property returns true if the control value has been edited; otherwise it returns false.

Secondly, it checks the invalid property of the userName form control. The invalid property returns true if the control contains invalid value; otherwise it returns false.

Only when both the conditions evaluate to true an error message is displayed. You can further check the kind of validation error and accordingly display error messages. The userName form control has two validators attached to it – required and maxLength. To check their validity status, you can use the errors collection of the userName form control. For example, if errors.required is not null, then it indicates that the form control is empty. Similarly, if errors.maxlength is not null, then it indicates that the control contains a value more than the maximum permissible length. Accordingly the respective <div> elements with error messages are displayed.

Notice the use of the ngClass directive that applies the message CSS class to the <div> elements to heighten the error messages.

This markup displays error messages for the userName form control. You can use the same technique to display error messages for password form control also.

Now that you know how to display field-level validation error messages, let's proceed to the code that invokes the Security Web API (Listing 7-32).

Listing 7-32. Sign-in form calls Security Web API

```
signin_click() {
  if (this.signinForm.invalid) {
    this.message = "One or more values are invalid.";
    return;
  }
  this.securityApi.signIn(this.signinForm.value)
  .subscribe(token => {
    sessionStorage.setItem('token', token.token);
    sessionStorage.setItem('userName', this.signinForm.
    controls['userName'].value);
    this.router.navigate(["/employees/list"])
  }, error => this.message = "Unable to Sign-in");
}
```

Notice the code marked in bold letters. It calls the `signIn()` method of `SecurityApiService` by passing `signinForm` value (an object with userName and password properties). If the user validation is successful, the value handler function receives a JWT issued by the Security Web API. This token is persisted in `sessionStorage` object so that it can be passed to server while performing CRUD operations.

The code also sets `userName` entry in the `sessionStorage` so that current user's sign-in name can be displayed on other pages of the application. Current user's sign-in name is retrieved from the `userName` form control using its `value` property.

Upon successfully signing in to the system, the user is navigated to the employee listing page. If there is any error while calling the Security Web API, the error handler sets an error message in the `message` member.

Sign-Out Component

The sign-out component displays the user name of the currently signed-in user and also shows a Sign Out button so that the user can sign out of the application. This component is represented by `SignOutComponent` class and its associated view. You can get the complete code of this component from this chapter's code download. Here only the ngOnInit() method of the class and the click event handler of the Sign Out button are discussed (Listing 7-33).

Listing 7-33. SignOutComponent signs a user out of the application

```
ngOnInit() {
  this.userName = sessionStorage.getItem('userName');
}

signout_click() {
  sessionStorage.removeItem('token');
  sessionStorage.removeItem('userName');
  this.router.navigate(["/signin"]);
}
```

As you can see, the ngOnInit() method simply retrieves userName key stored in the sessionStorage object and stores it in userName member. This userName is displayed on the view.

Clicking the Sign Out button raises the signout_click() event handler. Inside, the code removes token key from the sessionStorage. This way Web API calls will no longer have a JWT, and a user authentication will fail. The code also removes the userName key from the sessionStorage and navigates the user to the sign-in page.

This completes the sign-out component. The register component that displays a user registration page is quite similar to the components you developed earlier in this chapter and hence not discussed here. You can get the complete code of RegisterComponent from this chapter's code download.

Understanding app.module.ts

So far in this chapter, you created various components and services needed by the application. Now it's time to take a look at application's root module residing in the app.module.ts file.

If you open the app.module.ts file, you will find a series of import statements at the top followed by the module class – AppModule. These import statements can be categorized in three groups. The first group consists of import statements that import external modules that are necessary for the application to run. Listing 7-34 shows these import statements.

Listing 7-34. Importing modules required by the application

```
import { NgModule } from '@angular/core';
import { BrowserModule } from '@angular/platform-browser';
import { ReactiveFormsModule } from '@angular/forms';
import { HttpClientModule } from '@angular/common/http';
import { RouterModule } from '@angular/router';
import { AppRoutingModule } from './app-routing.module';
```

These import statements import Angular modules that are dependencies of the Employee Manager application. Especially `ReactiveFormsModule`, `HttpClientModule`, and `RouterModule` are worth noting because they are essential for reactive forms, HttpClient, and routing features, respectively.

The `AppRoutingModule` module is a custom module that houses application's routing configuration and is discussed in the next section.

The second group of import statements consists of services added during development and is shown in Listing 7-35.

Listing 7-35. Importing services

```
import { EmployeesApiService } from './employees-api/employees-api.service';
import { CountriesApiService } from './countries-api/countries-api.service';
import { SecurityApiService } from './security-api/security-api.service';
```

The third group of import statements imports components of your application (Listing 7-36).

Listing 7-36. Importing components

```
import { AppComponent } from './app.component';
import { EmployeeListComponent } from './employee-list/employee-list.component';
import { EmployeeInsertComponent } from './employee-insert/employee-insert.
component';
import { EmployeeUpdateComponent } from './employee-update/employee-update.
component';
import { EmployeeDeleteComponent } from './employee-delete/employee-delete.
component';
import { SignInComponent } from './signin/signin.component';
```

```
import { RegisterComponent } from './register/register.component';
import { SignOutComponent } from './signout/signout.component';
```

Except AppComponent all the other components were added during the development process. The AppComponent component is the default root component and is discussed in later sections.

Below these import statements, there is the AppModule class decorated with the @NgModule() decorator. An object containing module metadata is supplied to the @NgModule() decorator. Listing 7-37 shows the @NgModule() decorator.

Listing 7-37. Specifying module's metadata

```
@NgModule({
    declarations: [
        AppComponent,
        EmployeeListComponent,
        EmployeeInsertComponent,
        EmployeeUpdateComponent,
        EmployeeDeleteComponent,
        SignInComponent,
        RegisterComponent,
        SignOutComponent
    ],
    imports: [
        BrowserModule,
        ReactiveFormsModule,
        HttpClientModule,
        RouterModule,
        AppRoutingModule
    ],
    providers: [
      EmployeesApiService,
      CountriesApiService,
      SecurityApiService
    ],
```

```
    bootstrap: [AppComponent]
})
export class AppModule { }
```

This object consists of four array properties – declarations, imports, providers, and bootstrap. Although detailed discussion of these properties is beyond the scope of this book, it suffices to say that

- **declarations** section lists all the components that are part of this application

- **imports** section lists all the external dependencies of this application

- **providers** section lists all the services of this application

- **bootstrap** section specifies the root component of the application

---

Note   If your services contain the @Injectable() decorator that specifies { providedIn: 'root' } in the metadata, then you don't need to list them again in the providers section. Here, they are listed just for the sake of clear understanding.

Routing

While developing various components of the Angular application, you used routes such as /employees/list and /signin at several places. Now it's time to look into the routing configuration.

In addition to the app.module.ts file, you will also find the app-routing.module.ts file. This file contains a module for setting up routing of the application. Listing 7-38 shows the initial content of this module.

Listing 7-38. Content of app-routing.module.ts

```
import { NgModule } from '@angular/core';
import { Routes, RouterModule } from '@angular/router';

const routes: Routes = [];
```

```
@NgModule({
  imports: [RouterModule.forRoot(routes)],
  exports: [RouterModule]
})
export class AppRoutingModule { }
```

Notice the code shown in bold letters. The code declares an empty routes array. The routes array is supplied to the forRoute() method of RouterModule. Angular's RouterModule handles the routing and navigation for your application. The forRoot() method prepares the module to use the specified routes.

In order to define routes for an application, you need to modify the routes array to contain the required routing configuration (you will also need to add import statements that import components mentioned in the route configuration). Listing 7-39 shows the routing configuration required for the application being developed.

Listing 7-39. Routing configuration for an application

```
const routes: Routes = [
  { path: "", redirectTo: "employees/list", pathMatch: 'full' },
  { path: "register", component: RegisterComponent },
  { path: "signin", component: SignInComponent },
  { path: "employees/list", component: EmployeeListComponent },
  { path: "employees/insert", component: EmployeeInsertComponent },
  { path: "employees/update/:id", component: EmployeeUpdateComponent },
  { path: "employees/delete/:id", component: EmployeeDeleteComponent },
  { path: '**', component: EmployeeListComponent }
];
```

As you can see, the router array contains objects that define various routes. Various properties of the route objects used in this configuration are listed as follows:

- **path**: Indicates a path from a URL that is typically mapped to a component. If no path is specified, you can redirect to another path as specified in the redirectTo property. If path value of wild card (**) indicates a path not matching with any other defined path. Notice how id route parameter is specified for update and delete routes using :id syntax.

- **redirectTo**: Specifies a URL to redirect upon matching a path.

- **pathMatch**: Indicates the path-matching strategy; a value of full means the whole path is to be used during matching.

- **component**: Indicates a component that is instantiated to handle a path. For example, if you navigate to /employees/list URL, EmployeeListComponent will be invoked.

Note   Detailed discussion of Angular's routing capabilities is beyond the scope of this book. Consider reading `https://angular.io/guide/router` for more details.

This completes client-side routing configuration required for the application. The application still won't display components as per this configuration. You need to specify a placeholder where these routes are loaded. This is done using Angular's RouterOutlet directive. To use the RouterOutlet directive, open the root component view file – app. component.html – and write the markup shown in Listing 7-40.

Listing 7-40. Placing the RouterOutlet directive in the root component's view

```
<h1>Employee Manager</h1>
<hr />
<router-outlet></router-outlet>
```

As you can see, the `<router-outlet>` directive marks the place where routing configuration is expanded to show various "pages" of the application.

It should be noted that Angular routing is a client-side mechanism. Although it allows us to access the application in a "page-by-page" manner, client-side routing has its own problems. What if the user manually enters a client-side URL in the address bar? What if the user bookmarks a client-side URL and tries to access it sometime in the future? In such cases you will get 404 (Not found) error from ASP.NET Core application because these URLs aren't known to the server. You need to deal with such conditions in your ASP.NET Core application. One possible way to deal with such situations is added to this chapter's source code. It's not discussed here for the sake of brevity, but you can take a look at it by downloading the source code.

> **Note**   You used various CSS classes and styling in the components developed in this chapter. They exist in the styles.css file located under the src folder. So simply copy the complete CSS styling (site.css) from any previous version of Employee Manager, say MVC version, to this file.

Running the Angular Application

Now that you have completed the Angular application that represents Employee Manager's front-end, it's time to run the application and check whether everything works as expected or not.

To run the application, first you need to run the ASP.NET Core Web API project that contains Employees Web API, Countries Web API, and Security Web API. So open Visual Studio command prompt, navigate to the EmployeeManager.Angular project folder, and issue this .NET CLI command:

```
> dotnet run
```

This will run the application at `http://localhost:5000`. Now, open Node.js command prompt and navigate to the Angular project root folder. Then issue this Angular CLI command:

```
> ng serve --open
```

This command starts and serves an Angular application at `http://localhost:4200`. The `--open` switch indicates that a browser window will be opened and the application will be launched in it.

If all goes well, you will be presented with a sign-in page. Sign in using valid credentials (you can use a user account created while testing the jQuery app since the Angular application also uses the same Users table) or create a new account. Upon successful sign-in, you can try performing CRUD operations. Also, check whether the browser address bar shows URLs as per the routing configuration.

Integrating Angular Application with ASP.NET Core Application

In the previous section, you ran the ASP.NET Core application and Angular application as two independent applications. This is alright during development and testing stages. However, once the development is over, you would like to integrate the Angular application with the ASP.NET Core application.

To do so, first of all go to all the Angular services you created in this application and change the baseUrl member to this:

```
baseUrl: string = '/api/employees';
```

As you can see, the baseUrl no longer contains host and port information because the Angular application is going to be merged with the ASP.NET Core application. You need to make this change in EmployeesApiService, CountriesApiService, and SecurityApiService classes.

Then build the Angular application using the following Angular CLI command:

```
> ng build --prod = true
```

This command compiles the Angular application. The --prod switch is set to true indicating that the application will be compiled using production configuration. By default, the output of compilation is stored in the dist folder under the project root. Figure 7-12 shows the output of compilation.

Name	Date modified	Type	Size
3rdpartylicenses.txt	7/7/2019 10:14 AM	Text Document	24 KB
favicon.ico	7/7/2019 10:13 AM	ICO File	6 KB
index.html	7/7/2019 10:14 AM	Firefox HTML Doc...	1 KB
main-es5.04d25a61ce489d7c3031.js	7/7/2019 10:14 AM	JS File	381 KB
main-es2015.d88d95f25c910b6ec8fc.js	7/7/2019 10:13 AM	JS File	334 KB
polyfills-es5.ee0d5f960ce47213e70c.js	7/7/2019 10:14 AM	JS File	134 KB
polyfills-es2015.585ff42b5603db69e08c.js	7/7/2019 10:13 AM	JS File	58 KB
runtime-es5.ba44b74264daa95943c7.js	7/7/2019 10:14 AM	JS File	2 KB
runtime-es2015.c53cfa7e76780343722f.js	7/7/2019 10:13 AM	JS File	2 KB
styles.72fbc74fc75807d3ad17.css	7/7/2019 10:13 AM	CSS File	2 KB

Figure 7-12. *Output of compilation is stored under the dist folder*

Notice the index.html file that acts as the start page of the Angular SPA application.

Next, copy all these files and place them directly under the wwwroot folder of the ASP.NET Core application. Open the `Startup` class and change the `Configure()` method as shown in Listing 7-41.

Listing 7-41. Enabling the default page for the ASP.NET Core application

```
...
app.UseDefaultFiles();
app.UseStaticFiles();
...
```

When you integrate the Angular application with the ASP.NET Core application, it would be great if you set the index.html file of the Angular application as the default page of your ASP.NET Core application. To do this, you use `UseDefaultFiles()` middleware. Once you do this, ASP.NET Core will look for standard default pages such as default.htm, default.html, index.htm, and index.html inside the wwwroot folder. In this case you have index.html and hence it will be used as the application's default document.

You can now run the ASP.NET Core application and use the Angular SPA as before.

Summary

In this chapter you created the Employee Manager application using ASP.NET Core and Angular. ASP.NET Core Web APIs provided core application functionality, and the Angular SPA provided a front-end that consumed those Web APIs.

You learned to use Angular CLI and created Angular components and services. To implement CRUD functionality, you created `EmployeeListComponent`, `EmployeeInsertComponent`, `EmployeeUpdateComponent`, and `EmployeeDeleteComponent`. User authentication was provided through JWT authentication scheme. `SignInComponent`, `SignOutComponent`, and `RegisterComponent` were used while implementing the authentication features of the application.

You were familiarized with the overall Angular application architecture and also implemented routing and navigation. Finally, you integrated the Angular application with the ASP.NET Core application.

Blazor

In the previous chapters, you learned to use jQuery and Angular to build JavaScript front-ends of ASP.NET Core applications. So your application was a mix of server-side C# code and client-side JavaScript code. Wouldn't it be great if you can use C# on the server side as well as on the client side? That's what Blazor allows you to accomplish. Blazor is a framework for building rich and interactive client-side web user interfaces with ASP.NET Core. Using Blazor, you create UI components using C#, HTML, and CSS. This chapter teaches you how this is done. Specifically, you will

- Learn about Blazor hosting models

- Understand what Razor Components are

- Create Blazor UI that performs data validations and data binding

- Use lifecycle methods, dependency injection, and routing

- Integrate ASP.NET Core Identity in Blazor server-side applications

Let's get going.

Blazor Hosting Models

Before you go ahead and start developing a Blazor application, you need to decide where the application is going to be executed. That's where Blazor hosting models come into picture.

By now, you are aware that Blazor is a framework for building rich client-side user interfaces. Before beginning your Blazor development, you need to decide on the hosting model you want to use for an application. A Blazor application's code can execute inside a browser or on the server. Depending on where the application code runs, Blazor offers two hosting models: client-side (Blazor WebAssembly) and server-side (Blazor Server).

© Bipin Joshi 2019
B. Joshi, *Beginning Database Programming Using ASP.NET Core 3*,
https://doi.org/10.1007/978-1-4842-5509-4_8

Selection of a hosting model is typically done before you begin your application development. That's because there are certain differences between the two hosting models. Even the Visual Studio project templates are different for these hosting models. The following sections describe these hosting models in more detail.

Client Side (Blazor WebAssembly)

In this mode, a Blazor application and its dependencies are downloaded on the client side by the browser, and the application runs within the browser's boundaries. The client-side hosting model uses WebAssembly for its working.

WebAssembly (often abbreviated as Wasm) is a compact binary format that gives good performance (almost like a native execution) for web applications. WebAssembly is designed in such a way that any programming language can compile to WebAssembly format. Currently, all the major browsers support WebAssembly, so your application is not tied to a particular browser.

Note   Detailed discussion of WebAssembly is beyond the scope of this book. If you want to know more, consider visiting `https://webassembly.org` and `https://developer.mozilla.org/en-US/docs/WebAssembly`.

Once the application is downloaded on the client side, it is executed by the browser. Rendering of UI and user interactions (such as clicking of a button) are handled by the browser just like any other web application.

While evaluating whether you would like to go for client-side hosting or not, consider these points:

- Since the application is downloaded on the client side, this model utilizes client-side resources effectively giving good overall performance.

- The application runs within the boundaries of a browser. So all the limitations of a browser apply to the application.

- For bigger applications, the download time can be longer resulting in longer initial load time.

- This hosting model depends on a browser that supports WebAssembly.

Server Side (Blazor Server)

In the server-side hosting model, a Blazor application is executed on a web server inside an ASP.NET Core application. Changes to DOM and event handling are performed using a SignalR connection.

SignalR is a library that adds real-time functionality to ASP.NET Core applications. Using SignalR, the server can push notifications to the client. SignalR utilizes modern browser features such as WebSocket and HTML5 for this communication. If WebSockets aren't supported, SignalR can also use other techniques to get its job done.

Note   Detailed discussion of SignalR is beyond the scope of this book. If you want to know more, consider visiting `https://dotnet.microsoft.com/apps/aspnet/real-time`.

While evaluating whether you would like to go for server-side hosting or not, consider these points:

- Since the browser doesn't download the application and its dependencies, the initial load time is quite faster.

- Since the application runs on ASP.NET Core server, you can use many of the capabilities of ASP.NET Core (such as ASP.NET Core Identity) just like ASP.NET Core MVC or ASP.NET Core Razor Pages applications.

- Since the application is running on the server, every user interaction requires a small server communication.

- If you intend to support a very huge user base for your application, the server-side hosting model can be challenging.

As mentioned earlier, deciding on the hosting model to use should be done prior to beginning your development. Visual Studio provides distinct project templates that cover these hosting models. First, you need to select Blazor App in the Create a New Project dialog (Figure 8-1).

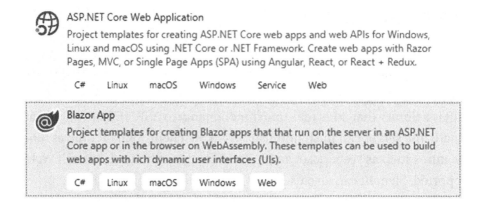

Figure 8-1. *Creating a new Blazor application*

After selecting this project type and after specifying a project name, you need to pick a project template as shown in Figure 8-2.

Create a new Blazor app

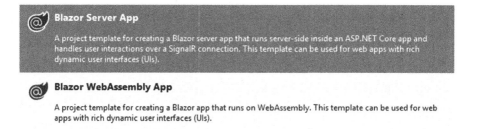

Figure 8-2. *Visual Studio Blazor project templates*

The purpose of each Blazor project template follows:

- **Blazor Server App:** This project template uses the server-side hosting model for the application. A Visual Studio project is created with a default set of files.

- **Blazor WebAssembly App:** This project template uses the client-side hosting model. The client code can call server-side Web APIs to perform server-side processing.

The remainder of this chapter uses the Blazor server-side hosting model to build a version of Employee Manager that uses Razor Pages (for user registration and sign-in), Razor Components (for CRUD pages), Entity Framework Core (for data access), and ASP. NET Core Identity (for user authentication).

Razor Components are building blocks of a Blazor application. The next section gives you more details about Razor Components.

Overview of Razor Components

A Blazor application consists of what are known as Razor Components. A Razor Component exists as a .razor file and contains a C# code and HTML markup. When compiled, these two pieces are combined to make a component class.

The C# code typically consists of members such as variables, properties, methods, and event handlers. You can also use C# constructs (such as a for loop or if statements) to dynamically generate HTML output. The former type of C# code exists in the @code block(s), whereas the latter type of C# code is intermingled with the HTML markup.

Note   You might find Razor Components quite similar to Razor Views (.cshtml) in many aspects. In fact, you can also integrate Razor Components into Razor Pages and Razor Views. However, in this book, you will stick to .razor files for the sake of clear understanding and uniformity.

When a Razor Component is initially rendered in the browser, it generates its HTML response. If any of the events causes the HTML response to change (say, an HTML element gets added as a result of the click event handler), then the Razor Component regenerates the new HTML response. The Blazor engine then determines the differences between the older HTML response and the newly generated HTML response by comparing both the DOM (Document Object Model) trees. Any modifications found as a part of this comparison are reflected in the browser.

Once created, a Razor Component can be used in two ways:

- It can be placed inside another component as a markup element. For example, a component named HelloWorld can be placed inside another component using markup: <HelloWorld></HelloWorld>.

- A Razor Component can be marked to be a page using the @page directive and is associated with a route. In this case, the component can be invoked using its route. For example, the HelloWorld component marked as a page can be made accessible at /HelloWorld.

The non-page Razor Components can reside anywhere in the project folder, whereas Razor Components acting as pages are placed inside the Pages folder under the project root (this is similar to how Razor Pages are placed inside the Pages folder).

Note   Since a Razor Component can be housed inside another Razor Component, you can also create a tree of Razor Components that have parent-child relationship.

Razor Components also support data binding and event binding. For example, you might data bind the Message property of a Razor Component with a textbox. When the component is rendered initially, it displays the value of the Message property into the textbox. Any changes made to the value of the textbox are reflected in the Message property. You can also handle client-side events by supplying an event handler function. For example, you might bind the onclick (In HTML, most of the events are represented by corresponding attributes in the markup. For example, the click event is represented by an onclick attribute in the markup.) event of a button to an event handler method – OnButtonClick().

Component Lifecycle Methods

A Razor Component undergoes a series of events during its lifecycle. These lifecycle events are marked by certain methods that a component author can override while creating a component. These lifecycle methods are summarized as follows:

- **OnInitialized:** This method can be used to perform some initialization tasks. For example, you might set component members to some default values.

- **OnParametersSet:** A component can have parameters. A parameter is represented by a property and can be set from an external world (say, a component's parent). The OnParametersSet() overridden method gets executed when a parameter property is assigned a value.

- **OnAfterRender:** This method is called after a component is rendered. Rendered content is accessible at this stage. You can use this method if your initialization logic involves rendered content.

All the methods mentioned in the preceding text have their asynchronous counterpart. For example, `OnInitializedAsync()` can be used to asynchronously handle initialization tasks.

Employee Manager Project Structure

In the sections that follow, you build Employee Manager that utilizes Blazor's server-side hosting model. Since the application uses a server-side hosting model, you can also use ASP.NET Core server-side features such as ASP.NET Core Identity.

In fact, the Employee Manager application built in this chapter uses ASP.NET Core Identity and associated Razor Pages that you developed in earlier chapters. To perform data access operations, the application uses Entity Framework Core. The data access happens through repositories. These repositories are quite similar to the ones you developed while working with the Web API project earlier in this book. You also need pages that perform CRUD operations. These pages are built using Razor Components and use the repositories to list, insert, update, and delete employee details from the database.

The Employee Manager application developed in this chapter exists as the
EmployeeManager.Blazor.ServerSide project and is shown in Figure 8-3.

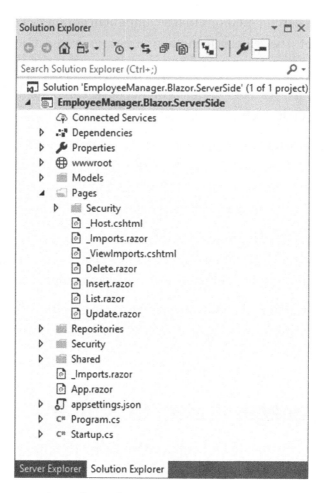

Figure 8-3. *Blazor version of Employee Manager*

You might find the project organization quite similar to a Razor Pages application.
Take a look at the Pages folder that contains all the Razor Components you develop in
this chapter. Notice the Razor Components that exist as .razor files. The Security folder
contains a set of Razor Pages (Register.cshtml, SignIn.cshtml, and SignOut.cshtml)
that are used for user registration and signing in to the application. These Razor Pages
are essentially the same pages you built while developing the Razor Pages version of
Employee Manager.

The Models folder contains EF Core model classes such as Employee and Country. The Repositories folder contains repository classes such as EmployeeRepository and CountryRepository. The Security folder contains identity-related classes such as AppIdentityUser and AppIdentityUser.

Now that you are familiar with the project organization, let's begin developing this project by adding an EF Core model and repositories. Make sure you have created the EmployeeManager.Blazor.ServerSide project based on the Blazor Server App project template discussed earlier. You may also remove the default Razor Components and classes included in the project template to reduce the clutter.

Entity Framework Core Model and Repositories

To perform CRUD operations, you use Entity Framework Core. So you need to have a custom DbContext and entity classes (Employee and Country) in the project.

Add the Models folder under the project root folder and place AppDbContext. cs, Employee.cs, and Country.cs files there from any previous project (say, MVC version of Employee Manager). After adding these files to the project, make sure to change their namespace to EmployeeManager.Blazor.ServerSide.Models. You are already familiar with the EF Core model required for data access, and hence it is not discussed here again.

Note   You can get the complete code of the Employee Manager application being developed in this chapter from the book's source code download.

Rather than directly using the `AppDbContext` class in the Razor Components, you create repositories to encapsulate CRUD operations. To create repositories, add the Repositories folder and add two interfaces to it named `IEmployeeRepository` and `ICountryRepository`. These interfaces should look familiar to you because you created them while learning Web APIs. For your quick reference, they are shown in Listing 8-1.

Listing 8-1. IEmployeeRepository and ICountryRepository interfaces

```
public interface IEmployeeRepository
{
    List<Employee> SelectAll();
    Employee SelectByID(int id);
    void Insert(Employee emp);
    void Update(Employee emp);
    void Delete(int id);
}

public interface ICountryRepository
{
    List<Country> SelectAll();
}
```

Next, add a new class to the Repositories folder named EmployeeRepository and implement the IEmployeeRepository interface in it. Listing 8-2 shows the completed EmployeeRepository class.

Listing 8-2. EmployeeRepository encapsulates CRUD operations on the Employees table

```
public class EmployeeRepository : IEmployeeRepository
{
    private AppDbContext db = null;

    public EmployeeRepository(AppDbContext db)
    {
        this.db = db;
    }

    public List<Employee> SelectAll()
    {
        return db.Employees.ToList();
    }
```

```
public Employee SelectByID(int id)
{
    return db.Employees.Find(id);
}

public void Insert(Employee emp)
{
    db.Employees.Add(emp);
    db.SaveChanges();
}

public void Update(Employee emp)
{
    db.Employees.Update(emp);
    db.SaveChanges();
}

public void Delete(int id)
{
    Employee emp = db.Employees.Find(id);
    db.Employees.Remove(emp);
    db.SaveChanges();
}
}
```

This code should look familiar to you since you have already used EF Core methods such as Add(), Update(), Remove(), and SaveChanges(). The EmployeeRepository class injects AppDbContext in the constructor and stores it in a class member. The db member variable is used by all the other methods while performing CRUD operations. The CountryRepository implements ICountryRepository and is shown in Listing 8-3.

Listing 8-3. CountryRepository returns all the countries from the Countries table

```
public class CountryRepository : ICountryRepository
{
    private readonly AppDbContext db = null;

    public CountryRepository(AppDbContext db)
    {
        this.db = db;
    }

    public List<Country> SelectAll()
    {
        return db.Countries.ToList();
    }
}
```

You need to register the AppDbContext, EmployeeRepository, and CountryRepository classes with the DI framework. That's because you want to inject the repositories into the Razor Components you develop in later sections. To do so, open the Startup class and add code to the ConfigureServices() method as shown in Listing 8-4.

Listing 8-4. Registering AppDbContext and repositories with the DI container

```
public void ConfigureServices(IServiceCollection services)
{
    services.AddRazorPages();
    services.AddServerSideBlazor();

    services.AddDbContext<AppDbContext>(options => options.
    UseSqlServer(this.Configuration.GetConnectionString("AppDb")));
    services.AddScoped<IEmployeeRepository, EmployeeRepository>();
    services.AddScoped<ICountryRepository, CountryRepository>();
}
```

Notice the code shown in bold letters. The first line registers AppDbContext for DI. The code picks the database connection string from the appsettings.json file (you need to add the connection string to the appsettings.json file in case you haven't done that already).

The second and third lines register EmployeeRepository and CountryRepository with DI using the AddScoped() method. Recollect from earlier chapters that services added using the AddScoped() method are created once per request.

Note   You created this application using the Blazor Server App project template. You will observe that ConfigureServices() calls AddRazorPages() and AddServerSideBlazor() methods to register services required by the Blazor server-side application. Similarly, the UseEndpoints() call inside the Configure() method uses MapBlazorHub() and MapFallbackToPage() methods to set up Blazor's routing.

Display a List of Employees

To display a list of employees (Figure 8-4), you need to create a Razor Component named List.razor.

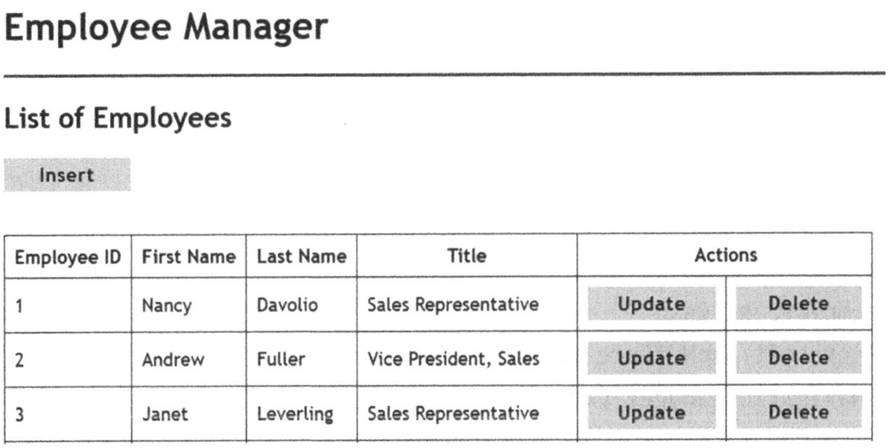

Employee Manager

List of Employees

Insert

Employee ID	First Name	Last Name	Title	Actions	
1	Nancy	Davolio	Sales Representative	Update	Delete
2	Andrew	Fuller	Vice President, Sales	Update	Delete
3	Janet	Leverling	Sales Representative	Update	Delete

Figure 8-4.   *Displaying a list of employees*

To add List.razor, right-click the Pages folder and select Add ➤ New Item to open the Add New Item dialog as shown in Figure 8-5.

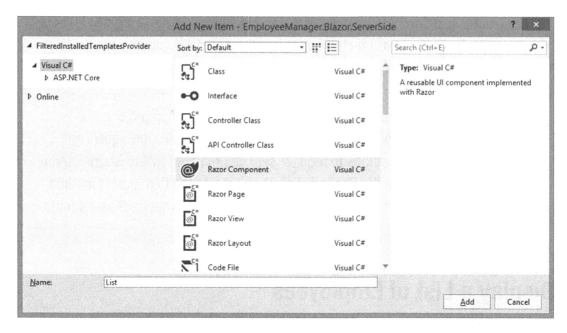

Figure 8-5. *Adding a new Razor Component*

From the list, select the Razor Component entry, specify the name as List, and click the Add button.

Once List.razor gets added, open it in Visual Studio editor and add the code shown in Listing 8-5 at the top of the Razor Component.

Listing 8-5. Defining route and injecting services

```
@page "/"
@page "/Employees/List"
@using Microsoft.AspNetCore.WebUtilities
@inject NavigationManager UriHelper
@inject IEmployeeRepository EmpRepository
```

The code consists of a series of directives. You want to use the List.razor component as a "page" rather than housing it inside other components. So the @page directive is used to associate this component to route templates. Notice that the code uses two @page directives, each specifying a route template. The first @page directive makes this component available as the default page of the application, so its route template is "/." The second @page directive makes the component accessible at /Employees/List. Blazor routing is integrated with ASP.NET Core's endpoint routing.

The @using directive specifies a namespace you want to use (Microsoft. AspNetCore.WebUtilities in this case). You could have specified this namespace inside the _Imports.razor file also in which case all the components would have been able to use it without the need of the @using directive. The QueryHelpers class from this namespace is used later in the code.

Then the @inject directive is used to inject an object of Microsoft.AspNetCore. Components.NavigationManager class. The @inject directive specifies two things: a type to be injected followed by a property name to receive the injected type (this property is automatically created by the compiler). You use this property name in your C# code to access the injected object.

The NavigationManager object injected into the component can be used to handle URLs and programmatic navigation. You use this object to read query string values (if any) as discussed later in this section.

On the same lines, the code injects the IEmployeeRepository object that can be accessed using the EmpRepository property.

Next, add a @code block below the directives just discussed and write the code shown in Listing 8-6 into it.

Listing 8-6. @code block fetches a list of employees

```
@code {
    List<Employee> Employees { get; set; }
    string Message { get; set; }

    protected override void OnInitialized()
    {
        Employees = EmpRepository.SelectAll();
        var uri = new Uri(UriHelper.Uri);
        if (QueryHelpers.ParseQuery(uri.Query).Count > 0)
        {
            Message = QueryHelpers.ParseQuery(uri.Query)
                .First().Value;
        }
    }
}
```

The @code block declares two properties, namely, Employees and Message. The former property is used to store a list of employees returned by the EmpRepository, whereas the latter property is used to store a message to be displayed to the user (if any).

Then there is the OnInitialized() lifecycle method that is called when a component is initialized. Inside the OnInitialized() method, the code calls the SelectAll() method of the EmpRepository object to retrieve a List of Employee objects. The return value of SelectAll() is assigned to the Employees property.

The next piece of code checks whether the URL contains a message or not. You need to do this because the delete component (discussed later in this chapter) passes a message to the employee listing page through query string. If this message exists in the query string, you need to display it to the user.

First, a Uri object is created based on the current URL. The current URL is obtained using the Uri property of the UriHelper object. The URL returned is passed to the constructor of the Uri class.

The next if statement checks whether the query string contains any parameters or not. This is done with the help of the QueryHelpers class and its ParseQuery() method. The ParseQuery() method parses a query string to obtain its key-value pairs. The Count property returns the number of key-value pairs. Inside, the code picks the first query string value (in this case, there is only one key-value pair) and assigns it to the Message property. The message is displayed to the user.

Note   In this example, you used a query string parameter to pass a message from the delete employee page to the employee listing page. However, you could have also used a route parameter instead of using query string. Route parameters are discussed in later sections. In more real-world situations, you should also include some error checking and validation for query string parameters being passed.

This completes the @code block. Below the @code block, write the HTML markup and intermingled C# code that displays a list of employees in a table (Listing 8-7).

Listing 8-7. Displaying a list of employees in the HTML table

```
<h2>List of Employees</h2>
<h3 class="message">@Message</h3>
<a href='/employees/insert' class="linkbutton">Insert</a>
```

```
<br /><br />
<table border="1" cellpadding="10">
    <tr>
        <th>Employee ID</th>
        <th>First Name</th>
        <th>Last Name</th>
        <th>Title</th>
        <th colspan="2">Actions</th>
    </tr>
    @foreach (var item in Employees)
    {
        <tr>
            <td>@item.EmployeeID</td>
            <td>@item.FirstName</td>
            <td>@item.LastName</td>
            <td>@item.Title</td>
            <td>
            <a href='/employees/update/@item.EmployeeID'
                class="linkbutton">Update</a>
            </td>
            <td>
            <a href='/employees/delete/@item.EmployeeID'
                class="linkbutton">Delete</a>
            </td>
        </tr>
    }
</table>
```

Below the page heading, the Message property value is displayed on the page. An anchor element points to the Insert.razor component (discussed later in this chapter) accessible at /employees/insert.

Note   In this example, you used the anchor element because the navigation is quite simple and straightforward. Blazor also provides the <NavLink> component that can be used to render hyperlinks to Razor Components. It has some additional features such as automatically setting the active CSS class for the link if the href attribute matches the current URL.

Then a <table> is rendered for displaying a list of employees. Notice the use of the @foreach loop to generate table rows. Every row generated displays EmployeeID, FirstName, LastName, and Title of the employee. Each row also has Update and Delete links. The Update link points to Update.razor accessible at /employees/update, and the Delete link points to Delete.razor accessible at /employees/delete. EmployeeID is also passed in these routes.

This completes the List.razor component.

Insert a New Employee

Clicking the Insert link on the employee listing component takes you to another component where you can insert a new employee (Figure 8-6). 

Figure 8-6. *Inserting a new employee*

To develop this component, add a new Razor Component named Insert.razor into the Pages folder.

Then add the directives shown in Listing 8-8 at the top of Insert.razor.

Listing 8-8. Defining routing and injecting repositories for Insert.razor

```
@page "/Employees/Insert"
@inject IEmployeeRepository EmpRepository
@inject ICountryRepository CtryRepository
```

Here, the @page directive specifies the route template to be /Employees/ Insert. The @inject statements inject two repositories that can be accessed as EmpRepository and CtryRepository properties, respectively.

Next, add a @code block to the component and write the code shown in Listing 8-9.

Listing 8-9. @code block with properties and event handlers

```
@code {
    Employee EmployeeModel { get; set; }
    List<Country> Countries { get; set; }
    string Message { get; set; }

    protected override void OnInitialized()
    {
        EmployeeModel = new Employee();
        Countries = CtryRepository.SelectAll();
    }

    private void OnSaveClick()
    {
        EmpRepository.Insert(EmployeeModel);
        Message = "Employee inserted successfully!";
    }
}
```

The @code block defines three properties, namely, EmployeeModel, Countries, and Message. The EmployeeModel property is of type Employee and is used for data binding with the data entry form (discussed latter). The Countries property holds a List of Country objects and is used to populate the Country dropdown list. The Message string property is used to display a success or error message to the user.

The @code block then proceeds to override the OnInitialized() lifecycle method. Inside, the code assigns a new Employee object to the EmployeeModel property. The code also calls the SelectAll() method of CtryRepository which fetches a list of all the countries from the Countries table.

Next, the @code block contains an event handler method named OnSaveClick(). This event handler method handles the OnValidSubmit event of the data entry form (discussed latter). Inside, the code calls the Insert() method of EmpRepository by passing the Employee object data bound with the form (as represented by the EmployeeModel property). A success message is displayed to the user by assigning it to the Message property.

This completes the @code block. Now proceed to add the markup shown in Listing 8-10.

Listing 8-10. Creating the data entry form using the <EditForm> component

```
<h2>Insert New Employee</h2>
<h3 class="message">@Message</h3>
<EditForm Model="EmployeeModel" OnValidSubmit="OnSaveClick">
  <DataAnnotationsValidator></DataAnnotationsValidator>
  <ValidationSummary></ValidationSummary>
</EditForm>
<br /><br />
<a href="/employees/list">Back to Employee Listing</a>
```

Notice the markup shown in bold letters. It shows the <EditForm> component of Blazor used to define a data entry form. The Model attribute of the <EditForm> element specifies a model object used for data binding with the form. Notice how the EmployeeModel property is used for this purpose. The OnValidSubmit attribute represents an event that is raised when a form contains valid entries and is submitted by a user. The OnSaveClick() method created earlier in the @code block is specified as the event handler of the OnValidSubmit event.

Inside the <EditForm> element, there are two components in the form of <Data AnnotationsValidator> and <ValidationSummary> elements. The <DataAnnotations Validator> component enables data annotation–based validations for this form. The Employee model class uses data annotations such as [Required] and [StringLength]. Using <DataAnnotationsValidator> means that the form can be validated on the basis of those data annotations. The <ValidationSummary> component renders a list of validation errors (if any) from the form.

The other parts of the form should look familiar to you since you used them on the List.razor component also.

Next, add the markup shown in Listing 8-11 in between the <DataAnnotationsValidator> and <ValidationSummary> components. For the sake of clarity, only the first name field is shown; other fields are discussed later.

Listing 8-11. Defining form fields and validations

```
<table border="0" cellpadding="10">
    <tr>
        <td class="right">
            <label for="FirstName">First Name :</label>
        </td>
        <td>
            <InputText id="FirstName"
            @bind-Value="EmployeeModel.FirstName" />
            <ValidationMessage
            For="(() => EmployeeModel.FirstName)" />
        </td>
    </tr>
    . . .
    . . .
```

Notice the code shown in bold letters. It shows the <InputText> component used to render a textbox (HTML <input> field with type of text). The <InputText> is to be data bound with the FirstName property of the Employee object. This is done by setting the @bind-Value attribute of the component to the FirstName property of the Employee object.

To display field–level validation errors (if any), the `<ValidationMessage>` component is used. The `For` attribute of the `<ValidationMessage>` element specifies a lambda expression representing an associated model property (`FirstName` in this case).

Just like the `<InputText>` component, there are a few more including `<InputDate>`, `<InputSelect>`, and `<InputTextArea>`. These components render an `<input>` field of type `date`, `<select>` element, and `<textarea>`, respectively. In this example, BirthDate and HireDate model properties are displayed using the `<InputDate>` component, the Country property is displayed using the `<InputSelect>` component, and the Notes property is displayed using the `<InputTextArea>` component, respectively.

The markup to display BirthDate and HireDate properties is shown in Listing 8-12.

Listing 8-12. Displaying BirthDate and HireDate using the <InputDate> component

```
<InputDate id="BirthDate"
@bind-Value="EmployeeModel.BirthDate" />
<ValidationMessage For="(() => EmployeeModel.BirthDate)" />

<InputDate id="HireDate"
@bind-Value="EmployeeModel.HireDate" />
<ValidationMessage For="(() => EmployeeModel.HireDate)" />
```

This markup is quite similar to the previous one except that it uses the `<InputDate>` component. Use of the `@bind-Value` attributes data binds `BirthDate` and `HireDate` properties, respectively. The `<ValidationMessage>` elements display validation messages for `BirthDate` and `HireDate` properties.

Note   Components such as <InputText>, <Inputdate>, <InputSelect>, and <InputTextArea> are collectively called input components. Input components are validated (if validation logic is associated with them) when a field value is changed and when a form is submitted. You can also use plain HTML <input> elements to render data entry fields.

To display the Country property, you use the `<InputSelect>` component. You also need to add a bit of code because the `<option>` elements are to be added depending on the Countries list. Listing 8-13 shows how this is done.

Listing 8-13. Displaying Country using the <InputSelect> component

```
<InputSelect id="Country"
@bind-Value="EmployeeModel.Country">
    <option value="">Please select</option>
    foreach (var c in Countries)
    {
        <option value="@c.Name">@c.Name</option>
    }
</InputSelect>
<ValidationMessage For="(() => EmployeeModel.Country)" />
```

The <InputSelect> element is data bound with the Country property using the @bind-Value attribute. An empty <option> element – Please select – is added to the resultant <select> element. Moreover, a foreach loop iterates through the Countries list and adds the <option> element for every available country. A validation message is displayed using the <ValidationMessage> component as before.

To display the Notes property, add the markup shown in Listing 8-14.

Listing 8-14. Displaying Notes using the <InputTextArea> component

```
<InputTextArea id="notes"
@bind-Value="EmployeeModel.Notes"
rows="5"
cols="40" />
<ValidationMessage For="(() => EmployeeModel.Notes)" />
```

Notice that in addition to the @bind-Value attribute, the <InputTextArea> element also specifies rows and cols attributes to specify rows and columns for the resultant <textarea>.

Finally, there is also a Submit button at the bottom of the data entry form that submits the form. You can get the complete context of Insert.razor from this chapter's code download.

Note   You might notice that while inserting an employee, the insert component initially displays DateTime.MinValue in the BirthDate and HireDate input components. If you want to show these fields empty, just make the BirthDate and HireDate properties of the Employee class nullable. For example, the BirthDate property can be changed to public DateTime? BirthDate { get; set; }, and HireDate can be changed to public DateTime? HireDate { get; set; }.

Update an Existing Employee

Clicking the Update button on the employee listing page takes you to the update existing employee Razor Component where existing details of an employee are presented for editing (Figure 8-7).

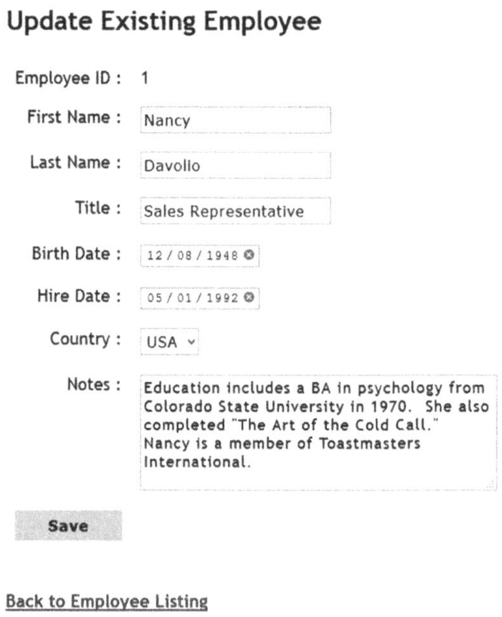

Update Existing Employee

Employee ID :   1

First Name :   Nancy

Last Name :   Davolio

Title :   Sales Representative

Birth Date :   12 / 08 / 1948

Hire Date :   05 / 01 / 1992

Country :   USA

Notes :   Education includes a BA in psychology from Colorado State University in 1970. She also completed "The Art of the Cold Call." Nancy is a member of Toastmasters International.

Save

Back to Employee Listing

Figure 8-7. *Updating an existing employee*

To create this page, add a new Razor Component named Update.razor and place the @page and @inject statements as shown in Listing 8-15.

Listing 8-15. Defining page route for the update component

```
@page "/Employees/Update/{EmployeeID:int}"
@inject IEmployeeRepository EmpRepository
@inject ICountryRepository CtryRepository
```

Notice the code shown in bold letters. It defines a route template for the update component. The update component needs to accept an EmployeeID whose details are to be updated. So the route template also includes a route parameter named EmployeeID. EmployeeID is an integer value, and hence the parameter constraint specifies its data type to be int. The @inject statements are identical to the insert component created earlier and inject EmployeeRepository and CountryRepository objects into the component.

Next, add a @code block and the code shown in Listing 8-16 in it.

Listing 8-16. EmployeeID is marked with the [Parameter] attribute

```
@code {
    [Parameter]
    public int EmployeeID { get; set; }
    Employee EmployeeModel { get; set; }
    List<Country> Countries { get; set; }
    string Message { get; set; }

    protected override void OnInitialized()
    {
        Countries = CtryRepository.SelectAll();
        EmployeeModel = EmpRepository.SelectByID(EmployeeID);
    }

    private void OnSaveClick()
    {
        EmpRepository.Update(EmployeeModel);
                Message = "Employee updated successfully!";
    }
}
```

Notice the code shown in bold letters. First, there is the public EmployeeID integer property. The EmployeeID route parameter's value is to be assigned to this property. The [Parameter] attribute marked on top of it does that job.

In addition to fetching a list of all countries, the OnInitialized() lifecycle method also fetches an existing employee from the database. This is done by calling the SelectByID() method of EmpRepository and passing EmployeeID to it. The returned Employee object acts as the model for the <EditForm> component and is stored in the EmployeeModel property.

The OnSaveClick() method acts as the OnValidSubmit event handler of the <EditForm> element. Inside, it calls the Update() method of EmpRepository and passes the modified Employee object (as represented by the EmployeeModel property) to it.

Below the @code block, you need to write the markup that renders the update form. This markup is quite similar to the insert component markup and uses the <EditForm> component and other input components such as <InputText>. The only difference is that it also shows the EmployeeID being modified in the table (Listing 8-17).

Listing 8-17. <EditForm> component that renders the update form

```
<h2>Update Existing Employee</h2>
<h3 class="message">@Message</h3>
<EditForm Model="EmployeeModel" OnValidSubmit="OnSaveClick">
    <DataAnnotationsValidator></DataAnnotationsValidator>
    <table border="0" cellpadding="10">
        <tr>
            <td class="right">
                <label>Employee ID :</label>
            </td>
            <td>
                @EmployeeModel.EmployeeID
            </td>
        </tr>
        ...
        ...
    </table>
    <ValidationSummary></ValidationSummary>
</EditForm>
<br /><br />
<a href="/employees/list">Back to Employee Listing</a>
```

As you can see, the EmployeeID being modified is outputted on the page. The other markup is identical to the insert component, and you can grab it from the Update.razor file available with this chapter's code download.

Delete an Existing Employee

Upon clicking the Delete button on the employee listing page, you navigate to the delete existing employee Razor Component (Figure 8-8).

Delete Existing Employee

Warning : You are about to delete an employee record.

Employee ID : 1

First Name : Nancy

Last Name : Davolio

Title : Sales Representative

Birth Date : 08 December 1948

Hire Date : 01 May 1992

Country : USA

Notes : Education includes a BA in psychology from Colorado State University in 1970. She also completed "The Art of the Cold Call." Nancy is a member of Toastmasters International.

Delete

Back to Employee Listing

Figure 8-8. *Seeking delete confirmation from the user*

To create the delete component, add a new Razor Component named Delete.razor and set it up as shown in Listing 8-18.

Listing 8-18. Defining routing and injecting EmployeeRepository

```
@page "/Employees/Delete/{EmployeeID:int}"
@inject IEmployeeRepository EmpRepository
@inject NavigationManager UriHelper
```

This code should look familiar to you since it is quite similar to the update component. Just like the update component, the route template contains the EmployeeID parameter. Also notice that in addition to injecting EmpRepository, it also injects the NavigationManager object. You need this object to programmatically navigate to the employee listing page once an employee record is deleted.

Below the @page and @inject directives, you need to write the @code block as shown in Listing 8-19.

Listing 8-19. Deleting an employee record and navigating to the employee listing page

```
@code {
    [Parameter]
    public int EmployeeID { get; set; }
    Employee EmployeeModel { get; set; }
    string Message { get; set; }

    protected override void OnInitialized()
    {
        EmployeeModel = EmpRepository.SelectByID(EmployeeID);
    }

    private void OnDeleteClick()
    {
        EmpRepository.Delete(EmployeeID);
        Message = "Employee deleted successfully!";
        UriHelper.NavigateTo
        ($"/employees/list?Message={Message}");
    }
}
```

The @code block declares the EmployeeID public property and marks it with the [Parameter] attribute. This way EmployeeID passed in the route is assigned to the EmployeeID property.

The EmployeeModel property gets assigned in the OnInitialized() lifecycle method. This is done by calling the SelectByID() method of EmpRepository by passing an EmployeeID value.

Upon clicking the Delete button, the OnDeleteClick() event handler method gets called. Inside, the code calls the Delete() method of EmpRepository by passing an EmployeeID. A success message is assigned to the Message property.

Once an employee record is successfully deleted, you need to take the user back to the employee listing page. Additionally, you also want to display a success message on the employee listing page that indicates the outcome of the delete operation. To accomplish this, the code uses the UriHelper object. The NavigateTo() method of UriHelper accepts a URL to navigate and redirects a user to that URL. Here, the code also passes a query string parameter named Message that holds the value of the Message property. Recollect that you have written code in List.razor to read this query string parameter and render on the screen.

Below the @code block, you need to write the markup that displays employee details from EmployeeModel into the HTML table. You also need to seek delete confirmation from the user. You could have used the <EditForm> component here also. However, since there are no editable controls on this page, you use a variation as shown in Listing 8-20.

Listing 8-20. Displaying employee details and seeking delete confirmation

```
<h2>Delete Existing Employee</h2>
<h3 class="message">
    Warning : You are about to delete an employee record.
</h3>
<form>
    <table border="0">
        <tr>
            <td class="right">
                <label>EmployeeID :</label>
            </td>
            <td>
                @EmployeeModel.EmployeeID
            </td>
        </tr>
        ...
        ...
```

```
        <tr>
            <td colspan="2">
                <button type="button"
                        @onclick="OnDeleteClick">
                  Delete
                </button>
            </td>
        </tr>
    </table>
</form>
<br /><br />
<a href="/employees/list">Back to Employee Listing</a>
```

Notice the code shown in bold letters. Here, you use the <form> element rather than the <EditForm> component. Inside, a table displaying employee details is rendered. For the sake of clarity, only the first and last rows of the table are shown (you can get the complete markup from this chapter's code download). The first row shows EmployeeID, and the last row contains a <button> element. The type of the button is button rather than submit. Moreover, the @onclick event attribute is assigned a value of OnDeleteClick (name of the event handler method you wrote in the @code block). This way clicking the Delete button will invoke the OnDeleteClick() event handler method.

Note   The onclick event handler method can accept a parameter of type MouseEventArgs. This event argument object supplies additional information about the event such as state of Ctrl, Shift, and Alt keys, screen coordinates of the mouse pointer, mouse button that was pressed, and so on. In the code shown in the preceding text, you don't need any such information, and hence that parameter was not used.

This completes all the four Razor Components (List.razor, Insert.razor, Update. razor, and Delete.razor) required to perform the CRUD operations. Before you run the application and confirm their working, you need to apply the CSS style sheet and layout to the application. This is explained in the following section.

Apply CSS and Layout to Razor Components

In the examples from the previous chapter, you know that Employee Manager's styling information resides in the Site.css file located under the /wwwroot/Styles folder. So firstly, place the Site.css file inside the /wwwroot/styles folder of the Blazor project.

Then locate the _Host.cshtml file from the Pages folder and modify it as shown in Listing 8-21.

Listing 8-21. Applying the CSS style sheet

```
@page "/"
@namespace EmployeeManager.Blazor.ServerSide.Pages
@addTagHelper *, Microsoft.AspNetCore.Mvc.TagHelpers
<!DOCTYPE html>
<html lang="en">
<head>
    ...
    <title>Employee Manager</title>
    <base href="~/" />
    <link href="~/Styles/site.css" rel="stylesheet" />
</head>
...
</html>
```

The _Host.cshtml file contains top-level HTML elements such as `<html>`, `<head>`, and `<body>`. Notice the markup shown in bold letters. It sets the application's title to Employee Manager and also adds the `<link>` element that points to Site.css from the /wwwroot/Styles folder. Make sure to remove other `<link>` elements that apply Bootstrap CSS framework to the application.

The `<ValidationMessage>` and `<ValidationSummary>` components use a CSS class named `validation-message` while displaying the error messages. So add that to your Site.css file:

```
.validation-message {
    color: red;
    font-weight: bold;
}
```

Next, locate the MainLayout.razor file from the Shared folder and modify it as shown in Listing 8-22.

Listing 8-22. MainLayout.razor contains layout applied to the components

```
@inherits LayoutComponentBase

<h1>Employee Manager</h1>
<hr />
<div>
    @Body
</div>
<br />
<hr />
```

The markup is quite straightforward. Blazor layouts inherit from the LayoutComponentBase class. Here, the layout sets the main heading of the application. To render the output of various Razor Components at a particular location in the layout file, you use @Body syntax.

You will revisit MainLayout again after integrating ASP.NET Core Identity with the application.

Note   You might wonder where exactly MainLayout.razor is applied to the Razor Components. That's done inside the App.razor file residing under the project root folder. All the components are applied MainLayout based on this setting.

Integrating ASP.NET Core Identity

In the preceding sections, you developed Employee Manager using the Blazor server-side hosting model. Although the application is able to perform CRUD operations, it lacks user authentication. As far as user authentication is concerned, Blazor server-side applications can utilize ASP.NET Core Identity just like ASP.NET Core MVC and ASP.NET Core Razor Pages applications.

While integrating ASP.NET Core Identity support into the Employee Manager Blazor application, you need to add the same Identity DbContext, models, Razor Pages, and startup configuration as you did with the Razor Pages version of Employee Manager earlier in this book. You could have also used the MVC version, but the Razor Pages version is more suited here because Blazor syntax closely matches to the Razor Pages syntax. Since all the pieces required are ready with you, just copy them into this project as instructed in the following. And then fine-tune them at a few places as explained in the later sections.

In order to integrate ASP.NET Core Identity in this project, you need to carry out the following steps.

Add IdentityDbContext and Associated Classes

Add a new folder named Security under the Employee Manager Blazor application's root folder. Then copy these files from the Razor Pages version of Employee Manager to it:

- AppIdentityDbContext.cs

- AppIdentityUser.cs

- AppIdentityRole.cs

After adding these files, make sure to change their namespace to EmployeeManager. Blazor.ServerSide.Security. The first file represents AppIdentityDbContext that communicates with the underlying data store. The other two files represent custom user and role, respectively.

Note   You also need database tables used by ASP.NET Core Identity. If you worked through the earlier versions of Employee Manager discussed in this book, you already have these tables in the Northwind database. Otherwise, you need to install the dotnet-ef tool and EF Core migrations to create the required tables. You may refer to Chapter 3 for more details.

Add Register and SignIn View Models

The project root folder already has the Models folder containing entity classes such as Employee and Country. Add Register.cs and SignIn.cs files from the Razor Pages version to this folder.

After adding the files, change their namespace to EmployeeManager.Blazor. ServerSide.Models. These files represent view models for the user registration page and sign-in page, respectively.

Add Register, SignIn, and SignOut Razor Pages

Under the Pages folder, create a subfolder named Security. Then copy these files from the Razor Pages version:

- Register.cshtml and Register.cshtml.cs

- SignIn.cshtml and SignIn.cshtml.cs

- SignOut.cshtml and SignOut.cshtml.cs

The .cshtml files contain the Razor Pages markup, whereas .cshtml.cs files contain PageModel classes. As before, change the namespace of the page model classes to EmployeeManager.Blazor.ServerSide.Pages.Security.

After adding these files, open SignIn.cshtml.cs and go to the OnPostAsync() page handler method. If sign-in operation is successful, the user should be redirected to the default Razor Component (List.razor). So change the line as shown in Listing 8-23.

Listing 8-23. User is redirected to List.razor upon successful sign-in

```
public async Task<IActionResult> OnPostAsync()
{
    if (ModelState.IsValid)
    {
        var result = await signinManager.PasswordSignInAsync
        (SignInData.UserName, SignInData.Password,
            SignInData.RememberMe, false);

        if (result.Succeeded)
        {
            return Redirect("/Employees/List");
        }
```

```
    else
    {
        ModelState.AddModelError("", "Invalid user details");
    }
}
return Page();
}
```

Recollect that List.razor is associated with the /Employees/List route template.

Now open SignOut.cshtml.cs and rename the OnPostAsync() page handler method to OnGetAsync(). You need to do this because in this case the Sign Out button resides inside MainLayout.razor (external to Razor Pages). And clicking the Sign Out button should invoke the SignOutAsync() method of SignInManager. The modified page handler is shown in Listing 8-24.

Listing 8-24. OnGetAsync() page handler of the SignOut page

```
public async Task<IActionResult> OnGetAsync()
{
    await signinManager.SignOutAsync();
    return RedirectToPage("/Security/SignIn");
}
```

As you can see, the OnGetAsync() removes the authentication cookie by calling the SignOutAsync() method of SignInManager and redirects the user to the sign-in page.

Add _Layout, _ViewStart, and _ViewImports Files

Earlier in this chapter, you worked with MainLayout.razor and _Imports.razor files. They are applied to Razor Components. The Register, SignIn, and SignOut Razor Pages also need their layout page, view start page, and view imports page. So copy these files from the Razor Pages version and place them in the Pages ➤ Security folder:

- _Layout.cshtml
- _ViewStart.cshtml
- _ViewImports.cshtml

Then open _ViewImports.cshtml and modify it to have the Security namespace as shown in Listing 8-25.

Listing 8-25. Add the Security namespace to _ViewImports.cshtml

```
@using EmployeeManager.Blazor.ServerSide.Pages.Security
@addTagHelper *, Microsoft.AspNetCore.Mvc.TagHelpers
```

As you can see, the using statement now specifies the EmployeeManager.Blazor. ServerSide.Pages.Security namespace. Due to this statement, you can simply specify the page model class name in the @model directive rather than specifying a fully qualified class name. There is also a @addTagHelper statement since Razor Pages use Tag Helpers to render their user interface.

Register and Configure ASP.NET Core Identity

In order to use ASP.NET Core Identity, you need to register it in the ConfigureServices() method of the Startup class. This is shown in Listing 8-26.

Listing 8-26. Registering ASP.NET Core Identity services

```
public void ConfigureServices(IServiceCollection services)
{
    services.AddRazorPages();
    services.AddServerSideBlazor();
    services.AddDbContext<AppDbContext>(options => options.UseSqlServer
    (this.Configuration.GetConnectionString("AppDb")));

    services.AddDbContext<AppIdentityDbContext>(options =>
    options.UseSqlServer(this.Configuration.GetConnectionString
    ("AppDb")));
    services.AddIdentity<AppIdentityUser, AppIdentityRole>()
            .AddEntityFrameworkStores<AppIdentityDbContext>();
    services.AddScoped<IEmployeeRepository,EmployeeRepository>();
services.AddScoped<ICountryRepository, CountryRepository>();
}
```

Notice the code shown in bold letters. Firstly, it registers `AppIdentityDbContext` with the DI container using the `AddDbContext()` method. Secondly, it registers ASP.NET Core Identity services using the `AddIdentity()` method. This also sets the security scheme for the application to ASP.NET Core Identity. This code should look familiar to you because you used it in earlier versions of Employee Manager also.

Next, go in the `Configure()` method and modify it as shown in Listing 8-27.

Listing 8-27. Add authentication and authorization middleware

```
public void Configure(IApplicationBuilder app, IWebHostEnvironment env)
{
    ...
    app.UseStaticFiles();
    app.UseRouting();

        app.UseAuthentication();
        app.UseAuthorization();

    app.UseEndpoints(endpoints =>
    {
        endpoints.MapBlazorHub();
        endpoints.MapFallbackToPage("/_Host");
    });
}
```

The `UseAuthentication()` method adds authentication middleware to the request pipeline. Similarly, the `UseAuthorization()` method adds authorization middleware. You can now decide which parts of your application require authentication and authorization.

Secure CRUD Razor Components

As far as the Employee Manager application being developed is concerned, you need to secure all the Razor Components that participate in CRUD operations. This includes List. razor, Insert.razor, Update.razor, and Delete.razor.

To enable user authentication in these Razor Components, you use the @attribute directive. The @attribute directive is followed by an attribute that gets added to the generated component class. Listing 8-28 shows how @attribute can be added to the List.razor component.

Listing 8-28. *@attribute directive adds an attribute to a component*

```
@page "/"
@page "/Employees/List"
@using Microsoft.AspNetCore.WebUtilities
@inject NavigationManager UriHelper
@inject IEmployeeRepository EmpRepository
@attribute [Authorize(Roles = "Manager")]
```

Notice the line shown in bold letters. It has the @attribute directive followed by the [Authorize] attribute. The [Authorize] attribute specifies the Roles property to Manager. You will find the [Authorize] attribute syntax identical to previous examples. Recollect that in MVC applications [Authorize] is applied to actions or controllers and in Razor Pages applications it is applied to page model classes. Here in Blazor, it is applied using the @attribute directive.

Add the [Authorize] attribute using the @attribute directive to other Razor Components. At this stage, if you run the application, the default component (recollect that List.razor is associated with the "/" route template) displays an error message as shown in Figure 8-9.

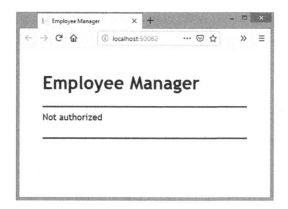

Figure 8-9. *Error while accessing the List.razor component*

As you can see, if a user is not authenticated or a user is not authorized to access a component, an error message (Not authorized) is displayed in the browser. This is the default error message, and you can customize it as described shortly.

To get rid of the error, navigate to /security/signin and sign in using a valid user account. Once you successfully sign in to the system, you will be taken to List.razor again, and this time the employee list will be displayed as expected.

Display the User Name and Sign Out Button

Once a user successfully signs in to the application, its user name is to be displayed at the bottom of all the Razor Components along with the Sign Out button. This is done in the MainLayout.razor file. Listing 8-29 shows how this is done.

Listing 8-29. Displaying the user name and Sign Out button

```
@inherits LayoutComponentBase

<h1>Employee Manager</h1>
<hr />
<div>
    @Body
</div>
<br />
<hr />

<AuthorizeView>
    <Authorized>
        <h2>You are signed in as @context.User.Identity.Name</h2>
        <a href='/security/signout'
            class="linkbutton">Sign Out</a>
    </Authorized>
</AuthorizeView>
```

Notice the <AuthorizeView> component placed at the end of the MainLayout.razor file. The <AuthorizeView> component is capable of displaying a user interface depending on whether a user is authorized or not. In this case, the <Authorized> section contains a user interface markup that is displayed only if a user is authorized to access a component.

The markup inside the `<Authorized>` section displays the user's sign-in name using context variable. The context variable is an object of the AuthenticationState class. You can use the context object to access user information.

The markup then renders a hyperlink that acts as a Sign Out button. The link points to the SignOut Razor Page you added to the Security folder in the earlier section.

Configure Initial Sign-In Prompt

From earlier discussion, you are aware that when you access Razor Components without signing in to the system, you are shown a "Not authorized" error message. You can customize this behavior by adding a friendlier message and a link to the sign-in page.

To do so, open the App.razor file from the project root folder. This file represents the Router component of Blazor. The App.razor file allows you to render custom user interface if it cannot find the component associated with a route or if user authorization has failed. Modify App.razor as shown in Listing 8-30.

Listing 8-30. Render custom user interface if authorization fails

```
<Router AppAssembly="@typeof(Program).Assembly">
    <Found Context="routeData">
        <AuthorizeRouteView RouteData="@routeData" DefaultLayout=
        "@typeof(MainLayout)">
            <NotAuthorized>
                <h2>You are not authorized to view this page.</h2>
                <h3>To sign in click <a href="/security/signin">here</a>.</h3>
            </NotAuthorized>
        </AuthorizeRouteView>
    </Found>
    <NotFound>
        <CascadingAuthenticationState>
            <LayoutView Layout="@typeof(MainLayout)">
                <p>Sorry, there's nothing at this address.</p>
            </LayoutView>
        </CascadingAuthenticationState>
    </NotFound>
</Router>
```

The App.razor file contains the <Router> component. Inside, there are two sections as defined by <Found> and <NotFound> parameters.

The user interface that you want to render in the browser if a route is not associated with any component is governed by the <NotFound> parameter. The <AuthorizeRouteView> component and its <NotAuthorized> parameter control the user interface displayed if a user is not authorized to access a component. The content from the <NotAuthorized> section informs the user of authorization status and provides a link to the sign-in page. Also notice that DefaultLayout and Layout values render the components using the specified layout.

After making these changes, if you run the application, you will be displayed a user interface as shown in Figure 8-10.

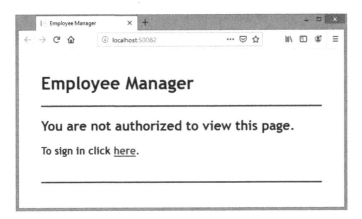

Figure 8-10. *Custom user interface is shown if the user is not authorized*

You can now click the sign-in link to reach the sign-in page and sign in with valid credentials to access the employee listing.

This completes the application. Run it, sign in with valid user credentials, and confirm the working of CRUD operations.

Use Policy-Based Authorization

So far in this book, you used role-based authorization to ensure that only users belonging to the Manager role can access the CRUD pages. Role-based authorization works great in many cases. However, at times your authorization needs are a bit more complex.

Suppose you have defined three roles in your system, say, Manager, Operator, and Administrator. As your application evolves, you might find it difficult to fit all the authorization rules into these three predefined roles. For example, you might want to authorize a few pages based on the user's role and a few more additional conditions. In such cases, you can't simply authorize users based on their roles. That's where ASP.NET Core's policy-based authorization can be used.

Policy-based authorization uses a policy to authorize users. A policy is a bundle of one or more requirements. A requirement is an object that implements the IAuthorizationRequirement interface. It would be interesting to know that ASP. NET Core's role-based authorization and claims-based authorization internally use a requirement and a predefined policy.

An authorization policy is defined in ConfigureServices(). Listing 8-31 shows a policy named MustBeManager being defined.

Listing 8-31. Defining a custom policy

```
public void ConfigureServices(IServiceCollection services)
{
    ...
    services.AddIdentity<AppIdentityUser, AppIdentityRole>()
            .AddEntityFrameworkStores<AppIdentityDbContext>();

    services.AddAuthorization(config =>
    {
      config.AddPolicy("MustBeManager",
          policy =>
          {
            policy.RequireRole("Manager");
          }
      );
   });
    ...
}
```

Notice the code shown in bold letters. The AddAuthorization() method defines a new policy using the AddPolicy() method. The AddPolicy() method takes two parameters: name of a policy and a set of requirements. As far as Employee Manager is concerned, the requirement is that a user must belong to the Manager role. To specify this requirement, the code uses the RequireRole() method. You could have used the RequireClaim() method to specify claim(s) as requirements, or you could have also used the Requirements collection to add custom IAuthorizationRequirement objects.

Now you have MustBeManager policy ready. The next step is to specify this policy while authorizing users. This is done in the [Authorize] attribute added in various components. Listing 8-32 shows the modified [Authorize] attribute in the List.razor component.

Listing 8-32. Applying a policy to a Razor Component

```
@page "/"
@page "/Employees/List"
@using Microsoft.AspNetCore.WebUtilities
@inject NavigationManager UriHelper
@inject IEmployeeRepository EmpRepository
@attribute [Authorize(Policy = "MustBeManager")]
```

As you can see, the [Authorize] attribute now uses its Policy property to specify an authorization policy (MustBeManager in this case). Users can access List.razor only if they meet the requirements set by the specified policy.

Note   You can use policy-based authorization in MVC and Razor Pages applications using the same technique. Detailed discussion of policy-based authorization is beyond the scope of this book. You may read more at https://docs.microsoft.com/en-us/aspnet/core/security/authorization/policies.

Summary

Blazor is a relatively new addition to the ASP.NET Core family and allows you to develop rich client applications that run in the browser. What's more, you can do the entire development (server side and client side) using C#, HTML, and CSS.

Blazor provides two hosting models: client side and server side. The client-side hosting model uses WebAssembly, whereas the server-side hosting model uses SignalR for its working. This chapter used Blazor's server-side hosting to build Employee Manager. You were introduced to many Blazor features such as lifecycle methods, creating custom Razor Components, using built-in components, routing, and dependency injection. After developing the CRUD components, you also integrated ASP.NET Core Identity support with the application.

So far in this book, you used local installation of SQL Server for your data storage needs. Modern applications often resort to cloud-based data stores. Moreover, NoSQL databases are also becoming more and more common. To that end, the next chapter is going to show you how to deal with three different data stores: Azure SQL Databases, Cosmos DB, and MongoDB.

CHAPTER 9

Azure SQL Database, Azure Cosmos DB, and MongoDB

So far in this book, you have been using a local instance of SQL Server which houses the Northwind database. In this chapter, you will move the Northwind database to the cloud using Azure SQL Database. The Employee Manager application then uses this database to perform the CRUD operations. Although relational databases are commonly used to store application data, non-relational and NoSQL databases are becoming more and more common. This chapter covers two such data stores: Cosmos DB and MongoDB. Specifically, this chapter teaches you to

- Create an Azure SQL Database using the Azure portal and connect with it using SQL Server Management Studio

- Perform CRUD operations on Azure SQL Database using the Microsoft.Data.SqlClient data provider

- Understand what NoSQL databases are and where do Cosmos DB and MongoDB fit into the picture

- Perform CRUD operations on Cosmos DB using the Microsoft Azure Cosmos DB client library and EF Core provider for Cosmos DB

- Perform CRUD operations on MongoDB using the MongoDB .NET driver

- Use custom cookie authentication without using ASP.NET Core Identity

Let's begin this chapter's journey with Azure SQL Database.

© Bipin Joshi 2019
B. Joshi, *Beginning Database Programming Using ASP.NET Core 3*,
https://doi.org/10.1007/978-1-4842-5509-4_9

Creating Azure SQL Database

Traditionally, you use SQL Server installed locally on your development or somewhere within a known network. Azure takes the SQL Server databases to cloud. Azure SQL Database is a relational database-managed service and provides the same set of functionality that you have been using with the local SQL Server. One of the advantages of using Azure SQL Database is you don't need to change your application code just because you are moving your data to the cloud. It's the same database engine, but the data is hosted and managed by Azure data centers.

Since these SQL databases are hosted and managed by Azure, you need to have an Azure account to create and work with them. So I encourage you to get an Azure account before you proceed with the example discussed in the following sections.

Here, I am going to assume that you have an Azure account and are able to sign in to your account for the purpose of creating an SQL database. Figure 9-1 shows the initial page of the Azure portal displayed upon successful sign-in.

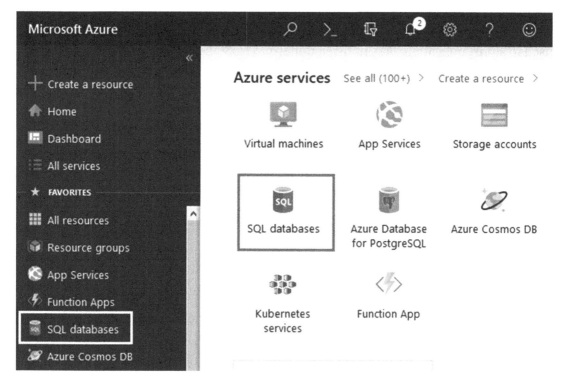

Figure 9-1. *SQL databases option in the Azure portal*

As you can see, there is an SQL databases option at the top of the main page as well as on the left side. Clicking the SQL databases option takes you to another page shown in Figure 9-2.

Figure 9-2. *Creating a new SQL database*

On this screen, click the Add button at the top. Doing so will open another screen where you need to fill a form with various settings for creating a new SQL database (Figure 9-3).

Create SQL Database
Microsoft

Basics   Additional settings   Tags   Review + create

Create a SQL database with your preferred configurations. Complete the Basics tab then go to Review + Create to provision with smart defaults, or visit each tab to customize. Learn more ☑

Project details

Select the subscription to manage deployed resources and costs. Use resource groups like folders to organize and manage all your resources.

* Subscription ❶	Visual Studio Enterprise	⌄

└─── * Resource group ❶	MyResourceGroup	⌄

Create new

database details

Enter required settings for this database, including picking a logical server and configuring the compute and storage resources

* Database name	Northwind	✓

Figure 9-3. *Specifying settings for a new SQL database*

At a minimum, you need to specify the following settings as per your Azure account setup:

- Subscription
- Resource group
- Database name (Northwind in this case)
- Server

Make sure to specify these details as per your Azure account setup. After specifying these details, click the Review + create button at the bottom of the page and complete the new database creation process. Upon successful creation of the database, you will be shown a success notification.

You can now see the newly created database on the main page of the SQL databases section. You can take a look at the basic database settings by clicking the Overview option (Figure 9-4).

Figure 9-4. *Database overview page*

You don't need to go into too much detail of this page. What's important for you is the Connection string section on the right side. Clicking the Show database connection string link will take you to another page where the ADO.NET connection string can be seen. Keep this connection string at a handy location because you will use it while connecting with the database.

One last step before you complete this section, you need to configure the server firewall to allow your client IP address. To do that, go to the Northwind database overview page and click the Set server firewall option (Figure 9-5) available at the top.

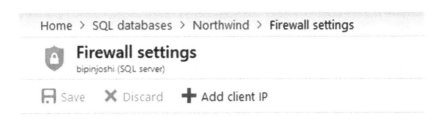

Figure 9-5. Setting the server firewall

Click the Add client IP button and add the client's IP to the list of allowed IP addresses. Your database is now ready to be accessed from SQL Server Management Studio.

Connecting to Azure SQL Database Using SQL Server Management Studio

Now, let's connect with the Northwind database you just created in Azure. Open SQL Server Management Studio and specify the connection details such as server, user name, and password based on the connection string you obtained earlier. Figure 9-6 shows the empty Northwind database upon successful connection.

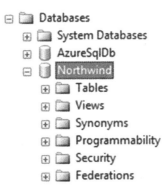

Figure 9-6. Northwind database in SQL Server Management Studio

You can now create the Employees and Countries tables in the Northwind database (you can use the CREATE TABLE statement to do that). You can also add some sample data in Employees and Countries tables.

Note   You can also take help from the T-SQL script of the Northwind database (you obtained this script from GitHub in Chapter 1) to add sample data to the Employees table.

Figure 9-7 shows a query being executed on the Northwind database hosted in Azure that returns employee records.

Figure 9-7. *Fetching employee records from the Azure SQL Database*

Employee Manager Using Azure SQL Database

In the sections that follow, you build the Employee Manager application (EmployeeManager.AzureSql) that performs the CRUD operations on the Northwind database that is hosted in Azure. The application is going to follow the same process as with the MVC version that you developed earlier. However, there are a few differences:

- The application uses the Northwind Azure SQL Database rather than the local installation of Northwind.

- The application uses the Microsoft.Data.SqlClient object model to perform the CRUD operations instead of using EF Core.

- The data access code is wrapped in repositories, and the EmployeeManagerController invokes the repositories to get the job done.

- The ASP.NET Core Identity tables are created in the Azure SQL Database.

Since the application is now familiar to you, I am going to focus only on the CRUD operations. You can get the complete code of this example from the book's source code download.

Note   This example uses Microsoft.Data.SqlClient classes to perform the CRUD operations. Although Entity Framework Core is a preferred way of accessing data in ASP.NET Core, at times you might want to have more control on the overall data access logic. For example, you might want to quickly migrate ADO.NET code to the newer framework, or you might want to work with queries and stored procedures directly rather than through an object relational mapper.

Employee and Country Model Classes

In order to work with this example, you need the Employee and Country model classes as before. However, since you aren't using EF Core in this example, these model classes are not entity classes. They are POCOs with validation attributes. Recollect that while building the client application for the ASP.NET Core Web API, you developed such model classes. You can grab the same classes and place them in the Models folder, or you can create them again. If you wish, you can also get them from the book's code download. Since these classes are already familiar to you, they are not being discussed here again.

Creating EmployeeRepository and CountryRepository

The CRUD operations are wrapped inside two repositories, namely, EmployeeRepository and CountryRepository. These repositories are based on the same interfaces (IEmployeeRepository and ICountryRepository) that you created in Chapter 5 earlier and reside inside the Repositories folder. So I am not going to discuss the interfaces in detail here. For your quick reference, these interfaces are shown in Listing 9-1.

Listing 9-1. IEmployeeRepository and ICountryRepository interfaces

```
public interface IEmployeeRepository
{
    List<Employee> SelectAll();
    Employee SelectByID(int id);
    void Insert(Employee emp);
    void Update(Employee emp);
    void Delete(int id);
}

public interface ICountryRepository
{
    List<Country> SelectAll();
}
```

Now add the EmployeeRepository class inside the Repositories folder. The Listing 9-2 shows the skeleton of this class.

Listing 9-2. Skeleton of the EmployeeRepository class

```
public class EmployeeRepository : IEmployeeRepository
{
    private string connectionString;

    public EmployeeRepository(IConfiguration config)
    {
        this.connectionString = config.GetConnectionString("AppDb");
    }
    ...
    ...
}
```

As you can see, the EmployeeRepository constructor accepts an object of IConfiguration. This is required because you need the database connection string while performing the CRUD operations. The connection string is stored in a member variable for later use.

SelectAll( ) Method

The SelectAll() method of EmployeeRepository returns all the Employee objects to the caller and is shown in Listing 9-3.

Listing 9-3. SelectAll() returns all the employees

```
public List<Employee> SelectAll()
{
    using (SqlConnection cnn = new SqlConnection(connectionString))
    {
        SqlCommand cmd = new SqlCommand();
        cmd.Connection = cnn;
        cmd.CommandType = CommandType.Text;
        cmd.CommandText = "SELECT EmployeeID, FirstName, LastName, Title,
        BirthDate, HireDate, Country, Notes FROM Employees ORDER BY
        EmployeeID ASC";

        cnn.Open();
        SqlDataReader reader = cmd.ExecuteReader();
        List<Employee> employees = new List<Employee>();
        while (reader.Read())
        {
            Employee item = new Employee();
            item.EmployeeID = reader.GetInt32(0);
            item.FirstName = reader.GetString(1);
            item.LastName = reader.GetString(2);
            item.Title = reader.GetString(3);
            item.BirthDate = reader.GetDateTime(4);
            item.HireDate = reader.GetDateTime(5);
            item.Country = reader.GetString(6);
```

```
            if (!reader.IsDBNull(7))
            {
                item.Notes = reader.GetString(7);
            }
            employees.Add(item);
        }
        reader.Close();
        cnn.Close();
        return employees;
    }
}
```

The code begins by creating a new SqlConnection object. The SqlConnection class represents a database connection and is available in the Microsoft.Data.SqlClient namespace. To access classes from this namespace, you need to install the NuGet package – Microsoft.Data.SqlClient – for your project (if you install Microsoft. EntityFrameworkCore.SqlServer, then this assembly is also installed). Notice that the whole code is put inside the using block so that the SqlConnection object is disposed once the method completes.

Inside the using block, the code creates a new SqlCommand object. The SqlCommand object represents a database command that you want to execute. Three properties of SqlCommand are then configured. Executing a database command requires an open database connection. The Connection property points to the SqlConnection object that you want to use while executing the database command.

The CommandType property is used to specify the type of database command you want to execute such as an SQL statement (Text) or a stored procedure (StoredProcedure).

The CommandText property specifies the database command to be executed. In this case, the code executes a SELECT statement that fetches required data from the Employees table.

In order to execute the SELECT statement, the database connection is established using the Open() method of SqlConnection. The query is executed using the ExecuteReader() method of the SqlCommand object. The ExecuteReader() method executes the query and returns the data in the form of the SqlDataReader object.

The SqlDataReader object is read-only and forward-only cursor, and the code iterates through it using the Read() method. The Read() method advances the current record pointer to the next record and allows you to read that record. Read() returns false if the end of records has been reached.

Inside the while loop, the code reads various column values using methods such as GetInt32(), GetString(), and GetDateTime(). These methods accept the column number (according to the SELECT query) to read value from. Which of the available GetXXXXXXX() methods to use depends on the data type of the column. For example, EmployeeID is an integer value, and hence the code uses the GetInt32() method. On the same lines, HireDate is a DateTime value, and hence GetDateTime() has been used. The column values obtained from these methods are filled into an Employee object, and the Employee object is added into a List. The IsDBNull() method accepts a column index and returns true if the specified column contains database NULL value.

Finally, the data reader and the database connection are closed using the Close() method, and the List of Employee objects is returned to the caller.

SelectByID() Method

The SelectByID() method is similar to SelectAll() but returns only a specific Employee to the caller. Listing 9-4 shows this method.

Listing 9-4. SelectByID() method returns a specific employee

```
public Employee SelectByID(int id)
{
    using (SqlConnection cnn = new SqlConnection(connectionString))
    {
        SqlCommand cmd = new SqlCommand();
        cmd.Connection = cnn;
        cmd.CommandType = CommandType.Text;
        cmd.CommandText = "SELECT EmployeeID, FirstName, LastName,
        Title, BirthDate, HireDate, Country, Notes FROM Employees WHERE
        EmployeeID=@EmployeeID";

        SqlParameter p = new SqlParameter("@EmployeeID", id);
        cmd.Parameters.Add(p);

        cnn.Open();
        SqlDataReader reader = cmd.ExecuteReader();
        List<Employee> employees = new List<Employee>();
```

```
        while (reader.Read())
        {
            Employee item = new Employee();
            item.EmployeeID = reader.GetInt32(0);
            item.FirstName = reader.GetString(1);
            item.LastName = reader.GetString(2);
            item.Title = reader.GetString(3);
            item.BirthDate = reader.GetDateTime(4);
            item.HireDate = reader.GetDateTime(5);
            item.Country = reader.GetString(6);
            if (!reader.IsDBNull(7))
            {
                item.Notes = reader.GetString(7);
            }
            employees.Add(item);
        }
        reader.Close();
        cnn.Close();
        return employees.SingleOrDefault();
    }
}
```

The `SelectByID()` method accepts an `EmployeeID` as its parameter. This time the SELECT query contains a WHERE clause and fetches only that employee whose `EmployeeID` matches with the supplied value. Note that the `EmployeeID` is represented by the `@EmployeeID` parameter.

The value of the `@EmployeeID` parameter is wrapped inside an object of `SqlParameter` and then added to the `Parameters` collection of the `SqlCommand` object.

Insert( ) Method

The `Insert()` method inserts a new employee to the Employees table and is shown in Listing 9-5.

Listing 9-5. Insert() method inserts a new employee

```
public void Insert(Employee emp)
{
    using (SqlConnection cnn = new SqlConnection(connectionString))
    {
        SqlCommand cmd = new SqlCommand();
        cmd.Connection = cnn;
        cmd.CommandType = CommandType.Text;
        cmd.CommandText = "INSERT INTO Employees(FirstName, LastName,
        Title, BirthDate, HireDate, Country, Notes)  VALUES(@FirstName,
        @LastName, @Title, @BirthDate, @HireDate, @Country, @Notes)";

        SqlParameter[] p = new SqlParameter[7];
        p[0] = new SqlParameter("@FirstName", emp.FirstName);
        p[1] = new SqlParameter("@LastName", emp.LastName);
        p[2] = new SqlParameter("@Title", emp.Title);
        p[3] = new SqlParameter("@BirthDate", emp.BirthDate);
        p[4] = new SqlParameter("@HireDate", emp.HireDate);
        p[5] = new SqlParameter("@Country", emp.Country);
        p[6] = new SqlParameter("@Notes", emp.Notes ?? SqlString.Null);

        cmd.Parameters.AddRange(p);

    cnn.Open();
    int i = cmd.ExecuteNonQuery();
    cnn.Close();
  }
}
```

The Insert() method accepts an Employee object representing a new employee to be added to the database. This time the CommandText specifies an INSERT query that contains several parameters such as @FirstName and @Notes. To supply these parameter values, an array of SqlParameter is declared (seven array elements), and all the parameter values are wrapped in the SqlParameter object.

The SqlParameter array is added to the Parameters collection of SqlCommand using the AddRange() method.

To execute the INSERT statement, the code uses the ExecuteNonQuery() method of the SqlCommand object. The ExecuteNonQuery() method executes an action query and returns the number of records affected by the query. In this case, since one record is being inserted, it will return 1 (if successful). Although here the value of i is not used, you can use it for further processing if needed.

Update() Method

The Update() method is quite similar to the Insert() method discussed earlier. But it executes an UPDATE statement as shown in Listing 9-6.

Listing 9-6. Update() method updates an employee

```
public void Update(Employee emp)
{
    using (SqlConnection cnn = new SqlConnection(connectionString))
    {
        SqlCommand cmd = new SqlCommand();
        cmd.Connection = cnn;
        cmd.CommandType = CommandType.Text;
        cmd.CommandText = "UPDATE Employees SET FirstName=@FirstName,
        LastName=@LastName, Title=@Title, BirthDate=@BirthDate, HireDate=
        @HireDate, Country=@Country, Notes=@Notes WHERE EmployeeID=
        @EmployeeID";

        SqlParameter[] p = new SqlParameter[8];
        p[0] = new SqlParameter("@FirstName", emp.FirstName);
        p[1] = new SqlParameter("@LastName", emp.LastName);
        p[2] = new SqlParameter("@Title", emp.Title);
        p[3] = new SqlParameter("@BirthDate", emp.BirthDate);
        p[4] = new SqlParameter("@HireDate", emp.HireDate);
        p[5] = new SqlParameter("@Country", emp.Country);
        p[6] = new SqlParameter("@Notes", emp.Notes ?? SqlString.Null);
        p[7] = new SqlParameter("@EmployeeID", emp.EmployeeID);

        cmd.Parameters.AddRange(p);

        cnn.Open();
```

```
        int i = cmd.ExecuteNonQuery();
        cnn.Close();
    }
}
```

The Update() method accepts an existing Employee that needs to be updated in the database. Inside, an UPDATE statement is formed and executed using the ExecuteNonQuery() method.

Delete( ) Method

The Delete() method deletes an existing employee from the database and is shown in Listing 9-7.

Listing 9-7. Delete() method deletes an employee

```
public void Delete(int id)
{
    using (SqlConnection cnn = new SqlConnection(connectionString))
    {
        SqlCommand cmd = new SqlCommand();
        cmd.Connection = cnn;
        cmd.CommandType = CommandType.Text;
        cmd.CommandText = "DELETE FROM Employees WHERE EmployeeID=@EmployeeID";

        SqlParameter p = new SqlParameter("@EmployeeID", id);
        cmd.Parameters.Add(p);

        cnn.Open();
        int i = cmd.ExecuteNonQuery();
        cnn.Close();
    }
}
```

The Delete() method accepts an existing EmployeeID and deletes that record from the Employees table. This time it executes a DELETE statement using the ExecuteNonQuery() method.

> **Note** The CountryRepository contains a single method – SelectAll() – that returns all the countries to the caller and should look familiar to you. For the sake of brevity, CountryRepository is not discussed here. You can grab it from the book's code download.

Once the repositories are ready, you need to register them with the DI container inside the ConfigureServices() method. Listing 9-8 shows how that is done.

Listing 9-8. Registering repositories using AddScoped()

```
public void ConfigureServices(IServiceCollection services)
{
    ...
    services.AddScoped<IEmployeeRepository, EmployeeRepository>();
    services.AddScoped<ICountryRepository, CountryRepository>();
    ...
}
```

This code should be familiar to you since you used the AddScoped() method earlier.

EmployeeManagerController Class

Now that the EmployeeRepository and CountryRepository are ready, you can use them in the EmployeeManagerController. So add EmployeeManagerController in the Controllers folder and inject both the repositories into its constructor (Listing 9-9).

Listing 9-9. Injecting repositories into the EmployeeManagerController

```
public class EmployeeManagerController : Controller
{
    private IEmployeeRepository employeeRepository;
    private ICountryRepository countryRepository;

    public EmployeeManagerController(IEmployeeRepository empRepository,
    ICountryRepository ctryRepository)
```

```
{
    this.employeeRepository = empRepository;
    this.countryRepository = ctryRepository;
}
...
}
```

As you can see, the EmployeeRepository and CountryRepository instances are injected into the constructor. The employeeRepository and countryRepository members are used by other actions of the EmployeeManagerController to get their job done. As an example, the Update() actions of EmployeeManagerController are discussed in the following.

The Update() action that handles the initial GET request is shown in Listing 9-10.

Listing 9-10. Update() action that handles a GET request

```
public IActionResult Update(int id)
{
    FillCountries();
    Employee model = employeeRepository.SelectByID(id);
    return View(model);
}
```

The Update() action calls the SelectByID() method of the EmployeeRepository by passing an EmployeeID to it. The returned Employee object is passed to the Update view.

Upon clicking the Save button of the Update existing employee page, the form is submitted to the POST version of Update(). This is shown in Listing 9-11.

Listing 9-11. Saving the modifications using Update()

```
[HttpPost]
public IActionResult Update(Employee model)
{
    FillCountries();

    if(ModelState.IsValid)
    {
        employeeRepository.Update(model);
```

```
        ViewBag.Message = "Employee updated successfully";
    }
    return View(model);
}
```

The Update() invokes the Update() method of the EmployeeRepository by passing an Employee object to it. A success message is then displayed to the user.

You can complete the other actions of the EmployeeManagerController and also add the views yourself or get them from the book's source code.

Note   The process of adding support for ASP.NET Core Identity is exactly same as before and hence not discussed here. However, remember that this time the Northwind database is hosted in Azure. So tables such as AspNetUsers and AspNetRoles are also created in the Azure SQL Database. The book's source code contains the completed Employee Manager application.

Database Connection String

Earlier in this chapter, you created a new Azure SQL Database. That time I asked you to grab the ADO.NET database connection string from the Azure portal (get that now if you haven't done that earlier). Now it's the time to use that connection string. Open the appsettings.json file and replace the AppDb key with your connection string. The following sample connection string shows how AppDb should look like after the said modification:

```
"ConnectionStrings": {
  "AppDb": "Server=your_server_address_here;
           Initial Catalog=Northwind;
           Persist Security Info=False;
           User ID=your_user_id_here;
           Password=your_password_here;
           MultipleActiveResultSets=False;
           Encrypt=True;
           TrustServerCertificate=False;
           Connection Timeout=30;"
}
```

Just substitute the placeholders for user ID, password, and other details with your values; and you are ready to run the Employee Manager application.

Overview of NoSQL Databases

So far in this book, you used the Microsoft SQL Server database to store data. SQL server is a relational database management system (RDBMS). Any RDBMS such as SQL Server stores data in tables. A table has rows and a row has columns. You need to decide the structure of a table (often called schema) in advance before you store any data in it. If there is any change in the table schema, it affects all the rows stored in that table.

In order to query the data stored in RDBMS and to manipulate it, you typically use Structured Query Language or SQL. The SQL statements such as SELECT, INSERT, UPDATE, and DELETE are quite commonly used while performing CRUD operations on RDBMS.

In modern computing, a new generation of databases is increasingly becoming common and popular. They are called NoSQL databases. NoSQL databases do not store the data in the rigid schema-based tables, rows, and columns. Rather, they store data in non-relational ways such as documents and key-value pairs. Due to this shift in the storage model, NoSQL databases do not use SQL to query and manipulate data. They typically use an object-oriented API to access the data store.

Although a detailed discussion of NoSQL databases is beyond the scope of this book, the following features are worth noting:

- NoSQL databases store data in different ways. Some common ways include document storage, key-value pairs, and graph stores.

- A NoSQL database that stores data as documents is often called a document database. Some examples of document databases are MongoDB, CouchDB, RavenDB, and Cosmos DB.

- Document databases typically store documents in the JSON format.

- NoSQL databases use a dynamic schema. This means you don't need to define storage schema in advance. Pieces of data that are different in terms of structure can be stored together. For example, you can store two JSON documents with different structures together.

- To perform CRUD (and other data access) operations, NoSQL databases provide a database-specific object-oriented API. For example, MongoDB and Cosmos DB both provide their own API for data access.

- NoSQL databases are easy to scale horizontally. For example, to increase the capacity of a database, you can simply add more servers. The database data can then span additional servers.

Now that you have some idea about what NoSQL databases are, let's quickly get introduced to the document databases you are going to use in this chapter: Cosmos DB and MongoDB.

Cosmos DB

Cosmos DB is an Azure-based database service. That means your Cosmos DB database is hosted in Azure and you get all the benefits of cloud environment for your database. An interesting feature of Cosmos DB is it can support multiple data models using one backend. For example, Cosmos DB can be used for storing documents, key-value pairs, and graph models.

Cosmos DB is often classified as a NoSQL database because you don't need to define any schemas to store data. However, it comes with a JSON-oriented query language that is similar to SQL. What's more, Cosmos DB provides native support for various popular NoSQL APIs including MongoDB, Cassandra, and Gremlin.

There are two options to access data residing in the Cosmos DB database. You can use the Cosmos DB SQL API exposed through the client library – `Microsoft.Azure.DocumentDB.Core`. This client library is available as a NuGet package and enables ASP.NET Core applications to connect to Azure Cosmos DB via SQL API (also called DocumentDB).

Microsoft has also developed an Entity Framework Core provider for Cosmos DB and is available through the `Microsoft.EntityFrameworkCore.Cosmos` NuGet package. If you use this provider, the development process becomes quite similar to EF Core. That means you create a custom `DbContext` and entity classes that map to your JSON document. The methods such as `Add()`, `Remove()`, and `SaveChanges()` can be used to perform the CRUD operations.

Note   Prior to Cosmos DB, Microsoft offered DocumentDB as a NoSQL document database. After the release of Cosmos DB, DocumentDB became a part of Cosmos DB. DocumentDB uses terms such as collection and document while describing the data. On the other hand, Cosmos DB uses terms container and item for the same purpose. I am going to use the same terminology while using the respective data access technique.

MongoDB

MongoDB is a popular NoSQL database engine that stores data as documents. The documents are stored in JSON-like format. MongoDB is designed to be a distributed database and aims at high availability and horizontal scaling. You can download and install the MongoDB server on your machine for working with the example discussed in this chapter. MongoDB provides a driver for .NET that allows you to perform data access and manipulation. This driver is available as a NuGet package – MongoDB.Driver.

Note   Discussion of Cosmos DB and MongoDB in more detail is beyond the scope of this book. You may read their official documentation at https:// docs.microsoft.com/en-us/azure/cosmos-db and www.mongodb.com respectively. The remainder of this chapter assumes that you have access to Azure Cosmos DB and have also installed MongoDB on your computer.

Creating a Cosmos DB Account

In this section, you create a new Cosmos DB account that can be used to create the Northwind database needed by the Employee Manager application.

In order to create a Cosmos DB account, you need to sign in to the Azure portal as you did previously. This time, however, you select the Azure Cosmos DB option as shown in Figure 9-8.

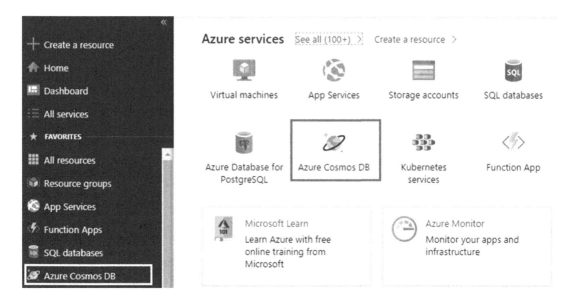

Figure 9-8. *Option to create and manage Cosmos DB accounts*

Then click the Add button to create a new Azure Cosmos DB account. The account creation screen looks as shown in Figure 9-9.

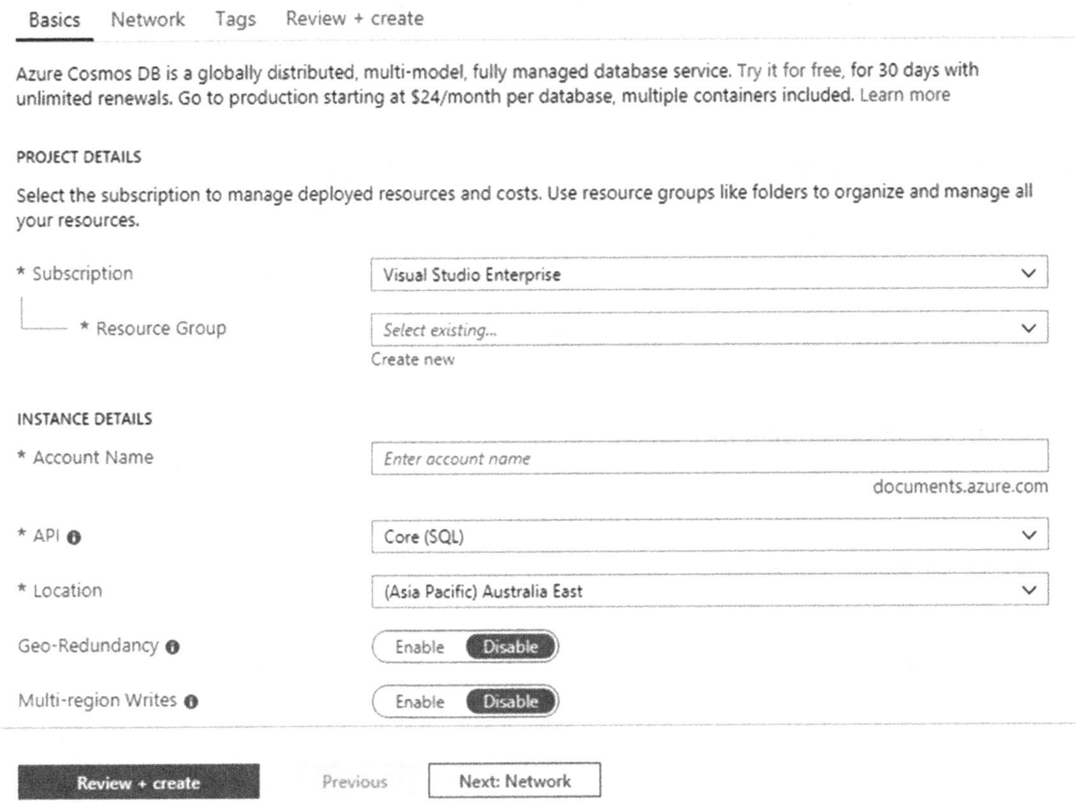

Basics   Network   Tags   Review + create

Azure Cosmos DB is a globally distributed, multi-model, fully managed database service. Try it for free, for 30 days with unlimited renewals. Go to production starting at $24/month per database, multiple containers included. Learn more

PROJECT DETAILS

Select the subscription to manage deployed resources and costs. Use resource groups like folders to organize and manage all your resources.

* Subscription

Visual Studio Enterprise

* Resource Group

Select existing...

Create new

INSTANCE DETAILS

* Account Name

Enter account name

documents.azure.com

* API ❶

Core (SQL)

* Location

(Asia Pacific) Australia East

Geo-Redundancy ❶

Enable   Disable

Multi-region Writes ❶

Enable   Disable

Review + create   Previous   Next: Network

Figure 9-9. *Creating new Cosmos DB account*

On this screen, select (or create) a resource group and also enter an account name of your choice. You can keep other settings to their default values. Complete the account creation process by clicking the Review + create button.

Once the Cosmos DB account is ready, navigate to the account and click the Keys option to reveal the keys and connection strings as shown in Figure 9-10.

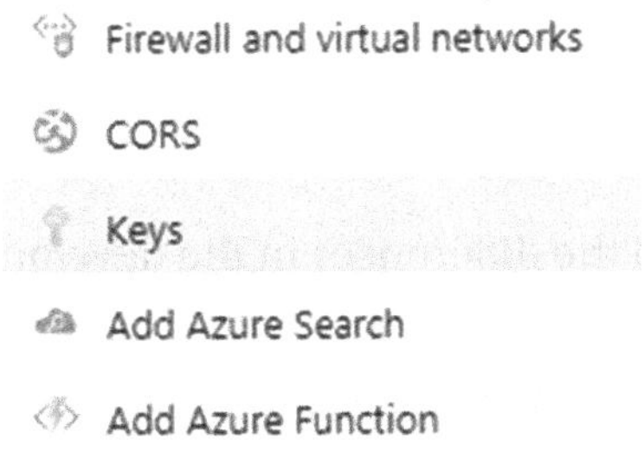

Firewall and virtual networks

CORS

Keys

Add Azure Search

Add Azure Function

Figure 9-10. *Get Cosmos DB account keys and connection strings*

Keep your keys and connection strings handy because you will need them while developing the Employee Manager application.

Employee Manager Using Cosmos DB

In the sections that follow, you develop Employee Manager using Cosmos DB. Although the overall development process remains the same, there are a few differences:

- The employee data now resides in a Cosmos DB database named Northwind.

- The application uses a custom cookie authentication without ASP. NET Core Identity. The user details such as user name, password, and role are also stored in the Cosmos DB database.

- A Cosmos DB database contains collections and documents. For the sake of analogy, you can think of a document as a record and a collection as a set of documents. The database, collections, and documents are created programmatically from within the Employee Manager application.

- Cosmos DB stores data in JSON documents. Each document has a unique string ID. Therefore, the Employee documents will have an extra property named DocumentID (this is in addition to the EmployeeID integer property) that stores a string GUID.

- Due to the preceding change, the insert and update pages will display EmployeeID in editable textboxes. You could have avoided EmployeeID altogether since DocumentID plays the role of a primary key, but for the sake of consistency with other versions of Employee Manager, you will still have it as a part of the JSON document.

- The application uses the Microsoft.Azure.DocumentDB.Core client library to perform CRUD options and more.

Now that you are aware of the differences in the development process of Employee Manager, let's get started by creating a new ASP.NET Core web application named EmployeeManager.CosmosDB based on the Empty project template. Since you are quite familiar with the overall development by now, only the differences outlined in the preceding text are discussed in the following sections.

Cosmos DB Connection Details

Employee Manager needs Cosmos DB account connection details for performing the CRUD operations. So store them in the appsettings.json file. Listing 9-12 shows a configuration section named CosmosDBSettings that goes into the appsettings.json.

Listing 9-12. Cosmos DB account connection details

```
"CosmosDBSettings": {
  "Uri": "your_uri_here",
  "PrimaryKey": "your_primary_key_here",
  "DatabaseName": "Northwind",
  "EmployeeCollectionName": "Employees",
  "CountryCollectionName": "Countries",
  "UserCollectionName": "Users"
}
```

The Uri key specifies the Cosmos DB account endpoint URI. You can get this URI from the Azure portal (read the earlier discussion). The PrimaryKey key specifies the primary key as obtained from the Azure portal.

The DatabaseName key specifies the name of the database used by the Employee Manager application. Note that the Northwind database is not yet created in the Cosmos DB account. You do that programmatically in later sections. To avoid hard-coding of the database name, you keep it in the configuration file. Just in case you want to give some different name for the sake of testing, you can just change it here.

Cosmos DB stores data in collections. Collections store JSON documents. Here, you specify three collection names using EmployeeCollectionName, CountryCollectionName, and UserCollectionName keys. Note that since this example uses a custom cookie authentication rather than ASP.NET Core identity, you need to store user details somewhere. The example prefers to store them in the Users collection. For the sake of simplicity, user details such as user name, password, and roles are stored as plain JSON documents. However, in a more realistic situation, you should consider strong encryption techniques to protect the user data. You might even prefer to store user details in some other data store. Data encryption and security techniques are beyond the scope of this book.

Microsoft.Azure.DocumentDB.Core Client Library

As mentioned earlier in this chapter, Cosmos DB is a multi-model database. It allows you to store and retrieve data using multiple APIs. One of the data access models of Cosmos DB is a dialect of SQL called SQL API. The `Microsoft.Azure.DocumentDB.Core` client library is built around the SQL API, and that's what you are going to use in this example. The `Microsoft.Azure.DocumentDB.Core` library allows your application to deal with the data as C# objects (say, Employee or Country), and it handles all the necessary background processing of serializing and de-serializing data to and from JSON format.

The `Microsoft.Azure.DocumentDB.Core` client library is available as a NuGet package, and you need to add it to your project.

Employee and Country Model Classes

The `Employee` model class is a POCO that takes the form as shown in Listing 9-13.

Listing 9-13. Employee class is serialized as JSON document

```
public class Employee
{
    [JsonProperty(PropertyName = "id")]
    public Guid DocumentID { get; set; }

    [Required]
    [Display(Name ="Employee ID")]
    [JsonProperty(PropertyName ="employeeID")]
    public int EmployeeID { get; set; }

    [Required]
    [StringLength(10)]
    [Display(Name = "First Name")]
    [JsonProperty(PropertyName = "firstName")]
    public string FirstName { get; set; }

    [Required]
    [StringLength(20)]
    [Display(Name = "Last Name")]
```

```
[JsonProperty(PropertyName = "lastName")]
public string LastName { get; set; }

[Required]
[StringLength(30)]
[Display(Name = "Title")]
[JsonProperty(PropertyName = "title")]
public string Title { get; set; }

[Required]
[Display(Name = "Birth Date")]
[JsonProperty(PropertyName = "birthDate")]
public DateTime BirthDate { get; set; }

[Required]
[Display(Name = "Hire Date")]
[JsonProperty(PropertyName = "hireDate")]
public DateTime HireDate { get; set; }

[Required]
[StringLength(15)]
[Display(Name = "Country")]
[JsonProperty(PropertyName = "country")]
public string Country { get; set; }

[StringLength(500)]
[Display(Name = "Notes")]
[JsonProperty(PropertyName = "notes")]
public string Notes { get; set; }
}
```

As you can see, the Employee class has all the properties such as EmployeeID, FirstName, LastName, Title, BirthDate, HireDate, Country, and Notes. In addition, it also has the DocumentID property that represents the JSON document's unique identifier in the form of a Guid.

Notice the code marked in bold letters. The Employee properties are decorated with the [JsonProperty] attribute. The [JsonProperty] attribute comes from the Newtonsoft.Json namespace and indicates that the underlying property is to be included during the JSON serialization. The PropertyName property of [JsonProperty] specifies the JSON property name of the underlying property. For example, the EmployeeID property will be represented as employeeID. Note that the PropertyName for the DocumentID property is id because it is going to act as the JSON document's unique identifier.

The Country class is created likewise and is shown in Listing 9-14.

Listing 9-14. Country class with [JsonProperty] attributes

```
public class Country
{
    [JsonProperty(PropertyName = "id")]
    public Guid  DocumentID { get; set; }

    [JsonProperty(PropertyName = "countryID")]
    public int CountryID { get; set; }

    [JsonProperty(PropertyName = "name")]
    public string Name { get; set; }
}
```

Creating the EmployeeManagerController

Now that the Employee and Country model classes are ready, let's proceed to creating the EmployeeManagerController. As before, EmployeeManagerController will have actions for performing the CRUD operations.

Note   In the examples that follow, you write data access code in the controller itself. This is done for the sake of simplicity and to remain focused on the data access logic. However, once you are comfortable working with NoSQL databases, you should consider moving the data access code to repositories.

The EmployeeManagerController class declares a set of variables that are needed by the other parts of the code. These variables are shown in Listing 9-15.

Listing 9-15. Variables that store Cosmos DB account details

```
public class EmployeeManagerController : Controller
{

    private DocumentClient client;
    private Uri employeeCollectionUri;
    private Uri countryCollectionUri;
    private string databaseName;
    private string employeeCollectionName;
    private string countryCollectionName;

    ...
}
```

The `DocumentClient` class is from the `Microsoft.Azure.Documents.Client` namespace and represents a client that can be used to connect with the Cosmos DB account and to perform data access operations.

The `employeeCollectionUrl` and `countryCollectionUri` objects are of type `Uri` and hold the address of the `Employees` and `Countries` collections (remember that a Cosmos DB collection consists of JSON documents).

The `databaseName`, `employeeCollectionName`, and `countryCollectionName` variables hold the respective names; and their values come from the appsettings.json file (we stored these values earlier).

The constructor of `EmployeeManagerController` does an important task – it creates the database and collections (if they do not exist already) and is shown in Listing 9-16.

Listing 9-16. Creating the Cosmos DB database and collections

```
public EmployeeManagerController(IConfiguration config)
{
    var uri = new Uri(config.GetValue<string>("CosmosDBSettings:Server"));
    var primaryKey = config.GetValue<string>("CosmosDBSettings:PrimaryKey");
    databaseName = config.GetValue<string>("CosmosDBSettings:DatabaseName");
    employeeCollectionName = config.GetValue<string>("CosmosDBSettings:
    EmployeeCollectionName");
    countryCollectionName = config.GetValue<string>("CosmosDBSettings:
    CountryCollectionName");
```

```
    client = new DocumentClient(uri,primaryKey);

    this.client.CreateDatabaseIfNotExistsAsync(new Database
    { Id = databaseName }).Wait();

    this.client.CreateDocumentCollectionIfNotExistsAsync(UriFactory.Create
    DatabaseUri(databaseName), new DocumentCollection
    { Id = employeeCollectionName }).Wait();

    this.client.CreateDocumentCollectionIfNotExistsAsync(UriFactory.Create
    DatabaseUri(databaseName), new DocumentCollection
    { Id = countryCollectionName }).Wait();

    this.employeeCollectionUri = UriFactory
        .CreateDocumentCollectionUri(
            databaseName, employeeCollectionName);

    this.countryCollectionUri = UriFactory
        .CreateDocumentCollectionUri(
            databaseName, countryCollectionName);

}
```

The code begins by retrieving Cosmos DB account details such as Uri and primary key stored in the appsettings.json. Based on those details, uri and primaryKey Uri objects are formed. The values of databaseName, employeeCollectionName, and countryCollectionName are also retrieved from the configuration file. (For the sake of simplicity, IConfiguration injected into the controller is used to access the configuration information. You could have also used strongly typed configuration as discussed in Chapter 5.)

Then the code creates an object of DocumentClient by passing the Cosmos DB endpoint URI and the primary key.

Then the code calls the CreateDatabaseIfNotExistsAsync() method of DocumentClient. As the name of the method suggests, it creates a Cosmos DB database if it doesn't exist already. This method accepts a Database object specifying the database Id (name of the database). The Database class is from the Microsoft.Azure.Documents namespace. In this example, the Northwind database will be created when you run the application for the first time.

Then the code proceeds to creating Employees and Countries collections. This is done using the CreateDocumentCollectionIfNotExistsAsync() method. The first parameter to this method is a database Uri, and the second parameter is a DocumentCollection object. The DocumentCollection object specifies the name of the document collections (Employees and Countries, respectively). The specified collection is created in the database whose Uri is being supplied.

While performing the CRUD operations, you frequently need the Uri of the Employees collection and Countries collection. Therefore, those Uri objects are created using the CreateDocumentCollectionUri() method. The CreateDocumentCollectionUri() accepts a database name and a collection name and returns a Uri for that collection.

Displaying a List of Employees

The List() action fetches employees from the Northwind database and is shown in Listing 9-17.

Listing 9-17. Fetching Employee documents from the database

```
public IActionResult List()
{
    var model = client.CreateDocumentQuery<Employee>
                (employeeCollectionUri)
                .OrderBy(e=>e.EmployeeID).ToList();
    return View(model);
}
```

In order to retrieve employees from the database, the code uses the CreateDocumentQuery<T>() method of the DocumentClient object. The call specifies that the JSON data is to be mapped with the Employee type and accepts a collection URI. The CreateDocumentQuery() method returns IOrderedQueryable. The code orders the employees on the basis of their EmployeeID and materializes the data into a List<Employee> using the ToList() method. The List<Employee> is then passed to the List view.

The List view that displays the employees in a table is quite similar to the MVC version of Employee Manager except that the Update and Delete links use DocumentID to uniquely identify an employee. These links are shown in Listing 9-18.

Listing 9-18. Using DocumentID for rendering the Update and Delete links

```
...
<td>
    <a asp-controller="EmployeeManager"
        asp-action="Update"
        asp-route-id="@item.DocumentID" class="linkbutton">Update</a>
</td>
<td>
    <a asp-controller="EmployeeManager"
        asp-action="Delete"
        asp-route-id="@item.DocumentID" class="linkbutton">Delete</a>
</td>
...
```

As you can see, the `asp-route-id` attribute uses `DocumentID` instead of `EmployeeID`. The remainder of the List view is quite similar to what you already know and hence not discussed here. You can get the complete code of List.cshtml from this book's code download.

Inserting a New Employee

The `Insert()` action that renders a blank Insert New Employee page is shown in Listing 9-19.

Listing 9-19. Insert() renders an Insert New Employee view

```
public IActionResult Insert()
{
    FillCountries();
    return View();
}
```

The `Insert()` action calls `FillCountries()` to populate the Country dropdown list and is discussed in a later section. When you click the Save button of the Insert New Employee page, the `Insert()` action shown in Listing 9-20 gets called.

Listing 9-20. Insert() adds a JSON document to Cosmos DB

```
public async Task<IActionResult> Insert(Employee emp)
{
  FillCountries();
  if (ModelState.IsValid)
  {
    Employee obj = client.CreateDocumentQuery<Employee>(employee
    CollectionUri).Where(e => e.EmployeeID == emp.EmployeeID).
    AsEnumerable().SingleOrDefault();

    if (obj == null)
    {
        emp.DocumentID = Guid.NewGuid();
        await client.CreateDocumentAsync(employeeCollectionUri, emp);
        ViewBag.Message = "Employee inserted successfully!";
    }
    else
    {
        ViewBag.Message = "EmployeeID already exists!";
    }
  }
  return View(emp);
}
```

Notice the code marked in bold letters. Since EmployeeID is now being accepted from a user, the code ensures that the EmployeeID isn't already there in the database. This is done by querying the database for a specific EmployeeID. The CreateDocumentQuery() method should look familiar to you since you used it earlier. The where condition filters the data based on a specific EmployeeID.

If there is no matching Employee object found by the query, the code inserts a new Employee document in the database. This is done using the CreateDocumentAsync() method of the DocumentClient class. Since you want to add a new document to the Employees collection, employeeCollectionUri is passed to the CreateDocumentAsync() method along with an Employee object to be inserted. Note that the DocumentID property of the Employee object is set to a new GUID before it is passed to the CreateDocumentAsync() method.

413

The remainder of the code is quite straightforward and hence not discussed here. The Insert view that displays the Insert New Employee screen is quite similar to that of the MVC version of Employee Manager. The only difference is that EmployeeID is now accepted from the end user. For the sake of brevity, the Insert view is not discussed here. You can get the complete code of Insert.cshtml from this chapter's code download.

Updating an Existing Employee

When you click the Update link from the employee listing page, the Update Existing Employee page is displayed with details of the employee pre-populated in various data entry fields. The Update() action that does this is shown in Listing 9-21.

Listing 9-21. Update() action fetches an existing employee to be updated

```
public IActionResult Update(string id)
{
    FillCountries();

    Guid docId = new Guid(id);

    Employee emp = client.CreateDocumentQuery<Employee>(employeeCollection
    Uri).Where(e => e.DocumentID == id).AsEnumerable().SingleOrDefault();

    return View(emp);
}
```

The Update() action receives a DocumentID as its parameter. Notice the code marked in bold letters. The code converts the id into a Guid since DocumentID is a GUID. The code then uses the CreateDocumentQuery() method of DocumentClient to fetch only that Employee document whose DocumentID matches with the specified docId. The Employee object is then passed to the Update view.

When you click the Save button of the Update Existing Employee page, the Update() action (POST) is called and is shown in Listing 9-22.

Listing 9-22. Update() saves the changes to the database

```
public async Task<IActionResult> Update(Employee emp)
{
    FillCountries();
    if (ModelState.IsValid)
```

```
    {
    await client.ReplaceDocumentAsync(UriFactory.
    CreateDocumentUri(databaseName, employeeCollectionName, emp.DocumentID.
    ToString()), emp);

    ViewBag.Message = "Employee updated successfully!";
    }
    return View(emp);
}
```

The code uses the ReplaceDocumentAsync() method of DocumentClient to replace the existing Employee document with the new one. The existing Employee document is identified by the DocumentID. The first parameter of ReplaceDocumentAsync() forms a Uri to that specific document. The second parameter of ReplaceDocumentAsync() passes the modified Employee document.

The Update view is quite similar to the one you developed earlier and hence is not discussed here. You can also get it from this chapter's code download.

Deleting an Existing Employee

When you click the Delete link for an employee on the employee listing page, a confirmation page is displayed. The action that is responsible for displaying the confirmation page is shown in Listing 9-23.

Listing 9-23. Displaying a delete confirmation page

```
[ActionName("Delete")]
public IActionResult ConfirmDelete(string id)
{
    Guid docId = new Guid(id);
    Employee emp = client.CreateDocumentQuery<Employee>(employeeCollection
    Uri).Where(e => e.DocumentID == docId).AsEnumerable().SingleOrDefault();
    return View(emp);
}
```

This code is identical to the first Update() action and hence not discussed again.

Upon clicking the Delete button on the confirmation page, the Delete() action shown in Listing 9-24 is invoked.

Listing 9-24. Deleting an Employee document

```
public async Task<IActionResult> Delete(string documentID)
{
await client.DeleteDocumentAsync(UriFactory.CreateDocumentUri(databaseName,
employeeCollectionName, documentID));
    TempData["Message"] = "Employee deleted successfully!";
    return RedirectToAction("List");
}
```

The Delete() action accepts a DocumentID of an Employee document to be deleted. Inside, the code calls the DeleteDocumentAsync() method of the DocumentClient object to delete the specified document. The DeleteDocumentAsync() method accepts a Uri that points to the Employee document to be deleted. The Uri is formed based on the databaseName, employeeCollectionName, and the documentID.

For the sake of brevity, the Delete view is not discussed here. It's quite similar to the one you developed earlier, and you can get it from this chapter's code download.

FillCountries( ) Helper Method

The Insert() and Update() actions discussed in the preceding text use a helper method – FillCountries(). The FillCountries() method creates a list of countries to be displayed in the Country dropdown list. The FillCountries() method is shown in Listing 9-25.

Listing 9-25. FillCountries() creates a list of countries

```
public void FillCountries()
{
    if (client.CreateDocumentQuery<Country>(countryCollectionUri).
    Count() == 0)
    {
        Country usa = new Country() { DocumentID = Guid.NewGuid(),
        CountryID = 1, Name = "USA" };
                Country uk = new Country() { DocumentID = Guid.NewGuid(),
                CountryID = 2, Name = "UK" };

        client.CreateDocumentAsync(countryCollectionUri, usa).Wait();
```

```
    client.CreateDocumentAsync(countryCollectionUri, uk).Wait();
}

var ctry = client.CreateDocumentQuery<Country>(countryCollectionUri).
ToList();

List<SelectListItem> countries = (from c in ctry select new
SelectListItem() { Text = c.Name, Value = c.Name }).ToList();

ViewBag.Countries = countries;
}
```

The code first checks whether the Countries collection contains any documents or not. This is done using the Count() method on the IOrderedQueryable returned by the CreateDocumentQuery() method.

Initially, there won't be any countries in the Countries collection, and hence the Count() will return 0. If so, the code adds a couple of Country documents to the Countries collection using the CreateDocumentAsync() method.

Next, the code gets all the Country documents from the database using the CreateDocumentQuery() method and forms a List<SelectListItem>. The List is then stored in the ViewBag.Countries property.

At this stage, your application can perform CRUD operations. I encourage you to take a pause and test all the functionality added so far. Once you confirm that CRUD operations are working as expected, you can wire authentication and authorization to the application as outlined in the following sections.

The Azure portal also allows you to view and manipulate a Cosmos DB database using Data Explorer (accessible from the Cosmos DB database management page). Figure 9-11 shows Data Explorer with a sample Employee document.

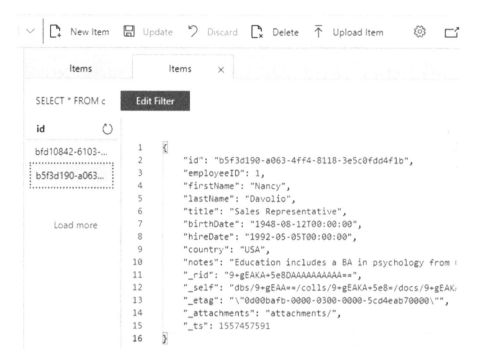

Figure 9-11. *Data Explorer showing a newly added employee*

Notice that in addition to document properties available in the Employee class, a few more properties such as _rid and _self are automatically added by Cosmos DB for its use. Also notice that the JSON property names are as per the ones specified in the [JsonProperty] attribute.

Adding Support for Authentication and Authorization

In the MVC version of Employee Manager, you used ASP.NET Core Identity to implement authentication and authorization. That time, user details such as user name, password, and roles were stored in the SQL Server database. In this example, you use Cosmos DB to store those details. Instead of using ASP.NET Core Identity (that requires certain tables in an SQL Server database by default), you use custom cookie authentication.

The custom cookie authentication and authorization follows the same overall flow as that of ASP.NET Core Identity. However, you need to device your own mechanism for user and role management.

To enable custom cookie authentication, you need to add the configuration mentioned in Listing 9-26 in the `ConfigureServices()`.

Listing 9-26. Enabling custom cookie authentication

```
public void ConfigureServices(IServiceCollection services)
{
    ...
    ...
    services.AddAuthentication
(CookieAuthenticationDefaults.AuthenticationScheme)
.AddCookie(o =>
{
    o.LoginPath = "/Security/SignIn";
    o.AccessDeniedPath = "/Security/AccessDenied";
});
}
```

Notice that the code uses the `AddAuthentication()` method to register services related to custom cookie authentication. The `AuthenticationScheme` property of `CookieAuthenticationDefaults` (`Microsoft.AspNetCore.Authentication.Cookies` namespace) passes the default name of the authentication scheme (Cookies). The `AddCookie()` configures the authentication cookie that is issued.

The `Configure()` method looks identical to the previous examples and hence not discussed here.

Storing User Details

While working with ASP.NET Core Identity, the details such as users, roles, and user-role mapping are stored in SQL Server tables. Since this example doesn't use ASP.NET Core Identity and resorts to Cosmos DB database store user details, you need to decide how these details are stored.

You could have used three Cosmos DB collections such as Users, Roles, and UserRoles to persist the respective details. However, for the sake of simplicity, this example uses only a single collection – Users – to store details such as `UserName`, `Password`, `Email`, `FullName`, `BirthDate`, and `Role` of a user. Although Employee Manager uses role-based security, there aren't too many roles involved. So this simple document structure serves the purpose. In a more realistic case, however, you would consider a more complex and fine-tuned arrangement.

To represent a JSON document that is persisted into the Users collection, you need a class that has all the properties mentioned in the preceding text. Listing 9-27 shows the AppUser class that wraps all these details.

Listing 9-27. AppUser class stores user details

```
public class AppUser
{
    [JsonProperty(PropertyName = "id")]
    public Guid DocumentID { get; set; }

    [JsonProperty(PropertyName = "userName")]
    public string UserName { get; set; }

    [JsonProperty(PropertyName = "password")]
    public string Password { get; set; }

    [JsonProperty(PropertyName = "email")]
    public string Email { get; set; }

    [JsonProperty(PropertyName = "fullName")]
    public string FullName { get; set; }

    [JsonProperty(PropertyName = "birthDate")]
    public DateTime BirthDate { get; set; }

    [JsonProperty(PropertyName = "role")]
    public string Role { get; set; }
}
```

The AppUser class contains several properties, namely, DocumentID, UserName, Password, Email, FullName, BirthDate, and Role. These properties are decorated with the [JsonProperty] attribute.

Once the AppUser class is ready, you can go ahead and add SecurityController that takes care of user registration, signing-in, and signing-out operations.

Creating the SecurityController

The SecurityController includes actions for creating a new user account, signing in a user by issuing an authentication cookie, and signing the user out by removing the authentication cookie. The following sections discuss the Register(), SignIn(), and SignOut() actions of SecurityController that take care of these operations. You can get the complete code of SecurityController from this chapter's code download.

Creating a New User Account

In order to create a new user account, you need to add a JSON document to the Users collection of the Cosmos DB database. This is done by the Register() action as shown in Listing 9-28.

Listing 9-28. Creating a new user account

```
[HttpPost]
public async Task<IActionResult> Register(Register model)
{
    if (ModelState.IsValid)
    {
        AppUser usr = client.CreateDocumentQuery<AppUser>(userCollection
        Uri).Where(u => u.UserName == model.UserName).AsEnumerable().
        SingleOrDefault();

        if (usr != null)
        {
            ModelState.AddModelError("", "UserName already exists!");
        }
        else
        {
            AppUser user = new AppUser();
            user.DocumentID = Guid.NewGuid();
            user.UserName = model.UserName;
            user.Password = model.Password;
            user.Email = model.Email;
            user.FullName = model.FullName;
```

```
                user.BirthDate = model.BirthDate;
                user.Role = "Manager";

                await client.CreateDocumentAsync(userCollectionUri, user);
                ViewData["message"] = "User created successfully!";
            }
        }
        return View();
}
```

The code first checks whether the user with a specific UserName already exists in the Users collection. This is done using the CreateDocumentQuery() method of DocumentClient.

If the UserName doesn't exist, the code proceeds to creating a new AppUser object and setting its properties. Recollect that AppUser represents a JSON document you want to store in the Users collection.

Once the AppUser object is ready, the code adds in to the Users collection using the CreateDocumentAsync() method. Notice that the Users collection's Uri is passed to the CreateDocumentAsync() method along with the AppUser object.

Signing a User In to the Application

In order to sign a user in to Employee Manager, you need to validate the user credentials and issue an authentication cookie. Since you aren't using ASP.NET Core Identity in this example, you resort to ASP.NET Core's HttpContext.SignInAsync() method and what is known as ClaimsPrincipal. Listing 9-29 shows how this is done.

Listing 9-29. Signing a user in by issuing the authentication cookie

```
[HttpPost]
public async Task<IActionResult> SignIn(SignIn model)
{
    AppUser usr = client.CreateDocumentQuery<AppUser>(userCollectionUri).
    Where(u => u.UserName == model.UserName && u.Password==model.Password).
    AsEnumerable().SingleOrDefault();

    bool isUserValid = (usr == null ? false : true);
```

```
    if (ModelState.IsValid && isUserValid)
    {
        var claims = new List<Claim>();
        claims.Add(new Claim(ClaimTypes.Name, usr.UserName));
        claims.Add(new Claim(ClaimTypes.Role, usr.Role));
        var identity = new ClaimsIdentity(claims,
        CookieAuthenticationDefaults.AuthenticationScheme);
        var principal = new ClaimsPrincipal(identity);
        var props = new AuthenticationProperties();
        props.IsPersistent = model.RememberMe;

        await HttpContext.SignInAsync(CookieAuthenticationDefaults.
                                AuthenticationScheme, principal, props);

        return RedirectToAction("List", "EmployeeManager");
    }
    else
    {
        ModelState.AddModelError("","Invalid UserName or Password!");
    }

    return View();
}
```

The code first checks whether UserName and Password as supplied by the user are valid or not. This is done by querying the Users collection using the CreateDocumentQuery() method for a specific UserName and Password combination.

If the user credentials are valid, the code proceeds to the sign-in operation. In order to sign a user in to the application, you need to construct the ClaimsPrincipal object. To construct a ClaimsPrincipal, you need a ClaimsIdentity and a List of Claim objects.

Note   Detailed discussion of security concepts such as claims-based security, ClaimsIdentity, and ClaimsPrincipal is beyond the scope of this book. You can read more about these concepts in the official documentation at https://docs.microsoft.com/en-us/dotnet/api/system.security.claims.claimsprincipal.

Take a look at the code shown in bold letters. Two Claim objects are being created and added to the List<Claim>. These Claim objects store UserName and user's Role, respectively.

Based on these claims, a ClaimsIdentity object is constructed. Then a ClaimsPrincipal is constructed by passing the ClaimsIdentity just created.

Next, an object of the AuthenticationProperties class is created. The AuthenticationProperties class is used to store properties of an authentication session. In this case, the IsPersistent property is set to either true or false depending on the Remember Me checkbox of the sign-in page.

Finally, the SignInAsync() method of the HttpContext class is called to sign the user in to the application. The SignInAsync() method accepts three parameters – the authentication scheme, ClaimsPrincipal object, and AuthenticationProperties object. It then issues authentication cookie to the user. This authentication cookie is passed between the browser and the server along with every request so that the server knows that a user has signed in to the application.

Signing a User Out of the Application

The SignOut() action of SecurityController signs the user out of the application by removing the authentication cookie. The SignOut() action is shown in Listing 9-30.

Listing 9-30. Signing a user out of the application

```
[HttpPost]
public async Task<IActionResult> SignOut()
{
    await HttpContext.SignOutAsync(
    CookieAuthenticationDefaults.AuthenticationScheme);
    return RedirectToAction("SignIn", "Security");
}
```

As you can see, the SignOutAsync() method of HttpContext does the job of signing the user out of the application. The SignOutAsync() accepts the name of the authentication scheme used as its parameter.

Securing the EmployeeManagerController with the [Authorize] Attribute

Once you integrate the custom cookie authentication as discussed in the preceding text, you can secure the EmployeeManagerController with the [Authorize] attribute. You can also protect the controller POST actions from the CSRF/XSRF attacks using the [ValidateAntiForgeryToken] attribute. This process is identical to what you did for the MVC version of Employee Manager. Just for your quick reference, a part of the EmployeeManagerController with these attributes applied is shown in Listing 9-31.

Listing 9-31. Using the [Authorize] attribute to EmployeeManagerController

```
[Authorize(Roles = "Manager")]
public class EmployeeManagerController : Controller
{
    ...
    [HttpPost]
    [ValidateAntiForgeryToken]
    public IActionResult Insert(Employee emp)
    {
        ...
    }
    ...
}
```

Using the EF Core Provider for Cosmos DB

Earlier, it was mentioned that you can also use the EF Core provider for Cosmos DB (available through the Microsoft.EntityFrameworkCore.Cosmos NuGet package) to work with Cosmos DB. In this section, you learn how to use it in Employee Manager. Rather than discussing the whole Employee Manager in the light of Microsoft.EntityFrameworkCore.Cosmos, only the CRUD operations are discussed here. But this book's code download contains a complete Employee Manager application developed using the Microsoft.EntityFrameworkCore.Cosmos provider.

Creating the AppDbContext

Have a look at Listing 9-32 that shows a custom DbContext named AppDbContext created for Cosmos DB.

Listing 9-32. DbContext for Cosmos DB

```
public class AppDbContext:DbContext
{
    public AppDbContext(DbContextOptions<AppDbContext> options) :
    base(options)
    {

    }
    public DbSet<Employee> Employees { get; set; }
    public DbSet<Country> Countries { get; set; }
    public DbSet<AppUser> Users { get; set; }
}
```

As you can see, the AppDbContext class looks quite similar to any other DbContext you created in earlier examples. The Employee, Country, and AppUser entity classes used by the DbSet properties are also created similar to any other entity class. As an example, the Employee class is shown in Listing 9-33.

Listing 9-33. Employee entity class

```
public class Employee
{
    [Key]
        [Required]
        public Guid DocumentID { get; set; }

    [Required]
    [Display(Name ="Employee ID")]
    public int EmployeeID { get; set; }

    [Required]
    [StringLength(10)]
```

```
        [Display(Name = "First Name")]
        public string FirstName { get; set; }

        [Required]
        [StringLength(20)]
        [Display(Name = "Last Name")]
        public string LastName { get; set; }

        [Required]
        [StringLength(30)]
        [Display(Name = "Title")]
        public string Title { get; set; }

        [Required]
        [Display(Name = "Birth Date")]
        public DateTime BirthDate { get; set; }

        [Required]
        [Display(Name = "Hire Date")]
        public DateTime HireDate { get; set; }

        [Required]
        [StringLength(15)]
        [Display(Name = "Country")]
        public string Country { get; set; }

        [StringLength(500)]
        [Display(Name = "Notes")]
        public string Notes { get; set; }
}
```

Notice that the DocumentID property is of type Guid and is also marked with the [Key] attribute indicating that it's the unique identifier for the document. The Country and AppUser entity classes are quite straightforward and are not discussed here.

You can inject the AppDbContext into any controller by registering it in the ConfigureServices().Listing 9-34 shows how this can be done.

Listing 9-34. Registering AppDbContext in ConfigureServices()

```
services.AddDbContext<AppDbContext>(options =>
    options.UseCosmos(
    "your_account_uri",
    "your_account_secret_key",
    "your_database_name"
));
```

The `UseCosmos()` method supplies three pieces – your Cosmos DB account endpoint URI (same as your server configuration setting), your account's secret key (same as the PrimaryKey stored in the configuration file), and the database name. These details are necessary to establish a connection with the database. For this example, it's better to use a different database name since Northwind is already created in the previous example.

Performing CRUD Operations

While using the `Microsoft.Azure.DocumentDB.Core` client library, you created the Northwind database programmatically. You can accomplish the same thing while using the EF Core provider for Cosmos DB as shown in Listing 9-35.

Listing 9-35. Creating a database if it doesn't exist

```
public class EmployeeManagerController : Controller
{

    private readonly AppDbContext db;

    public EmployeeManagerController(AppDbContext db)
    {
        this.db = db;
        db.Database.EnsureCreated();
    }
    ...
}
```

The `EmployeeManagerController` constructor gets an instance of `AppDbContext` and stores it in a member variable (`db`). Then the `EnsureCreated()` method of the `Database` object is invoked. The `EnsureCreated()` method creates the database specified in the

UseCosmos() method if it doesn't already exist. When you use the EF Core provider for Cosmos DB, it stores various Employee items under a container named AppDbContext. This container is automatically created for you.

You can insert a new Employee item into the AppDbContext as shown in Listing 9-36.

Listing 9-36. Inserting a new employee in the AppDbContext container

```
[HttpPost]
[ValidateAntiForgeryToken]
public IActionResult Insert(Employee emp)
{
   FillCountries();
   if (ModelState.IsValid)
   {
    Employee obj = (from e in db.Employees
           where e.EmployeeID == emp.EmployeeID
           select e).SingleOrDefault();
    if (obj == null)
    {
        emp.DocumentID = Guid.NewGuid();
        db.Employees.Add(emp);
        db.SaveChanges();
        ViewBag.Message = "Employee inserted successfully!";
    }
    else
    {
        ViewBag.Message = "EmployeeID already exists!";
    }
   }
   return View(emp);
}
```

Notice the code marked in bold letters. It first checks whether an EmployeeID being added already exists in the database or not. It does so by querying the container for items with a specific EmployeeID. As you can see, this query is quite similar to any other LINQ to Entities query.

If the `EmployeeID` doesn't already exist in the database, the code proceeds to creating a new `Employee` entity. The `DocumentID` property is assigned a new `Guid` value. The newly created `Employee` is added to the `Employees` DbSet using the `Add()` method, and `SaveChanges()` is called to persist the changes.

In order to update an existing employee, you need an `Update()` action as shown in Listing 9-37.

Listing 9-37. Updating an existing employee

```
[HttpPost]
[ValidateAntiForgeryToken]
public IActionResult Update(Employee emp)
{
    FillCountries();
    if (ModelState.IsValid)
    {
     Employee obj = db.Employees.Find(emp.DocumentID);
     obj.EmployeeID = emp.EmployeeID;
     obj.FirstName = emp.FirstName;
     obj.LastName = emp.LastName;
     obj.Title = emp.Title;
     obj.BirthDate = emp.BirthDate;
     obj.HireDate = emp.HireDate;
     obj.Country = emp.Country;
     obj.Notes = emp.Notes;
     db.SaveChanges();
     ViewBag.Message = "Employee updated successfully!";
    }
    return View(emp);
}
```

Notice the code marked in bold letters that updates an existing employee in the Cosmos DB database. First, the code retrieves the entity that matches a specified `DocumentID` using the `Find()` method. It then assigns various properties of the `Employee` to their modified values. The code then calls the `SaveChanges()` method to save the changes in the database.

If you wish to delete an Employee item from the AppDbContext container, you could write code as shown in Listing 9-38.

Listing 9-38. Deleting an employee item

```
[HttpPost]
[ValidateAntiForgeryToken]
public IActionResult Delete(string documentID)
{
    Employee emp = db.Employees.Find(new Guid(documentID));
    db.Employees.Remove(emp);
    db.SaveChanges();
    TempData["Message"] = "Employee deleted successfully!";
    return RedirectToAction("List");
}
```

The code retrieves an Employee entity that needs to be deleted using the Find() method. The retrieved entity is passed to the Remove() method to remove it from the Employees DbSet. Finally, the SaveChanges() method removes it from the database.

If you have Employee items in the AppDbContext container, you can fetch them as shown in Listing 9-39.

Listing 9-39. Retrieving all the employees

```
public IActionResult List()
{
    var query = from e in db.Employees
                orderby e.EmployeeID
                select e;
    return View(query.ToList());
}
```

A LINQ to Entities query grabs all the employees, and they are sent to the List view for display.

Note   As you can see from the preceding code snippets, the overall process of performing CRUD operations using the EF Core provider for Cosmos DB is quite similar to the SQL Server database. Therefore, other parts of this Employee Manager example are not discussed here. You can get the complete source code of this example from the book's code download.

If you run this Employee Manager application and add a few Employee items, you can view them from Data Explorer also. Figure 9-12 shows such a sample Employee item.

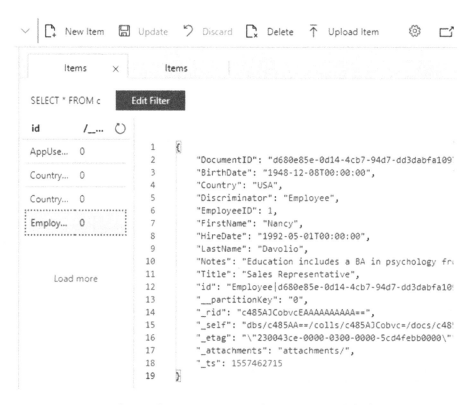

Figure 9-12. *Data Explorer showing an Employee item added to the AppDbContext container*

Installing and Running MongoDB

In the preceding sections, you used Cosmos DB to build the Employee Manager application. In this section, you will use another popular NoSQL database – MongoDB. Before you start writing code to perform CRUD operations, you need to install MongoDB on your local machine. In this section, you will do so and also run the database engine so that your ASP.NET Core application can connect with the database.

The first step is to visit the official MongoDB web site and download the MongoDB database server. You can either download the database server as an MSI file or a ZIP file. Figure 9-13 shows the content of the Bin folder after the ZIP file has been extracted.

Name	Date modified	Type	Size
bsondump.exe	3/28/2019 9:35 PM	Application	17,819 KB
Install-Compass.ps1	3/28/2019 10:04 PM	Windows PowerS...	2 KB
libeay32.dll	4/3/2018 6:58 PM	Application extens...	2,405 KB
mongo.exe	3/28/2019 9:53 PM	Application	18,020 KB
mongo.pdb	3/28/2019 9:53 PM	Program Debug D...	146,348 KB
mongod.exe	3/28/2019 10:04 PM	Application	31,879 KB
mongod.pdb	3/28/2019 10:04 PM	Program Debug D...	351,508 KB
mongodump.exe	3/28/2019 9:41 PM	Application	18,894 KB
mongoexport.exe	3/28/2019 9:38 PM	Application	18,398 KB
mongofiles.exe	3/28/2019 9:37 PM	Application	18,243 KB
mongoimport.exe	3/28/2019 9:39 PM	Application	18,582 KB
mongorestore.exe	3/28/2019 9:40 PM	Application	18,962 KB
mongos.exe	3/28/2019 10:03 PM	Application	16,503 KB
mongos.pdb	3/28/2019 10:03 PM	Program Debug D...	184,276 KB
mongostat.exe	3/28/2019 9:36 PM	Application	18,484 KB
mongotop.exe	3/28/2019 9:42 PM	Application	18,082 KB
ssleay32.dll	4/3/2018 6:58 PM	Application extens...	350 KB

Figure 9-13. *Using mongod.exe to run the database engine*

Notice the mongod.exe file. It's the build of the MongoDB daemon for the Windows platform. A simple way to start the MongoDB server is to run this executable using a command prompt. By default, the MongoDB server is run at port 27017. You can also specify a folder where the data is stored. For example, the following command starts the MongoDB server and specifies the data directory to be Data (create the Data folder under the MongoDB installation folder before running this command):

```
> mongod --dbpath ..\Data
```

Figure 9-14 shows the command prompt when the MongoDB server is successfully started.

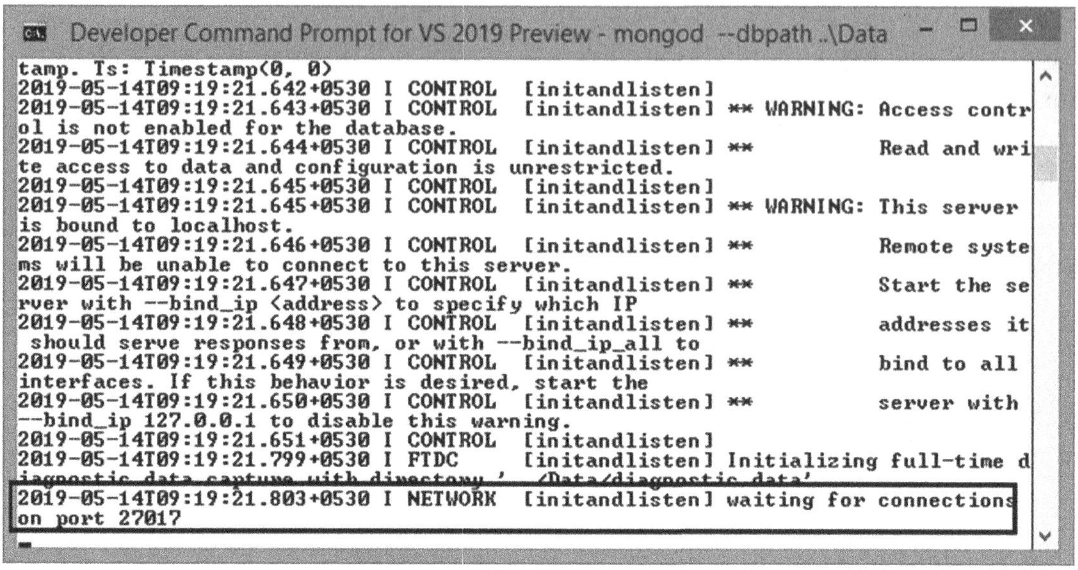

Figure 9-14. *Successful run of the MongoDB server*

Once the MongoDB server is started, you can proceed to performing the CRUD operations.

Note   Teaching you MongoDB and the MongoDB driver in detail is beyond the scope of this book. The following sections focus on performing the CRUD operations. For more details, visit the official documentation at `https://docs.mongodb.com/ecosystem/drivers/csharp/`.

Performing CRUD Operations

In this section, you learn to perform CRUD operations on a MongoDB database named Northwind. You haven't created the Northwind database and its collections yet. That will happen through the MongoDB driver. So after creating and configuring a new project (EmployeeManager.MongoDB), make sure to add the NuGet package – `MongoDB.Driver` – that represents the MongoDB driver for .NET.

For the sake of brevity, the following sections discuss only the CRUD operations from the EmployeeManagerController.

Configuring MongoClient

In order to connect to a MongoDB server, you use the MongoClient class. Listing 9-40 shows how MongoClient can be configured and used in an application.

Listing 9-40. Connecting with the MongoDB server using MongoClient

```
public class EmployeeManagerController : Controller
{
    private IMongoCollection<Employee> employees;
    private IMongoCollection<Country> countries;

    public EmployeeManagerController(IConfiguration config)
    {
        var client = new MongoClient(config.GetValue<string>
        ("MongoDBSettings:Server"));
        IMongoDatabase db = client.GetDatabase(config.GetValue<string>
        ("MongoDBSettings:DatabaseName"));
        this.employees = db.GetCollection<Employee>(config.GetValue<string>
        ("MongoDBSettings:EmployeeCollectionName"));
        this.countries = db.GetCollection<Country>(config.GetValue<string>
(       "MongoDBSettings:CountryCollectionName"));
    }
}
```

Inside the constructor of EmployeeManagerController, the code creates a new instance of MongoClient by passing the server endpoint URI. By default, this URI is mongodb://localhost:27017, and it's stored in the appsettings.json file.

Once a connection is established with the server, the code gets hold of the Northwind database using the GetDatabase() method of MongoClient. The GetDatabase() method accepts a database name. If the specified database already exists, it is returned as IMongoDatabase implementation. If the database doesn't already exist, it is created and then returned as IMongoDatabase.

The code then proceeds to retrieve two document collections – Employees and Countries – using the GetCollection() method. If a collection already exists, it is returned in the form of IMongoCollection; otherwise, the collection is created and returned as IMongoCollection.

Employee and Country Model Classes

The Employee and Country model classes are similar to the ones you created for the Cosmos DB example. However, this time they use [BsonId] and [BsonElement] attributes. Listing 9-41 shows the Employee class with these attributes.

Listing 9-41. Using [BsonId] and [BsonElement]

```
public class Employee
{
    [BsonId]
    public ObjectId DocumentID { get; set; }

    [BsonElement("employeeID")]
    [Required]
    [Display(Name ="Employee ID")]
    public int EmployeeID { get; set; }

    [BsonElement("firstName")]
    [Required]
    [StringLength(10)]
    [Display(Name = "First Name")]
    public string FirstName { get; set; }

    [BsonElement("lastName")]
    [Required]
    [StringLength(20)]
    [Display(Name = "Last Name")]
    public string LastName { get; set; }

    [BsonElement("title")]
    [Required]
    [StringLength(30)]
```

```
[Display(Name = "Title")]
public string Title { get; set; }

[BsonElement("birthDate")]
[Required]
[Display(Name = "Birth Date")]
[BsonDateTimeOptions(DateOnly = true)]
public DateTime BirthDate { get; set; }

[BsonElement("hireDate")]
[Required]
[Display(Name = "Hire Date")]
[BsonDateTimeOptions(DateOnly = true)]
public DateTime HireDate { get; set; }

[BsonElement("country")]
[Required]
[StringLength(15)]
[Display(Name = "Country")]
public string Country { get; set; }

[BsonElement("notes")]
[StringLength(500)]
[Display(Name = "Notes")]
public string Notes { get; set; }
}
```

Earlier, it was mentioned that MongoDB stores data in the form of JSON documents. For efficient storage of these documents, MongoDB uses a binary format called BSON (Binary JSON).

The DocumentID property of the Employee class is marked with the [BsonId] attribute (MongoDB.Bson.Serialization.Attributes namespace), and its data type is ObjectId. This indicates that the DocumentID property is going to act as a unique identifier for the JSON document. (In MongoDB, the _id property of JSON documents acts as a unique identifier. The [BsonId] attribute automatically saves the underlying property as _id.) The ObjectId type is defined by the MongoDB driver and represents a 12 byte value.

The other properties are decorated with the [BsonElement] attribute (MongoDB. Bson.Serialization.Attributes namespace) indicating that the underlying property will be serialized as a JSON element. You can also specify an alternate name for the JSON property using the parameter of the [BsonElement] attribute. If you don't specify an alternate name, the name of the underlying property is used.

Note that BirthDate and HireDate properties are also decorated with the [BsonDateTimeOptions] attribute. The DateOnly property of [BsonDateTimeOptions] is true indicating that only the date part is to be considered while serializing and de-serializing those properties.

The Country class can be created on the same lines and is shown in Listing 9-42 for your quick reference.

Listing 9-42. Country class

```
public class Country
{
    [BsonId]
    public ObjectId DocumentID { get; set; }

    [BsonElement]
    public int CountryID { get; set; }

    [BsonElement]
    public string Name { get; set; }
}
```

Displaying a List of Employees

In order to retrieve a list of Employee documents from a MongoDB database, you use employees IMongoCollection as shown in Listing 9-43.

Listing 9-43. Retrieving a list of employees

```
public IActionResult List()
{
    var model = this.employees.Find(FilterDefinition<Employee>.Empty)
    .ToList();
    return View(model);
}
```

The Find() method called on the employees IMongoCollection takes a filter condition in the form of the FilterDefinition object. Since we don't want to set any filter, an empty filter condition is passed. The Find() method returns a fluent find interface in the form of IFindFluent. To get the data as a List<Employee>, the ToList() method is called.

Inserting a New Employee

In order to insert a new Employee into the database, you use the InsertOne() method of IMongoCollection. This is shown in Listing 9-44.

Listing 9-44. Inserting a new employee

```
[HttpPost]
[ValidateAntiForgeryToken]
public IActionResult Insert(Employee emp)
{
    FillCountries();
    if (ModelState.IsValid)
    {
      Employee existing = this.employees.Find(e => e.EmployeeID == emp.
      EmployeeID).FirstOrDefault();

      if(existing == null)
      {
          this.employees.InsertOne(emp);
          ViewBag.Message = "Employee inserted successfully!";
      }
      else
      {
          ViewBag.Message = "EmployeeID already exists!";
      }
    }
    return View();
}
```

   The POST Insert() action first uses employees IMongoCollection to check whether an EmployeeID being inserted already exists or not. If the EmployeeID doesn't exist, the InsertOne() method of employees IMongoCollection is called by passing the new employee to be added.

Updating an Existing Employee

In order to update an existing employee, you can use the ReplaceOne() method of IMongoCollection. There is also the UpdateOne() method that can be used if you wish to change particular properties rather than updating the whole document. The use of ReplaceOne() is shown in Listing 9-45.

Listing 9-45. Updating an employee

```
[HttpPost]
[ValidateAntiForgeryToken]
public IActionResult Update(string documentID, Employee emp)
{
   FillCountries();
   if (ModelState.IsValid)
   {
     emp.DocumentID = new ObjectId(documentID);
     var filter = Builders<Employee>.Filter.Eq(e => e.DocumentID, emp.
     DocumentID);
     var result = employees.ReplaceOne(filter, emp);

     if (result.IsAcknowledged)
     {
         ViewBag.Message = "Employee updated successfully!";
     }
     else
     {
         ViewBag.Message = "Error while updating Employee!";
     }
   }
   return View(emp);
}
```

Notice that the Update() POST method not only takes the Employee object but also the documentID string. This is because model binding can't automatically convert a string DocumentID into an ObjectId instance. So the code gets the string DocumentID and converts it into an ObjectId and assigns it to the DocumentID property of Employee.

Then the code builds a filter that filters the employees based on the DocumentID. In this case, since the filter is based on the DocumentID, only one Employee will be filtered. This filter is passed to the first parameter of the ReplaceOne() method. The second parameter of ReplaceOne() is the modified Employee document.

Deleting an Existing Employee

In order to delete an existing employee, you use the DeleteOne() method of IMongoCollection. This is shown in Listing 9-46.

Listing 9-46. Deleting an employee

```
[HttpPost]
[ValidateAntiForgeryToken]
public IActionResult Delete(string documentID)
{
    ObjectId docID = new ObjectId(documentID);
    var result = this.employees.DeleteOne(e => e.DocumentID == docID);

    if (result.IsAcknowledged)
    {
        TempData["Message"] = "Employee deleted successfully!";
    }
    else
    {
        TempData["Message"] = "Error while deleting Employee!";
    }
    return RedirectToAction("List");
}
```

The Delete() action receives a string documentID and converts it into an ObjectId instance. Then the DeleteOne() method is called on the employees IMongoCollection by passing the deletion condition in the form of a LINQ expression.

441

This completes the CRUD operations. You may get the complete source code of this example from the book's code download.

Implementing Authentication and Authorization

Implementing user authentication and role-based security in this example is quite similar to the Cosmos DB example because this example also uses a custom cookie authentication. The user data such as UserName, Password, and Role are stored in a MongoDB collection named Users. However, in a more realistic situation, you should consider strong encryption techniques to protect the user data. You might even prefer to store user details in some other data store. Data encryption and security techniques are beyond the scope of this book.

The SecurityController contains the same set of actions – Register(), SignIn(), and SignOut() – to take care of the respective operations. Usage of the [Authorize] attribute also remains as before. For the sake of brevity, those implementation details are not discussed here. You can get the SecurityController from the book's code download.

Summary

This chapter introduced you to three data stores – Azure SQL Database, Cosmos DB, and MongoDB. Azure SQL Database is the same SQL Server database that you are familiar with, but it's hosted and managed by Azure. Nowadays, NoSQL databases are also quite common, and you learned two of them – Cosmos DB and MongoDB. Both store data in the form of JSON documents. To perform CRUD operations on a Cosmos DB database, you used the Cosmos DB client library as well as the EF Core provider for Cosmos DB. You also learned to use the MongoDB driver for .NET to handle data access. Together, this chapter made you familiar with cloud-based and NoSQL data stores.

You have been developing various flavors of Employee Manager throughout this book. In the next chapter, you learn to deploy Employee Manager to IIS and Azure App Service.

CHAPTER 10

Deployment

Your journey in this book, so far, involved developing the Employee Manager application using various technology options available in the ASP.NET Core family of technologies. You used the IIS Express web server while developing the applications. Once you finish developing an application, you want end users to use it. This calls for deploying the application in some hosting environment and making it accessible to the end users.

If you developed ASP.NET web applications before, you might be aware of Internet Information Services (IIS)–based hosting. This traditional way of deploying ASP.NET applications is still available to ASP.NET Core developers. Additionally, many modern web applications are hosted in Azure App Service. To that end, this chapter teaches you to

- Deploy Employee Manager in Internet Information Services or IIS
- Deploy Employee Manager in Azure App Service

This chapter uses two projects you developed earlier, namely, EmployeeManager. Mvc and EmployeeManager.AzureSql, for the sake of illustrating the deployment options mentioned in the preceding text. So keep them ready with you.

Note   This chapter assumes that you have installed IIS and Web Deploy on your machine. To know more about Web Deploy, visit `https://docs.microsoft.com/en-us/iis/publish/using-web-deploy/introduction-to-web-deploy`. It is also assumed that you have access to the Azure portal and Azure App Service.

© Bipin Joshi 2019
B. Joshi, *Beginning Database Programming Using ASP.NET Core 3*,
https://doi.org/10.1007/978-1-4842-5509-4_10

Deploy Employee Manager to IIS

In this section, you learn to deploy the Employee Manager application to IIS. So first of all, open the EmployeeManager.Mvc project in Visual Studio. While opening the project, you need to open it in administrator mode since you want to use Web Deploy to deploy the web application. You can do that by right-clicking the Visual Studio entry in the Windows Start screen and then picking Run as administrator (Figure 10-1).

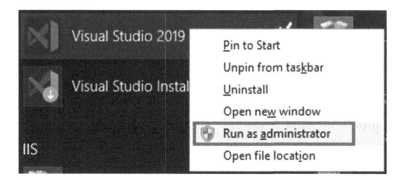

Figure 10-1. *Run Visual Studio as administrator*

Then build the project just to make sure that there are no compilation errors. Just for your quick reference, Figure 10-2 shows the EmployeeManager.Mvc open in Solution Explorer.

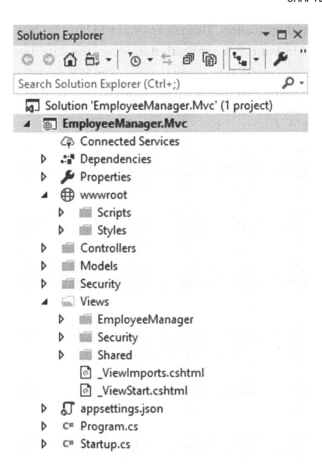

Figure 10-2. *EmployeeManager.Mvc open in Solution Explorer*

Recollect that you have stored the database connection string in the application configuration file – appsettings.json. While developing Employee Manager, you used the local installation of SQL Server. Your database connection looked like this:

```
"ConnectionStrings": {
    "AppDb": "data source=.;
             initial catalog=Northwind;
             integrated security=true;
}
```

As you can see, the integrated security option is set to true indicating that SQL Server will use Windows Authentication. This is alright during development because your web application and SQL Server are running on the same machine. However, in many real-world situations, SQL Server is installed on some different server and you want to access it using SQL Server Authentication. This means you will have an SQL Server user ID and password that is used by your web application to access the data. In such cases, you need to modify your database connection string to reflect the SQL Server details. Consider the following connection string that uses such credentials:

```
"ConnectionStrings": {
    "AppDb": "data source=your_sql_server;
             initial catalog=Northwind;
             user id=your_sql_server_userid;
             password= your_sql_server_password"
}
```

As you can see, the data source setting now specifies the name or the IP address of the target SQL Server. The user ID and password settings specify the respective values. Make sure to change these settings as per your setup and save the appsettings.json file.

Create a Target SQL Server Database

As far as this example is concerned, this step is an optional step. However, in most of the real-world applications, you need to transfer database and data from your local installation of SQL Server to the production installation of SQL Server. There can be multiple ways to accomplish this task including these:

- You might generate database scripts using SQL Server Management Studio and run those scripts in the target SQL Server.

- You can use Import/Export Data features of SQL Server Management Studio to transfer the data from the local database to the target database.

- You can use the Copy Database feature of SQL Server Management Studio to copy the database objects and data from the local database to the target database.

Discussion of these database deployment techniques is beyond the scope of this book. If you want to use an SQL Server instance other than that running on your local machine, use any of these techniques to deploy your database to the target server. Make sure to change the database connection string from the appsettings.json as per the target database (see the previous section for more details).

Create an IIS Site

Before you use Web Deploy to deploy Employee Manager to IIS, you need to create an IIS site that will host your web application files. To do so, open Internet Information Services (IIS) Manager (Figure 10-3).

Figure 10-3. *Internet Information Services (IIS) Manager*

Then right-click the Sites folder and select the Add Website shortcut menu option to open a dialog shown in Figure 10-4.

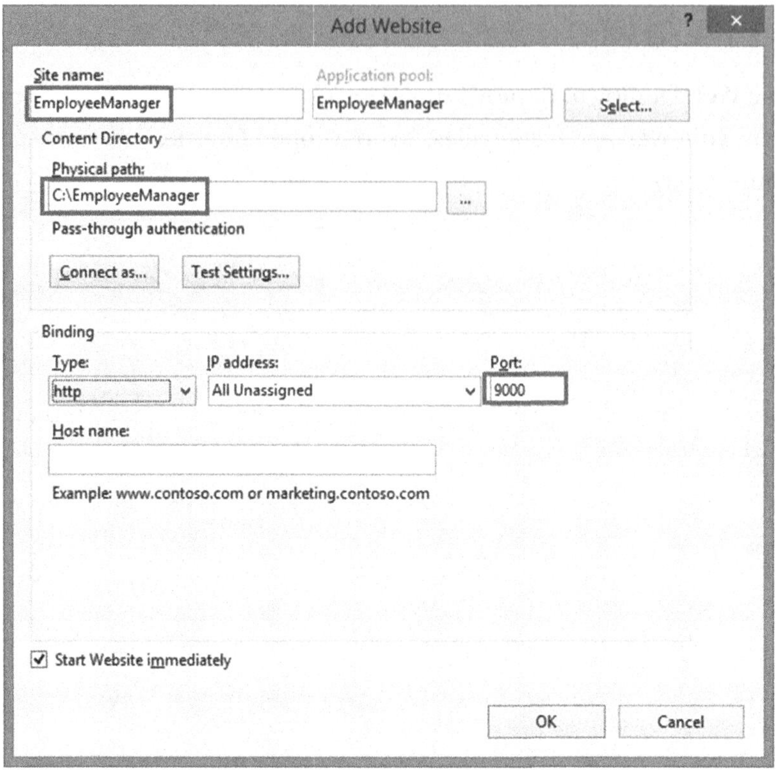

Figure 10-4. Configuring a new IIS web site

In this dialog, specify the site name to be EmployeeManager. Then pick a physical file system folder where the site's files are to be stored (C:\EmployeeManager in this example). The default site under IIS listens at port 80, and to avoid interfering with it, specify some unused port number, say 9000. In a more real-world situation you should set up an SSL certificate in IIS and enforce HTTPS in your application as described in `https://docs.microsoft.com/en-us/aspnet/core/security/enforcing-ssl`. Now, click the OK button to create the site.

Once the site is created, click the Application Pools option to reveal the IIS application pools (Figure 10-5).

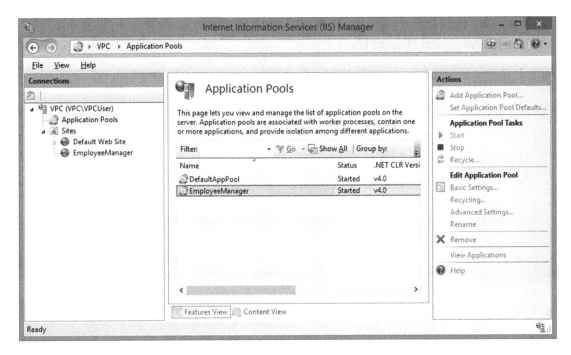

Figure 10-5. *IIS application pools*

Here you should see an entry for the EmployeeManager. Double-click the EmployeeManager application pool to reveal its settings. Change the .NET CLR version to No Managed Code (Figure 10-6) and then close the dialog.

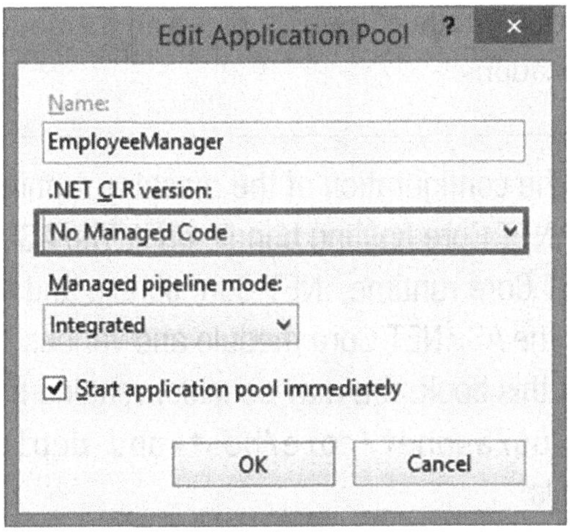

Figure 10-6. *Change application pool properties*

Next, click the EmployeeManager site in the IIS Manager and double-click Modules from the Features view (Figure 10-7).

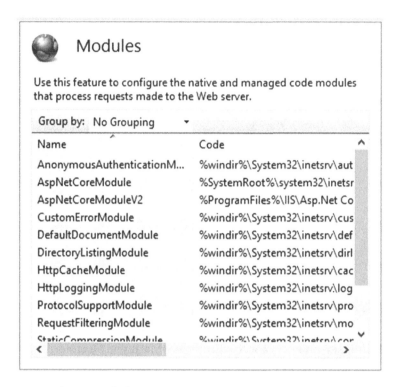

Figure 10-7. *List of IIS modules*

Notice the ASP.NET Core Module listed there. It's an IIS module that handles the ASP.NET Core web applications.

Note   Depending on the configuration of the machine running IIS, you might need to install the ASP.NET Core hosting bundle on it. The ASP.NET Core hosting bundle installs the .NET Core runtime, .NET Core library, and ASP.NET Core module. Detailed discussion of the ASP.NET Core module and various hosting models is beyond the scope of this book. You may consider reading `https://docs.` `microsoft.com/en-us/aspnet/core/host-and-deploy/aspnet-core-` `module` for more details.

Publish Employee Manager from Visual Studio

Now that the EmployeeManager site has been created in IIS, you can deploy your application to the site. Switch back to the Visual Studio IDE that has the EmployeeManager.Mvc project loaded. Click the Build menu and select the Publish EmployeeManager.Mvc menu option.

When you do so, you are asked to pick a publish target (Figure 10-8).

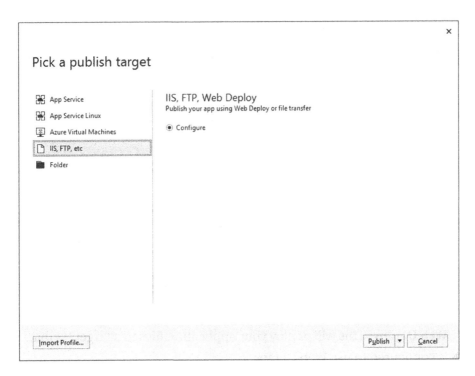

Figure 10-8. *Selecting a publish target*

In this dialog, select the IIS, FTP, etc. option from the left-side list and click the Publish button. This will open a dialog as shown in Figure 10-9.

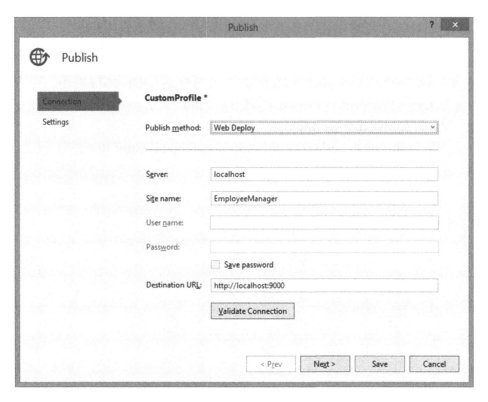

Figure 10-9. *Specify Web Deploy settings*

At the top of this dialog, you can select a publish method. Although you are going to use Web Deploy, it's worthwhile to enumerate the available options:

- **Web Deploy:** This will deploy your application files to a target IIS that is configured to use Web Deploy.

- **Web Deploy Package:** This option generates a ZIP file containing all the files and settings to be deployed. You can then install the package in the target IIS.

- **FTP:** This option allows you to upload your web application files to an FTP location.

- **File System:** This option allows you to publish a web application to a file system folder. You can then copy these files to IIS.

So pick Web Deploy in the Publish method dropdown list and fill out the following details:

- **Server:** This is the name or IP of the target server that has IIS and Web Deploy installed. In this example, the application is being deployed to the local installation of IIS, and hence the server is specified to be localhost.

- **Site name:** It's the name of the IIS site that you created and configured earlier – EmployeeManager.

- **User name and password:** If the target server requires a user name and password to connect, you also need to specify them in the respective textboxes.

- **Destination URL:** Specifying a destination URL is optional. If specified, Visual Studio will launch this URL in a browser once the deployment is over. In this example, the destination URL is http://localhost:9000 since the EmployeeManager site is configured to use port 9000.

Once you enter all these details, click the Validate Connection button so that Visual Studio validates the connection settings specified in the various fields and informs you of the success or error.

If the connection is validated successfully, click the Next button to go to the next step of the wizard (Figure 10-10).

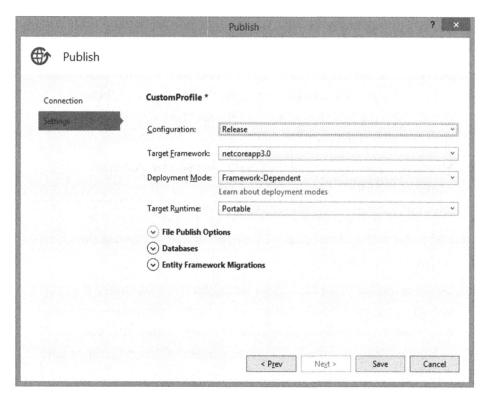

Figure 10-10. *Specify publish settings*

In the publish settings dialog you can specify various settings as described in the following:

- **Configuration:** Visual Studio allows you to build your applications in two modes – Debug and Release. The former is useful during development and debugging stages, whereas the latter is suitable once the application development is complete. The release mode output is more optimized in terms of performance and physical disk size. Therefore, select Release in this dropdown list.

- **Target Framework:** This dropdown list allows you to select the target version of the framework. For the Employee Manager application, it's netcoreapp3.0.

- **Deployment Mode:** This dropdown list contains two options for deploying your web application – Framework-Dependent and Self-Contained. The former option assumes that your application will run on top of .NET Core installed on the server. Therefore, only your application files and third-party dependencies are deployed.

The latter mode, in addition to application-specific files, also bundles the .NET Core framework files with which the application was build. Depending on your choice, select an option from the list.

Note   To know more about framework-dependent and self-contained deployment modes, you may read `https://docs.microsoft.com/en-us/dotnet/core/deploying`.

- **Target Runtime:** This setting can be used to specify the target runtime environment for the application. There are various options such as win-x86, win-x64, linux-x64, and Portable. Default selection is Portable. We don't want to target a specific runtime, and hence the default selection is maintained.

- **File Publish Options, Databases, and Entity Framework Migrations:** Options from these categories can be used to perform some additional tasks such as removing additional files from the target machine and running EF Core migrations from your project. The Employee Manager application doesn't need any of these options. So keep all of them unchecked (default).

After specifying these options, click the Save button. This will save your deployment preferences and start the deployment process. The Web Publish Activity window displays the status of the deployment process (Figure 10-11).

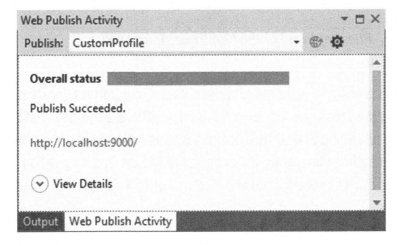

Figure 10-11. *Web Publish Activity window shows the status of deployment*

455

Once the deployment is complete, Visual Studio will also launch the application in the browser. Figure 10-12 shows the files that got deployed to the EmployeeManager folder.

Name	Date modified	Type	Size
runtimes	5/27/2019 9:08 AM	File folder	
wwwroot	5/27/2019 9:08 AM	File folder	
appsettings.Development.json	12/6/2017 9:52 AM	JSON File	1 KB
appsettings.json	3/22/2019 8:37 AM	JSON File	1 KB
EmployeeManager.Mvc.deps.json	5/27/2019 9:08 AM	JSON File	145 KB
EmployeeManager.Mvc.dll	5/27/2019 9:08 AM	Application extens...	55 KB
EmployeeManager.Mvc.exe	5/27/2019 9:08 AM	Application	330 KB
EmployeeManager.Mvc.pdb	5/27/2019 9:08 AM	Program Debug D...	8 KB
EmployeeManager.Mvc.runtimeconfig.js...	5/24/2019 9:06 AM	JSON File	1 KB
EmployeeManager.Mvc.Views.dll	5/27/2019 9:08 AM	Application extens...	128 KB
EmployeeManager.Mvc.Views.pdb	5/27/2019 9:08 AM	Program Debug D...	11 KB
Microsoft.AspNetCore.Identity.EntityFra...	4/28/2019 2:55 AM	Application extens...	97 KB
Microsoft.EntityFrameworkCore.Abstract...	4/27/2019 8:31 PM	Application extens...	21 KB
Microsoft.EntityFrameworkCore.dll	4/27/2019 8:31 PM	Application extens...	1,555 KB
Microsoft.EntityFrameworkCore.Relation...	4/27/2019 8:32 PM	Application extens...	779 KB
Microsoft.EntityFrameworkCore.SqlServe...	4/27/2019 8:32 PM	Application extens...	247 KB
Remotion.Linq.dll	5/24/2019 6:17 AM	Application extens...	173 KB
System.Data.SqlClient.dll	4/24/2019 10:03 PM	Application extens...	251 KB
System.Interactive.Async.dll	12/25/2018 10:47 ...	Application extens...	246 KB
System.Text.Encoding.CodePages.dll	4/24/2019 9:51 PM	Application extens...	735 KB
web.config	5/27/2019 9:08 AM	CONFIG File	1 KB

Figure 10-12. *Files deployed to the EmployeeManager site*

Note   In the preceding example, you used the most common deployment options for deploying the Employee Manager application. There are many configuration settings that allow you to fine-tune the deployment. Discussion of all these configuration settings is beyond the scope of this book. You may read more at `https://docs.microsoft.com/en-us/aspnet/core/host-and-deploy/iis`.

Let's quickly enumerate some of the important output files obtained as a result of the publish operation:

- **appsettings.json** is the application configuration file, and it is deployed as it was during developing the application. If you change the configuration settings from this file (say, database connection string), the changed settings will be used by the application.

- **EmployeeManager.Mvc.dll** is an assembly that contains the compiled C# application code. This includes the EF Core model, controllers, and any other C# code that you might have.

- **EmployeeManager.Mvc.exe** is an executable that represents a process that listens for HTTP requests. Depending on your publish configuration, this executable is typically used by the <aspNetCore> section of web.config.

- **EmployeeManager.Mvc.Views.dll** is an assembly that contains compiled output of all the Razor files (*.cshtml) including view files, view imports file, View Start file, and layout file.

- All the **NuGet packages** and **dependencies** needed by your application are also deployed. For example, Microsoft. EntityFrameworkCore.dll and Microsoft.AspNetCore.Identity. EntityFrameworkCore.dll are deployed to the target location.

- There is also a **web.config** file generated by the publish operation. This file is not used directly by your application code, but it contains certain settings that are used by the IIS. For example, the web.config specifies the ASP.NET Core Module configuration and the hosting model used by the application.

- There is also the **wwwroot** folder that contains static resources used by your application. For example, Site*.css and jquery*.js files that you placed under wwwroot during development are deployed to the target location.

After successfully deploying the application, Visual Studio launches http:// localhost:9000. You can try signing in to the application and test the CRUD operations. Figure 10-13 shows the launched web application after successful sign-in.

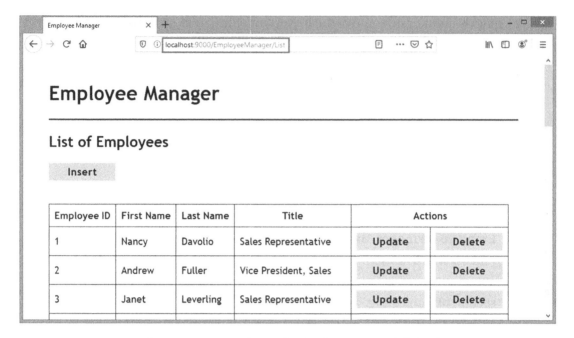

Figure 10-13. *Employee Manager launched after successful deployment*

Redeploying the Application

In the preceding sections, you deployed the Employee Manager application to IIS. Many a times after deploying an application, you make changes to the code base. This calls for redeploying the application to the server. To assist you in the redeployment process, Visual Studio remembers your previous publish settings in a publish profile.

If you again select the Build ➤ Publish EmployeeManager.Mvc menu option, you will be shown a dialog as per Figure 10-14.

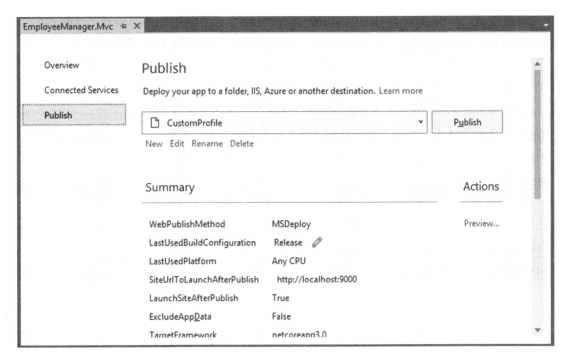

Figure 10-14. *Publish settings are stored in a custom publish profile*

As you can see, the dropdown list has a custom publish profile selected. Below the dropdown list, there are New, Edit, Rename, and Delete buttons that can be used to perform the specific action on the publish profile.

If you want to redeploy the web application without making any changes to the publish settings, you can simply click the Publish button to begin the redeployment.

If you want to make any changes to the publish settings, you can click the Edit button to make the necessary changes. Upon making the changes, you can then click the Publish button to redeploy the application.

Deploy Employee Manager to Azure App Service

In this section, you deploy the Employee Manager application to Azure App Service. Earlier in this book, you developed a version of Employee Manager that uses the Azure SQL Database (EmployeeManager.AzureSql project). Although that application used the Azure SQL Database as a data store for employee data, the web application was running on your local machine. In this section, you deploy the application to Azure App Service.

Azure App Service is an Azure service that works on a platform as a service (PaaS) model. It can run and manage web applications, mobile applications, APIs, and business logic applications. You can think of Azure App Service as a managed hosting environment for your ASP.NET Core web applications.

Note   Detailed discussion of Azure App Service is beyond the scope of this book. You may read more at `https://azure.microsoft.com/en-in/services/app-service`.

For this example, you use the EmployeeManager.AzureSql project created earlier. Just for your quick reference, Figure 10-15 shows that project opened in Solution Explorer.

Figure 10-15. *EmployeeManager.AzureSql opened in Solution Explorer*

Since this project already uses an Azure SQL Database, you don't need to make any changes to the database connection string stored in the appsettings.json. Just for your quick reference, the connection string is given in the following:

```
"ConnectionStrings": {
  "AppDb": "Server=your_server_address_here;
            Initial Catalog=Northwind;
            Persist Security Info=False;
            User ID=your_user_id_here;
            Password=your_password_here;
            MultipleActiveResultSets=False;
            Encrypt=True;
            TrustServerCertificate=False;
            Connection Timeout=30;"
}
```

Just ensure that your values for server, user ID, password, and other details are correct before you continue further.

To deploy EmployeeManager.AzureSql to Azure App Service, you essentially run the same wizard that you ran while deploying to IIS earlier in this chapter. However, selection of various options and settings is different.

So begin by opening the Build menu and then select the Publish EmployeeManager. AzureSql menu option to start the wizard. Figure 10-16 shows the first step of the wizard where you pick a publish target.

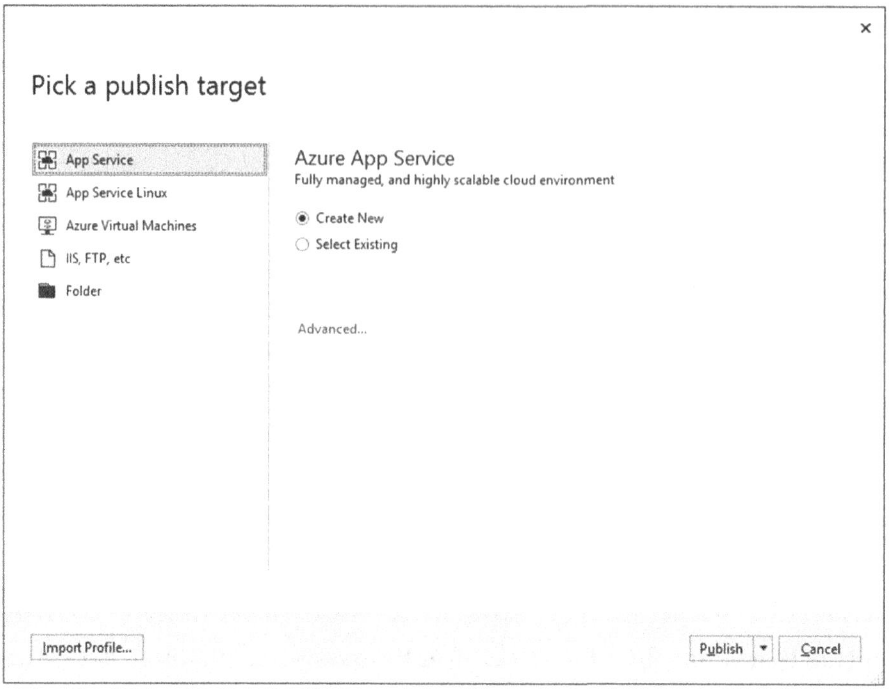

Figure 10-16. *Publishing to Azure App Service*

In this step, select App Service from the left-side options and then pick the Create New radio button to indicate that you want to deploy the application to a new Azure App Service. Then click the Publish button to go to the next step (Figure 10-17).

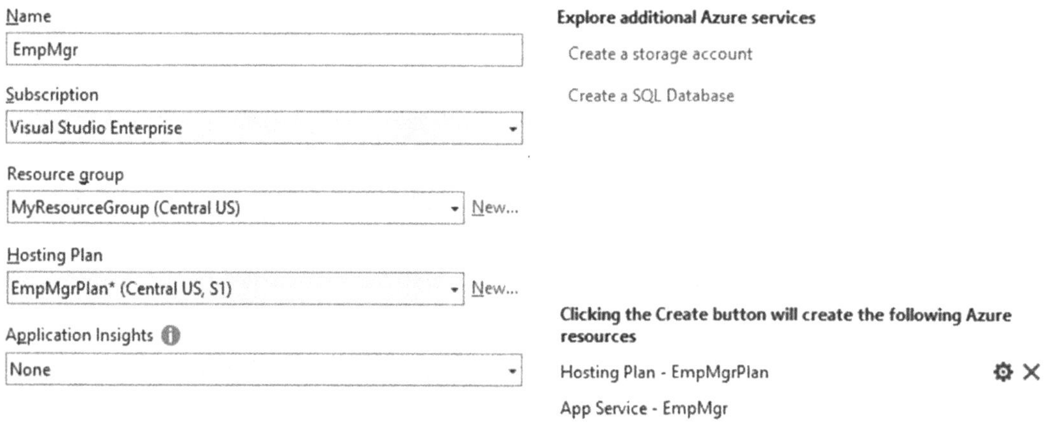

Figure 10-17. *Specify Azure App Service details*

In this screen, you specify various details about the new Azure App Service such as follows:

- **Name:** Indicates the name of the new Azure App Service being created. This name needs to be unique. You will be informed in case the name you specify is already in use. This name also appears in the URL of the resultant web site. So make sure to enter some short yet meaningful name here.

- **Subscription:** Select your Azure subscription from this dropdown list.

- **Resource group:** A resource group is a logical grouping of resources. If you have already created some resource group, pick its name or create a new one by clicking the New button.

- **Hosting plan:** You also need to pick a hosting plan for your web application. You can either keep the default hosting plan selection or create a new hosting plan by clicking the New button. You should pick or create a hosting plan based on your requirements. Figure 10-18 shows a new hosting plan defined using the default size.

Figure 10-18. *Creating a new hosting plan*

- **Application insights:** If you are interested in analyzing your application's performance, you can pick an application insight. For this example, you can keep the Vdefault selection of None.

Notice that on the right side of the screen, there are options to create a new storage account and Azure SQL Database. You don't need one for this example because your data is already into an Azure SQL Database.

Next, click the Create button to create a new Azure App Service as per given specifications. Upon creating the App Service, the necessary files will be deployed to it. You will be notified once the deployment is complete (Figure 10-19).

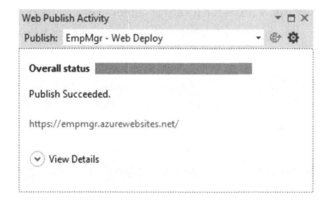

Figure 10-19. *Successful deployment to Azure App Service*

Notice the URL given in the Web Publish Activity window. It takes this form:

```
https://your_app_service_name.azurewebsites.net/
```

If you navigate to this URL (make sure to substitute your Azure App Service name) using a browser, you should see the application sign-in page. You can then sign in to the system and test the CRUD operations as before. Figure 10-20 shows the employee listing page of the application upon successful sign-in.

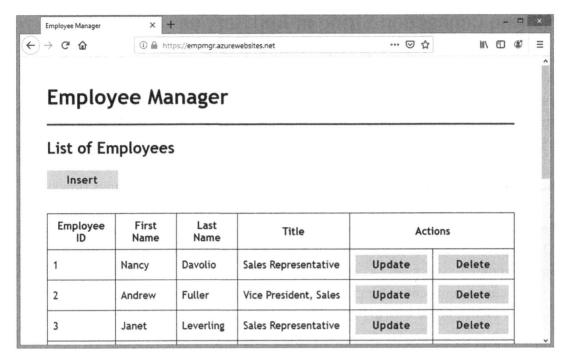

Figure 10-20. *Accessing Employee Manager hosted in Azure App Service*

If you log in to the Azure portal and go to the App Services section, you will find that newly created App Service listed there (Figure 10-21).

App Services
Default Directory

+ Add   **≣≣** Edit columns   **↻** Refresh | **◆** Assign tags   **▶** Start   **ↆ** Restart   **■** Stop   **🗑** Delete

Subscriptions: Visual Studio Enterprise – Don't see a subscription? Open Directory + Subscription settings

| empmgr | All resource groups | ⌄ | All locations | ⌄ |

1 of 1 items selected

NAME	STATUS	APP TYPE	APP SERVICE PLAN	L
🌐 EmpMgr	Running	Web App	EmpMgrPlan	(

Figure 10-21. *Newly created App Service listed in the Azure portal*

Storing Connection String in App Service

In the preceding section, you stored the database connection string in the appsettings. json file. However, for security reasons, you might want to avoid storing the database connection string in the appsettings.json file. Moreover, your development connection string and production connection string might be different. Luckily, Azure App Service allows you to store database connection in a more secure way.

You can define a database connection string in your App Service using the Azure portal. This connection string will have the same name as the appsettings.json key (AppDb in this example). At runtime, the connection string defined in the App Service will be used instead of the connection string defined in the appsettings.json. This happens automatically for you, and there is no need to make any change to the source code.

To define a connection string in an App Service, go to the App Service and click the Configuration option shown in Figure 10-22.

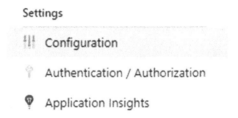

Figure 10-22. *Azure App Service configuration*

Then you can add a database connection string by clicking the New connection string button (Figure 10-23).

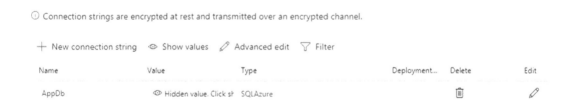

Figure 10-23. *Adding a database connection string*

Specify the connection string name, its value, and its type. Then save the configuration by clicking the Save button at the top. As you can see in the figure, a connection string named AppDb has been added to the App Service configuration. Make sure that this connection string name matches with what you used in your appsettings.json file and code. That's it. Now the deployed web application will use this connection string.

Redeploying the Application

In case you need to redeploy the application, the overall process remains the same as in the case of deploying to IIS. Figure 10-24 shows the publish wizard with previous settings selected.

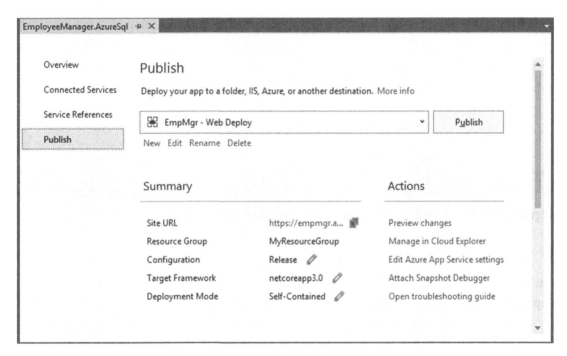

Figure 10-24. *Redeploying the web application using the publish wizard*

As before, you can use New, Edit, Rename, and Delete buttons to perform the respective operation on the publish profile. You can click the Publish button to redeploy the web application based on the selected publish profile.

Click the Edit button to open a dialog as shown in Figure 10-25.

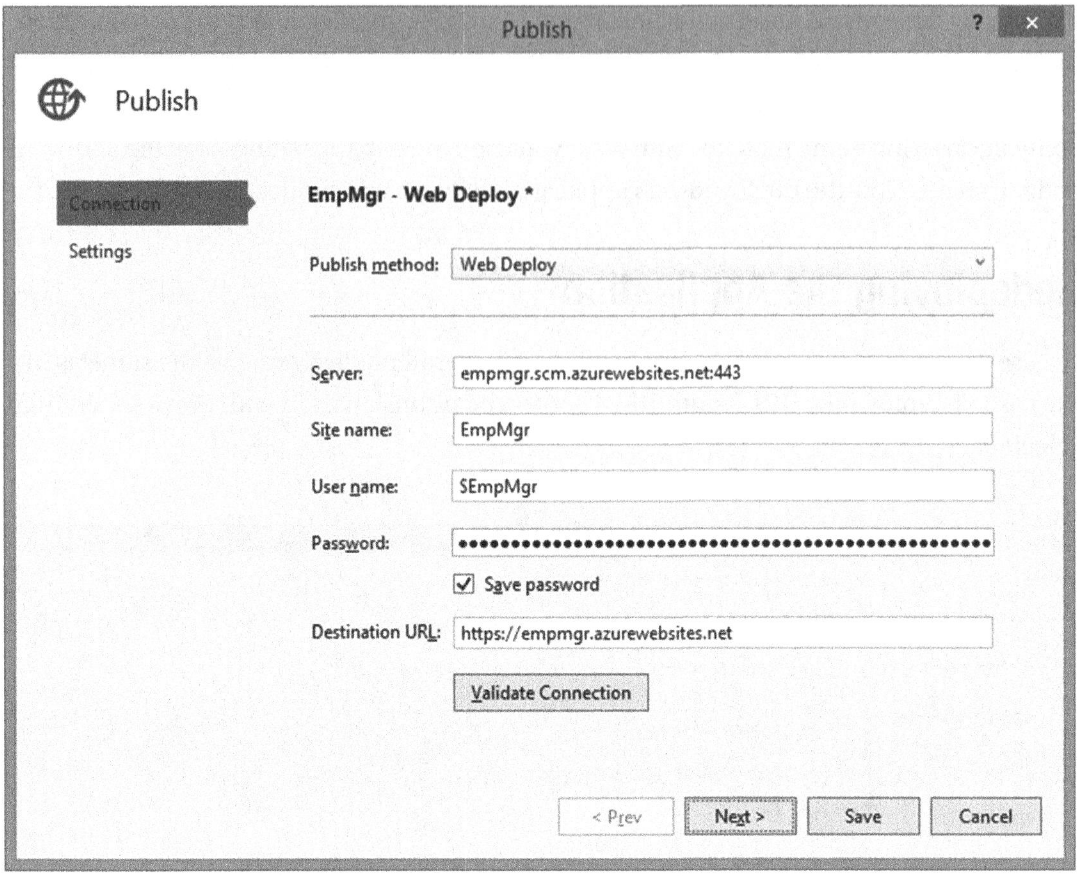

Figure 10-25. *Changing the deployment connection settings*

As you can see, it's Web Deploy being done to the Azure App Service. If you click the Next button of the wizard, you can configure the same settings as you did while deploying to IIS. These settings are shown in Figure 10-26.

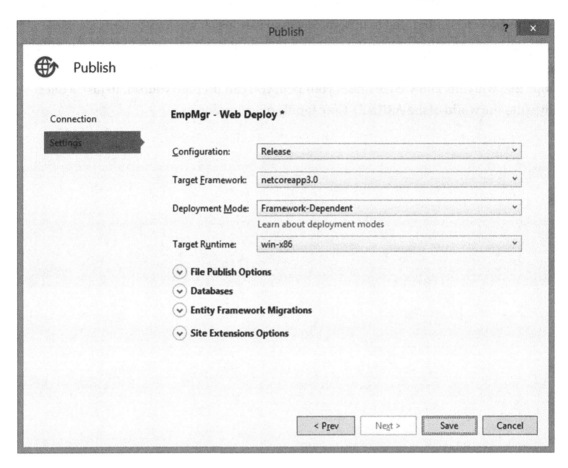

Figure 10-26. *Changing deployment configuration settings*

You can complete the deployment by following the wizard steps and rerun the application by launching a browser.

Summary

In this chapter, you learned to deploy ASP.NET Core web application. Two common deployment options were discussed, namely, deploying to IIS and deploying to Azure App Service. In order to deploy a web application using any of these options, you used the Publish menu option under the Build menu. You also learned about various configuration settings available during the deployment operation such as target framework and deployment mode.

This book has attempted to introduce you to various technology options available while building ASP.NET Core web applications including MVC, Razor Pages, Web APIs, jQuery Ajax, Angular SPA, Blazor, Azure SQL Database, NoSQL databases, and more. I hope that with this knowledge under your belt, you can prepare yourself to take a deep dive into the world of the ASP.NET Core family of technologies.

Index

A

© Bipin Joshi 2019
B. Joshi, *Beginning Database Programming Using ASP.NET Core 3*,
https://doi.org/10.1007/978-1-4842-5509-4

W, X, Y, Z

Printed in the United States
By Bookmasters